REAL ETHICS

John Rist surveys the history of ethics from Plato to the present and offers a vigorous defence of an ethical theory based on a revised version of Platonic realism. In a wide-ranging discussion he examines well-known alternatives to Platonism, in particular Epicurus, Hobbes, Hume and Kant, as well as contemporary 'practical reasoners', and argues that most post-Enlightenment theories of morality (as well as Nietzschean subversions of such theories) depend on an abandoned Christian metaphysic and are unintelligible without such grounding. He also argues that contemporary choice-based theories, whether they take a strictly ethical or more obviously political form, are ultimately arbitrary in nature. His lively and accessible study is informed by a powerful sense of philosophical history, and will be of interest to both students and scholars of ethics.

JOHN M. RIST is Professor Emeritus of Philosophy and Classics at the University of Toronto. His publications include *Plotinus: The Road to Reality* (Cambridge University Press, 1967), *The Mind of Aristotle* (University of Toronto Press, 1989), *Augustine: Ancient Thought Baptized* (Cambridge University Press, 1994), and many journal articles.

REAL ETHICS

Reconsidering the Foundations of Morality

JOHN M. RIST

CAMBRIDGE
UNIVERSITY PRESS

PUBLISHED BY THE PRESS SYNDICATE OF THE UNIVERSITY OF CAMBRIDGE
The Pitt Building, Trumpington Street, Cambridge, United Kingdom

CAMBRIDGE UNIVERSITY PRESS
The Edinburgh Building, Cambridge CB2 2RU, UK
40 West 20th Street, New York, NY 10011-4211, USA
10 Stamford Road, Oakleigh, VIC 3166, Australia
Ruiz de Alarcón 13, 28014 Madrid, Spain
Dock House, The Waterfront, Cape Town 8001, South Africa

http://www.cambridge.org

First published 2002

Printed in the United Kingdom at the University Press, Cambridge

Typeface Baskerville Monotype 11/12.5 pt.   *System* LATEX 2ε   [TB]

A catalogue record for this book is available from the British Library

Library of Congress Cataloguing in Publication data
Rist, John M.
Real Ethics: Reconsidering the Foundations of Morality / John M. Rist.
p. cm.
Includes bibliographical references and index.
ISBN 0 521 80921 5 (hc) – ISBN 0 521 00608 2 (pbk.)
1. Ethics. 2. Realism. 3. Ethics – History. I. Title.

BJ1012.R53   2001
170 – dc21   2001035254

ISBN 0 521 80921 5 hardback
ISBN 0 521 00608 2 paperback

Contents

Acknowledgements

During the dozen or so years in which I have been thinking specifically about the themes of this study, I have incurred many philosophical debts: not least because, after three or four years, I realized that I should be much better equipped if I had a deeper knowledge of Augustine, on whom I eventually published a book in 1994. I should therefore thank those students in Toronto who took PHI 200 and 300 (Ethics), and those who followed my tortuous attempts to give graduate seminars on Augustine which made both historical and philosophical sense.

Of the many colleagues and friends who helped at different stages I should first mention Elmar Kremer, who properly savaged parts of the second version of the text. A precursor of parts of chapters 1 and 2 was discussed at a Boston Area Colloquium in Ancient Philosophy meeting at Holy Cross College, Worcester, Massachusetts, and I should thank all those who took part in the constructive debate, especially Rachel Barney. Some of my more wide-ranging suggestions were offered and published as an Aquinas lecture at Marquette University, and I thank John Jones and the Marquette Department of Philosophy – not to mention their visiting professor Arthur Madigan SJ of Boston College – for providing such a comfortable location to try things out and for asking awkward questions about the notion of the common good. The Augustinianum in Rome has provided me with an appropriate locale for the final stages of the book, and I owe a special debt to its Director, Professor Angelo di Berardino, and to Professors Robert Dodaro, Allan Fitzgerald and George Lawless, all of the Order of Saint Augustine, for all kinds of help and encouragement.

Dr Hilary Gaskin of the Cambridge University Press has always been a most helpful editor, and I should like to indicate my appreciation to the two anonymous Press readers for their very constructive comments, which led to substantial improvements, particularly in my treatment of Epicurus and Hume.

One always kicks philosophical ideas around in the family, and my children have often contributed (wittingly or unwittingly) to the debate I have tried to record, and I close with my regular homage to the merciless survey of both language and argument to which Anna Rist subjected two would-be final versions of my entire text. She has shared the thinking with me and in hundreds of places has helped me get the argument right and lucid.

With non-professional readers in mind, I have tried to ensure that the text can be understood without reference to the footnotes.

Introduction: Ethical crises old and new

The present book is in part, and necessarily, a reflection on topics in the history of ethics from the time of Socrates and even earlier, but its core concern is what is widely admitted to be a crisis in contemporary Western debate about ethical foundations. *Discussion* of this crisis – including the status of older claims that coherent moral propositions must be grounded in metaphysical truths, and the consequences for all of us if they cannot – is at present carried on largely within academic departments of philosophy, where it is widely believed that not only transcendental realism – the belief in an absolute good – but even much weaker forms of moral objectivism have already been emasculated if not killed off outright. We – whoever 'we' may be, and here too anti-realism soon raises its head[1] – must now resort for 'meaningfulness' and 'fulfilment' to some sort of critical *choice* among what we see as goods and ourselves rationally 'construct' the values on which moral theorizing will rest.[2] The *effects* of this crisis in ethical theory are already visible in the world outside the universities as well as inside: in reassessments of our responsibility for the poor in Western states (not to speak of those in the Third World), in arguments over the 'ethics' of the market economy or of modern warfare or arms trading, in debates about what, if any, public policies should be adopted to control research in genetics and about the increasing number of 'quality of life' issues which arise in the practice of medicine.

The perception in many academic and professional circles of the seriousness and ramifications of the theoretical crisis, combined with the ignorance of ordinary people, makes way for deceptions, equivocations

---

[1] See for example O. Flanagan and A. O. Rorty (eds.), *Identity, Character and Morality* (Cambridge, Mass.: Harvard University Press, 1990), 3, where we are told that we need a 'more robust conception of identity' but that 'the trouble is that the objective point of view may assume an unwanted metaphysical realism'.

[2] *Ibid.*: 'A life lived according to ... ideals might be meaningful because it is a self-chosen life or because there is a certain consonance and consistency between a person's ideals and her character and mode [*sic*] of life.'

and outright lying and humbug in public debate. For the public always lags behind the opinion-makers in its *underlying* 'moral' attitudes, as well as in its self-awareness concerning them. In Western societies, despite ubiquitous and ill-defined appeals to rights and to the priority of choice and 'freedom', the ethical hangover from a more homogeneous Christian past is still relatively influential outside élite circles, and that fact still, though diminishingly, restrains academics, media people and lawyers from making unabated statements (say in defence of direct lying or misinforming) which, even if plausible, would as yet be widely considered unacceptable among non-professionals. Most people are still largely uninformed or apathetic about the possible practical effects of the insights now claimed by our intellectual élites, except where these may seem to entail an increase in crime – especially against the person – or where some underlying intellectual trend is seen as promoting (perhaps via prominent figures from Hollywood or the music industry) a too blatantly hedonistic or manipulative sexual behaviour, or – and more commonly as a source of concern – a decline in basic educational skills. Even in these debates, however, deception is already rife, as when it is asserted that there can be no connection between unwanted teenage pregnancies and contempt for 'Victorian values'.

At the beginning of recorded moral enquiry in the West, Plato identified analogous problems about the foundations of ethics and about the serious effects if it were widely believed that nothing religiously or metaphysically substantive lies beneath current moral fashions and orthodoxies – themselves rationally – even, if need be, irrationally – replaceable by radically different alternatives. He came to believe that if morality, as more than 'enlightened' self-interest, is to be rationally justifiable, it must be established on metaphysical foundations and in the *Republic* he attempted to put the nature of these foundations at the centre of ethical debate. His book was too challenging for its day and in the short term this project foundered.

Part of Plato's failure – which I shall begin to consider in chapter 1 – can be attributed to his deliberately unsystematic approach to philosophical questions, to his wish to instruct without inducing parrot-fashion learning of the 'right' answers, and to the fact that the apparent connections between moral philosophy on the one hand and theories of the person and personal identity on the other are approached in Platonic dialogues by indirection rather than by statement, justification and accompanying argument; the Greeks were but little disposed to write treatises on methodology. A further factor was that many of Plato's own followers became so engrossed in his metaphysics that they inclined to forget that this was originally developed to provide the groundwork for 'the best life', for the good of the soul. As for his opponents, they so concentrated on what they saw as his metaphysical inadequacies that they overlooked or misconstrued the consequences for ethics if his apparently defective foundationalism is set aside, or they surreptitiously appropriated parts of that foundationalism while rejecting other essential elements needed to make the theory coherent.

There is reason to believe that in our times, as in those of Plato, the theoretical crisis about moral foundations underlies many of the immediate disagreements about personal and political decision-making, and that the confusion in much contemporary moral debate depends in part on a systematic unwillingness outside academia – and often within it – to look squarely at this crisis. A good example of such 'ostrichism' can be recognized in the fact that even many religious writers seem to wish to explain away, if not merely to ignore, the radically 'foundationalist' threat to their entire ethical belief systems, and that even when they are themselves highly skilled in the techniques of contemporary – and especially Anglo-American – philosophy.

Some of them suppose that by making a few compromises, by broad-mindedly supping with the devil, they can beat their opponents at their game; others expect that *principled* agreement on the foundations of morality between theists and atheists is possible. One of the conclusions of the present study will be that however much the two groups may agree on the practical implementation of their theories, at the level of theory itself agreement can only be reached if one group – and it is invariably the theists – gives away most of its position at the outset: a 'Catch-22' effect of the Christian ethic is that 'charity' may seem to imply an exaggerated deference to one's opponent! In thus combining an apparently secular, often nominally Kantian, moral theory with a strict religious code of practice, our theists prop up an attempted rationalism in philosophy with a fideism in theology, thus indulging in a moral absolutism for which their account of human nature, human circumstances and human reason provides inadequate support. It is then hardly surprising that they fail to convince their secular debating partners of the coherence of their philosophical claims.

The distinction between theists and secularists or de facto atheists, even if not recognized by the theists, is often clear to their opponents, and not merely to those – such as 'emotivists' and other 'non-cognitivists' – who hold that truth and falsehood have no place in moral discourse. It is not only among consequentialists, who identify the good solely in effects, but also among 'Kantians', who think that a working morality can be 'constructed' through examination of the concept of rational agency, that it is widely held that attempts to identify the 'essence' of humanity, dependent as they must be on theism or some 'realist' metaphysics, have failed, and hence that in our Brave New World 'deep' claims of theoretical reasoning must be replaced by purely practical and secular reflection on our capacities, capabilities and activities.[3]

That might seem a discouraging prospect, yet secular humanists, unless ambushed by post-modernism, are necessarily optimists. Derek Parfit, a bold contemporary thinker who has done much to expose the nature of the current chaos in ethics, is unambiguously hopeful in his conclusions, not only holding that the crisis about foundations in ethics is already in process of resolution (or dissolution), but maintaining it a mark of philosophical progress that we can now see reflection on moral questions as still in its infancy. At the end of *Reasons and Persons* he writes:[4]

Belief in God, or in many gods, prevented the free development of moral reasoning. Disbelief in God, openly admitted by a majority, is a very recent event, not yet completed. Because this event is so recent, Non-Religious Ethics is at a very early stage. We cannot yet predict whether, as in Mathematics, we will all reach agreement. Since we cannot know how Ethics will develop, it is not irrational to have high hopes.

Our present chaos in ethics has no single begetter but, both developing and subverting Kant and Bentham, Nietzsche, with his assault on 'Enlightenment values' can claim to have played a major role in its genesis – though at times he saw himself merely as the enthusiastic chronicler of stupendous events. A second contemporary philosopher, David Gauthier – no reconstructed utilitarian like Parfit but a neo-Hobbesian – has cited him as the prophet of our times: 'As the will to truth thus gains self-consciousness – there can be no doubt of that – morality will gradually perish now: this is the great spectacle in a hundred acts reserved for the next two centuries in Europe – the most terrible, most questionable, and perhaps also the most hopeful of all spectacles.'[5]

---

3 Note the perceptive summary of O. O'Neill, *Towards Justice and Virtue* (Cambridge University Press, 1996), 95: 'Without a more explicit vindication of some background perfectionism, or more generally of the necessary metaphysics, it may quite simply be impossible to establish necessary and sufficient conditions for qualifying as an agent (or person), or as a subject (or holder of rights). Yet most contemporary universalists are uninclined [*sic*] to argue for this type of background position.'

4 D. Parfit, *Reasons and Persons* (Oxford University Press, 1986), 454.

5 *On the Genealogy of Morals*, trans. Walter Kaufmann and R. J. Hollingdale (New York, 1967), third essay, section 27, p. 161; cf. D. Gauthier, 'Why Contractarianism?' (unpublished lecture).

Prescind from Parfit's claim that most of mankind is now sufficiently enlightened as to admit to open disbelief in God (for Parfit – not alone in this – seems to identify mankind with a self-anointed vanguard group of middle-class European and North American intellectuals and opinion-formers) and concentrate on his observation that philosophical enquiry into matters ethical is now at a new and crucial stage. This part of his claim is true, even though, as noted, many of the more traditionally minded moral philosophers he controverts are – to judge at least by their writings – hardly aware of the significance of what is happening around them. Certainly puzzled and often appalled by what they see in political and moral *behaviour*, and hence tempted to various types of moral fundamentalism, they yet fail to recognize the relation of such public changes to the debunking of any form of intellectual objectivism not only in ethics but throughout the humanities as a whole – unless perhaps they notice the morass of contemporary New Testament studies or the hypothesized absence of an author from their favourite works of literature.[6]

That is not to say nor to imply that the 'post-modern' world has come upon us out of the blue; that world is in important respects merely a late stage of the world of 'modernity'. Yet it is now easier for Westerners, after many years of attempted self-delusion, to come to an awareness of the extent of the change in their personal outlooks and behaviours to which unchecked anti-transcendentalism (whether nominally naturalist, emotivist, constructivist, perspectivist or more traditionally relativist) has given birth: not, of course, parthenogenically, but coupled first with in-dustrialization and the development of technology, and more recently with economic globalization. Just as it is apparent from any Western campus cafeteria or from any 'quality' newspaper that the language and images of Parfit's 'mankind' have become proletarianized[7] – no need now to look in the public lavatory for the lowest common denominator – so the habits of what was 'low-life' morality (often under high-sounding

---

[6] Cf. M. Foucault, 'Qu'est-ce un auteur?', *Bulletin de la Société Française de Philosophie* 63 (1969). An interesting examination of the seriousness of the challenge of this kind of writing is offered by G. Steiner, *Real Presences* (London: Faber, 1989).

[7] N. Boyle, *Who Are We Now?: Christian Humanism and the Global Market from Hegel to Heaney* (Notre Dame University Press, 1998), stresses the role of economic globalization in our being prole-tarianized (as producer/consumers). No-one now is just a bourgeois or an official, an owner or a regular employee, or possessed of an old-style vocation or profession. Boyle's analysis (except insofar as it leads to economic determinism in a stronger sense than I would allow) is often compatible with mine. An issue between us, however, might be the full range of characteris-tics of the new 'proletarians'. I shall return to the social and economic aspects of our current moral chaos, and their interaction with the ascendancy of anti-transcendentalism, in my political chapter 8.

names) fast become the norms of moral and political discourse. In the wake of the loss of any clear sense of what 'low-life' might suggest, intellectuals are becoming 'downwardly mobile', and while losing their grip on an overall concept of virtue, often see such a direction as in itself virtuous and high-minded, or sentimentally as solidarity with the marginalized or dispossessed.

Thus Western philosophers and their opinion-forming disciples have come to resemble midwives – to borrow Plato's metaphor – to the birth of a class of intellectual lager-louts. What deserves consideration is whether, personal comfort, expediency and even safety apart, there is anything 'inappropriate' (if not 'wrong') about the changes in the fundamental moral beliefs and attitudes of such opinion-formers – changes visible equally on the 'left' and on the 'right' of what used to be the conventional spectrum – or whether we are merely growing wiser about the illusionless 'truths' to which intellectual integrity demands we acclimatize ourselves. If where I have normally spoken of 'moral', as in 'moral agents', perhaps I should have highlighted the seriousness of the problem by using the apparently broader term 'spiritual', it is that, bowing to the *Diktat* of our liberal times, I have myself preferred to speak, at least in the first instance, in current parlance. However, I shall argue not only that 'moral' is an insufficiently broad notion but that the concept of agency suggests a Procrustean diminution of human nature which has proved a convenient means both of diminishing the problems of ethics and of giving a spurious impression of success in solving them.[8]

Exception may be taken to Plato and the Greeks more generally being given priority in this book. If that objection were sustainable, the book would fail. Throughout his life Plato thought that 'How should I live?' is *the* philosophical question and that in theory and in practice there are only two honest answers to it, attempts to mediate between these two being but ignorant, incoherent, trivializing or all of these. In his last work, the *Laws*, he was still attempting to describe how, in the absence of an incorruptible philosopher-king – by then relegated to wishful thinking – the implications of the answer to 'How should I live?' could best – albeit often tragically – be given a practical and inevitably institutional form.

The philosophical thrust of the present work does not depend on whether my reading of Plato is historically correct. Plato's use of the dialogue form can make it peculiarly difficult to determine which views

---

[8] Despite its perhaps still excessive (or misleading) emphasis on human *action*, the phrase 'acting person' has its attractions, but I prefer to avoid as far as possible the definitional problems which arise when we speak of 'persons'.

of his characters are those of their creator.⁹ Yet although philosophically I am not committed to the historicity of my account, I believe the views I attribute to Plato to be indeed his own. It will require a further book to explain why this is so, but a brief, unargued introduction to my reasons is not out of place here.¹⁰

The best interpretation of Plato's dialogues will accept that their author held philosophical truth to be a way of life and irreducible to any set of propositions. Any defender of that way of life must defend it propositionally, that is by analysis, argument and reference;¹¹ yet all of these methods involve pulling material out of the life context in which it is embedded, and hence will be reductionist at least in the sense of being incomplete. If some of the positions of, say, Socrates are the positions which Plato himself would have always attempted to defend, he would also have known that his defences would be limited. Though they would be effective in the context of the arguments he is from time to time controverting and as a reply to the type of individual who would mount rival positions of particular sorts, they would stand in need of substantial restatement in differing social and intellectual circumstances.

Consider a parallel case. Francis of Assisi would have denied that living a Christian life is merely the equivalent of knowing and accepting the decrees of the Church as formulated in its creeds and by its Councils, yet he would have appealed to creeds, Councils and other theological sources if asked to provide an explanation of his Christian life. While refusing to equate such sets of theological propositions with being a Christian, he could maintain that they had been arrived at in the hope of resolving particular problems. The parallel can help us to see why Plato would not wish to identify living a philosophical life with whatever propositions Socrates, or any other character of his dialogues, might successfully defend; hence his proper cautions about *writing* philosophy. Plato's view would be that certain basic propositions, often but not always defended or advanced by Socrates himself, help to move the reader in the right direction, and that anyone who would reject (rather than

---

⁹ For a challenging recent treatment see C. H. Kahn, *Plato and the Socratic Dialogue* (Cambridge University Press, 1996).

¹⁰ I made a tentative beginning in 'On the Aims and Effects of Platonic Dialogues', *Iyyun* 46 (1997), 29–46.

¹¹ Reference is particularly important since Plato conspicuously refers to the Good (especially in the *Republic*) while refusing to describe it, allowing himself only to identify it via its effects, and also by analogy, his very claims about the Good implying that it cannot be defined. It is, of course, possible to refer to things without knowing what they are (whether essentially or in some other way); I do not need to 'know' the physical qualities and structure of iron to recognize and point out a piece of iron.

amend and improve) those propositions is moving in the direction of metaphysical and – here I will venture the word – spiritual error.

The present book is about foundationalism in ethics, and discussions of foundationalism were often deeper, more perceptive and more honest among the ancients, operating without Jewish or Christian theological *assumptions*, though not necessarily without what I would call theological *conclusions*. However, I do not wish merely to retrieve ancient philosophical theses, even those of Plato and the Platonists; my purpose is to build on those theses and those of their continuators, in our present revived and revised debate. For all its ancient material, this is offered as a book about ethics and politics, not about the history of philosophy. Only it is futile to expect to do ethics if we refuse to remember what we have been taught; thus if Plato is fundamentally right about transcendental moral realism, any 'modern' reconstruction of ethics must reduce to some form of 'choice theory', tied to relativism or perspectivism. The major issues in moral philosophy, as Plato realized, are comparatively simple and cannot be fudged. Much of the sheer complication and difficulty of contemporary moral philosophy serves to blur this simplicity.

There is a further way in which the historical material in this book is intended directly as a contribution to philosophy itself. The history of Western thought is not to be drawn in a continuous line from Thales to the late twentieth century. There are many radical breaks in the continuity – not least that associated with Kant – but the most radical of all, and the most enduring, is to be located between the fourteenth and the seventeenth centuries. The scientific and other objective advances of that period were achieved at the price of enormous philosophical setbacks, some of which – not least the gradual sacrifice of teleology in the pursuit of the 'how' to the exclusion of the 'why' both in physics and in ethics – are gradually being recognized. Much of 'antiquity' was lost and needs to be retrieved as a corrective to the emphases and directions of 'modernity' and its 'post-modern' entail, and nowhere is this more apparent than in the metaphysics of morals and in moral philosophy itself.

Thus this book is also intended to further the process of setting straight the historical record and returning us, chastened, to earlier and more promising journeyings. And in so proceeding I must emphasize another tactic in which throughout the present study I am systematically following a Greek path: not, in this case, that of Socrates and Plato, but that of Zeno, the disciple of Parmenides of Elea. Opponents of Parmenides' claim that 'being is one' argued that his views are wildly counter-intuitive, and that, if true, they would offer us an extraordinary world. On Parmenides' behalf Zeno countered that if he is wrong the world is very much *more* extraordinary and paradoxical. I shall similarly suggest that Plato's moral realism is strange, and makes striking demands on us, but that if he and his more developed philosophical successors are radically mistaken, the world is far stranger – and I mean unintelligible as well as more dreadful – than some of us find conceivable.

Finally, the present work being a discussion both of ethics and of its political entailments, I shall follow Plato's strategy in the *Republic* in a further particular sense: chapters 1–7 are partly historical and largely directed to ethical theory; chapter 8 turns to political implications of ethics, while foundational issues, in a more directly theological context, return in the concluding chapter 9. Within chapters 1–7 I shall first explicitly consider the two essential aspects of any 'Platonizing' position: (1) Plato's theory of the Good and its subsequent adaptations (1–2); (2) Plato's theory of love and the 'divided soul' (3–4). Chapters 5–7 will treat of the more interesting and promising contemporary alternatives to 'Platonic' realism.

CHAPTER I

Moral nihilism: Socrates vs. Thrasymachus

The raw material of ethical reflection is provided by human behaviour as we experience and observe it and as it is recorded directly by historians, journalists, TV cameramen and film-makers, writers and, less directly, by other sorts of 'creative' artists. An argument might be developed that it is preferable that such people not be philosophers, for the more philosophical they are, the more they are likely to overlay their observations with theory, and theories have a way of bending facts to their own convenience. A possible reply would be that a philosopher might approach historical or descriptive writing more conscious of such dangers, and thus take more precautions to be dispassionate.

Many people believe that it is vain to hope to produce narratives of the past or present unburdened by theory, and thus conclude that the only significant difference between the 'philosophical' observer and his lay counterpart is that the former will produce more self-conscious, more sophisticated and even novel theories with which to wrap up the 'facts', while the latter is more likely to reproduce the 'ordinary' prejudices of his time. Such a conclusion is premature and simplistic. While the historian or other direct assembler and assessor of the raw material of ethical enquiry cannot entirely avoid a limited and personal point of view (though he can certainly avoid crude propaganda), the literary artist, especially the tragedian, is able to present moral dilemmas the more poignantly – or the more unfairly – since he enjoys the luxury of not having to argue, or even perhaps insinuate, any resolution in moral terms; he need only describe an example of human chaos, perhaps from different perspectives, thereby evoking our sympathy, hatred or contempt, though not always our rational judgement.[1]

Contemporary perspectivism, however – advancing beyond the view that we can only describe 'events' partially, and that our viewing is

---

[1] See the discussion of Sophocles' *Philoctetes* in A. MacIntyre, *Whose Justice? Which Rationality?* (London: Duckworth, 1988), 58–62.

irremediably determined by our subjective stance, its history and the tradition to which it belongs – is more than a powerful description of the difficulties of historiography and of 'unbiased' thinking. It is a philosophical theory that 'truth' itself, in history as in morality, is unobtainable and therefore an illusion; indeed that the past itself is to be collapsed into the present or constructed out of our desires and wishes for the future. Such bold inferences, of course, are far from self-evident and face dialectical threats – as can be recognized if we deconstruct the project itself. The claim that, since our knowledge is limited by our perspective as viewers, any complete and overarching 'truth' is impossible to attain, let alone that it does not exist, cannot itself be treated as 'neutral' or 'context-free': *ex hypothesi* perspectivism is a thesis with a history and the perspectivist (whether he admits it or not) is himself an agent with a history whose own views cannot be privileged, however immediately attractive they may seem – and they attract because they contain a degree of truth.

Perspectivism is a post-modern theory claiming to transcend its own limitations and intended to bolster prior insights about the impossibility in principle of objective knowledge, metaphysical truth, historical fact, and especially of objective values in morals and aesthetics. It is a form of special pleading for seeing man, and each man, as a timeless will, and like all special pleading it can hardly avoid overstating its case, thus using the 'facts' it reveals to insinuate a greater degree of applicability than they warrant. For quite apart from the irrationality of any privileging of the perspectivist as a historical critic, a claim that our understanding is limited by our perspective says nothing compelling about the more interesting questions of whether some perspectives are more informative and ultimately more fruitful – 'truer' even – than others, or how, if they are more informative, fruitful or true, they might be recognized as such. To be a perspectivist about the *means* of discerning truth does not commit me to believing truth an illusion, nor to the Nietzschean claim that we cannot distinguish facts from images or metaphors from literal truths.

Nevertheless, there are ways in which perspectivist ideas, misleading though they often are, can be put to good use. They may for example challenge the cosy, contemporary perspective whereby philosophers are assumed to have always been concerned with the same questions, even if they have approached them from differing starting-points and with more or less skill. At a broad level of generality there is truth in that, but to make the point at such a level is of little practical help, and it is actually harmful if accompanied by uncritical claims as to the steady and unchanging meaning of philosophical terms (and concepts) across centuries of reflection: whether these terms exist within some single language and culture, or whether they or their translated 'equivalents' are held to persist as we move from one language and culture to the next.

It is easy to forget that significantly different philosophical enquiries may make use of similar 'technical' terms: famously, words like 'being' (which in classical Greek refers to *finite* being, though it is not so restricted in English) and 'reason' (which can refer merely to discursive reasoning in English but may include 'intuition' in classical Greek) are of this sort. Such examples would suggest that from whatever perspective we view the history of philosophy we can increase the depth and seriousness of our enquiries by considering, so far as possible, not merely how we believe we rightly deploy words and concepts, but how they were deployed in those other historical epochs relevant to our subject-matter. While granting to the perspectivist that for such a work we cannot entirely remove our own distorting spectacles, we have no need to grant either that we are unaware that we are wearing them or that we cannot begin to correct the distortions they produce. That is, there is no need to concede that old-fashioned philology does not have its uses – not least because, thanks to the perspectivist, we can be more aware of its limitations.

Supported by such generally consoling awareness of the difficulties confronting those who essay to interpret alien cultures, whether contemporary or of the past, let us turn to the Greek origins of Western philosophy. Though not the first ethical thinker in Greece – indeed a thinker already reacting both to the often explicit practices of his own society and to the boldly subversive views of the Sophists – Socrates, a practical man and a craftsman both by upbringing and by philosophical profession, has a good claim, as Aristotle recognized, to be hailed if not as the founder, then at least as the re-founder, of Western moral debate – though not, of course, of Western moral belief. Socrates apparently wanted to be as clear about what kinds of acts are good and just and about how to perform them as shoemakers are about what shoes are and how to make them. He wanted to be able to identify who knows how to act justly, what kind of knowledge such a man possesses and the kind of acts he will typically perform. He looked for some kind of identifying mark on bits of behaviour by which he could recognize unerringly a morally good act when he saw it, and hence posit a good class of acts. He accepted (perhaps for the sake of argument) that in the good old days an Athenian gentleman knew how to behave, knew his code of behaviour, in the same way as an eighteenth-century English gentleman knew that he should pay his card debts and make 'calls'.

By the time of Socrates such assured awareness of a code of behaviour, albeit a narrow one, could not pass without challenge. In his comedy *The Clouds* Aristophanes presents a character who, when charged with adultery, is able to say 'What's wrong with that?' Or, anticipating Moore's 'open question' argument, when charged with beating his father and mother, something like: 'I know that this stick is striking father's back and hurting him, and that a lot of people, including father, find that offensive, but what's *wrong* with it?' In a notorious line of Aristophanes' contemporary Euripides, a character asks, 'What's wrong except what the audience think to be wrong?' Rightly or wrongly, such attacks on the traditional moral code were associated with those called 'sophists', professional teachers, sometimes of rhetoric, who often claimed to distinguish between what is conventionally wrong and what, if anything, is really or 'naturally' wrong. Some of them were inclined to encourage clever politicians or other opinion-makers to play on such antitheses. They could persuade people that what they had always been taught to think wrong is only wrong by convention, by man-made law or custom, and they might add that such customs and laws are worth no more than the interests or wills or wisdom of their makers. Thus if a law or custom could make parricide a vice, a new version, if accepted through force, fraud or deliberate choice of some or more human beings, could make it a virtue. Once it is widely accepted that the significance of moral terms can fluctuate in this way, a traditional society has collapsed. Socrates seems to have divined such a collapse, actual or impending, and his pupil Plato to have characterized it in detail.

The *Republic* is Plato's most ambitious attempt to explain the seriousness of the issues at stake if moral words (and therefore moral concepts) are freed from their traditional moorings, though, as we have seen, he was not the only or even the first observer of the phenomenon as it appeared in its Greek setting. After the fictions of Aristophanes, consider the historian Thucydides describing (3.82.4) the effects of civil war in Corcyra (Corfu): the struggle of oligarch against democrat, which is to say of those who advocated a dictatorship of the few against those favouring a dictatorship of the majority:

Men changed the ordinary accreditation of words to things at their own discretion. Mindless audacity was considered to be the courage of a true party-man, thoughtful hesitation to be specious cowardice, restraint an excuse for lack of virility ... careful planning a plausible pretext for failing in one's responsibilities ... The political leaders on each side took up pretty slogans, one speaking of equal civic responsibilities and obligations for the people under the law, the other of a moderate aristocracy.

Thucydides has reduced the world of politics and public policy to that of the gang boss who, observing one of his men unwilling to cut the throat of a bystander whose mistake is to have seen too much, taunts him with 'lack of guts'. He merely *narrates how* moral language can be twisted by demagogues and military adventurers to their own purposes, for who can say what is correct usage? In the *Republic*, Plato himself, apprenticed by a political background on both sides of his family, develops the Thucydidean theme for his own purposes. There is no immediate context of civil war, in Corcyra or anywhere else, nor is he merely drawing attention to the manipulation of the public by demagogues and adventurers; Plato makes the subtler point that demagogues fall victim to their *own* propaganda. In deceiving others, they cannot but diminish their identity by being themselves deceived. The example shows something of the nature of the world in which we must live if the abuse of moral language becomes endemic: though that world will not arise from nothing, and Plato rehearses a version of the stages of the degeneration of society from the rule of aristocrats holding office to serve others and lead them towards the Good to that of the 'tyrannical' man whose only aim is to use others to promote what he takes to be his own advantage. Plato holds that the tyrant is the last person to know what that advantage is.

Before composing the *Republic*, Plato had published a number of smaller and slighter dialogues treating of how to recognize a virtue (such as self-control or courage) when you see it. The more basic challenge to morality as such – put in the mouth of Thrasymachus in the *Republic* – was still in the future. In the *Gorgias*, in some respects a trial run for the *Republic*, we find that Callicles, judged by Nietzsche to get the better of Socrates,[2] believes that there is an objective 'natural justice'

---

[2] Cf. E. R. Dodds, *Plato's Gorgias* (Oxford University Press, 1959), 387–91. But Nietzsche's account of the Nietzscheanism of Callicles is misleading. He failed to notice that Callicles shows no interest in the creativity on which he himself placed such emphasis. Nietzsche's primary hero was – eventually – Goethe, not Napoleon; Callicles admires not literary figures as creative artists, but politicians as direct wielders of power.

Nevertheless, we should recognize Nietzsche's perspicacity in identifying Socrates and Plato as his greatest philosophical foes, and the tradition which they inaugurated as a supreme challenge to his own position. For Socrates and Plato established much of the framework – including much of the metaphysical framework – within which Greek ethics was constructed and without which most of it is unintelligible. Which makes it the more surprising that J. Annas, *The Morality of Happiness* (Oxford University Press, 1993), especially 17–20, declines to discuss Plato in five hundred pages of small print on ancient ethics. Her reasons, however, become clearer in light of her more recent study, *Platonic Ethics, Old and New* (Ithaca: Cornell University Press, 2000), a book concerned largely with Middle Platonic readings of Plato, but where, in chapter 5, she denies – in what seems to be an atomizing of the text, an unwillingness to consider the structure of the *Republic* as a whole – that the metaphysics of the *Republic* is intended to sustain the ethics.

recognizable by the strong and taking the form of a law that the superior pursues and should pursue his own will. Not only does Callicles hold to this claim about the objectivity of justice, thus appearing less radical than Thrasymachus, but he allows himself to concede to Socrates that there are certain sorts of behaviour (such as that of passive homosexuals) which are simply shameful. That is a fatal admission analogous to that of the would-be relativist or perspectivist who nevertheless allows himself to say and believe, for example, that the Holocaust was simply wrong.

The *Republic* is a complex book with many themes; it is arranged like a set of Russian dolls, one inside the other such that the innermost doll, the 'metaphysical' claims about the Good in books 6 and 7, is the core of the work. As we move from book 1 towards book 6, Plato progressively opens up the stronger and eventually metaphysical claims he believes to be necessary if the position of 'his' Thrasymachus – that 'justice is nothing other than the advantage of the stronger' – is to be rebutted.[3]

It is not clear from what we know of the historical Thrasymachus why Plato has selected him to present – if ultimately incoherently – the position of the moral nihilist,[4] the man who believes that, since the sense of all moral terms is determined by the social and political context in which they are uttered, it is only fools (and especially fools duped by those more astute in the 'propaganda' struggle) who take them seriously in the sense of believing themselves to be not merely imprudent in breaking the rules and acting 'unjustly', but objective evil-doers. Views rather like that of Thrasymachus can be found in the extant fragments and citations of the sophist Antiphon – who might thus seem to have been a candidate for enhanced fame through a personal appearance in

---

3 Not least because of the nature of his earlier arguments for the existence of Forms (especially the 'one-over-many' argument: if a, b and c are good, then there is a Form of Goodness; if x, y and z are men, then there is a Form of Man), Plato developed a broader metaphysical realism than he needed to defeat his ethical opponents. His view that there are realities answering to every sort of general term is unnecessary – and depends on (at least) two false propositions: (1) that general terms of 'fact' and 'value' can be treated similarly, and (2) that there is no need to introduce a 'bearer' of moral terms (who would need only be a *maker* or *creator* of physical objects). A Fregean realism limited to non-moral and non-evaluative terms would resolve some of the difficulties of proposition (1) in exactly the opposite way to that required for a successful defence of the foundations of ethics. Proposition 2, as I shall argue in chapter 2, was corrected by later Platonists.

4 A version of what follows in this and the following chapter on the *Republic* was tested at a meeting of the Boston Area Colloquium on Ancient Philosophy meeting at Holy Cross College, Worcester, Mass., and appears as 'The Possibility of Morality in Plato's *Republic*', in J. Cleary and G. Gurtler (eds.), *Boston Area Colloquium in Ancient Philosophy* 14 (1999), 53–72, together with a thoughtful (but, I think, ultimately unsuccessful) critique by Rachel Barney: 'Is Plato Interested in Meta-Ethics? Commentary on Rist', *ibid.*, 73–81.

the *Republic*.[5] Plato may have wanted to demonstrate that the historical Thrasymachus, author of writings on rhetoric, was retailing in systematic form the kind of education which, emphasizing persuasion rather than truth, must always lead (perhaps unbeknown to its professors) to nihilist attitudes and behaviour.[6] Or Plato's selection of Thrasymachus for his notorious role could be an ironic parody or in-joke, the significance of which is now lost.

I turn to the text. After Socrates has given comparatively short shrift to Polemarchus' traditional and unthinking appeals, in an attempted account of justice, to notions like helping one's friends and harming one's enemies,[7] Thrasymachus, snorting with indignation at the 'simplistic' attitudes of the speakers, is induced to make the cryptic remark that justice is the advantage of the stronger. He is not presented as offering this as a definition of justice, but as a truth about justice, and by justice he refers to a set of other-regarding attitudes *which are called* justice, for as he goes on to explain, he thinks justice is no more than the name for whatever the laws (and customs) prescribe as appropriate to our dealings with one another. Part of his position, it soon turns out, is clear and devastating: whatever type of régime happens to be in power, whether democratic, oligarchic or despotic, makes laws designed to profit itself, and mainly to keep itself in power. These laws it presents as just (338E1, cf. 2.359B3), and the gullible public – relying on the assumption that when the word 'just' is used, reference is made to something objective and prescriptive – is inclined to obey them. Thus Thrasymachus combines the brutal view that all law is positive law with the assumption that those astute enough to rule play on the folly (noble or otherwise) of the human race, and specifically on their supposition that 'law' indicates objective moral norms.[8]

---

5 Cf. D. Furley, 'Antiphon's Case Against Justice', in *Cosmic Problems* (Cambridge University Press, 1989), 66–76. Furley is right to argue that (despite his use of the notion of 'nature') Antiphon's view is closer to that of Thrasymachus than to that of Callicles.

6 The *Phaedrus* lends colour to this possibility.

7 Polemarchus fails to think his position through in at least the following ways:

1. Like characters in earlier dialogues, he starts from too restrictive an account of the kind of behaviour that is just.
2. In allowing himself to be led into accepting that the good guard is the good thief, he fails to understand the moral force of 'cannot', as in 'I cannot bring myself to do that.'
3. He uses, rather than makes sense of, the notion of helping your friends and harming your enemies.
4. He fails to distinguish between 'punish' and 'harm'.

8 Thus my account of the position of Thrasymachus is nearest to that of T. J. D. Chappell, 'The Virtues of Thrasymachus', *Phronesis* 38 (1993), 1–17. Cf. also A. Flew, 'Responding to Plato's Thrasymachus', *Philosophy* 70 (1995), 436–47, e.g. 443.

Plato's genius as an observer of the human scene is literary as well as philosophical: he presents Thrasymachus as claiming that such objective and non-arbitrary justice is a fiction, and yet as unable to express himself about 'justice' (the fiction) without using the language of justice (the reality) (347, 352A ff.). This ironic depiction is certainly one of the causes of the disagreement among scholars as to what exactly Thrasymachus is trying to propose – though this is less obscure if his claims are viewed in the light of the project of the *Republic* as a whole.

That project is to show – and it is also my project here – that a position roughly similar to that of Thrasymachus is one of only two coherent attitudes to the first principles of 'morality': a position which itself may appear in two different forms. The more inchoate version will be recognizable when its advocate is too good-natured or confused to see the full implications of his approach – not least concerning the 'shocking' language in which human behaviour should properly be discussed. The clear and unambiguous version, on the other hand, will be expressed in terms which the ordinary public will find hard to stomach, or perhaps unacceptable. Hence, Thrasymacheanism is of only limited *direct* concern to the observer of the surface of the *practical* world of power politics, though of paramount importance in any theoretical account of the nature of morality.[9] For what philosophers can debate more or less unashamedly among themselves can be introduced only gradually into publicized policies. Except in such brutalized conditions of society as obtain, as Thucydides noted, in times of civil war or other fundamental social upheaval, the public needs to be softened up (deliberately or otherwise) to accept the 'unacceptable'.

Since it is impossible to defend an irrational position rationally, Plato probably thought of Thrasymachus' position as rationally indefensible. That may be why he both allows Thrasymachus to be discomfited by Socrates' use of arguments which – unless recognized as in part necessarily *ad hominem* – seem often less than compelling (though Thrasymachus himself, being the sort of character who would hold the sort of theory he holds, lacks the wit or skill to see through them), and why he also admits that Thrasymachus has let Socrates off too lightly and could have done a good deal more for his own position.[10] For that position, Plato knows, wins support not merely because of what can rationally be said

---

[9] Cf. Flew, 'Responding', 443.
[10] Thrasymachus unnecessarily weakens his position by ignoring a specifically instrumentalist account of reason (though Glaucon and Adeimantus correct him) and by tending to suggest that the 'stronger' will *always* act 'unjustly' (e.g. at 349CD).

for it, but because of its all-too-human, albeit not 'moral', attractiveness –
especially to half-educated sophisticates and those who admire political
goals they conventionally dread to espouse and political crimes they lack
the boldness to attempt.

The claim of Thrasymachus that particular political régimes use
'moral' language and promote 'moral' beliefs as a means of ensuring
their own survival is a special version of the broader claim that the will
of any individual or group of individuals, however arrived at, is sufficient to determine the reference of a prescriptive 'moral' term. When
Thrasymachus observes that justice (that is, what people hold or believe to be justice in some prescriptive sense) is the advantage of the
stronger, he is drawing a legitimate conclusion from the claim that the
dominant elements in any society, be they groups or individuals, will
legislate about what is 'just' with their own interests (however defined)
in mind – unless they believe that there is some superior 'moral' reason why they should not do so. This broader claim is perhaps less
self-evident than Thrasymachus believes. Most people, as Hume recognized, do seem to have limited reserves of generosity, and of course
it may also turn out that our own interest is also the interest of some
(or even of all) members of our society, even if that is a matter of
chance.

Thrasymachus holds that there are no non-arbitrary values ('goods
in themselves'), and that we are free, if we wish, to work out, determine
or construct whatever 'values' will please and profit ourselves from time
to time – including a system of morality to which other people can
be induced to subscribe. What can the Platonic Socrates say in reply?
The main point of the ensuing books of the *Republic* – down to the
core books 6 and 7 – is that unless claims about the proper application
of terms like 'just' and 'good' can be grounded in the transcendent
reality of something perfectly good and just (which Plato calls a 'Form'),
then Thrasymachus has won an important argument: not perhaps the
argument that what is conventionally called injustice makes one happier
than what is conventionally called justice, but that we are deluded if
we believe that justice and goodness (or, to give it a modern context,
'human rights') enjoy any objectively prescriptive status, in the sense of
existing outside the human mind (where they are more or less rational
possibilities) or apart from the human will (where they are practices or
conventions, whether beneficial or the reverse). We may be *useful* idiots
in subscribing to moral objectivism, and in particular to transcendental
realism, but philosophically we are still idiots.

In the interests of historical verity we should disarm a lurking objection to this reading of the *Republic*. In refutation of the view that Plato offers (through his account of the Good) a thesis that a transcendental meta-ethics is required if moral nihilism is to be defeated, it might be objected – especially if book 1 is read in comparative isolation – that the argument with Thrasymachus has nothing to do with meta-ethics at all; Socrates and Thrasymachus simply represent two radically different approaches within the parameters of normative ethics. They agree that we all seek happiness (*eudaimonia*), but they disagree about how such *eudaimonia* is to be attained.

The argument between Socrates and Thrasymachus is not primarily about how *eudaimonia* is to be attained, but whether Thrasymachus rightly denies the objectivity of moral values. Socrates (eventually) comes to suggest that no search for *eudaimonia* can possibly be effective if there are no man-independent realities or Forms to make talk either of happiness or of morality coherent and intelligible. If that is right, although Thrasymachus *talks* about *eudaimonia*, he not only does not know what is conducive to *eudaimonia*; he is simply inadequately equipped to consider the matter at all. It is not that Socrates and Thrasymachus are 'eudaimonists' who disagree how to secure their end; rather Thrasymachus will not admit the world of discourse in which, for Socrates, *eudaimonia* must be located. Since he will know nothing of that universe, he repels consideration of how values, including those he thinks his own, can be secured, and any coherent notion of what we *ought* to do if we want to be happy.

The debate between Socrates and Thrasymachus cannot then be characterized as between two realists, one of whom – Socrates – later shows that he thinks that *eudaimonia* has a strong connection with the harmony of the psyche, while the other denies that; it is a debate between a transcendental realist and an anti-realist who disagree about the possibility of morality, and therefore, necessarily, its connection with happiness. It is not merely that Thrasymachus wants judgements of right and wrong to be arbitrary; the implication of his view – to which Socrates eventually offers transcendental realism as the only adequate reply – is that 'right' and 'wrong' are the result of human confusions and human manipulations and that therefore happiness (if distinct from 'success') is unreal.

In both its origins and its goals the *Republic* is pre-eminently a practical book: Plato fears what follows if he cannot show that Thrasymachus is wrong. For Plato, the tyrant is the Thrasymachean anti-hero at his most fully developed – we notice how astutely Thrasymachus speaks of our hidden or less hidden admiration of crime on a grand scale – with the shreds of 'bourgeois' or other 'virtue' removed. Thus Plato makes two claims, which together produce a paradoxical scenario. The first is that unless transcendental realism and the corresponding sense of moral language can be established, there is no logical reason, but only the residue of a discredited world-view – or in each new generation the rebirth of a purely pre-philosophical morality – in the way of the full-blooded pursuit of tyranny (or anything else) as the goal of human nature. The second is that with the loss of such an objective morality, any sense even of what is useful to us as we happen to be constituted must also be lost. Epicurus, an ardent anti-Platonist who supported the first of these claims, attempted – perhaps indeed under the influence of the speeches of Glaucon and Adeimantus in the *Republic* – to deny the second, thus resolving the paradox. Plato offers only limited comment on the second point – though what he says is of much interest – his main aim in the *Republic* being to see what philosophical claims are necessary to establish the first.

Plato thus sets up the problem of the objectivity of morality in the starkest possible terms. In the end, he holds, we have to decide between (an improved version of) the moral nihilism of Thrasymachus, for whom goodness is (objectively) whatever we are fool enough to believe if we believe it to be any other than made by man or some men, and the view of Socrates that moral terms, since and only since they have a fixed and transcendental point of reference, cannot be made to mean whatever we like, whatever is convenient, whatever seems to make sense at the moment or whatever we can get people to agree to. They refer to, and derive their force from, some primary 'reality' in the world (or 'beyond' it). For Socrates, if members of traditional societies have accepted a crude, simplistic and initially indefensible morality, their critics have merely shown them to be wrong in detail and application, not in principle. They – and in our pre-philosophical selves we are like them – have merely not understood what they are trying to formulate.

Little of substance can be added to a tightened-up version of the radical challenge which Thrasymachus throws out, but there is now a fashionable corollary which indirectly sheds further light on it. Even if moral 'realism', in the shape of belief in an ultimate moral standard like a Form, is a superstition, it may be a valuable superstition not only for the stronger or dominant party in society but for everyone. That would certainly be so if the alternative *non-realist* theories of moral objectivism were inadequate to save our moral foundations and, in that case, it would follow that it is best for us to believe the lie that there are objective, indeed realist, standards, and to believe it with full emotional commitment. Any alternative would lead to 'moral' and social anarchy – and in the paradox inherent here lies the 'realist's' securest foundation. In our contemporary society failure so to 'believe' would be to encourage terrorism in social and political life, and an inability on the part of anyone to condemn – unless on grounds of expediency – crimes ranging from genocide to the threat and use of chemical, biological or nuclear weapons in international disputes.

Plato would hold that this kind of 'virtual' or 'as-if' morality[11] falls on the Thrasymachean side of the divide which the *Republic* has identified. It might be expedient that many, if not all of us, should believe 'emotionally' that some acts (e.g. genocide) are just wrong, even if there is no such category and they can only be deemed horrifying or inconvenient, but Thrasymachus would still be telling the truth. Plato would also mention that Thrasymachus might be happy to see such deception practised and encouraged by everyone other than himself. And we shall note that Sidgwick and several other recent philosophers have proposed varying forms of the thesis that the generality of men are better off ignorant of certain seeming truths and consequently reasoning in the dark.[12]

Plato is aware of the social threat if moral language is allowed, and especially if it is known to be allowed, to float free. It would not follow that, if he were right about the starkness of the alternatives confronting us, he would be right about 'realism' itself, but whether or not a philosophical account of transcendental moral realism is finally defensible, he would claim that any such theory must either subsume or reassert the arguments of the *Republic*. Nor, of course, even if his strongest claims are more or less correct, will that alone make it simple to determine in any instance whether this act is better or more just than that, less still to know more generally how to act rightly. What he would have shown is that there exists, at least in principle, a canon or measuring stick by which to test such determinations.[13]

---

[11] S. Blackburn, *Spreading the Word* (Oxford University Press, 1984), supplies a contemporary version of which Hume is an ancestor. For more on such positions see chapter 6 below.

[12] B. A. O. Williams, in J. J. C. Smart and B. A. O. Williams, *Utilitarianism: For and Against* (Cambridge University Press, 1973), 16, comments on this kind of 'Government House Consequentialism'.

[13] Aristotle and other virtue-ethicists often seem to suggest that there will be times when only when confronted by the need for a particular decision will the good man know what he should do. Such a view need not be mere intuitionism, only a claim that the good man cannot always predict how his 'disposition' will instruct him to act. Obviously such difficult situations will be rare. In any case Aristotelian 'intuitionism' – as distinct from more recent versions – depends on the cultivation of 'virtue' over many years of disciplined life.

The debate between Socrates and Thrasymachus – and its ramifications in the rest of the *Republic* – not only dramatizes the problem of the
objectivity of moral judgements and the possible realism of moral truths;
it also links such questions closely with those of power and its rewards in
human affairs. To be noticed too is a significant parallel between Platonic
theorizing and the procedures of contemporary perspectivism. Though
the latter as such demands no such necessary linkage, many of its advocates (simultaneously following and subverting Nietzsche) are inclined to
turn Hobbesian in reducing all the social attitudes and behaviours which
are the context within which traditional moralities develop to functions
of power, and hence to insist on the 'politicization' of all aspects of human
behaviour. Plato would agree that politics is fundamentally concerned
with the nature, uses and abuses of power, and that, given man's social
nature, any power relationships are 'political'.

There is a certain difference, however, of at least historical importance,
between contemporary talk of all social relations being 'political', and
the views Plato attributes to Thrasymachus himself. Speaking the language of Greek culture, Thrasymachus has no view of the private sphere
as a mere *part* of the public, a part where public power relationships
work themselves out through social institutions, including the family.
Those modern critics are right who hold that much of the separation of
public and private spheres is constructed arbitrarily by convention and
legislation, and that the practices of public life, including assumptions
about domination and subordination, frequently carry over into the private sphere and the family – and are reinforced in their turn by similar
practices which have grown up within that sphere.[14]

Insofar as Thrasymachus separates the public and the private, his
'ideal' world is less 'totalitarian' than would be the case were he to
redesign it for the twenty-first century. He allows a little 'low-grade'
autonomy to the family world of private life and, despite the example of contemporary Sparta, is less aware than his latter-day avatar
of the risks to the 'real ruler' if the private sphere – 'woman's' world,
as he would contemptuously note it – is allowed as much autonomy
over against the public as he seems prepared to concede. But a reconstructed Thrasymachus need admit only to having made a mistake in

---

[14] That is not to admit, however, that even were impersonal justice of necessity the most basic
condition of sound public life, the relationship between love and justice in family life should
merely reflect this public necessity. Insofar as justice is necessarily impersonal, I shall argue
(especially in chapters 5 and 6) that it can and should be transcended: at least in private life, and
where possible in public life as well.

social psychology:[15] not about the rational principles of politics but about their application.

Despite the differences between Thrasymachean and modern views of moral nihilism, the similarities are far greater: as much as any contemporary deconstructionist Thrasymachus would found every rational version of 'morality' (whether public or private) and every rational account of the nature of moral language on power relationships, in particular on the type of constitution and social structure (dictatorial, oligarchic or democratic) which happens to be desirable or in place at any given time. And as much as any contemporary political operator Thrasymachus holds those who believe in any objective basis for concern for others to be good-natured fools. In the *Gorgias* too, we find Callicles, the pre-Thrasymachean advocate of the pursuit of personal satisfaction by the effective use of force and fraud, alluding to such fools and reproaching Socrates with immaturity.[16] Talking political philosophy and ethics is kids' stuff; if you 'grow up and live in the real world' you can join the struggle and, if you combine strength of purpose with the appropriate ruthlessness, you can dominate. What other goal makes sense?

Plato has identified in broad terms what he believes to be the only two possible coherent attitudes in the debate about moral foundations. Either moral language is more or less stable and the proper and transcendent referents of moral terms can be inferred, or it is free-floating and ultimately arbitrary in its prescriptions, moral terms signalling only the rationalized expression of (someone's) perceived (and even genuine) needs, desires, wishes and preferences. If the latter alternative is to be upheld, users of moral language can be divided into two groups: those 'stronger' people, the 'movers and shakers' (including the 'as-if' moralists) who invent or exploit it to support their own preferences, wants and needs – whether or not objective or basic – and those who uncritically accept the evaluations which others, whether or not in good faith, hand out to them.

---

[15] Thrasymachus would quickly see his 'error', if he read a few pages of S. Talmon's *The Origins of Totalitarian Democracy* (Harmondsworth: Penguin, 1986) on the advantages to the powerful of an all-embracing reduction of the private to the public during the French Revolution and later. He would similarly profit from S. Schama's *Citizens* (Toronto: Random House, 1989).

[16] As already noted, the positions of Callicles and Thrasymachus differ in that Callicles thinks that 'might' (as he understands it) really is right, while Thrasymachus holds that claims about what is naturally right are as naive as claims about what is naturally good. The two anti-Socratics are identical in the importance they place on power and the advantages it brings, but for Thrasymachus Callicles is at bottom just another type of misguided objectivist, even if the effects of his 'natural' objectivism are more rational.

In later chapters we shall consider whether Plato's basic alternatives form the complete set of possibilities, but two currently popular attempts to circumvent the starkness of the choice he offers can be immediately rejected. The reflex has developed among many professional philosophers – presumably under the influence of Wittgenstein – of proscribing as impossible the discussion of such 'Thrasymachean' claims as that 'dishonesty is good' under pain of being excluded from the community of moral reasoners. Such fiats and delimitations certainly enable foundationalist questions to be dismissed, but at the price of *assuming* some sort of 'reality' for that very morality with which the community of moral reasoners is here supposed to be concerned: in other words of 'begging the question'. But the challenge of Thrasymachus is precisely the radical one that morality is a foolish assumption and the community of moral reasoners a mere assembly of fools, and none the less foolish even if they comprise the vast majority of the human race.[17]

A second way of evading Plato's stark options is commonly found among contemporary 'communitarians' in the wake, perhaps consciously, of the followers of Leo Strauss. These start out by assuming that we learn our morality within moral traditions normally embedded in socio-political structures, perhaps preferably in nation-states. Since all our moral thinking occurs within the limitations of these structures, we cannot transcend or – the extreme view – legitimately criticize moral items within them, but must wait until defective traditions, confronted by superior alternatives, lose confidence in themselves and die out. Objections to this are that without such piecemeal criticism – normally from hostile sources – any tradition, however vicious, is likely to perpetuate itself, and more fundamentally that it is folly to encourage people to suppose their particular tradition morally complete and perfectly defensible – not least because most of us are content, while assuming unexamined foundations, to embed our traditions in apparently unchallengeable socio-political institutions.[18]

Such attitudes among 'communitarians' seem to arise from a failure to integrate two common features of 'communitarian' schemata: an

---

[17] I adapt the example of a Thrasymachean treatment of dishonesty from E. L. Pincoffs' *Quandaries and Virtues* (Lawrence: University Press of Kansas, 1986), 248: not because Pincoffs' book is generally typical of the type of moral thinking I like to repudiate; indeed insofar as Pincoffs polemizes against the ethics of problem-solving and advocates an ethics of dispositional development I find his approach sympathetic. Rather I cite him to indicate that even among those most critical of what I believe to be unhelpful features of much modern ethics, this particular question-begging approach to foundationalism is widespread.

[18] See the interesting comments of N. K. Badhwar, 'Social Agency, Community and Impartiality', *Social Philosophy and Policy* 13 (1996), 1–26.

anti-individualist emphasis on tradition and the naive belief that traditions develop 'legitimately' over time. The first element may induce a cavalier attitude about objectively secure foundations, the second a failure to differentiate between essential and incidental features of individual traditions. To which Plato would add what communitarians can only ignore or deny:[19] that in the absence of a transcendental metaphysics of morals, secure foundations for the ideals of communitarianism *cannot* be established – from which it follows that our communitarians should limit themselves to identifying the flaws in and evil effects of liberal individualism rather than pretending to offer a viable alternative.[20]

It is reasonable to assume that Plato was unaware of the magnitude of the task he had set himself and the number of subsidiary problems which must arise if his original 'Socratic' defence against Thrasymachus is eventually to be sustained. That in no way diminishes the importance of his challenge that, unless some sort of transcendental theory of moral values can be defended, it is impossible to identify or adequately to motivate and justify the pursuit of a good life. It is with the problem of justification that the *Republic* in general, and specifically its account of the Form of the Good, is concerned. Plato is not wanting to claim that it is impossible to live – at least given what he called a 'divine dispensation', what Christians call 'grace' or providence and pagans *fortuna* or just luck – what in appearance and even in reality is a good life in 'good faith'; what he does want to urge is the impossibility of the non-realist's offering a compelling rational justification of such a life. Yet justification of behaviour is a primary concern of ethics, at least in the sense that when we think about why what is 'wrong' is wrong, we may be less immediately concerned with our own ability to live a good life (though our reflections may sometimes help with that) than with our ability to persuade or influence others *to* that life and to defend it against intellectual challenge.

Our discussion thus far has been limited to a partial set of 'values', namely moral values. Plato hardly distinguishes between moral and

---

[19] Typical are the remarks of M. Walzer, *Spheres of Justice: A Defence of Pluralism and Equality* (New York: Basic Books, 1983), xv ('Justice is relative to social meanings'); cf. 312–13.

[20] We shall return to this uncomfortable corollary in the final chapter. Liberals sometimes claim that they can operate from uncontroversial foundations: cf. J. Rawls, *Political Liberalism* (New York: Columbia University Press, 1993). That such claims are normally tendentious is argued by J. Haldane, 'The Individual, the State and the Common Good', *Social Philosophy and Policy* 13 (1996), 59–79. That they trivialize differences of opinion in the interest of securing a 'democratic' consensus is certain. For Rawls' influential distinction between 'comprehensive' and 'political' liberalism (and the latter's emphasis on the neutrality of the state) see recently J. Skorupski, 'Liberty's Hollow Triumph', in J. Haldane (ed.), *Philosophy and Public Affairs* (Cambridge University Press, 2000), 66.

aesthetic evaluation, and would certainly accept that if his case about objectivity fails in the case of ethics it also fails in aesthetics. Whether, if it can be preserved in ethics, it will necessarily also be saved in aesthetics is another, more difficult matter. Plato himself would have wished to argue to that effect, and there is no doubt that he could construct a powerful case, elements of which will become apparent as we proceed.

In the *Cratylus*, a dialogue perhaps slightly earlier than the *Republic*, Plato considered problems of the 'correctness' of names. The chief points he had tried to establish are first that if names are 'applied' in any sense correctly, such 'correctness' can only be determined by an investigation of the things named and not merely of the words which name them. His second point is that it is the man who can think straight (the 'dialectician') who will best be able to determine the fit between words and things, or rather the firmness of the bond between various conventional linguistic signs, differing from language to language (Plato toys with, and presumably rejects, the possibility of an 'ideal' language), and the objective items, including moral 'items', to which these words refer. His implicit conclusion here too is that only a free-standing moral universe, not a set of man-made moral concepts, can supply any basis for moral discourse as for morality itself.

Such Platonic themes will recur in the present discussion, as they do in other contemporary discussions, more or less overtly: a good example of the broad and reassuring claim that in philosophy we less often discover new problems than review old ones. What is more challenging, however, is that we review them from different starting-points, as we meet them in different surroundings and from different perspectives. We may find further reasons for accepting or rejecting long-current theories after going down new and exciting alleys, and learning – in a way we could hardly have imagined without the experience of trying them out – that they are ultimately blind. So as we go down the road of investigating the contemporary crisis in ethics, we shall come surprisingly often to remember that Plato and those who developed his insights were there before us.

CHAPTER 2

Morals and metaphysics

PLATO'S METAPHYSICAL GROUNDING OF MORALITY

There is a traditional and popular 'objective' understanding of 'morality' and 'ethics' which has immense emotional appeal. It is acceptable both to the 'man in the street' when he says something like 'That's just wrong' or 'Hitler was an evil man' and to the philosopher in his unguarded moments when he indulges in similar sentiments, not glossing them with anything like 'We all agree that we do not like what Hitler did, and *therefore* we call him evil', or 'Since what Hitler did contributes to the maximization of harms rather than of benefits in the world, we count him as evil', or 'What was "wrong" with Hitler's genocidal schemes was that they were irrational and inconsistent.' But this ordinary understanding of 'common morality'[1] is changed, wittingly or unwittingly, in philosophical talk; for reasons of 'public relations', or a residual sense of shame which the example of Hitler makes apparent, many philosophers who would wish to gloss their comments on Hitlerian behaviour in the ways just indicated decline to state that 'Morality should be superseded', preferring to use the word 'morality' (or 'ethics') as if it referred to something esoteric.

From time to time there are protests against this sleight of hand: Finnis entitled a chapter in an introductory book on moral philosophy, 'Utilitarianism, Consequentialism, Proportionalism... or Ethics?'.[2] Such protests, however, seem to have little effect, because for differing reasons both those who want to change much of the traditional content of ethics and the ordinary non-philosophical public have too strong an emotional investment in the older way of speaking to be willing openly – rather than, for the philosophers, in select company – to avow or accept any radical redescription of what we do when we behave 'rightly' or 'wrongly'.

---

[1] The phrase has been popularized by A. Donagan, *The Theory of Morality* (University of Chicago Press, 1977).
[2] J. M. Finnis, *Fundamentals of Ethics* (Washington: Georgetown University Press, 1983), chapter 4.

Clear-headed philosophers, especially those committed to an 'objective' morality, have always recognized the problem facing the non-objectivist when confronted with the challenge of whether Hitler ever really did anything *wrong* or whether genocide is *just wrong*. At the beginning of the objective tradition Plato, both as philosopher and dramatic artist, highlighted it magnificently in the later books of the *Republic* with his descriptions of developing evil, culminating in the portrait of the tyrannical man. We have already considered the prophetic significance of the views which in book 1 Plato attributes to Thrasymachus; we must now look in more detail at the narrative of the *Republic* as a whole.

Readers of the *Republic* have often been puzzled at what happens at the end of the first book. Plato's brothers, Glaucon and Adeimantus, insist that Thrasymachus has not done justice to his own position, and attempt to restate it. In the course of their restatements they mention a number of *ideas* about justice which seem at first sight to have only limited connection with Thrasymachus' own thesis. One is that justice perhaps emerges when the weak band themselves together against the strong; it would thus be the result of a contract. Thrasymachus himself never says that (though his refusal to commit himself to anything like a 'higher' justice of nature, over and above conventional justice, leaves such an option open), but it is reasonable to hold that this is one of the less unappealing ways in which his position, if correct, could be given practical application. For if there is no possibility of a Platonic account of justice, there are a variety of devices by which some of the work which 'justice' is traditionally supposed to perform can be parcelled out. In a Thrasymachean democracy a belief in the importance of obeying laws could be justified by reference to such a contract – 'ideally' in bad faith if the democrats are de facto 'stronger'. Thrasymachus himself might doubt if they would be strong *enough* for such bad faith; more likely they would believe their own fantasies about such a contract's historicity.

Neo-Thrasymachean 'applications' of the second book of the *Republic* can be envisaged in a more modern setting. If there is no Justice in the traditionally assumed sense for which Plato will attempt a philosophical defence in the rest of the *Republic*, some sort of utilitarianism, or rights theory, or contract theory, with or without a Hobbesian despotism, are among the more plausible ways of saving something from the wreckage: Hobbes thought that we could at least salvage our personal security. Plato's fundamental thesis is that either there is a transcendental aspect to morality or morality is somehow man-made; the different ways in which we can develop distinctions within what is man-made are of less interest to him.

While Plato explicitly emphasizes the primary importance of this dichotomy, many other philosophers – interestingly including Aristotle in the *Ethics* – do not.[3] Although Aristotle holds that the goods we seek and the obligations we have to pursue them are objective, dependent not only on man's nature but on his conforming of that nature to a right end which is (naturally) also a possible end, unlike Plato he did not raise the radical question, 'What if "morality" is but a comforting and useful delusion?' – which is precisely the subject of the *Republic* and precisely the question which Socrates must try to answer when Thrasymachus poses it in its strongest form. Unlike Plato, Aristotle *assumes* some sort of objectivist (perhaps even realist) aspect to morality ('There are some things which the good man – who acts for the sake of the noble or fine – simply will not do'), and he *assumes* a general knowledge of what the best society and the best upbringing 'for the sake of the noble' would be like, concerning himself not with justifying such assumptions, but specifically with the human 'function' and the nature of characteristically human acts and virtues.

At the end of book 1 of the *Republic*, Thrasymachus sulks, indicating that he is unconvinced. He knows that he has lost the battle but thinks that somehow he has been tricked and could still win the war. Part of the explanation of his puzzlement is that his character is such that he cannot understand where he went wrong. The challenge now facing Plato as dramatic philosopher is to restate much of what Thrasymachus has said, but in such a way that the *ad hominem* arguments and tactics used so effectively by Socrates against him can be abandoned, or at least modified, in the next, more obviously constructive, stage of the debate. To achieve that, Socrates must be given a different kind of interlocutor, one who is impressed by Thrasymachus' arguments but who wishes he could be honestly convinced that they fail. Such an interlocutor must therefore be without those defective character traits which prevent Thrasymachus from seeing his own weaknesses; he must be the product of a better moral universe, which he would dearly love to justify, albeit fearing that the anti-moralist could be right.

Plato does not produce a second debate. Had he done so, further advances might have been made, but the argument would begin to

---

[3] Interestingly, because it is an example of what seems a significant feature of the history of philosophy: that some of the major claims and insights of a philosopher may be the most readily ignored, underestimated or misinterpreted by his successors, however able. Another striking example is the neglect – by his own followers and within a decade or two of his death – of some of Aquinas' most original claims about existence.

look interminable and the *Republic* would run not to ten books but to a lifetime! What then is Plato's complementary strategy after book 1? He clearly would not allow that book 1 has failed, since he has designed it to show that if a position like that of Thrasymachus generates people like Thrasymachus, or can only be credibly held by people like Thrasymachus, it is identifiable, though indefensible, by its own advocates. What then is Plato's complementary strategy, and by extension what might be *our* complementary strategy? He must show that a certain sort of metaphysics, together with a very specific theory of man, are the necessary foundations for morality, and highlight the disastrous personal and social consequences if such foundations cannot be laid. For Plato an adequate account of morality has to depend both on an exposition of our human nature and of how it is now 'divided', as on a metaphysical theory about the proper object of human knowledge and human love. Yet the reader of the *Republic* is still innocent of what is to unfold when in book 2 Glaucon and Adeimantus revive what they suppose the position of Thrasymachus, beginning their renewed challenge to Socrates by charging Thrasymachus, as he had earlier charged Polemarchus, with conceding too much, with letting Socrates have his way too easily.

Thrasymachus himself never appeals to natural justice as opposed to bourgeois or conventional justice; that, we have suggested, is because he thinks justice merely a name, a convenient fiction. As this position is the most radical possible, it is not unreasonable that Glaucon and Adeimantus are able to allude to other theories of justice, including 'natural justice' (of the might-is-right type as espoused by Callicles in the *Gorgias*) and justice by contract, because these are possible ways in which the 'justice' Thrasymachus has exposed as a useful fiction can be turned into a concrete political and social programme. The examination of a number of variant versions which the fiction of justice may take helps to flesh out the seriousness of the multifaceted challenge to objective and real justice, and the necessity of facing that challenge in its starkest form.

It might be supposed that the 'natural justice' (or 'injustice') theory, whether in the form offered by Callicles in the *Gorgias* or in the version alluded to in the *Republic* – or, for that matter, as the principle to which Plato refers once again, and for the last time, in the *Laws* (714DE) – is itself not a 'Thrasymachean' theory of any sort. Rather it is an objective theory, in that while the power of the stronger 'rightly' prevails, it is not up to us who is the stronger; that is objectively given. Plato's view seems to be that such a theory of 'natural justice', though somehow objective, is not prescriptive, and so is not an objective theory *in ethics*, for it suggests no reason why what often *is* the case, namely that the strong compel the weak to do what they wish, *ought* – among humans, as opposed to among animals – to be the case. Hence while such a theory can be presented as, and even believed to be, both moral and objective, it remains essentially Thrasymachean in that its advocates *choose* to apply the (perhaps partial) facts to which it refers as norms for their conduct. Such choice leaves unexamined the supposedly factual assertion that mere power is a specifically human kind of 'strength', a natural good which we should therefore rationally and rightly choose to endorse.

Hume might see the Calliclean move as the illicit deduction of an 'ought' from an 'is'. Plato's not unrelated objection – on the lines of his account in the *Meno* of the difference between opinion (not rationally or experientially defensible) and knowledge (which will involve an account of the 'cause' of whatever is to be explained) – would be that Callicles, and anyone like him, is unable to give a rational account of justice as prescriptive. Indeed, so far from being rational, it is arbitrary, in the spirit of Goering's dictum that 'Power is my fist on your throat.' If we pass beyond the obvious truths about the effect in nature of the physically strong upon the weak, on which a Calliclean position rests, we have no reason to hold that anything about those truths provides us with reasonable grounds for obligations – except perhaps for feeling obliged to perform whatever actions are minimally required to defend ourselves against people like Callicles. If we are Callicleans or Nazis, what we have left is no argument, no reason why we should use our strength to abuse others, merely the assurance that we *like* power to do as we will. It should come as no surprise – though it has often surprised the commentators – that Plato presents Callicles as appealing to so simplistic a principle.

In any case, as Plato implies in passages of the *Republic*, Callicles and his like equivocate on the meaning of 'nature' and further equate 'stronger' not only with 'better' but with 'successful' crudely understood and without due explanation as to why such 'success' is worth pursuing. All Callicles offers in the *Gorgias* – since he relies on the observed fact that the people he admires *like* power – is an unanalysed attitude to pleasure presented as assertions like, 'We should maximize our pleasures and try to fulfil all our desires.' The strict unintelligibility of that latter objective – mocked in the *Gorgias* itself as like trying to fill a leaky pitcher – is also rehearsed in the latter part of the *Republic*.

The revival of applied Thrasymacheanism by Glaucon and Adeimantus leaves Plato with two fundamental challenges. First he must show that 'nature' – taken to be that which is always the case – is not to be understood solely, if at all, in terms of 'Nature red in tooth and claw'. And secondarily, if not that, then what? Or, to put it slightly differently, what, if anything, is there in the world (properly understood (cf. 6.501 B)) which is eternal and unchanging, and how does what is eternal and unchanging affect ethics? These are clearly metaphysical questions, and although as we read on in the second and third books of the *Republic* we are not yet warned that metaphysical considerations are inescapable if Thrasymachus and his alluring alternative 'morality' are to be rejected, we should not be surprised when Plato eventually chooses to unveil them.

Socrates must unravel the notion of nature, or the most basic nature of things, but he must *also* show specifically that such nature provides us with grounds for believing that there is indeed a 'natural', objective *morality*, and that hence the metaphysical enquiry will be inseparable from the moral enquiry. If Plato is to defend the Socratic proposition that we ought to live in such a way as to make our souls as good as possible, that must be understood in light of an insistence that the moral world is at least as much an objective reality (he should have added, much more specifically, a different kind of objective reality) as is the realm of 'nature' studied by physicists: and also that physical (including psychological) nature itself, as he later claims in the *Timaeus*, is morally and teleologically governed.

As we have observed, Socrates does not attempt to refute the positions of Glaucon and Adeimantus directly; there is no 'dialectical' examination of the anti-moral views on offer. That suggests that the kind of difficulties Socrates now wants to consider are such that strictly demonstrable conclusions are unable to be mounted. In any case, step by step dialectic, though necessary in philosophic life – but also incomplete without such imaginatively presented sketches of possible behaviour as are offered by the later books of the *Republic* – cannot go on indefinitely within the framework of a deliberately literary work. Perhaps, as I suggested, this is one reason for Plato's suspicion of written philosophy; good philosophy *is* the narrative of a 'Socratic' life. Socrates has to repeat (and improve on) his solo performance at the end of the *Gorgias*; he has to speak at length, but without the even lengthier dialectical excursuses necessary if absolute and dependable conviction is to be achieved. Yet he can certainly take the opportunity to evoke, and largely to expose, the pseudo-primitivism of contractarian myths.

Since justice is supposed to be some kind of internal bond upon both individuals and human communities, Socrates invites us to approach it by considering how hypothetically it would be best for such communities to be formed. This is not the place for the details: the need for protection, the principle of the efficient division of labour, the difficulties involved in finding people who will both guard the city and themselves refrain from plundering it, the nostalgic looking back to the (very primitive) innocence of paradise and the dangerous effects of asking more sophisticated questions and living a more complex life. In the immediate context of the *Republic*, the chief point Socrates wants to make is that those who have the power in the city, if they are to be 'genuine guardians' and not predators, must understand the benevolent intentions of the original lawgivers and intend to carry them out. In other words, if a city is to survive and all its members are to flourish as much as their situations and capacities will allow, those with power must be educated and trained to be a certain sort of people. But what sort, apart from people who will not turn and rend their own?

Plato's answer necessarily includes the claim that those who do not want to rend their own and who see reason not to do so must possess a kind of 'knowledge' – in some sense of the word – of which the rest of us are largely 'ignorant'. If he cannot argue this successfully, he will appear to beg the question by merely presenting another 'conventional' city with the sort of morality which Thrasymachus and his supporters will instantly denounce as a fiction. Hence at the end of book 5 we shall meet important distinctions between two types of people and two kinds of cognitive objects.

'Lovers of opinion' spend their lives looking at what changes, what is 'put on', as in the theatre, from time to time. 'Lovers of reality' *also* look at an eternal and unchanging world on which the world of change ultimately depends. They are awake and no longer 'dreaming'. Ultimately they base their manner of living on the existence of the 'Form of the Good' itself. To understand this picture, we need a general grasp – without worrying too much over minor and largely culture-specific differences – of what sort of metaphysical, and even 'theistic', claim Plato is trying to make – even if he is grasping for what he cannot properly encompass.

Perhaps it is easier to come to grips with Plato's proposals if we look not at the Form of the Good but at the Form which he seems to have recognized first – because it is the object of love – and which, because of its physical manifestations, he says (in the *Phaedrus*) is the most obvious: the Form of Beauty. Plato holds that, whereas all objects of physical beauty are comparatively beautiful (Helen is beautiful when compared with the girl next door, but not when compared with Aphrodite), there is nothing that could be more beautiful than the Form of Beauty itself. It is not only incomparably beautiful, but it sets a standard by which all other beauties can be measured. Such a standard is not man-made, though any of us can, at least dimly, recognize it.

Plato declines to say exactly what Beauty is, but it exists independently of any mind, and cannot be a physical (and therefore perishable) object. Since Beauty itself is more beautiful than anything else, and since it is a feature of beauty to inspire us to act or to react, Beauty itself will be more inspiring than any lesser beauty. To grasp what Plato has in mind consider the following: if I claim to be in love with someone (and thus, in Platonic language, to recognize and admire his or her beauty), I want to do what is in the interest of that love object; if I said I loved someone but that I would not do anything for him, Plato would insist that I am not in love at all, though I might want to 'use' someone in some way and would for that reason say, and perhaps mistakenly believe, that I loved him or her. Hence if there is a Form of Beauty, it will be more likely than anything else to impel those who 'know' and love it to act well. Indeed the Forms as a whole are *both* inspirational realities *and* provide standards by which we may determine in our ordinary lives what would be just or kindly acts and what their counterfeits.

There are both simple and complex reasons why Plato introduces Forms in the *Republic*, and at a particular point in it. The simple reason is that he has reached a stage where he must either introduce Forms or leave Socrates' entire reply to Glaucon and Adeimantus hanging in the air; the more complex is that the Forms are introduced to clarify Socrates' apparently preposterous proposal that philosophers should become kings. Philosopher-kings are proposed because they will both know what to do and have the power to do it. Necessarily what the philosopher-king does is correct, and thus he will produce the best possible state. Since he understands the nature of the best political structure, he will succeed in making it an earthly reality as far as is possible. The best structure will be the perfect embodiment of justice and the other virtues, as will the lawgiver himself. If the philosopher-king is to be successful, he must have a perfect knowledge of what is just, where 'what is just' is such as will best develop the excellence of the souls who live in accordance with its dictates.

The perfect state demands not only that the just man be in power, but also a transcendent standard of justice by which he can be guided. Without both prerequisites, there can be no just society; we could only allude to a just society, not even, strictly, envisage it, for what would be 'envisaged' would be *comparatively* just – and that, as the philosopher-king knows, would not satisfy the requirements of justice. For what he needs is a standard, external *and moral* (and not merely, with luck, *prudential*), by which he can both establish his own state and measure each variety of existing state against alternative possibilities, themselves arranged in order of increasing inadequacy – as they are in the later books of the *Republic*. Plato attempts no strict demonstration of the existence of the Form of the Good; indeed, though it is possible to discern both from his own writings and from those of his critics – principally Aristotle – what arguments he was inclined to use and that they gradually grew more sophisticated, in the *Republic* he presents the Forms largely without argument. What he there wants to show is that the existence of the Form of the Good – or an effective equivalent – is the *sine qua non* of any well-grounded theory of virtue and moral obligation, as distinct from some theory of how to calculate as well as possible what seems (given certain assumptions about human nature) to be my own or someone else's interest. The very distinction between obligation and interest, Plato would claim, is intelligible only if we assume the answer to the separate problem of whether the 'content' of such interest can be assessed without appeal to some external 'final cause' of human nature.

Plato, in the persona of Socrates, not only claims that without an external standard of Goodness the threat posed by a Thrasymachus (and – the immediately practical point – by his disciples in social and political life) cannot be rationally defused, but *also* manages to show, in the persona of Thrasymachus himself (as also in the persona of Socrates elsewhere, most notably in the *Phaedo*), that 'bourgeois' virtue and justice are built on a lack of self-knowledge – built indeed on self-deception, deliberate or otherwise, and the deception of others. Here Plato is interestingly at one not only with Thrasymachus but to a considerable extent with Hobbes and many other of his more unsentimental philosophical opponents.[4] If there is no objective standard of Goodness by which moral structures can be secured, the so-called good man – he who according to the *Phaedo* (82 B) will be reincarnated next time round as a social animal like an ant or a bee – is merely someone with the 'luck' to be born in a respectable society and of a respectable family, and who has not been forced to stand by his indefensible beliefs in circumstances where it would be politically incorrect, even dangerous, to be 'good'.

Plato has now in effect envisaged that further problem to which we have alluded: if morals cannot be defended by metaphysics, 'bourgeois'

---

[4] As already noted, the case of Hobbes is especially informative, since, as MacIntyre observes of Foucault in *Three Rival Versions of Moral Enquiry* (London: Duckworth, 1990), 53, it is hard for extreme anti-Platonists, even Nietzscheans, not to collapse into Hobbesians. Hobbes is considered further below.

society may have to be defended by systemic self-deception and probably by outright lying about moral 'truths'. And in raising the question of the need for lying and self-deception in conventional societies Plato cannot avoid raising it for any society, including his own ideal projection.

Plato's is a revolutionary temperament, though people may distort this insight by failing to identify his objectives and collapsing his views into those of some contemporary ideologist.[5] Something of his radicalism can be recognized in the distinction between those few who acknowledge an objective, realist standard of morality – and who are thus able to ground their moral beliefs and stand by them in adversity – and the many who, usually because following popular and unexamined assumptions about such standards, abandon them readily when tested by political or social pressures or by intellectual sophistry. They abandon them because they 'know about' them (or perhaps, in Plato's own language, have true beliefs about them) but do not *know* them by direct and lasting experience of their inspirational source.

But what if such direct experience is hardly obtainable? The Forms may exist but be of small use to us. Then should ill-based convictions about morality nonetheless be deliberately (and misleadingly) encouraged? Can 'true belief' – belief with no possibility that an individual can go through the moral and intellectual education required to justify it – be effective in society? Can it be honestly promoted or in the long run attained at all?

A 'problem' about any revolutionary insistence on moral saints or heroes is that it seems to demand too much of the average man. Heroic moralities may be appropriate for a Weberian 'sect', but can never survive in a Weberian 'church' – and it is not only in religious contexts that the distinction between 'sect' and 'church' can be found; it exists within any political party which demands of its members high standards of personal conviction. Plato recognized the problem (where the Stoics, in some ways also Socratic, did not); hence he had no immediate desire to found an international community of the wise, a cosmopolitan 'city' composed exclusively of philosopher-kings. His original and continuing aims were always practical, never exclusively theoretical; he sought to cure what he diagnosed as a malaise in the Greek political and intellectual climate. Therefore there must be citizens wise in a secondary sense: not themselves philosopher-kings, but able to recognize and obey those who are. Arguably Plato was insufficiently aware of the practical difficulties of

5 K. R. Popper's *The Open Society and its Enemies* (second edition, London: Routledge and Kegan Paul, 1952) is only the most notorious of such simplistic misinterpretations.

getting people to understand (rather than merely accept) that for them the best life is the life of obedience.

Plato is certainly inclined to be contemptuous of 'second-best' individuals, but we can reasonably ask whether it is less his account of the Good than his view of the sort of training necessary to understand that Good which entails his particular version of aristocracy. Be that as it may, what 'matters' in Plato's realistically conceived universe is that, although all have to behave morally, not all have to be able to justify such behaviour.

Let me summarize the selection of Platonic themes that have appeared thus far: in addition to halting Thrasymachus at least temporarily in his tracks, Plato in his wider struggle with moral nihilism has proposed the following:

1. That a metaphysics of moral and transcendental realism is the only possible basis for a complete reply to the determined subverter of morality; if it fails, Thrasymachus wins.

2. That if Thrasymachus wins, various pseudo-moralities (contractarianism, Callicleanism, plus various modern versions) may compete with moral nihilism itself. All display common features: emphasis on pleasure and subjective preferences. Some introduce myths about an early unspoilt condition of mankind.

3. That conventional or 'bourgeois' societies depend at best on true beliefs, at worst on deception and self-deception about human nature and 'values'.

4. That the necessary metaphysical realities ('Forms') must reveal Beauty, provoke and inspire love, inspire and sustain action.

5. That in their combined moral and intellectual capacities, that is, in their character, men are significantly unequal, above all in their ability to *justify* their moral beliefs.

6. That the notion of a just society is only intelligible if a metaphysically defensible Good exists and if the citizen-body is able, in different ways, to profit from its existence by learning the craft of living well. Such learning – or rather understanding – will require time and emotional preparation.

7. That problems of deception and self-deception (including outright lying) are not limited to inferior societies. Plato admits the necessity of symbolic myths (that is, the 'noble lie') if the ideal society is first to be established and then to buttress the 'true opinion' of the lower classes. But if transcendental realism is abandoned, ignoble, self-serving lying, deception and self-deception will be ubiquitous in both public and

private life. They may even seem required as preconditions of social stability.

I

Though Plato's challenge to Thrasymacheans is powerful, it is incomplete as it stands. There is a general difficulty about 'Platonic' accounts of universal terms which arises from the fact that some such terms are evaluative, others merely descriptive. Some at least of Plato's arguments seem to generate a far wider range of Forms than is necessary for tackling the problems of moral nihilism – and thereby to manufacture unnecessary difficulties for the moral realist. Gradually, and often indirectly, later Platonists, both pagan and Christian, began to refine their Platonism.

As we have seen, there are in Plato form-suggesting, general terms for at least three different kinds of relevant items: (1) for artificial objects like tables which are made by man from pre-existing materials; (2) for natural objects like trees which a theist would normally hold ultimately to be created by God; (3) for evaluative notions like justice, which theistic Platonism will after some sort identify as God's nature or God's thoughts. Only the third category of candidate 'Forms' is mandatory for a realist metaphysic of morals; I can therefore neglect Platonizing treatments of Forms of the other two classes. In other words, in the metaphysics of morals by 'Platonism' I shall refer to a theory in which evaluative Forms, such as Goodness, are the essential requisite. Of course, if the *combination* of arguments for such 'Forms' entailed Forms for the other two classes, the Platonists' difficulties would be far more serious, but by good hap they do not: in a theistic world God can create trees and men, men can make tables, but goodness and justice are not created by God (nor, it follows, by man), but subsist in God's being or nature.

God and God's nature, Platonically understood, are the successors of the evaluative Forms and of the Good itself, and not merely are they successors, but they indicate metaphysical progress, for goodness looks like a quality, though Plato, as Aristotle realized, needs his Forms to be substances. Unless goodness is substantiated in and as some sort of 'good thing', it appears to be an ungrounded quality, and hence incapable of doing the philosophical work for which it was proposed.

Originally in pagan, later in Christian (and occasionally Jewish and Muslim) guise, Platonists developed Plato's defence of morality in two respects: firstly – our concern in this chapter – they improved on his account of the Good itself; secondly – as will be pursued later – they developed and corrected aspects of his account of the moral agent, his or her 'soul' and actions. In the third century AD, the Christian philosopher Origen drew attention to the problem of human inequality, claiming that while Platonism catered for an élite, Christianity could provide (at least adequately) for the rest of humanity *as well*.[6] If he was right, consideration should be given both to the historical question of how and why the organizational structures of primitive Christianity were more effective in reaching out to wider humanity – which is not our present concern – and at the more theoretical level to the question of whether Plato is too restrictive or inaccurate in his account of what he holds to be 'divine' in us: namely our capacity – to be developed over years by a correct moral and intellectual discipline – to recognize and love objective goodness.

For Plato thinks that an essentially intellectual[7] divine spark within us – and hence the 'value' of human beings will vary with their intelligence[8] – is buried beneath false ideas and practices, yet remains itself unharmed and perfect. Thus his version of absolute standards is tied to a highly questionable account of the nature of the unified human soul or person and of our native moral capacities. Happily such a thesis is no necessary part of a 'realist' moral theory as such.

I shall defer consideration of the soul – its unity and its purity – and of moral agency until chapter 3. Meanwhile (and normally), for a version of Christianized Platonism which tackles some of the difficulties about Plato's Form of the Good I shall refer to the writings of Augustine, not because he is the first Christian Platonist, but because his adaptation of Platonic metaphysics (as of important features of Plato's theories of love and the soul) has dominated all subsequent Christian philosophy in the West,[9] including, at relevant foundational points, that of the Thomists (as I shall indicate in chapter 6).

For while Plato's Form of the Good – assuming it to exist – is effective as a standard, it is an unusual kind of existent: as we have noted, it is quality

---

[6] See Origen, *Against Celsus* 5.43.

[7] Plato's understanding of 'intellectual', however, would involve a large affective component; he is not normally attracted to a Cartesian-style distinction between reason and the passions. The matter is complicated and cannot be discussed here; Plato's mature view is best approached from the ninth book of the *Republic* and the *Phaedrus*.

[8] Cf. J. M. Rist, *Human Value* (Leiden: Brill, 1982), 68–83.

[9] For my own general views of Augustine, see J. M. Rist, *Augustine: Ancient Thought Baptized* (Cambridge University Press, 1994).

rather than substance, impersonal moreover and apparently floating free outside the world of life. To understand the oddity of such claims, we must go back to Socrates' original concerns over moral language, which were probably directed as much towards descriptions of moral *acts* as towards descriptions of moral individuals. Now, though we too are as likely to speak of good acts as of good people, as philosophers we should presumably be ontologically austere, holding that the existence of 'acts' is dependent on the existence of agents and that hence if there is a standard of goodness independent of the human mind, the prime candidate would have to be not an 'object' like justice or – as a hostile critic would put it – a reified act, but a superior 'soul' or, as we might prefer, a superior 'person'. This supposition would be strengthened by a belief that if that standard is to be, as it is for Plato, the object of the highest form of love, it must *be* a person.[10]

The theory of Forms – certainly in its original version – seems to reify qualities of acts, not agents. Perhaps at the end of his life Plato identified the Form of the Good as a Divine Mind, that is as some kind of God,[11] but in the majority of his writings the gods, each a kind of soul, have identifiably different conceptual and 'cultural' origins from the Forms; as Plato himself puts it in the *Phaedrus* (249C), it is by virtue of knowing the Forms that the gods themselves are divine. Thus for him the gods are stronger and unchangeable versions of the human soul, morally stronger in that they do not 'fall', as well as in their more active capabilities. In Plato's language we are to become not 'like the Good' but 'like God' in as much as he is good.

Perhaps more questionable than (and not unrelated to) the apparent impersonality of the Platonic Good is the fact that Plato's account of the 'Forms' (including the Good) as moral exemplars leaves them in metaphysical limbo. They would exist as essentially intelligible ideas even if there were no mind, human or divine, to recognize them: as objects of thought, not mere constructs or concepts. But, as Augustine learned, and as the Greek Neoplatonists had asserted, the notion of an eternal object of *thought* (and thus for Plato a cause of thought) without a ceaseless thinking subject is unintelligible. Intelligible Forms, never proposed as mere concepts, cannot be proposed as Plato originally proposed them, as free-floating metaphysical items.

---

[10] One sense of impersonal 'love' would obviously be out of the question, that in virtue of which I would say that I 'love' Orvieto Classico: that is, that I 'love' to drink it.

[11] For a view of the evidence see J. M. Rist, *The Mind of Aristotle* (Toronto University Press, 1989), 196–204.

Although Plato, then, has pointed in the direction of a principle on which an objective and 'realist' moral system could be grounded, he has failed to identify it convincingly. If the Forms as originally proposed are rejected, those determined to make a 'Platonic' start on grounding morality are left with the mind, human or divine, or else with some other 'morality-sensing' or 'morality-identifying' power. Which is not to suggest that 'Forms' must be concepts after all, needing a mind to generate them, but to grasp that, since they are essentially recognized by thought, they demand a primary mind to recognize them: in fact, as in Augustine's development of Plotinus' more impersonal version of Platonism, to recognize them *in and as itself* as its own 'divine attributes'. Of course, as I have noted, such a personal Divine Mind would not recognize the Form of Table or the Form of Tree as such an attribute, and thus are eliminated some of the problems of a possible wider Platonism which we feared. It *would* so recognize the Form of Justice and, above all, of the Good.

Plato offered the Forms both to explain the nature of the contents of the physical universe and as an attempt to ground the objectivity of moral judgements. Why then did he refuse (at least until near the end of his life) to affirm – with many of his successors both Christian and non-Christian – the identity of the Forms, or at least of the Form of the Good, with God – seen as (at least) some kind of Divine Mind? In part certainly because of his restricted concept of God. It is easy to forget that the classical Greeks had a very different notion of God from that now long conventionally current in Western assumptions. For example, there is no concept of divine omnipotence in classical Greek thought. More specifically, post-classical writing about God or gods brings together two 'divine' features which Plato largely kept apart: namely, being and doing. Plato does not *call* his Forms gods because although they are at the summit of the hierarchy of being and value, they are not directly *active*. Now if we were to describe as 'god' whatever is most 'valuable', there would be many candidates, some of which, though not all, would also be active. Thus if we were to think power 'the most important thing' in the world, we should call the most powerful and (in this case) *active* being (say, Zeus) a god or 'divine'. *We* might think that since the Platonic Good is the highest reality, then that Good, even if not directly active, must be a god since – following Hebrew thought and Anselm rather than Plato – we associate the highest good with divinity; Plato, however, requiring direct activity if beings are to be labelled 'god', does not think of the Forms as gods, but as something higher.

Let us leave Plato's original Goodness for Augustine's improved version, to which the One of Plotinus, from whom Augustine largely learned to think immaterially, is a half-way house. Augustine's God, as the God of his Christian Platonist predecessors, is personal and therefore more readily understood as lovable. He represents the Platonic Form of the Good as the standard of goodness, but is less of an ontological curiosity. Like Plotinus' One, 'he' is no reified quality, but a living and self-knowing 'being' and the ultimate efficient cause of living beings; like the Platonic gods (and unlike the Platonic Forms which are not agents) the God of the Christians is that which we should strive to resemble and is thus at the same time a Platonic Form, an Aristotelian Mind 'in actuality', and an omnipotent, providential and 'moral' Jewish personal source of law and command – however incompletely the idea of omnipotence was still understood. He – it is convenient as well as expedient to accept the Old Testament's pronoun without prejudice to arguments as to applications of gender to the One who is *ex hypothesi* the Creator of gender – is not only the point of reference for moral language but also the active promoter of moral goodness. Unlike the gods of Greco-Roman thought, he may even 'ground' a morality viewed as a set of divine commands, yet would provide no warrant for the supposition that such divine commands must necessarily be arbitrary. Morality would on this view be not of his creation but a representation of his nature or being, that is, of the 'primitive' or first cause. Though now 'seen through a glass darkly' (as too we now apprehend objective moral truths), he would be unambiguously recognizable only (and eventually) via the 'faith' of those to whom he allows himself to be more clearly revealed.

Augustine's Judaic and Christian inheritance also tallies with another important Platonic moral theme – where the Stoics (by contrast) show themselves to be hyper-Platonic. The Jews, followed by the Christians, had divided mankind into two groups, the elect and those outside, the chosen and the rejected or damned (in whatever sense of 'damned' applied from time to time). Those who were elect both did the right thing (however defined) and were possessed of certain kinds of knowledge about the right thing to do. Primarily this was knowledge of God and knowledge, however obtained, about God's commands. Or perhaps not knowledge but belief which, according to Augustine, is normally the precondition for religious understanding, for in his view knowledge (in the strictly propositional sense) is limited in the here and now to logical and other analytic truths and to such propositions as 'This seems sweet to me'.

Not only do the elect have 'true belief', but their life is oriented in one of the only two possible directions: towards God though not in a straight line, yet overall. They are 'servants of God', the only alternative being to be 'servants of the devil'. Servants of God rest their belief on an objective reality, being in this like Platonic philosopher-kings; servants of the devil are all who do not, all who, in the words recorded of Jesus, 'scatter abroad'. But for Augustine such salvific 'belief' (*essentially accompanied in all cases* by a transmuted form of Platonic *eros*) is available to all, unlike Platonic knowledge which is limited to those possessed of special 'intellectual' powers – for, as Paul has it (1 Tim. 2.4), God wishes all men to be saved, and love of the Good is possible for anyone. *Pace* Plato there are naturally no second-class humans, though no-one can divine, by Platonic or other scrutiny, who are the elect. Baptism and membership of the Church greatly increase security, but are by no means a guarantee – though within a continuing Church authorizing truths partly if diminishingly unintelligible to us, we can perceive something akin to the successors in the college of philosopher-kings, renewing themselves through the generations to perpetuate their necessary institution.

Such institutional or indeed ecclesiastical questions are not our present concern, though they will recur. From the philosophical point of view what primarily matters, as for Plato so for Augustine in his richer Christian and Neoplatonized habit, is that unless there exists an objective and 'moral' transcendent reality by the recognition and inspiration of which alone we can live the good life, and by reference to which we can give a reasonable justification of that life, then once hard (or soft) times or probing challenges appear, Thrasymachus or his successors must be victorious: not always immediately, and perhaps never definitively in historical time, but the Thrasymachean position will remain the only honest alternative – whether we are the 'useful idiots' who fail to recognize this or the opportunists who take advantage of it.

Augustine's notoriously bleak picture of ordinary, 'fallen' life (dark even by Platonic standards because more obviously the opposite of a clearer-cut vision of the Good) highlights a stark contrast between the 'true' nature of the world if there is a moral 'Real' (or God) and if there is not. Reflect on the universe proposed by Augustine without Augustine's God and we are left in the universe of Sartre, where values are constructed at random whenever 'honest' folk see the necessity, where hell is other people seen as ineluctably predatory, and where life itself seems an absurdity which can only be transcended in the ultimately hopeless or destructive pursuit of a genuinely 'free' act. As a rule, Augustine is no more

than Plato prepared to demonstrate the existence of a principle such as
would genuinely ground a morality, and like Plato he thinks that the only
apparently alternative position cannot even be coherently presented, but
only shown up in ever more appalling terms through depiction of the
incoherent, loveless universe where Thrasymachus rules. Both Plato and
Augustine raise the same challenging questions: are there really only
two alternatives?; are all other possibilities good-natured muddles to be
collapsed by the clear-headed into Thrasymacheanism?

II

Plato has more than one goal in the *Republic*, but I have largely concentrated on his claim that, without an objective 'substantive' Good,
no moral obligation and no virtue can be supported. I also touched
on the self-deception and lying which he thinks will be endemic in all
non-Platonizing societies. These matters demand further consideration,
but in the *Republic* itself another important, as yet unexamined, question
takes precedence. Socrates argues that in this life what we ought to do
corresponds with what is to our advantage, that 'the good' is also 'the
useful'; even though, as he acknowledges, we are not to do what we ought
to do *merely* because it is to our advantage, whether in the long or the
short term, nonetheless the advantage needs to be recognized. To those
presenting the challenge of the utility of virtue, Socrates is obliged to
demonstrate the paradox of our obligation to pursue something for its
own pre-eminent sake while also recognizing its (ultimate) utility. Any
Platonizing account of ethics faces a similar challenge.

What significance, Plato asks, would the Good have in philosophy or
in life unless it were useful? This question might be put down to some
supposedly characteristic 'Greek pragmatism', but Plato has urgent and
recognizable philosophical and political reasons for asking it. He is pitting
himself against people who say that even if justice exists, it is of no 'use'
or of no 'benefit', or, as the Athenian spokesman puts it in Thucydides'
Melian Dialogue, that it is a concept only of use to the weak, who can
plead justice when all appeal to force is impossible. Dramatic seeings of
the error of their ways apart, such cynical or 'hard-nosed' opponents
can only be disarmed, as any 'eudaimonist' knows, if the realist can
demonstrate that to know the truth is supremely useful to us all.

There is already an ambiguity about 'advantage' in Thrasymachus'
claim that justice is the advantage of the stronger. There is a sense in
which Socrates would not want to dispute that to be just really is to the

advantage of the stronger, as of everyone else. Were he to argue that justice did not pay *in any sense*, Thrasymachus would simply jeer at a proposal not even worthy of debate. Thus Plato commits himself to the belief that the Good not only exists independently of our fallible concepts, but that knowledge of it is useful to all in a surpassing way such that in its absence nothing could be useful. Without it we can neither 'order' our souls nor establish a polity satisfactory for all. Hence, we can now add an eighth to the seven tasks which Plato thinks he has completed:

8. The Form of the Good is not only a prerequisite for moral goodness; it is also the only reliable point of reference by which all of us – though indirectly – can look after our best interests.

As Christian and Platonist Augustine of course accepts this, given that it is most clearly in our interest to be 'saved' and 'go' to God, and, historically speaking, the essentials of any possible realist metaphysic are now securely in place: there is no immediate need to pursue further refinements.

TOWARDS ALTERNATIVES TO PLATONIC REALISM

Epicurus and reductionist psychology

Many contemporary attempts to replace transcendental realism are significantly dependent on Kantian views of human autonomy; Kant will therefore require more extended discussion in a modern context. I shall consider more immediately other and still influential alternatives to Platonic ethics outside the various Kantian traditions which may be juxtaposed with the ethical and metaphysical structures which, founded by Plato and developed by Augustine, were enriched by later Christian thinkers at least down to the time of Aquinas' appropriation of a Platonized Aristotle, and more spasmodically – though in the case of Newman dramatically – in recent centuries. I shall argue that these alternatives are more or less radically Thrasymachean, not always in that they are explicitly varieties of moral nihilism, but because their foundations cannot be established; hence that they are open to 'cynical' Thrasymachean reduction: their claims (when not parasitic on realism) depend ultimately on assertions of a reductionist sort about psychology and/or on mere preferences about goods. They are therefore either morally nihilist or only desiderately though unjustifiably to be identified as non-nihilist.

Viewing them as precursors of contemporary post-Christian ethics and politics, I shall discuss aspects of the thematically connected thought of Epicurus, Macchiavelli and Hobbes. Finally I shall turn to Kierkegaard, whose defence of an apparently 'Augustinian' ethic was ironically recast as a source of anti-realist theories which emphasize the most radical version of the primacy of human *choice* and *preference*.

Of our anti-Platonic theorists it is philosophically as well as historically appropriate to consider Epicurus first. Not only was he, like Plato, an Athenian, but a number of his rival positions were foreshadowed in Plato's own works, especially in the *Republic*, *Phaedrus* and *Laws*. As well as denying Plato's 'providentialism' – his gods are too self-absorbed to be concerned with human morality – Epicurus was ready to confront Plato's claim that if we jettison the Good as fantasy (as he thought we must), we must also do away with anything like a 'moral' ought and the whole traditional notion of virtue. This latter, now viewed as a means to an end, he said that he 'spat on' unless it brought him pleasure, but he supposed that some kind of prudential and useful 'good', together with a satisfying lifestyle, could still be defended. At the political level Epicurean prudence can justify a contractarian view of society, as foreseen by Glaucon and Adeimantus in the *Republic*, and in a manner somewhat reminiscent of Hobbes. Epicurus' approach is reductionist not only about the cosmos but about the nature of man, which is why it is so interesting an alternative to Plato. More even than Parfit in our own day, Epicurus had the full courage of his convictions. He made no attempt to reconstruct or justify traditional morality but aimed to replace it. That was an honest aim, even if such an assessment is already paradoxical, honesty for its own sake being no virtue for an Epicurean.

Epicurus held that the chief prerequisite for happiness, or, as he would prefer to say, for adequate freedom from pain, is the stripping off of illusions (not least about richer or 'thicker' theories of human goods which would leave us emotionally dependent on the fortunes and behaviour of others) and a 'philosophical' willingness to face life as it 'really' is.[12] All metaphysical talk of an immaterial soul or of an afterlife – as of an immaterial Goodness itself – is to be abandoned; the therapy of 'philosophy' is to be applied to the traumas which such fantasies tend to bring about. In place of the Forms Epicurus, like many of his successors, evokes the concept of human nature and human 'interest'. We must

[12] A recent, if self-referential, treatment is that of M. Nussbaum, *The Therapy of Desire* (Princeton University Press, 1994), 102–279. Most Hellenistic philosophers were inclined towards something of Epicurus' reductionist account of goods.

recognize what we naturally want – that is, what we are such as to want – as matter of fact. But how do we know what we 'naturally' want, if we do not live in a state of nature but in a state of society? We have been surrounded since our birth, says Epicurus, by opinions, of which some few are true and the rest, especially those among philosophers, are false. In this, perhaps, we may follow him without too great difficulty, but Epicurus becomes more problematic when he proceeds to *identify* the few opinions which are true from the mass which are false, above all with respect to what is good and what is bad.

Epicurus claims that we all 'naturally' want to maximize our pleasure, at least in the sense of wanting to minimize pain. Let us grant, for the sake of argument, that this is indeed natural, yet it does not follow, as it must for Epicurus, that, given our physical and mental structure in an uncaring universe, there is no more to be said about what is natural, whether in our 'primitive' moral condition or when we are more mature: the Epicureans constantly engaged in polemic with Stoics who maintained that what is primitively good is not pleasure but self-preservation.

At the heart of the Epicurean system lies an inadequate and inadequately supported claim that if false opinion is stripped away, we all give priority to minimizing our own pain, and that we *should* have such priorities because it is rational to do so. Supposing it were true, however, that as babies we were once in this primitive and uncorrupted state, why should we believe that it is therefore either possible or desirable – let alone any sort of obligation of reason – for adults with developed powers of thought to remain thus situated? If it is impossible, it is irrelevant, and if it is held both possible and desirable, the Epicurean requires (at least) one further premiss: that our behaviour at an undeveloped stage of our human life provides compelling evidence for the similar value of pleasure in the life of a mature, thoughtful adult. But how (without recourse to a 'metaphysical' value theory) can the Epicurean answer the claim of an ascetic who wishes to pursue his chosen lifestyle, even though it gives him (at least indirectly) pain, perhaps both 'physical' and 'mental', with uncertain hedonistic rewards and satisfaction at the end? To dispose of this, Epicurus has to repeat his mere assertions (perhaps supplemented by a theory of psychopathology): that pleasure (or the absence of pain) is the only primary good; that the ascetic's acquired desires all involve misguided beliefs precisely insofar as they clash with our natural primary desire for pleasure – which constitutes begging the question. Unsupported axioms about the cognitive superiority of childhood 'beliefs' – even if these beliefs are correctly identified – are inadequate; they certainly cannot support the notion that absence of pain is what we (should) always seek as adults.[13]

Notice how Epicurus' difficulties come to a head, as has always been recognized, in his treatment of friendship: a topic discussed at length by all moral philosophers in antiquity, since it was universally recognized that the possession of friends has considerable bearing on our ability to flourish. Recall again that for Epicurus what we all seek is our own good, and that that good is to be identified as pleasure, that is, as absence of pain. Certainly the presence of friends gives us pleasure, and therefore, in Epicurean terms, friends are useful to us. And note here the 'objectivist' (though non-realist) claim: friends do not *seem* useful, they really *are* useful. Thus we have an attempt to ground preferred behaviour on an apparent fact about human nature as we find it, that friends are useful: their utility is not merely that they can be counted on to help out in the difficulties of life, but that we feel comfortable and relaxed in their company.

But it is of the essence of friendship to trust one's friends, and since in the Epicurean world it is each one's own and no-one else's comfort that is to be sought, what guarantee do we have that our friends will not let us down, and for good Epicurean reasons? The answer Epicurus provides is that if friends are good Epicureans they will have calculated that the advantages of friendship are so great that it would not pay to risk losing a friend by being untrustworthy, and Epicurus was prepared to go so far in this direction as to claim that in some circumstances a friend would die for his friend. Perhaps he would, but it is hard to see why in most circumstances an Epicurean would not reasonably change his mind, in the interest of saving his own life, and betray his friend or otherwise expose him to injury. The likelihood of this would be increased in light of another Epicurean claim, that the friends will not be passionately committed to one another; from the outset there will have been a pact for mutual convenience and satisfaction.

Plato had foreseen this sort of position, and repudiated it as precisely the opposite of his own view. In the *Phaedrus*, Socrates first argues that one should yield to the wooing of a non-lover rather than of a lover, for then entanglement can be avoided and each by consent can use the other to maximize his present and predictably future pleasures. In his recantation he argues how misleading such a suasion must be, since the non-lover

---

[13] For further interesting, though incomplete, discussion of the Epicurean treatment of childhood behaviour, see J. Brunschwig, 'The Cradle Argument in Epicureanism and Stoicism', in M. Schofield and G. Striker (eds.), *The Norms of Nature* (Cambridge and Paris: Cambridge University Press, 1986), 113–44.

cannot but use the beloved entirely for his own convenience without serious consideration of whether his partner is harmed or benefited in the process. We should note the parallel dichotomies: in Plato the non-lover and the lover; in Epicurus the wise philosopher and the crazy non-'philosopher'.

Thus Epicurus ties himself in knots over the utility of friendship: necessary as a source of pleasure but arguably attainable *if and only if* strict Epicurean claims about nothing being good in itself are suspended – for who would trust his partner if he knew that he was only valued instrumentally?[14] Plato, though, can rejoice in that the Epicurean alternative to his own standard points to the impossibility of Epicurean happiness: moreover, that it does so even if happiness is defined in such reductionist terms, even if deception by and of the wise is allowed to be a part of the good life, and even if we grant the Epicureans (or other consequentialists) that an intelligent calculation of goods and harms can indeed be achieved – at least if only one's own good is to be considered. Epicurus indeed is on stronger ground in calculating goods than is a common consequentialist such as the modern utilitarian, who has undertaken to try to optimize every aspect of the situation for the whole of humanity. Plato could claim that the case of Epicurus is especially interesting in that if *he*, the professed egoist, cannot do his felicific calculus, then what other consequentialist can hope to do so? Still, the inability to *calculate* whether or not to betray a friend (in practice) is a main cause of Epicurus' impasse over friendship.[15]

As the case of friendship shows, it is the view of Epicurus that if a coherently anti-Platonic position is to be established, one must give up 'romantic' or 'sentimental' ideas of doing good to other people, unless such acts are convenient or pleasing to oneself. On the contrary, others must be ruthlessly sacrificed when reason points in that direction. And Epicurus' alternative to Platonism is prophetic in other ways too, not least in that his position depends on the claim that we know what it is

---

[14] Note the comment in P. Mitsis, *Epicurus' Ethical Theory* (Ithaca and London: Cornell University Press, 1988), 128: 'Like Mill, Epicurus believes that we can value something for its own sake apart from its instrumental contribution to our satisfaction. This position is inconsistent with the claims of his hedonism.' Mitsis has persuaded me that my earlier attempts to save Epicurus' consistency were in part misguided.

[15] For reasons which may be identified from my discussion of Epicurus, I shall say little in this book (but see chapter 6 below) about utilitarianism and other modern forms of consequentialism; the inability of utilitarians to do the requisite calculations is notorious, as is the problem that the content of utilitarian claims must be derived from outside utilitarianism itself, hence the tendency of modern utilitarians to function in a purely formal mode: maximize the good whatever the good happens to be.

natural to do. But why ought we to behave naturally if what is natural is merely what human beings would do unless 'misled' by conventions and philosophers? Epicurus' answer, of course, is that we can recognize that such behaviour will give us the most comfort. In other words because certain behaviours give the most comfort, we *ought* to follow through with them. Clearly there is no moral obligation here: what Epicurus claims is that we ought to do what is rational, and what is rational is what leads to pleasure. But to move from 'is' to 'ought' in this way depends simply on the assertion (as we have seen inadequately defended) that in the last analysis pleasure is all that matters. Epicurus' failure might be averted by a better account of the natural, though in remaining anti-Platonist, such an account must steer clear of any realist assumptions. Still, since it is often supposed that Epicurus is an inadequate naturalist, I must defer further treatment of naturalism until I can consider Hume, its most influential advocate. More immediately I turn to two very different thinkers, both of them significantly appearing on the European scene when the Augustinian consensus on God the Good as the foundation of morality was breaking up and beginning to be replaced by an ever more radical individualism – in its varying ways often surprisingly reminiscent of Epicureanism as well as of other non-realist forms of pre-Christian thought.

Macchiavelli and choice

Macchiavelli was writing when the Reformation was in its opening phases and, like its Renaissance background, still spreading. He is thus able to stand at several crossroads. He knows that traditionally two ways of life are regularly pitted against each other: the Christian love of God and the 'pagan' love of glory. As is typical of Renaissance man, Macchiavelli's view of the love of glory is deeply influenced by what the classical moralists, Plato and Aristotle, as well as their Roman, Christian and above all Augustinian successors, often thought the most 'attractive' alternative to the good life: while the love of honour in the *Republic* itself is the 'second-best' option, in the *Nicomachean Ethics* Aristotle recognizes that such a life, in contradistinction to the 'bestial' life of pleasure-seeking, has a curious attractiveness to the nobler part in man, though he rejects it, for it makes a man's worth dependent on the often mistaken evaluation of one or more of his fellows. As for the early Christian writers, they were accustomed to observe – in a metaphor of Genesis – that the last of the coats of skin that the good man must abandon is the coat of fame.

Though Macchiavelli tries to distinguish acceptable and unacceptable forms of 'princely' immorality – his determining factor is the end
for which harsh and deceitful means are necessary[16] – he knows that
even this most attractive alternative to the love of that Good now seen as
the Christian God is of a fundamentally different order, and he therefore proposes very different patterns of moral behaviour for those who
prefer it. The 'shocking' features of Macchiavelli's claims, such as (inevitably) the effective necessity for princes to make regular use of lying
and cruelty – albeit in an intelligent manner – are actually testimony
to their author's intellectual integrity and insight. He concludes that the
Augustinian Christian synthesis is of a fundamentally different order
from its secular rivals, that though the only 'moral' way of life, it equally
certainly is not the only attractive way of life, and therefore not the only
'good' way of life. Macchiavelli's doctrine is a kind of wholehog-ism; since
any alternatives to that 'moral' life which is based on realist claims about
the Good and God are of a fundamentally different order, it is mere
intellectual laziness or hypocrisy to cling (unless perhaps incidentally) to
hangovers from the old Christian way if one is intent on rejecting this in
favour of something more expedient.

Macchiavelli's raising of the possibility of an alternative to the
Christian way is not arbitrary, nor even entirely dependent on the simple
attractiveness of glory and honour. It both is driven by for him urgent
considerations and is dependent on an important strain in Augustinian
Christianity. The practical concern is the desire to free Italy from the
'barbarians' (in particular the French) and withal to promote certain
forms of republican government in Florence and beyond.[17] That is in
turn related to the theoretical concern. It has often been observed not
only that there is little 'political' construction in Augustine himself, but
that his moral rigorism and powerfully realistic analysis of human nature and society suggest that decent people can hardly be effective in
the political domain; in this 'darkness of social life' they have to do too
many things which leave them with 'dirty hands'. It is true that at times
Augustine seems to discourage political and military figures, impressed
by his moral demands, from leaving the world for the monastery, and perhaps he is swayed by consequentialist arguments about political practice

---

[16] See the helpful comments of S. Buckler, *Dirty Hands: The Problem of Political Morality* (Aldershot:
Avebury, 1993), 25–38.
[17] We shall return to Macchiavelli as one of the sources of modern 'republicanism' – which claims
to identify goodness and virtue within the limits of the free (nation-)state – in the final chapter.
Note the use of such ideas in Rawls, *Political Liberalism*, 205–6.

which he would rule out in private life. Nevertheless, the apparent thrust of much of Augustine's analysis of human nature and of the nature of society seems to suggest that the scrupulous Christian is doomed to be ineffectual in the public domain.

It is precisely this suggestion – noted and endorsed by many mediaeval theorists – which so affected Macchiavelli. Since he accepts both that the moral life will be politically ineffective and that the political life is desirable not simply as the source of glory but as means to the regeneration of society, he draws the conclusion that we must choose for or against the moral (= Christian) life. He thus raised questions about the very possibility of a moral politics which no advocate of a Platonic universe or of the theory that man is by nature a 'social animal' can evade.

As for Macchiavelli himself, whether his choice of glory is susceptible of a better defence than Epicurus' way of pleasure need not concern us. Insofar as he *prefers* the pursuit of glory – a matter on which he remains standing at the crossroads and intriguingly ambiguous – he agrees with Plato that on the primary issue of realism in morality there is no half-way house, and that the consequences of any anti-Platonic determination are 'shocking'. Clever lying by the rulers to their subjects will be mandatory; better for the prince if his subjects do not see the theoretical alternatives as clearly as he does.

For our immediate purposes differences between Epicurus and Macchiavelli are less important than similarities. We should notice, however, that where Epicurus claims to base his position on a supposed fact of human nature, namely that in a state of innocence uncorrupted by the false and delusive opinions of men, we all *in fact* pursue pleasure (understood as the absence of pain), Macchiavelli – in this one of the earliest spirits of the modern age – seems more or less to invite us to 'elect' glory as a good. Yet he seems not entirely 'pro-choice', but probably to retain or derive from classical antiquity a belief that there is something 'naturally' noble in the pursuit of fame for its own sake. This is the view which Plato, as we saw, presents in the person of Callicles in the *Gorgias* in a manner similar to that in which in the *Phaedrus* he foreshadows the view of Epicurus both in the speech of Lysias and in the first, 'corrupt', speech of Socrates himself.

Hobbes: power and contract

It is appropriate to turn from Epicurus and Macchiavelli to Thomas Hobbes, who died while translating Thucydides' unblinking portrayal of human history and whose moral philosophy accepts the challenge of depicting – without the props of Platonic realism – what 'natural' man must be like. Epicurus was a pagan who denied the existence of providence; Macchiavelli was divided, still admiring Christian objectivism but wanting room for an alternative. Hobbes seems to have combined the rejection of Christianity foreshadowed by Macchiavelli with an unabashed Epicurean individualism, and having reputedly abandoned Christianity, confronts a 'state of nature' not dissimilar to the Epicurean world. Life in the state of nature was and 'underneath' still is a struggle of all against all – though blending Epicurus with the Stoics Hobbes thinks both that 'good' indicates what is pleasurable, 'evil' what is painful, and that hence man's overriding and all-compelling drive is towards his own biological survival.[18] In this he is an ancestor of contemporary atheists like the geneticist Richard Dawkins, though one can hardly suppose he would commit himself to anything so philosophically naive as Dawkins' anthropomorphism about the gene!

Man, according to Hobbes, finds himself in an unavoidable social situation in which deals have to be made – and here too he resembles Epicurus, though their kinds of deals differ. Epicurus wishes to opt out of the city-state, hoping to be allowed to live in peace on condition that he plays no part in the life, and above all in the politics, of society as a whole. Sometimes, as we have seen, he will discuss from an 'Epicurean' point of view what is 'just' in society. Just are whatever laws we agree to be useful when we sign up to whatever social contract will engineer the minimum of pain.

Perhaps contrary to their expectations, Epicureans found their opting-out as unpopular in autocracies as under other régimes. Like the Christians of antiquity, they were supposed to be 'enemies of the human race' in that they did not share the civic 'ideals' of their contemporaries. Hobbes was wiser. Faced with not dissimilar social and political pressures and, as he supposed, unable to escape, he invokes the minimal rationality that will enable the subject to do an unavoidable deal in favour of despotism. When we grasp that above all we long for personal security and survival, we shall all be prepared to make a contract with our potential rivals to live under whatever arrangement will be most conducive to that security. Such an arrangement must issue in an autocracy

[18] For similarities and dissimilarities between Epicurus and Hobbes see Mitsis (note 14 above), 67, 87ff. Hobbes' account of the pre-contractarian world is superior to that of Epicurus precisely because of his better understanding of power and competition; its weakness, as Hume recognized, lies in its omission or underestimate of limited (even ultimately self-serving) feelings of generosity.

demanding unconditional (and therefore, insofar as it involves civic duties, un-Epicurean) loyalty on condition that it preserve the safety of those
who subscribe to it. If it does not, by an appeal to first principles it can
be legitimately overthrown.

In this calculation Hobbes, though generally more perceptive than
Epicurus, at key points recalls Epicurean errors. Epicurus appeals to a
hypothetical, inaccurate and misleading account of uncorrupted childhood for guidance as to the best life for man. Hobbes too appeals to
'nature' and 'liberty', but to that natural state of human life which is
'nasty, brutish and short'. One can see the attraction of this type of
thinking. Under pressure to survive – as any civil war or famine reveals,
and as Thucydides, we have noted, had famously described – men easily
revert to brutishness. Thus brutishness, it seems to Hobbes, is 'natural',
'when the chips are down'. But for Hobbes' analysis to work, as Hume
made clear, it would be necessary for *everyone* to exhibit a similar brutishness – if indeed *anyone* ever was historically in quite the original version of
the 'primitive' conditions Hobbes alludes to, and if, even more strangely,
mankind was exactly and entirely to revert to it.

What makes Hobbes' view seem plausible is that even in less barbarous
conditions we sometimes seem to be approximating to his nightmarish
vision. When President Richard Nixon observed that 'If you have them
by the balls, their hearts and minds will surely follow', he appeared
to speak a good deal of truth, at least about people involved in the
same political enterprise as he was. Neither Nixon nor Hobbes, however,
spoke of everyone or of every occasion, and apart from the fact that
inferences about how we would behave in a hypothetical and impossible
situation are no sure guide to rational or even likely behaviour in an
actual situation, there always are some whose behaviour is not as such
analysts predict. To be statistically true ('That is usually how men and
women behave') will not serve Hobbes' turn, for if even a few refuse the
contract – and even if they pretend (for whatever reason) to do so – they
will detract from the integrity of the schema. Hobbes' position depends
on the empirically implausible theory that all possible 'moral' saints and
heroes can be reasoned out of their beliefs and practices. But if they
cannot, no government will (or should) ever rest assured that, provided
only it looks after the survival of the citizens, it will be granted legitimacy.
Hobbes' view – dependent on its cynically reductionist psychology – that
at least much of the work of a realist morality can in practice be effected
by the power of autocracy, thus rests on insecure foundations. We recall
that Plato, in the second book of the *Republic*, had foreseen the attempt
to use the social contract as an escape from the dilemmas posed by the

ignoring of a secure basis for morality and virtue. But perhaps a better version of the contract than that proposed by Epicurus and Hobbes is available; I shall therefore return to it in chapter 6 when discussing the current influence of Hume.

The paradoxical position of Kierkegaard

I have compared Hobbes with Epicurus in respect of their radical substitutes for transcendental realism, and I have observed how Macchiavelli, insofar as he *opts* for glory as the most attractive alternative to the Christian life, reveals himself as something of a forerunner of those modern theorists whose ethic asserts the primacy of *choice* as a 'solution' to the vacuum generated by nihilism (or by the apparently indefinite variety of possible *goals* in life). But are there no ancient or mediaeval forerunners for claims about radical choice, and if not why not? Part of the answer is that all the ancient thinkers, even 'Thrasymachus', 'Callicles' (who believes that following the 'passions' is the rational course) and Epicurus, claim a certain ethical primacy – defensible or not – for reason as a guide for life. *Either* reason could focus on the good, *or* it could first identify our natural (as distinct from our conventional) inclinations, and then serve those instrumentally – *or* it could do both of those things. Thrasymacheans certainly have thought that we should invent (or contract into) some kind of morality, but they have wanted to select what they took to be the most reasonable 'ethical' stance. No more than Plato or Aristotle (who were far from using reason only instrumentally) were they choosing whether to be rational or whether rather to advocate freedom to choose for its own sake. If the course they followed could be shown to be 'irrational' – that is, not rationally defensible – they would have to own to having made a mistake. They accepted to be reasonable and would have been appalled to be supposed to have deliberately chosen against the rational in favour of the merely willed, or informed that what matters in life cannot or need not be identified by reason at all. They might have failed to think well; they would rightly have denied that they had merely 'plumped' or followed their passions without due reason.

Why, then, are many modern attitudes so apparently different – as may be observed in accounts of rights as either protected goods or protected choices?[19] Certainly there are multiple causes of the contemporary

---

[19] Cf. L. W. Sumner, *The Moral Foundation of Rights* (Oxford University Press, 1987), 45–53. For an illuminating introduction to the legal and moral difficulties buried in much contemporary (and especially American) debate about rights, see Mary Ann Glendon, *Rights Talk: The Impoverishment of Political Discourse* (New York: Free Press, 1991).

situation, but two are of special importance to us here. The first is the Kantian emphasis on the essential humanity of autonomous decision-making, and we shall be considering Kant at a later stage. But Kantianism alone could only have become the parent of certain contemporary views when allied with the notion of a 'leap of faith', a radical and basic decision to follow a particular course. Perhaps Macchiavelli needed such a leap to characterize how we decide between the way of Christ and the way of glory, but he contents himself with delineating the two ways with rather little consideration of the choice itself.[20]

More immediate origins of the contemporary emphasis on choice and preference can be traced back to eighteenth-century discussion of the truth or otherwise of Christianity – in fact to a further weakening of the Augustinian reconciliation of Christianity with Platonism. Theologians of the day made consistent attempts (Paley's *Evidences* is a good example) to offer a rationalist construction of Christianity – beyond mere arguments that Christianity is rationally defensible – and the intelligible and predictable result of such attempts was failure. Produced were defences for an emaciated deism with the supernaturalism largely eliminated and very unlike traditional accounts of Christianity.

The upshot of such failures was a growing suspicion that Christianity is not defensible, from which varying conclusions were drawn. The *philosophes* and their supporters outside as well as inside France saw the rational next step as the abandonment of Christianity altogether. Kant, too, attempted to demythologize much Christian doctrine so as to present it as a religion within the limits of reason alone.[21] A third and quite different position, especially associated with Kierkegaard, was that although Christianity is right religion, its apologists are misguided. In Kierkegaard this is no mere recurrence of a theme often preached (though more rarely practised) by Christian zealots and traditionally traced back to Tertullian in third-century Carthage:[22] as he put it, that there is nothing in common between Athens and Jerusalem or that it is one of the glories of Christianity that it wholly defies the philosophic mentality.

Kierkegaard's role in the history of Western thought is paradoxical. His aim seems to have been to free Christianity not only from the bourgeois

---

[20] Macchiavelli probably had in mind two distinct ancient 'choices' – that of Hercules between pleasure and virtue, and that of Augustine (in the *City of God*) between the city of God and the secular city: *aut servus Dei aut servus diaboli.*

[21] For an introduction to recent studies see Philip J. Rossi and Michael Wreen (eds.), *Kant's Philosophy of Religion Reconsidered* (Bloomington and Indianapolis: Indiana University Press, 1991).

[22] For a plausible corrective to the traditionally fideist picture of Tertullian, see especially E. Osborn, *Tertullian: First Theologian of the West* (Cambridge University Press, 1997).

and institutional trappings of 'Christendom' but from deist or naturalist transmutations, whether of Kantian or Hegelian origin, and to restore something like the pietist form of Augustinian and Lutheran beliefs in which he had grown up.[23] He was, however, largely neglected by his contemporaries and his influence in philosophy is a more or less twentieth-century phenomenon.

Recently friends and foes alike have read him as a prime source for theories of radical 'freedom'. Thinkers as diverse as Sartre and MacIntyre have seen him as proposing a choice,[24] for which no reason can be given, between the life of feelings, of 'aesthetic' man, and the life of rational morality. Since rationality is one of the two alternatives, it follows that it cannot be used as the means to determine between them. This interpretation of Kierkegaard has been so influential that it is worth trying to understand why it has arisen and why it is historically erroneous.

When considering Macchiavelli, we observed that he offered only *two* alternatives, the Christian (and moral) life and the life of 'princely' glory. In Kierkegaard's *Either/Or* there seem also to be two alternatives: the life of the 'aesthete' or sensualist, which according to its critics culminates in despair, and the life of morality – seen as work, marriage and rational duty – represented by Judge William. According to MacIntyre, as Kierkegaard sees it, we cannot come to a rational decision between these two lives. Hence he is the originator of theories of radical choice. However, there are three lives, not two, in *Either/Or*, though the third, the religious life, is only in the background of Judge William's world until, at the end of the book, it emerges in a brief sermon written by the Jutland pastor whose main theme is that man is always in the wrong before

[23] Kierkegaard's latest writings – it should be noticed – not only reject *institutional* Lutheranism, but also – more philosophically significant – his own earlier insistence on God's grace as the only means by which we can overcome the 'moral gap', as it has recently been called, between our understanding of moral demands and our capacity to perform them. For the nineteenth-century version of the 'moral gap' (and its origins in Kant) see John E. Hare, *The Moral Gap: Kantian Ethics, Human Limits, and God's Assistance* (Oxford University Press, 1996). More generally on Kierkegaard's relations with Kant see R. M. Green, *Kierkegaard and Kant: The Hidden Debt* (Albany: State University of New York Press, 1992), and more cautiously A. Rudd, *Kierkegaard and the Limits of the Ethical* (Oxford University Press, 1993). For MacIntyre's misconstrual of Kierkegaard's account of rationality see M. Piety, 'Kierkegaard on Rationality', *Faith and Philosophy* 10 (1993), 365–79; also N. Lillegard, 'Judge William in the Dock: MacIntyre on Kierkegaard's Ethics', in R. L. Perkins (ed.), *International Kierkegaard Commentary, Either/Or, part II* (Macon, Ga.: Mercer University Press, 1995), and C. K. Bellinger, 'Kierkegaard's Either/Or, and the Parable of the Prodigal Son: Or, Three Rival Versions of Three Rival Versions', in *ibid.*, 59–82.

[24] For the nineteenth-century neglect of Kierkegaard and the crucial role of Sartre in his transformation into the forerunner of theories of reasonless choice see Roger Poole, 'The Unknown Kierkegaard: Twentieth-Century Receptions' in A. Hannay and Gordon D. Marino (eds.), *The Cambridge Companion to Kierkegaard* (Cambridge University Press, 1998), 48–75, esp. 54–6.

God. In writings later than *Either/Or*, especially in *Fear and Trembling*, Kierkegaard develops his account of the religious life in much greater detail, even working out more than one level within that life itself.

How does Kierkegaard, within *Either/Or*, think that we move from one life to another? Not by reasonless choice, but because within the two lower lives (though the process is shown explicitly only in the case of the aesthetic life) we shall recognize contradictions which can only be resolved by a determination to transcend (not, be it noted, to abandon) the aesthetic lifestyle. It is that act of rational choice – that decision freely to act on one's beliefs – which constitutes the 'leap' of faith.[25] How then are the contradictions recognized? They are recognized in that the aesthetic lifestyle is perceived as unsatisfying to the whole man, and above all to what Kierkegaard thinks of as his passions, as representing his whole personality as distinct from his merely rational capacity. In thus bringing together the whole man, Kierkegaard rejects a tradition of rationalist accounts of what we are which goes back at least to Descartes and which receives its fullest ethical formulation through Kant's notion of those rational and moral duties which we must perform without concern for 'happiness', feeling or self-interest. Thus Kierkegaard's leap of faith is not a rejection of rationality as such but of the rationalist's narrower conception of that rationality, and it aims at the restoration of something much more like the erotic Platonic rationality of *Republic* book 9.

Yet ironically it is less this revivalist Kierkegaard – this Kierkegaard who would offer an account of how even the decision left unexplicated by Macchiavelli could be made – who has been influential in the history of recent Western ethics than his 'Sartrean' transfiguration.[26] It is further ironical that while Kierkegaard wished to register a protest against the aridities of the eighteenth-century version of rationalism, he should become instead a patron saint of twentieth-century irrationalism.

While, however, Kierkegaard tried to reform the concept of rationality, he also seems to have maintained, and in his anti-institutionalism even to have strengthened, the Protestant tradition of man as isolated ethical *individual* – not least in that, for whatever reasons, he eventually broke even with the established Lutheran Church of Denmark. For radical

---

[25] For *some* Kantian background to 'leaps' see Green, *The Hidden Debt*, 139–46. For more general treatment see M. Jamie Ferreira, 'Faith and the Kierkegaardian Leap', in *The Cambridge Companion to Kierkegaard*, pp. 207–34. There is no doubt that Kierkegaard's (similar but dissimilar) emphasis on freedom encouraged Sartre (not to speak of Heidegger) in his mistreatment of his predecessor's position. To pursue the matter further is beyond our present remit.

[26] Sartre would hardly have appreciated *Either/Or* (Hong and Hong) 2.215, where self-choice is specifically *not* identical with creating oneself.

choice, in and of itself, and, as we shall see, like many another modern ethical trend, is as much a bastard of the Protestant Reformation, of the thesis of man alone with his God, as are the sub-Kantian theories of autonomy with which it is now regularly associated.

Of course, radical choice, though a descendant of the 'faith alone' of the Protestant Reformers, as also of the fideism of some of the late Scholastics, would have been unacceptable to all these earlier thinkers, who had taken their beliefs to be based on the inescapable and readily intelligible evidences of Scripture as the direct and unmediated Word of God. For them faith is no chosen determination of human autonomy but a god-given confidence in the objective reality and significance of Christ. Yet the commands of God in both the Calvinist and Lutheran traditions often seemed to be arbitrary assertions of God's power as such, and contemporary secular theories of radical choice may be analogues (some would hold them a secular abuse) of extreme versions of Divine Command Theories of Ethics: theories, that is, which propose that what is right and wrong is so (or is known to be so) primarily, or even exclusively, because God has so determined it. In the secular version it is our autonomous selves which make such determinations of morality. If a Kierkegaardian 'leap of faith' is blended with pseudo-Kantian (or better Millian) autonomy, read as the power to choose 'freely', and if this blending creates us as human and valuable, we shall have arrived at the contemporary notion of radical choice. Given Kierkegaard's concern with human freedom, that blending is not unlikely.[27]

Plato, of course, lacking a strong version of divine omnipotence, could not have foreseen any such theological theory, let alone specifically rejected it, though he might have stumbled upon the possibility of radical choice in pursuing some other way. He did not, and neither did the other major philosophers of classical antiquity, all of whom must be viewed as moral naturalists and moral 'rationalists' of some sort.

Paradoxically, it would seem, a major effect of Kierkegaard's work has been to promote an approach to ethics entirely repugnant to his own expressed philosophical and theological aims: an approach under which much of the power of the anti-Platonist theses of Thrasymachus, Epicurus, Macchiavelli and Hobbes can be subsumed. For all alternatives to '*Platonic*' objectivity in ethics may be forms of the claim – becoming explicit only *after* Kierkegaard but much indebted to him – that what *matters* in the world is what we prefer, what we choose to be 'natural',

[27] See Green, *The Hidden Debt*, 147–50.

what we choose as our own – and precisely *because* we autonomous beings choose it as our own. Such a claim agreeably links choice with both pleasure and power, as Plato again had largely predicted, especially in the *Gorgias*.

This linkage will be considered in more detail. For the present, however, we must leave the realist metaphysics of the Good and its possible alternatives to look at Platonizing concepts of the *psyche*. For any ethic, Plato believes, must depend not only on a metaphysic of morals but on a specific philosophical psychology and concept of human nature. On the latter as an appropriate subject of enquiry Platonists and anti-Platonists can agree (as we have seen with Epicurus and Hobbes), as they can on the need to buttress their psychological theses with empirical appeals.

CHAPTER 3

The soul and the self

MULTIPLE SELVES

Every writer on ethics is an avowed or closet naturalist. Not even the positive lawyer tells us how we should live, what it is right to do, or what is good for us, unless he avows or assumes a thesis of what we are or could be. All such theorists provide a description, however incomplete, of the relevant features of human nature, and insofar as they presume knowledge of that nature, all prescriptions based on them are 'naturalist'. Even revisionists who argue that claims as to what is 'natural' are social constructs for purposes of control or exploitation – men, for example, may justify the subordination of women in terms of biological finality – must concede that although 'natural' accounts, in this case of 'gender', depend on social conditioning, there are limits to what socializing alone can do. Unless socializing can be extended to include gross surgical manipulation, no amount of it will permit males to conceive.[1]

All ethical theories are *also* natural-law theories in that they assume that the maxim 'Ought implies can' – though at times misleading – indicates an important truth: it is no use telling us we ought to walk more if we have no legs, or to think more if our mind is insufficiently educated. Anatomy is at least a condition of destiny, as generally are physiology and psychology insofar as they identify the parameters within which human beings can function, setting limits – within roughly accepted bounds of sanity – on the laws we prescribe and targets we set for ourselves – whether in the physical domain (no-one will ever run a one-minute mile) or in the moral (no-one will ever perform all his actions from entirely pure motives). Even the existentialist who thinks that we should create ourselves in achieving a series of free acts assumes a theory about the kind of beings who can contemplate this goal.

[1] Thus Shulamith Firestone argues that any society requiring gender blindness as sexual 'equality' must demand the widespread use of artificial reproduction (*The Dialectic of Sex* (London: Jonathan Cape, 1970)): a paradigm case of 'counter-natural' egalitarianism.

Thus human nature sets the parameters within which rational ethical enquiry must be pursued. Where 'Ought implies can' is misleading is in the case of ideals the more inspiring in that they are beyond our grasp. Yet to suggest that is to imply a notion of what our grasp might be, indeed of what 'we' are. If, with one of Browning's *dramatis personae*, we can declare 'Ay but a man's reach should exceed his grasp, / or what's a heaven for?', we are better placed to understand our goods and duties, or at least what is good for us and hence what can be reasonably expected of us.

'What is Truth?, asked jesting Pilate, and did not wait for an answer'. So wrote Francis Bacon, and the question is far older than Pilate and far younger than Bacon. Yet so is the word and the 'natural' concept it conveys in multiple languages. Either we repudiate it – effectively giving Pilate's envisaged answer – or truth about the world is to be taken as the foundation of theories about the world: hence theories in ethics should be connected with implicit or explicit views of man, and better moral theories will be connected with truer, more defensible accounts of human nature. For ethical theories are concerned with what is 'true' and therefore good and right for men in general and with what it is right for an individual man – not a dog or superman – to do or to experience.

This necessary grounding is lacking in discussions of morality governed less by theories of human nature than by analysis of the moral terms we pass from language to language. Philosophers who thus proceed either literally do not know or at least do not trouble to identify what they are talking *about*; since they offer no explicit account of human nature, they cannot but theorize on the basis of ideas uncritically assumed or culturally conditioned. Absurd though such presumption must be,[2] persistence in it can be understood as in part due to an unwillingness to introduce difficulties from the 'philosophy of mind' – the unfortunately Cartesian title for what should still be called the philosophy of human nature – into the already splintered and chaotic world of ethics. However well intentioned, such unwillingness is an omission making for triviality.

Contemporary philosophy of mind offers ethics disappointingly little help; indeed relevant ethical material is often excluded from its debates. We hear about personal identity, but little direct reference to moral identity. Those who discuss the continuing reality of the 'self' offer radically divergent theories of psychological or physiological connectedness over time, or they consider the possible lurking of a fixed internal item or

---

[2] For some especially influential comment see G. E. M. Anscombe, 'Modern Moral Philosophy', *Philosophy* 33 (1958), 1–19.

'further thing'[3] under the changing appearances of our personalities and actions. In all these discussions 'self' is a term of art, referring roughly either to a (Cartesian) centre of consciousness or to a bearer (or 'owner') of active and experiential capacities sometimes identified as a separable 'core'. This self is normally supposed to be 'unified' – even 'unitary' – at least at each moment in time, since we are 'aware of ourselves'. Yet paradoxically we are supposed to remain confident not just of our continuing identity as subjects of consciousness or as thinkers, but of our continuing moral identity, in the supposition that we have roughly the same moral beliefs, responsibilities and rights from one day to the next, and that these beliefs and awarenesses form a unity which *is* our moral character or mindset.

Analogies with the continuing, if temporally limited, unity of physical objects, including those which form various parts of our bodies, help to make the notion of personal and moral identity plausible. Consider the head – a physical item – and the thoughts which can loosely be said to occur and persist 'within' some part of it, namely the brain. Each of us, we know, has one head; each of us, we easily assume, has – at least at any particular time – one more or less consistent and unified set of continuing beliefs, habits and practices, moral and otherwise, though the moral are our immediate concern. This assumption is not weakened by our awareness that there will always be moral questions on which we remain undecided; in such cases indecision is allowed for within our assumption of unity. We are undecided, we think, because we do not yet know, and perhaps will never know, how to square particular moral difficulties with the beliefs and attitudes which are forming the structure of our moral universe. One head, we are sure, implies one moral universe; we are, we suppose, more or less morally coherent.

Nor is it that we forget that we 'change our mind', but that we do not always understand our changes, nor the view of the self to be presupposed by 'changing one's mind', let alone by speaking of ourselves as 'divided'. I leave aside phenomena of religious or political conversion to concentrate on what happens when we are persuaded, usually after a lapse of time since we first began to 'have our doubts', that a specific position we previously adopted – for example against remission of Third World debt – was mistaken. Here are three possible reasons why such a change might occur: we recognize that we were unduly harsh about other people's sufferings, or we decide that such relief would be far more effective than

---

[3] Cf. (e.g.) Parfit, *Reasons and Persons*.

we had previously supposed, or that it may 'pay dividends' over time. In each case we may adjust a moral outlook which we earlier believed to be coherent but which we now suppose defective. We may judge this defectiveness to have proceeded from lack of imagination, ignorance of facts, or from an inadequate view of life in general.

Perceptiveness about our psychological condition will be increased if we realize that our judgements have often been inadequate not simply because of errors of fact or defects of imagination but because of radical inconsistencies in what we supposed was a unified moral outlook. Such greater awareness may develop if we experience a conversion in our religious, political and social beliefs, since conversion involves the conviction – often accompanied by feelings of regret or remorse – that there was something fundamentally amiss with us. If that perceived wrongness be construed broadly as a wrong *moral* orientation, a *misdirection* of our most basic ethical beliefs, of our moral 'self' as a whole, it is only marginally our present concern, but if it involves the recognition that, all unawares, we have held radically opposed and self-contradictory moral beliefs, followed consequently contradictory moral courses, then we need to explore not only the nature of the opposition among these beliefs but its very possibility.

We may begin by supposing that it is especially likely in our contemporary pluralistic society that the mere possession of a single head is no guarantee that its moral contents form a unity – unless that of a heap or a conglomerate at best partially sorted, for by now we are 'educated' from a smorgasbord of traditions, practices and beliefs which themselves derive from variegated first principles: from Christianity in its various flavours, Marxism, liberalism and Darwinism, psychoanalysis in Freudian, Jungian and Adlerian forms, Kant and Nietzsche, perhaps exotically seasoned by a dash of what we at least take to be Zen Buddhism. It is near certain that most of us, while professing a series of strongly held moral beliefs about the contentious subjects of the day – abortion, euthanasia, just and unjust warfare, pacifism, capital punishment, the ecological threat – keep the first principles of our positions, if not the positions themselves, in watertight compartments, sealed off from each other. We are convinced that we have an 'overall' moral stance and there may indeed be a dominant tendency among our various individual beliefs, but we are widely capable of deriving one set of moral conclusions from a basic premiss p and at the same time – indeed almost in the same breath – others from versions of not-p.[4]

4 Cf. A. MacIntyre, *After Virtue* (London: Duckworth, 1981), 1–5.

A quick check – admittedly liable to be marred by the self-deception endemic in introspection – would do much to establish the plausibility of this claim.[5] But if it is even largely correct, then insofar as our foundational moral beliefs are incoherent or inconsistent, we remain divided, possessing no single identity, even though in promoting a moral programme we are unprepared to concede that we have no right to all its parts simultaneously. In what sense divided? Not as an apple or a house can be divided, for the parts of our divided self are at least potentially hostile to one another and self-contradictory, so that in a particular circumstance we may struggle over which course to follow, and 'hate' ourselves for reaching a certain conclusion. Nor will that hatred necessarily be superficial; it will arise when via my projected and accomplished actions 'I' *realize* my internal divisions and the differing moral selves 'I' must be nourishing. Thus our basic moral divisions may be seen as the development of potentially different personalities, each only partially achieved at any one time.

A given person, at a given time, may be tending to develop or alter in a specific direction, towards a less chaotic 'moral self'; in that very 'tending' he or she will be erratic, variable and unpredictable. The individual's diversity is probably greater than any moral check-up could reveal, and the more so now that the complexities of modern acculturation have helped to extend the range and variety of our differing selves. Nevertheless, it is these different 'personalities' or potential selves, revealed in part by introspection, that cause the ensuing self-hatred to which I have alluded. We also become aware of further causes of our division: not only the plurality of social and ideological elements in our culture, but those differing roles (brilliantly depicted by Sartre) which we assume in public and private life: at home, at work – and indeed within different contexts of our homes and places of work – and among differing groups of companions, friends and cronies.

As comedians have made it their business to notice, human beings have always tended to 'wear a different hat' for their public and private lives – for their 'love' life, their business life, their 'spiritual' life – and it is at least indisputable that different kinds of external behaviour and comportment, for example in matters of dress, are seen as appropriate for different human activities. But in the modern urbanized jungle – not least with the demand for 'flexibility' in the job market – we seem to need a radically different 'persona' as we move from one office to the next, let

---

5 I have several times asked students to identify any two strongly held moral beliefs and think about the reasons behind them. Most of them have admitted to holding p and not-p at the same time.

alone from one job to the next. Our variations are more complex than the mafia hit-man who goes home from 'work' to play happily (because, he hopes, forgetfully) with his children – and perhaps dons mourning for the elaborate funeral of his or his group's victim. What is puzzling is in what sense 'we' forget: who forgets whom and who is forgotten.

Every potential self will be a composite of newly experienced desires and beliefs and of further engrained beliefs, desires and practices arising from various habituations. Our compartmentalized selves will form without our fully realizing what is happening to us as we 'fit in' to our surroundings: in part because even when we become aware of our diverging beliefs and desires we lack the intelligence to organize ourselves harmoniously, in part because we lack the strength of will to do so and are overpowered by one or other version of *acrasia*; we 'know the better and do the worse', perhaps for what seems a short-term advantage, or we are indisposed to discard our fondest beliefs, however discredited our intellects may suspect them to be, retaining them as part of a 'second nature' or as wishful thinking. Or we may tell ourselves it is too late to do anything about it: 'the damage is done', and so we connive at self-deception.

In thus speaking of compartmentalization and of potential selves, I am not merely redescribing our performances of different kinds of actions at different times. Certainly our erratic behaviours will form a sequence, if only because we cannot focus on or carry out all our differing intentions at once. On the contrary, at any particular time and in virtue of the multiplicity which has developed within us and which can always expand still further, we can act in effect 'inconsistently' when called upon to act out any one of our varying but established roles. However, if we perform in differing roles in very rapid succession, we may come to seem to ourselves to be acting erratically and out of character; the ensuing puzzlement will increase the likelihood of our reconsidering larger segments of our life as a whole – and thus of the imbroglio of our 'selves' encroaching on each other's territory.

The divisions in the moral self under consideration do not correspond to Freudian distinctions between the pre-conscious, conscious and unconscious, though to propose them is not to reject those distinctions. Each of our 'selves' or developing personalities may be composed of conscious and unconscious elements, as the circumstances which seem to require our adoption of different *personae* fade from memory or are buried in originally deliberate and increasingly habitual self-deception. Nor should they be considered as subsystems of a single core personality or basic system, as warts or cysts are independent growths on or within a 'core' body. Such 'systems' or 'subsystems' would imply a fixed, prior – perhaps even pre-existing – core self, so that to propose them is to beg the question of the nature of the priority of the ultimate moral I who am the ultimate referent of the name 'John Rist' – and not least in that they leave it still uncertain why the original self should thus subdivide 'irrationally'.[6]

The consequences of this unavoidable uncertainty are considerable: firstly because, whether we are concerned with what *I* ought to do, with what principles *I* should follow, with whether *I* should attempt to maximize some form of good or with whether *I* try to live up to the course *I* believe to be rational or to the moral contract to which *I* believe *I* have subscribed, it is difficult to see how such concerns can be rationally met if it is not clear who *I*, the assumed moral agent, *am*, or whether there is a single *I*.

All moral theories are either agent-relative, agent-neutral or some mixture of the two. Very roughly, in an agent-neutral system we are concerned with calculating how to maximize a desired good or goods without reference to the moral status of those responsible for achieving them except insofar as that status may itself be counted among the goods to be achieved. Such systems will thus tend to challenge us to maximize goods (or effects) without much (or any) attention to the means required to secure them; or at least they will not allow anxieties about the 'morally' appropriate means to determine how to pursue the valued ends. Their 'agent-relative' critics – from Socrates to the present day – have thought that such calculations miss an essential characteristic of morality (and even humanity), namely that one can never neglect the importance of personal responsibility, thus dispensing with the questions 'What ought *I* to do now?' or 'Should any goal justify *my* doing *this* now?' or, more broadly, 'Am *I* morally unique among others who are also morally unique?' But what is the point of such concerns if the very notion of *I* as a moral subject remains unclear and confused? For mere legal purposes such anxiety about the complexity or otherwise of each moral 'self' is comparatively unimportant: statisticians and others can work with abstractions such as a 'legal person' or 'economic man', and for the identification of a legal person – an individual answerable in law – some physical, psychological or social criterion can easily be

---

[6] Such 'systems' are considered, for example, in the often helpful book of D. F. Pears, *Motivated Irrationality* (Oxford University Press, 1984), esp. 67–106.

stipulated; genetic or conventional fingerprinting might be satisfactory. Even a society in which moral categories can avowedly no longer be established needs a legal system, and so 'positive' lawyers work on the assumption that law as such merely needs its own instruments, and similarities between legal and moral prescriptions can be, perhaps ultimately must be, accidental.

But legal positivism entails a moral and psychological reductionism which philosophers must question. If, despite the moral divisions and potential selves we experience, each of us is entitled to refer to himself as a moral agent, we must reconcile our unity with our plurality. Here perhaps a reconstructed Hume can help us. Our moral self – and I might venture the older word 'soul' – must then be a 'narrative', and so in some respects at least, like a nation or club. But if our 'soul' is to be a meaningful moral – and metaphysical – narrative, it possesses, or can construct, a *telos* or goal at which we may and should deliberately aim. Only if we take *possession* of (and do not *merely* construct) such an individual *telos*, are we more than interchangeable moral units – 'legal selves' – and thus capable of fully agent-relative morality. Moreover only then – and whatever our present disintegration into a set of competing 'personalities' by which we live different lives and play a multiplicity of roles – shall we be more than an accidental bundle as we continue our passage through life. Only then shall we differ from the Hobbesian 'ship of Athens' – or any other inanimate object with all parts replaceable over time – insofar as each of us is able, and has reason as an unique organic agent, to identify with our unique past 'self' – even 'selves' – achieving this by our own activity, not simply in virtue of what is done to us, and with reference to the sort of soul we ought to become in the future.

The fact of such activity indicates that the moral 'bundle' in which resides whatever unity we possess cannot be merely accidental, thus contradicting our irreducible feeling that 'I' am more than accidental, in as much as I am still able to summon up sufficient 'purpose' – as most of us seem to – to move and want to move in one overall direction rather than another. Such movement, whether it be considered progress or decline, is distinct from mere ageing and can only be a process of moral and spiritual unification – or disunification – continuing as long as our physical condition allows. Its very possibility depends on our individual choices being made not in a vacuum but within a framework of more or less coherent past practices, habits and dispositions without which we could and would 'tend' randomly to the pursuit of any number of supposed goods.

If we are a set, less or more unified, of competing selves, those selves will have various typical 'goods' as goals. What then happens when two such goals collide and how do *we* determine which good should be given priority? The very question suggests that, whatever our decision in the individual case, we shall not be quite the same overall 'self' or bundle before as after the chosen act, but shall have strengthened the likelihood of resemblance to one or other of our possible selves, or else added a new potentiality. We shall continue to be a human being qualified in gradually diverging or converging ways as a dynamic continuum.

In that other type of moral circumstance where we cannot decide which of two 'good' deeds to perform, we shall again eventually make a choice – even if it is the choice not to act or to defer choice – and we shall normally choose in accordance with our previous overall character with its various proclivities and practices. It may be argued that only a theory of a (Cartesian or other) core self will explain how in such situations we retain any freedom – within the limits of human nature in general and of our own past decisions and habits – to be what we choose to be, but this would be to mislead, since the posited 'core' need be no more than what we happen to be overall and at any particular time; there is no need to introduce an unchanging self or fixed moral essence to guarantee the type of 'freedom' in question, for to be adequately ourselves is to be precisely no more than what, within the necessary parameters of our personal and genetic histories, we from time to time are. Of course, insofar as we become more unified, our possible 'freedom' will appear more morally restricted. That does not matter since, if we are to be 'single-minded', certain 'options' (all, that is, which would increase our multiplicity) will become morally nigh impossibilities since we could hardly bring ourselves to 'choose' them even where we have the physical capacity to do so.

Thus while we are multiple, we are constantly making choices between our possible selves and determining – however gradually – what we are likely to become, it may be to arrive at a fixed state in which certain habits are all-engrossing; then any agonizing over choices would cease and we would effectively pursue proper courses of 'action' – to include contemplation when appropriate. This has the further important implication that since uncertainty – and so choice – between alternatives of substantially distinct moral worth is only provisionally desirable, choice in itself cannot be a final good: that it will be not the power to choose, nor 'right to choose', which will finally matter, but what has been and is chosen and for what motive. If we were already in possession of a fixed core self, identifiable by introspection or in any other way, our right choices would be the self-restricted reflections of that core self and hence intrinsically *good* 'choices' (giving a more meaningful sense to 'choice') – not means to a further end. Insofar as we are a developing self – in whatever moral 'direction' – moral choices are not ends in themselves but instruments, on arrival at eventual perfection to be superseded.

In view of the apparently universal illusion of moral unity among human beings, despite their random diversifications of personality, it should be no surprise that it has been a persistent theme in moral philosophy and philosophy of mind (as in certain religious traditions) that insofar as a human agent is or becomes wicked he or she is or becomes 'multiple', and that insofar as he or she becomes good he becomes single, 'simple' and unified[7] (which does not mean that to be wicked is simply to be a complex, or that to be good is to be a self-sufficient, personality). Yet to become less complex is not to become single, and unless we are to claim that incoherences and inconsistencies can be eliminated from our moral beliefs and behaviour, and so simplicity attained, there is a significant sense in which we *cannot* become one person or 'self'. To be one person or 'self' thus understood would entail being incapable of moral regression, being aware of all that is required for the achievement of the best possible approach to 'singleness of heart' and so unable to lose sight of it. 'Choice' would have ended.

Complete simplicity would require not merely freedom from moral confusion and thus, at least in intention – ignorance of relevant facts, however, being sometimes impossible to avoid – total success in moral action, but precisely no *possibility* of *moral* failure: the possession of a god-like inability to do wrong (however wrongdoing is defined). In contrast to that is the present incoherence of the moral self, which, as I have argued, can be exhibited empirically. As we have also seen, it is impossible (and not merely in our present polymorphous society) to test our basic moral 'principles' introspectively and with complete honesty; our capacity for self-deception is apparently indefinite and – given our need to objectify ourselves in introspection – substantially irreducible. Thus we cannot even hope to discover within ourselves a fully coherent or settled pattern of belief, desire and habit, and even more dauntingly, there is no reason to believe that such a settled condition *could* exist during human life, hence

[7] The 'unity of the virtues' is best understood in this sense. The hypothetically perfect man would possess all the virtues integrated. This does not imply that it makes no sense to say that X is courageous but lacks self-control, merely that the courage X shows cannot be courage in an ultimate sense. The intelligibility of such 'secondary' uses of 'courageous' depends on the reference of all courage to a primary instance which would thus indicate, as Aristotle has explained, the focal meaning of 'courage'.

that our behaviour *could* ever cease being more or less erratic. Though we may be consciously tending towards one or more of our potential selves – the life-roles we play from time to time – we are unable entirely to identify with that self or selves.

That being so, we have to recognize what has been dubbed the 'surd-factor' within what we like to see as the self as a whole, and which we depict both as a moving organic narrative or 'tradition' and as a more or less unified bundle of beliefs and practices of which we are only partially conscious. Approaching this surd-factor from a rather different direction, MacIntyre identifies it as follows:[8] 'What one discovers in oneself and in all other human beings is something surd and unaccountable in terms of the rational understanding of human nature: a rooted tendency to disobedience in the will and distraction by passion, which causes obscuring of the reason and on occasion systematic cultural deformation.'

While MacIntyre's formulation relies too heavily on a 'Cartesian' distinction between reason and the 'passions', and thus accounts for 'surds' in terms of an undoubted tendency to disobedience and related problems of the 'will' – so raising the further question of why the will should be like that – my sketch has centred on the differing sets of beliefs, desires and habits which, seen as one varying set, indicate the total psychological 'shape' of this surd. My representation of the 'surd-factor' identifies it not as a quasi-separate element of the psyche, but as an *effect and sign of the ineradicability of division in our present nature itself.* One might even call it a 'shadow self': what we would be if everything went wrong with us! The continuing presence of our surd-factor might well be indicated by continuing desire for what is other than good or by any not wanting to know what are goods.

Apart from its manifestations in the empirically observable irrationality and sheer erratic madness of much human behaviour – quite incomprehensible to those who refuse to accept it[9] – the 'surd-factor' as

---

[8] MacIntyre, *Three Rival Versions*, 140. An earlier and somewhat narrower use is by Donald Davidson, 'How is Weakness of the Will Possible?', in *Essays on Action and Events* (Oxford University Press, 1980), 42. In view of our upcoming discussion of autonomy, it is worth noticing how far even Kant was prepared to go in recognizing radical evil within the human agent (cf. *Religion within the Limits of Reason Alone*, 25 (30), 32 (37), on the 'perversity of the human heart'). See recently D. Savage, 'Kant's Rejection of Divine Revelation and his Theory of Radical Evil', in *Kant's Philosophy of Religion Reconsidered*, 54–76, esp. 71–3. These ideas do not commit Kant to the Calvinist view that after the Fall man is totally depraved.

[9] Cf. P. Fussell, *Wartime: Understanding and Behavior in the Second World War* (Oxford University Press, 1989), 132: 'It [World War Two] was a savage, insensate affair, barely conceivable to the well-conducted imagination . . . and hardly approachable without some *currently unfashionable* theory of human mass insanity and inbuilt, inherited corruption' (emphasis added).

a signifier of our division is recognized less dramatically in the daily conflicts we experience between first- and second-order wishes: between what we want (say money) and what we want to want (say generosity).[10] Without the surd-factor, and so single-mindedly reflecting on our conflicts, we would easily bring about a moral progress which clearly is not readily available to most.

Which brings us back almost to our starting-point of separate potential selves within each 'moving' moral individual. Though it is not an immediately ethical question, we can hardly not go on to wonder about the ontological status of our potential 'selves'. Are we to say that we are 'nothing but' these sets of interlocking potential individuals, or are our 'selves' in fact the varying qualities of a primary core? I have already suggested that the 'I' is best explained as a dynamic continuum of which my 'selves', incomplete as I am, are the changing constituent parts. However, there seems no reason not to award the self a limited unity over and above these part selves nor to deny that these are at differing stages of 'growth', some being closer than others to our desirable moral personality as a whole, though none identical with it. Such an interpretation becomes the more plausible – and may appear the only option – the more firmly an essentialist 'core self' is rejected. Plato, of course, did subscribe to such a core self, and in view of my 'choice' for the Platonic tradition, it is incumbent on me to offer 'ethical' reasons for my view that in this he is mistaken.

CORE SELF OR FUTURE SOUL?

In Plato's *Apology* Socrates presents two particularly striking examples of agent-relative morality, both drawn from his own experience. In the year 406 BC the Athenians defeated the Peloponnesians in a sea-battle at Arginusae, but though victorious they lost some thirty-five ships and the Athenian generals were accused of making inadequate attempts to rescue their own sailors. The law in Athens was that where several participants in an alleged criminal act were to be put on trial, they must be tried separately, not as a group. Socrates, who by chance was president of the appropriate judicial body at the time, refused, at great personal risk, to allow consideration of an illegal proposal to try the accused together. In

---

[10] See H. Frankfurt, 'Freedom of the Will and the Concept of a Person', *Journal of Philosophy* 68 (1971), 5–20; E. Stump, 'Sanctification, Hardening of the Heart and Frankfurt's Concept of Free Will', *Journal of Philosophy* 85 (1988), 395–420; also C. Taylor, 'Responsibility of Self', in A. O. Rorty (ed.), *The Identities of Persons* (Berkeley: University of California Press, 1976), 281–98.

recording the incident Plato makes no comment on whether Socrates thought the men guilty or innocent; nor did Socrates allow his views about any best possible outcome to influence his determination not to countenance the use of illegal means to secure a (probably) just verdict: namely the condemnation of the generals.

The second incident occurred a few years later when the Athenian democracy had been overthrown and an oligarchic clique, supported by foreign troops, ruled in its place. It was the policy of the oligarchs to multiply the number of citizens implicated in their crimes – on the not unfamiliar principle of encouraging as many as possible to fear that in any counter-revolution they too will be destroyed. In accordance with this policy, Socrates and three others were ordered to arrest a prominent citizen, Leon of Salamis, who was then to be put to death on a trumped-up charge, but in reality for his money. Socrates disobeyed the order and went home while the other three proceeded to Salamis and made the arrest. What is important in this case, and what makes it a star example of agent-relative morality, is that, although Socrates himself refused to have any part in a crime, his action did not secure what would often be judged the best end state: the safety of Leon. What his stance achieved was to make the point that, although an injustice could not be prevented, it was not to be done 'through me'. In the *Gorgias* he had already argued explicitly that it is better to suffer wrong than to do it.

In such behaviour we see the Platonic and presumably the historic Socrates embracing the major principle of agent-relative morality, the notion of an individual's 'responsibility' for his actions: his choice of means as well as his ends. Plato's story also introduces the chief reason why Socrates thought such all-inclusive carefulness about our behaviour essential: as he put it, we should be concerned above all with the well-being of our 'souls', or with how our souls *are to become* as good as possible. Vicious behaviour is damaging not only to its external victims, but even more to its perpetrators. That of course implies that our 'souls' are valuable, or at least necessarily and properly to be valued and treasured by us. We may leave aside for the moment the justification of such ascription of value: whether it is that unless we look after our souls we shall be 'uncomfortable', whether such discomfort is connected with our desire for some form of self-preservation, or whether, as was the view of Socrates and Plato, some further explanation of that 'value' or 'goodness' is necessary. In any case, it is hard even to approach the question of whether we should be agent-relativists or agent-neutralists unless we have a theory of the 'morality' of the individual agent: a theory to explain its importance for the agent-relativist and its comparative unimportance for the agent-neutralist. Indeed the agent-relativist position can be painted as merely sentimental if we have no clear idea of what a *moral* agent is.

Does all this, as Plato seems to have supposed, make agent-relativism depend on the theory of a permanent core of the 'self', an uncorrupted interior man? We have already suggested that it does not, and disagreement with Plato here is of great importance, for it concerns the manner in which we should concern ourselves with the 'soul'. Plato himself offers two accounts of the purity of the soul, of which his first, naive model is developed into the second, more sophisticated version. The naive model, that of the *Phaedo*, is that the soul will be pure when it frees itself from the body. The second version depends on a critique of that position: if the soul is so weak as to be corrupted by the body which is its theatre of operations, there must be something seriously wrong with it. But how seriously? Very roughly, Plato came to think that we should be concerned to strip off *from the soul itself* the layers of corrupt practice and misguided belief which have caused us to become no longer single and unified but many and diversified persons. But if there is no such core self, such a process might be ultimately futile; however much we remove mistaken belief and bad habit, we shall never, by these or any means, recover what we already are. If 'cleansing' is to be undertaken – and Plato is only one of many who think it should – then its intelligible goal can only be, not to reveal what we really are (and always were) but to change the make-up of what we shall really (that is eventually) become.[11] In fact for Plato himself the matter is more complex than we have so far disclosed. In the next chapter we shall consider the difficulty that although there is certainly a core self theory in Plato, there is also a rival theory which in effect subverts it, though without inducing Plato himself to abandon it: he knew that much depended on his not doing so, and perhaps sensed the way out of the dilemma.

In any case, while dissenting from Plato's views over the core self, we should not underestimate agreements between our working hypothesis about a future 'soul' and other Platonic claims. An important area of agreement, as we have noticed, is the common emphasis on the theme

---

[11] It seems that Plato's core self, as presented, must also be immortal, in that no vice (= plurality) can destroy it. That is the point of what is often held to be a weak argument (and one not repeated by Plato himself) for the immortality of the soul in *Republic* book 10. If the soul is a 'core self', then the argument of *Republic* book 10 entails immortality. If the soul is what it is and what it 'really' is lies in the future, there is no such entailment, though the possibility is open.

of simplicity and the avoidance of 'multiplicity' in the soul – an emphasis afforded grudging admiration even by staunch anti-Platonists.[12] In the Platonic dialogues this theme is to be found most urgently in the *Republic*, and nowhere more elegantly and powerfully than in the portrayal in book 9 of the 'tyrannical man', the antithesis of the philosopher-king, or more properly the philosopher-king manqué. Plato holds that no-one would knowingly choose to resemble such a man and believes that unless his description of the tyrannical character can be shown to be mistaken, the tyrant provides in his own lineaments a devastating rebuttal of the claims of Thrasymachus that one 'flourishes' more if one behaves in ways which would conventionally and by 'ordinary' misguided people be condemned as 'unjust'.

The tyrannical man is presented as pulled in every direction by his unfulfilled (and unfulfillable) desires and passions. He is thus the perfect example of a 'multiple' moral personality, insofar as one can be divided against 'oneself' or one's potentially simple self, while still remaining a living human being (and presumably sane, though Plato hardly seems to want a distinction at this level between madness and criminality). So Plato's thesis, when assembled thus far, would appear to be (as we should now expect) that although we are all multiple personalities, we become the more evil as we become the more multiple. Evil at the moral level is thus identified with some anti-rational behavioural chaos in which no attempt at pruning or even at prioritizing one's desires, except in terms of their (non-moral) intensity, is feasible.

---

[12] Note the remarks of J. L. Mackie on Plato's claim that we injure ourselves by 'pluralizing' ourselves in *Morality: Inventing Right and Wrong* (Harmondsworth: Penguin, 1977) 191:

> Though Plato is wrong in suggesting that there is only one sort of leading motive around which a personality can be integrated, we can concede that one who, in pursuit of apparent self-interest, evades on special occasions a morality which he not only professes and encourages but allows ordinarily to control his conduct will probably be incurring costs in the form of psychological discomfort which he may not have taken adequately into account when calculating his self-interest. But we must not make too much of this. A completely harmonious soul, a fully integrated personality, is in any case an unattainable ideal [we have already raised the question of whether ideals are necessarily valueless if unattainable], and in the post-Freudian era we know that an appearance of harmony is likely to be achieved only by pushing conflicts out of sight.

> Mackie is certainly right that the unity which Plato desired is unattainable (at least in the present life, which is Mackie's entire frame of reference); indeed Plato may eventually have seen this himself. It is also true that if unity is unattainable in the present life, and *there is no possibility of its being attained in another*, then it has less (but not necessarily no) use in ethical theorizing. What at least is clear is that Plato may have been right in supposing that if there are objective and realist standards of morality, there may also be a future life in which we can live in ways which we can only dream of enjoying in our present existence. Yet if it is possible that there is some kind of necessary link between theories of an afterlife and a realist morality, then such a morality may well seem to some less plausible than ever.

Plato's claim, then, as we hypothesized above, is that we are disintegrated not simply insofar as we are multiple, but also insofar as this multiplicity has no possibility within itself for prioritizing, that is for securing an order and unity in and through the multiplicity. The point may turn out to be important for soul-making 'practice' as well as theory, since it leaves open the possibility (even the likelihood) that improvement is not merely a matter of restricting our desires but of properly channelling and diversifying them: in more contemporary terms, not of repressing them but of integrating or healthily 'cathecting' them. It may not be possible to determine how far Plato himself would have wished to go in that direction.

He seems to have identified goodness (as a metaphysical reality) with unity. No-one (at least now) can be quite clear what he meant by this, but we can certainly see something of his intention if we reconsider his account of the moral disintegration of the tyrant. His belief is that since all of us are potentially evil, there must be an at least potential 'multiplicity' of persons within each of us, for if we were correctly unified, we should be good. Plato's educational project and ambition, in the *Republic* at least, is to eliminate this 'potential' multiplicity, or rather this potentially multiple *disorder*, for a plurality ordered within a unity would be morally acceptable, at least if it involved a rejection of those 'personalities' which would not submit to such ordering. He later became convinced that success in this endeavour was beyond the range of human striving and only a god could achieve it. Man (at least in this life) will always retain an element of multiplicity that defies harmonization, and hence of imperfection, in the possibility, even if unrealized, of being divided against himself – the ineradicable surd-factor again. Yet despite his metaphysical claims about the relationship between 'unity' and goodness, Plato's treatment of men's unity or lack of it in the latter part of the *Republic* is at the level of phenomenology, of acute observation of what we are; he has little to say about why we are (or why we must be) as we are.

Nevertheless, there are historical implications in Plato's position, and since a Platonist (at least in antiquity) is someone who thinks it his task to bring out what is known but left implicit in what Plato taught, we should not be surprised to find later speculation – some of it of great value in its own right – as to the origin of the indeterminate moral condition in which we find ourselves. Clearly insofar as people in that tradition of exposition remain in any sense Platonists, they will retain, explicitly or implicitly, the principle of agent-relativity together with as much of

Plato's understanding of it as they can honestly accommodate when it comes under attack.

If we can only infer, on grounds of general plausibility and on the evidence of other writers, that Plato thought of goodness somehow as unity, we are in no doubt about the view of his greatest champion in antiquity, the founder of the revival and reformulation of Platonism which goes under the modern title of Neoplatonism, and which primarily mediated Platonism to Augustine. Writing in the third century of our era, Plotinus spells out in great detail how as the world 'declines' from the perfection of a unity which in a sense contains everything but which also transcends and exists apart from its productions, so the element of 'multiplicity' increases. We are not now concerned with Plotinus' metaphysical claims about the origin of our universe; my intention in considering him (as in considering Plato) is only to draw attention to certain features of a kind of thinking about moral and 'personal' issues as they first appear – and as they often startlingly and starkly appear – on the philosophical horizon.

That said, there are certain features of Plotinus' metaphysics which are strikingly different from the views of Plato even though their author did not believe this to be the case, and some of these must be evoked if we are to understand the Plotinian account of the multiplicity of the soul. First of all, in Plotinus' universe everything is caused by the One (that is, in modern terms, by God as Efficient Cause). Without the One, nothing of any kind would exist. Not that the temporal universe has a beginning, for there can be no reason why things should start at one time rather than another. On the contrary, if there is a One, then there are 'always' others, in their respective modes of existence.

That implies that the most important distinction in Plotinus' world is not that between the eternal and the changing, as in the universe of Plato – though Plotinus of course retains that distinction – but between the One and the others, between the necessary and the contingent and dependent. Insofar as this affects our present concerns, it means that the distinction between unity and multiplicity which, as we noticed, has moral significance in Plato's account of the soul, is even further emphasized in Plotinus'. But there is more than that, for Plotinus' enhanced status for his first principle enables him at least to suggest an explanation (and an argument) for the fact that we have such extraordinary potentiality for self-fragmentation, for losing our 'unity', for being many (potential) people at once, and none of them entirely. We can fragment, Plotinus thinks, because we are dependent on 'unity', or in his preferred language because we are other than unity; though insofar as we can be said to exist at all we retain a certain unity which binds us together as human and not merely as animal, let alone as vegetable or inanimate objects.

In Plotinus' complicated metaphysical schema, the level of Soul, that is, of all souls, is characterized as a 'unity and multiplicity'; by which he means *inter alia* that we are a unity of such a kind that without being to an extent transmuted into something 'higher' we cannot retain 'pure' unity; we shall always be simultaneously fragmented, and liable to further fragmentation into forms which are increasingly subhuman. The advantage Plotinus' metaphysic gives him (at least over the *typical* Plato) is that he can present a coherent (though not necessarily a true) explanation of our present perceived experience of multiplicity – without appeal to pre-existence – where Plato has merely noted a phenomenon. And we should recognize that the displacement of pre-existence undercuts Plato's account of the soul's *natural* immortality and indeed of its being a pure core self – though Plotinus does not develop this criticism, and indeed would repudiate it.[13]

Plotinus follows Plato in giving insufficient metaphysical weight to our historical experiences. This is best seen in his account of what we ought to be like. He distinguishes between our empirical 'self' (roughly what we are like in our embodied life) and some sort of 'real' or core self (or, as he would prefer, 'upper soul') which exists over and above our empirical self or ego – in his language the 'we'. The soul is hidden by the ego and apparently tainted by it, and when we are purified it reverts to what it is always 'really' like.

Besides believing this to be the view of Plato – it is indeed *one* of Plato's views – Plotinus has an interesting argument in its favour, an argument which we must tackle if we are to continue with the objection that it fails to account for the way we actually experience our apparent 'identity' and are to try to simplify and improve it. This argument is that without some sort of ever-pure moral self or core, if we ever become morally inferior or possessed of any sort of bad character, we have no way to moral improvement. Plotinus believes that this pure core or 'undescended soul' must exist because people do in fact achieve what would otherwise be impossible: that is, they become morally better. We ought not to be surprised by or contemptuous of this argument, even though – as we

---

[13] Pre-existence is retained in Plotinus, perhaps precisely because it is required if the soul is to last as long as the One; what has gone is its epistemological usefulness. For related questions see A. N. M. Rich, 'Reincarnation in Plotinus', *Mnemosyne* 7 (1954), 4, 10 (232–8).

shall suggest later – it may not take all the necessary issues of moral improvement into account and though I shall ultimately conclude it to be unsatisfactory. In its essentials it is an argument, or more often merely a view, which is still commonly current, even among people who know nothing or nothing good of Plato.

For some such belief underlies contemporary 'liberal' claims that human beings are 'really' or 'naturally' or 'underneath' good, or good at heart. Though there is no *a priori* or empirical reason to accept such a claim, to abandon it is to remove the underpinnings of a great deal of nineteenth- and twentieth-century progressivism and of prospective twenty-first-century secularism. It underlies such commonplace assumptions as that if good education, proper medical attention, adequate means of birth control and adequate housing were available to all, we should have something approaching an ideal society and certainly a happy one. Of course, to deny that such is the case is not to deny that good housing, education and the rest help promote better social circumstances with less crime and a more peaceful domestic life. It is, however, to deny that they guarantee it, being favourable conditions rather than either necessary or sufficient causes, and also to assert that since they do not guarantee it, the explanation of our current discontents, moral and otherwise, cannot be complete, or even anywhere near adequate, until it takes into account the basic weaknesses, the tendencies to multiplicity, the 'surd-factor' in human nature as we presently experience it. Bad social conditions – the phrase is intended to cover more than material poverty – will certainly impel the 'surd-factor' to reveal itself in the form of immoral, erratic and anti-social behaviour, but good social conditions for economic man can by now be known to be far from adequate to guarantee the opposite.

Plotinus needed an explanation of what seemed the facts about man's possibilities for moral improvement, but his explanation both collides with the thesis that it is hard to identify what we are, and seems to assert (not merely to imply) that we can discover our 'real' (or core) self, beyond all shadows and appearances, by some sort of introspection. Yet however closely Plotinus' position may resemble still influential Cartesian theories about the self,[14] it is very different from many of the attitudes of Socrates and Plato, despite their promotion of the Delphic precept 'Know thyself'. Plato, after all, had urged that we recognize the 'truth',

---

[14] Plotinus' closeness to Descartes should not be overemphasized; above all he engages in no 'epistemological' hunt for certainty. See generally E. K. Emilsson, *Plotinus on Sense Perception* (Cambridge University Press, 1988), and G. B. Matthews, *Thought's Ego in Augustine and Descartes* (Ithaca: Cornell University Press, 1992).

the intelligible world of unchanging Forms, not by introspection but by thinking about the world, including the moral world, around us. The objection to that had always been the sceptical one: how do we know that what we recognize, either by the mind or through the senses, is what the 'world' is really like? Can we get at the real world at all?

Plato may have an answer to that, but he does not give it explicitly, and I shall not attempt to reconstruct it for him. In any case and for whatever reason, Plotinus, who still recognizes Platonic Forms, thinks – in this respect like Descartes – that the 'truth' can best be seen not outside in the world, but 'within us'. That runs up against the now familiar objection that we do not know that we are able to look within ourselves without distorting what we see: just as it is hard to recognize our own motives, for we are always inclined to distort them in self-serving and self-flattering ways, and have no certain check against self-deluding defence mechanisms and wishful thinking. Even if there is a 'core' self – the point at issue – it will be impossible to be sure what it really is – or perhaps which one it really is.[15] In any case, who is doing the looking? Such difficulties in Plotinus' position did not remain long unobserved in more professional theological circles.[16]

Among these, Augustine thought he knew not only where Plotinus had gone wrong, but how what he had got right could be re-established more securely. Indeed he thought that any reconstruction other than the one he himself proposed could not be successful, and that if he were to be proven wrong, the whole attempt to do ethics in the Platonic 'tradition' of realism would be fatally undermined. In early days, when more uncritically influenced by Plotinus and the Platonists, Augustine too had supposed that an understanding of the true self could be established by introspection, but by the time he wrote his *Confessions* (AD 397–400), he had come to hold that we have no guarantee that the self we see is the self we hope or want to see – and we accordingly construct one to fit our rationalizing and self-indulging fantasy.[17] What is more, his rejection of Manichaeism, which held that our apparent moral conflicts are caused by our 'good' will being challenged and overcome by a second

---

[15] Difficulties about the moral nature of the core self recall problems raised by Hume's claim that by introspection he can see no substantive self but only a stream of perceptions (*Treatise* I.4, section 6). In the present study, these problems will be largely neglected, because (following the misleading footsteps of Descartes and Locke) Hume challenged what he saw as the traditional problem of the continuing self without immediate reference to our continuing *moral* personality and *moral* identity. Many philosophers consider the dissolution of morality as a possible consequence of the disappearance of the substantive self rather than precisely an aspect of that dissolution.

[16] Including those of the pagan Neoplatonists who followed Iamblichus.

[17] In the next chapter we shall return to the question of what we can and cannot see in introspection.

evil will which is not 'us', led him to focus firmly on the fact that it is 'we' who apparently want conflicting things at the same time (thus exhibiting our plurality), that it is we who must tackle the random, variegated and conflicting loves and desires that shiftingly dominate us. Such clashes, of course, include those between first- and second-order desires to which we alluded earlier, where the second-order desire is to want to want the proper object of a first-order desire, and are well illustrated by his famous prayer: 'Give me chastity, but not yet.'[18]

If we are thus conflicted, have we no way of seeing our (moral) 'self'? Certainly not directly, but Augustine's answer is that it is not our 'self' – core or otherwise – on which we must rely to get us out of the difficulty, for in view of our 'sinful' division that is impossible; rather it is on God. Since God (necessarily) cannot be changed and manipulated by us, and since God is a necessary condition of our own existence (as Plotinus also held), then if we see God (rather than imagine we see God), it is not because we strain to see him, but because he makes himself available and visible to us.

Thus Augustine's explanation of how we (or some of us) seem to improve is not that we improve ourselves, but that God enables us to improve. In other words, Plotinus and Plato were right to suppose that we need some inner core, untouched by sin, if we are to improve by our own efforts, but that since there is no such identifiable pure and inner core and yet – despite the surd-factor – some people do improve, that improvement cannot ultimately be explained in terms of our own efforts. This is, in effect, both a moral argument for the existence of God and at the same time an insistence that we do not possess a clearly demarcated and simple core self of the type the Platonists (and many later thinkers and assumers) had posited.

Augustine develops an important corollary to his argument, and one for which there may be further evidence. Moral improvement by chance being in the long run impossible, and since one needs help from outside to maintain even an approximation to the simple, consistent existence which Plato and Plotinus had recognized as the good life, it follows that such life (and the 'happiness' which characterizes it) can be achieved at best fleetingly in our earthly mode of existence. The good life is like a jelly which is being formed, as our 'soul' is growing better and thus more unified, but it is always liable to dissolve, since, as Augustine reiterates time and again, man is a proud and self-willed creature liable normally to abuse his responsibility to rule himself (let alone that of ruling other

---

[18] See D. D. Crawford, 'Intellect and Will in Augustine's *Confessions*', *Religious Studies* 24 (1988), 291–302.

people). Should the good life be finally achieved, it can only be in another mode of existence, which is to say after death and – for the Christian – through death. We have no kind of entitlement to any other such mode and, if we do possess it, can only owe it to some special act and intention of God, unpredictable in principle by us.

Augustine's position, if correct, would imply that the search for moral identity as a quality or characteristic, a substance or 'narrative' already unambiguously completed and possessed, is the search for a mirage. The question 'What am I now?' has no clear answer. Our moral (hence personal) identity, as usually discussed, is as yet unidentifiable and unattainable; hence the philosophical difficulties which it obviously generates. It can exist only in the hope that in place of our distracted 'self' we shall have a stable and unified soul, which will strictly 'exist' not in the past, as Plato had supposed, but in the future – or, if our present existence is all there is, not at all.

Here we return to our starting-point, for a real oddity about agent-relativity – if it is of the essence of morality and if morality is more than a prudential contract or rational arrangement to secure the apparent best for some or all of us – is that it is shot through with confusions and ambiguities which render moral identity, and hence personal responsibility, so problematic and indeed ultimately unintelligible in most of the contexts in which they are regularly discussed. And there is more, for agent-relative morality is posited as (among other things, and perhaps indirectly) such as to make the soul better. Yet apparently it cannot entirely succeed, and if it attains temporary success, that success will always be precarious and dependent on particular circumstances; these, therefore, will be considered in the next chapter.

The developments in Platonic ethics and philosophical psychology that occurred down to the time of Augustine highlight major difficulties in the thought of Plato himself. We have identified in passing one particularly damaging tension. As a matter of historical fact, Plato's version of agent-relative ethics seems to demand a core self (or 'soul'), but, as we shall see in the next chapter, some of his accounts of moral identity seem to imply (perhaps rightly) that we do not in fact possess such a core, but only the more or less conflicting selves we can recognize, no one of which has any guaranteed permanence though some, in the case of the 'better' among us, are more permanent than others. Such inconsistency should not surprise us; what is extraordinary is not that Plato has left major knots untied but that he has proceeded as far as he has along a number of paths holding much promise.

MORAL VS. ONTOLOGICAL ACCOUNTS OF MAN

An attraction of first-person descriptions of the world – by which I mean descriptions from my standpoint and including reference to that standpoint – is that they promote a greater awareness of the claims of that morality of responsibility and personal integrity which I have introduced as 'agent-relative'. Their apparent inconvenience is that they allow less room for scientific generalization and quantifiable data, while at the legal and moral level they may tend to privilege the agent's 'virtue' and importance in his own eyes, thus offending against humility and impartiality. Historically, as we have seen, it was Plato (or Socrates), always concerned with moral conflict and with man as a moral agent, man striving for 'likeness to God', who first among philosophers urged the necessary agent-relativity of the good life – or to restate this in another way: Plato recognized that man can develop non-moral excellences and moral – or perhaps better spiritual – excellences. His primary concern, however, was with man's capability for moral excellence, and he considered other excellences either less important or – more normally – inextricably involved with moral excellences and even as dependent on them.

While also an agent-relativist, Plato's pupil Aristotle usually discusses man in terms less obviously related to agent-relativity and indeed to ethics in general, and seems more concerned than was Plato with the whole range of man's capacities. Aristotle's ethics and 'theory of value' overlap with the views of Plato in many respects, but these are less our immediate concern. For along with such similarities – and quite apart from the question of the relation of moral capacities to human capacities as a whole – we find in Aristotle's metaphysical and psychological writings a very different approach to first- and third-person accounts of the universe and of man, and this different approach can spill over into ethics: the result, variously interpreted, would allow for theories either complementary or adverse to those of Plato.

Roughly speaking, Aristotle *assumes* the importance of man as a moral agent (and a possible moral unity) emphasized by Plato but, not least because of his dissatisfaction with Plato's theory of the soul as a separate substance, he works out a metaphysical account of the unity of the human being (whereby the soul is the form of the body) without much *specific* consideration of how this metaphysical unity should be related to man's peculiarly 'moral' nature and apparent moral unity. Hence a seeming 'Aristotelian' might come up with a powerful theory of man's metaphysical unity while having nothing to say about any moral identity – or indeed about human nature as specifically moral at all.[19] And as we have already noted, in the modern and contemporary debate about personal identity from Locke to Parfit, discussion of the moral aspects of any possible unity we may exhibit, whether through physical or psychological continuity, is minimal.

Aristotle's chief concerns are to sort, classify and explain the contents of the universe, and while he allows Plato's moral concerns (if not Plato's answers to them) to be of great importance, he offers an account of the human soul which, at least prima facie, gives no indication that man should be viewed primarily as moral agent. (Plato might comment that Aristotle has proposed a *useful* but not the *most* informative account of man.) To put it somewhat differently, Aristotle's formal and metaphysical account of the 'soul' and hence of man is a third-person view: man is a body–soul 'composite' and the soul is the first actuality of a living body 'possessed of organs'. Thus he calls up, for the first time, the problematic of the relationship between a 'scientific' account of man and the 'moral' account presented by Plato: by implication, one should add, because Aristotle does not seem to recognize the problem he has raised; indeed, when talking about man as a moral agent, he assumes much Platonic language, saying for example in the *Nicomachean Ethics* that we should strive for likeness to god as much as possible (10.1177B33), or that we should act 'for the sake of what is noble' (*kalon*).[20] We shall return later to this latter claim.

Aristotle's solution to the apparent divergence between the first-person (moral) and third-person (ontological) accounts of man should be sought in his description of the human mind and in his thesis that the better our mind (and thus the better our moral decisions) the 'better' or more valuable we are. The intricacies and difficulties of this need not concern us; what is important is that Aristotle offered at least the possibility of defining man without reference to his peculiar capacity for that first-person

[19] *Republic* book 10, provides good evidence for the differing approaches of Plato and Aristotle. Here, as we saw, Plato argues that if vice cannot destroy the soul then nothing can, thus assuming a certain ontological unity in the 'soul' beneath its moral multiplicity. Aristotle's ontological unity, however, is not just that of the soul but of the human being.

For a modern adaptation of Aquinas' version of Aristotle's theory of metaphysical unity see David Braine, *The Human Person: Animal and Spirit* (Notre Dame University Press, 1992). For its theological possibilities see especially chapter 14 (where attention to Plotinus' theory of the body's being 'in' the soul might have been fruitful). But while Braine puts great emphasis on man's linguistic capacities as powers of his soul which 'transcend' the body, he makes only the barest mention of moral 'transcendence' (e.g. at 494–5).

[20] See in particular J. Owens, 'The *kalon* in the Aristotelian Ethics', in D. O'Meara (ed.), *Studies in Philosophy and the History of Philosophy*, vol. ix: *Studies in Aristotle* (Washington, D.C.: Catholic University of America Press, 1981), 261–77.

view of the world necessary for an agent-relative morality. Although it would be to do him considerable injustice to say that he would think of an 'ontological' account of man as adequate, he has certainly opened the door to those who would.[21]

An advantage of distinguishing, in broad terms, the accounts of human nature, human rationality and human excellence given respectively by Plato and Aristotle, is that we can see both of them underestimating the complexity of the problem. Both at times adopt an approach to human nature guaranteed in advance to be incomplete. Aristotle says in *On the Soul* that a man is a composite of soul and body, and specifically that the soul is the first activity of an organic body capable of life. That is an impersonal, scientific statement not of what we are as moral agents, but of what we can physically and mentally enact. It could refer to any living organism, but let us assume we are concerned only with rational human life. Although Aristotle discusses moral dilemmas and the weakness of the will in *On the Soul*, the *Ethics* and elsewhere, in his more 'formal' account of the human being our 'moral' features are only implied, and only insofar as they are rational.

When Aristotle asks, 'What is it that makes a human being human?', he answers, 'The mind' (especially viewed in its deliberative capacity, its ability to devise means to ends): an answer which naturally and easily leads him to suppose that the less 'mind' one has the less 'human' one is. What he calls natural slaves (I would prefer 'manimals')[22] are the children of human beings but defective in those mental qualities which make a human being human and so unable to plan their own lives. Some of the ('illiberal') conclusions Aristotle professes about natural slaves are the de facto (if hidden) agenda of all who think of humanity in such impersonal and strictly rational terms; they are usually concealed in their modern reincarnations (to which we shall return) beneath the remains of a very different Christian (and partly Platonic) conception of what it is to be human. We can expect that the Aristotelian bluntness will, at convenience, come ever more to the fore as a post-Christian mentality becomes the norm.

Plato's account of man does not do justice to many of Aristotle's legitimate concerns, above all to his sense that we are a metaphysical unity

---

[21] Note the comments of C. Gill, 'Is there a Concept of Person in Greek Philosophy?', in S. Everson (ed.), *Psychology: Companions to Ancient Thought*, vol. II (Cambridge University Press, 1991), 166–93, especially at 169 – though Gill does not deal with the agent-relative implications of first-person descriptions.

[22] For the term and its explanation see Rist, *The Mind of Aristotle*, 249–51.

of soul and body. Indeed there is reason to think that the weaknesses in Plato's '*moral*' account of the 'soul' as some sort of core substance (a view to which in his youth Aristotle had subscribed) may have influenced Aristotle towards a more third-person and impersonal version. But it was by no mere chance – we could more reasonably invoke his own directly moral, social and political concerns and motivations and those of Socrates – that Plato concentrated on those features of humanity so important from the moral point of view: its capacity for individual moral decision-making and personal responsibility. Hence although Plato's overall picture of man may be as formally incomplete as that of Aristotle, and his emphasis on moral matters may have induced him to neglect man's ontological unity, it is his analysis of the *soul* as the agent of morality, and his account of the soul–body relationship, not his emphasis on *man* as a moral agent, which needs overhauling.

Plato's 'scientific' view of what it is to be human is significantly different from Aristotle's. 'Scientifically', for Plato, we are a compound of 'soul' and body, but these are ultimately separate substances. Plato's account of the empirical self, insofar as it is, even as experienced temporally, some sort of metaphysical unity, is far less advanced than that of Aristotle. Hence we find the externals – but not always the hard bits – of theory of action far better described by Aristotle. Plato is not greatly interested in the metaphysical unity (or 'unity', as he might prefer) of our present empirical structure, but in a separate soul and the problematic unity of even that. The real 'I' is the soul which can live best apart from the body, and is no mere 'self' in the sense of a Cartesian centre of consciousness.[23]

For Plato what matters most about human beings is less that they can reason (though to some degree they can and that is important) than that they are moral or 'spiritual' subjects, capable of loving the good (or the less than perfect) and hence determining for themselves what kind of life they should live:[24] that is, whether we should live in accordance with a transcendent (and in no way mind-dependent) Form of the Good (of which we shall find only a ghost or shadow in Aristotle) or whether we should opt for the alternative life of force, fraud and rationalization, with, as its theoretical counterpart, the denial of metaphysical truths and concentration on the maximization of our desires: a life in which reason

[23] See Gill, 'Is there a Concept of Person in Greek Philosophy?' – though Gill makes no specific mention of Plato.
[24] The notion of loving implies both that the human agent is in some sense radically incomplete and that he or she is, at some level, a sexual agent. Thus a full account of man as a 'moral' or 'spiritual' agent will require some account of sexuality and 'gender differentiation'. This will be developed further in the next chapter.

is and ought only to be (when 'ought' suggests 'What fool wouldn't see that?') the servant of the passions, tyrannical as those passions will be over both ourselves and others. One of the few things which *Socrates*, according to Plato, claimed to know about (and thought enormously important) was 'love matters' (*Symposium* 177D).[25] Astonishingly, although Aristotle assumes some kind of ghost of the Platonic *kalon* and discusses friendship at length, he has (at least in the texts which survive) virtually nothing to say – positive or negative – about Platonic *eros*. Any complete exposition of Aristotle would need to offer an explanation of this strange omission.

In what concerns our present enquiry, Aristotle differs from Plato in at least three ways: he has abandoned Platonic Forms except that within his version of moral realism he has retained their ghosts – a matter to which we shall return; he has moved towards a conception of the human being which comes closer to that of a purely rational agent; he has concentrated on man as a metaphysical unity rather than as a divided moral subject.

Aristotle points to the mind as that which distinguishes man from the beasts,[26] but to emphasize a peculiar feature is not necessarily to identify its peculiar importance, and Aristotle's valuable distinction between practical and theoretical reasoning – combined with a neglect of Plato's view of *eros* as motivator and with an inadequate treatment of the goals or ends of life (as distinct from the means towards them) which the 'eye of the soul' can recognize[27] – encourages him further to misdescribe, if not marginalize, those very human features which Plato had considered of paramount importance. It is interesting to notice, however, that when in *On the Soul* Aristotle raises a rather Platonic question – there are parallels in the *Phaedo* – about whether the soul–body relationship is like that of a sailor in a ship (413A8–9; cf. 408B25–27), he observes that a solution is not clear. He would seem to envisage the possibility of combining his

---

[25] On this fundamental point about Socrates, Plato's testimony is confirmed by other Socratics, especially Aeschines and Eucleides (see Kahn, *Plato*, 15, 18–29).

[26] For the differences here between Plato and Aristotle see R. Sorabji, *Animal Minds and Human Morals* (London: Duckworth, 1994), 12–16.

[27] In Aristotle deliberation is concerned (despite continuing wishful thinking among a number of contemporary scholars) only with means, not with ends; cf. *Nicomachean Ethics* 1145A6, 1144A8 and P. Aubenque, *La prudence chez Aristote* (Paris: Presses Universitaires de France, 1963), and 'La prudence aristotélicienne porte-t-elle sur la fin ou sur les moyens?', *Revue des Etudes Grecques* 78 (1965), 40–51; also W. W. Fortenbaugh, 'Aristotle's Conception of Moral Virtue and its Perceptive Role', *Transactions and Proceedings of the American Philological Society* 95 (1964), 77–87. Insofar as the confusion about Aristotle's treatment of means and ends is not ideologically driven or an explicit 'improvement' on Aristotle, it has partly arisen because at *Nicomachean Ethics* 1.1097A3off. he writes of an absolutely final end to be 'chosen' (note *haireton*, not *prohaireton*) for itself and never as a means. This is not, however, a choice arrived at by deliberation; it is given by the 'eye of the soul', the functioning of which depends on how we have been trained to look.

concern for an ontological account of the soul as the form of the body with a Platonic description of such a 'form' as giving moral commands to the body, but to be puzzled how to proceed with the limited 'dualism' that description implies.[28]

It can be argued that Plato's overriding concern with moral agency, and its function in knowing oneself and looking after one's 'soul', places too great an emphasis on the individual's evaluation of and concern with himself.[29] Perhaps Aristotle's more neutral manner (though, as we have seen, he is far from denying the importance of Plato's concerns in what he thinks of as their proper place) is less self-centred, less concerned to inflate man's importance in the universe as a whole. There is no need, at least as yet, to evaluate the strengths (and weaknesses) of Aristotle over Plato. In any case, an attack on one position does not in and of itself constitute a defence of another, and, if effective, may leave the object with the option of repair work, not merely of starting again.

The repair work may need to be substantial: thus, is Plato – or any other agent-relativist – committed to the view that the reason we should not be unjust is simply that injustice damages the self or one's own 'integrity'? I shall argue later that there is no reason to believe he need be so committed, and, importantly, my consideration of 'dirty hands' will suggest that self-division, when not caused by wrongful behaviour towards oneself, is necessarily a sign of objective wrongdoing to others: wrongdoing, that is, which really does injure its victims (though arguably less than its perpetrators). This discussion will be deferred, however, until I consider the place of rules in the good life; for the moment I conclude that third-person (ontological) accounts of man downplay our sense that we alone understand what it is like to be *us*, but also – and more disturbingly – undercut the Platonic agent-relativist's claim that our greatest concern should be for the moral decisions we make and the moral practices we develop.

AGENT-RELATIVE REDUCTIONISM

Though I have urged the importance of identifying man as a moral (and spiritual) agent, some such identifications are liable to promote vices of their own. Some agent-relative moralities are reductionist – not

---

[28] On such dualism see H. Robinson, 'Aristotelian Dualism', *Oxford Studies in Ancient Philosophy* 1 (1983), 123–44.

[29] Criticism somewhat along these lines is suggested by T. Nagel, *The View from Nowhere* (Oxford University Press, 1986), 195–7.

(usually) in that they sacrifice too much to the moral life, but because the 'good life' is too narrowly conceived. The discussion of rules and principles in chapter 5 will indicate one area in which such narrowness gives grounds for concern, and thereafter I shall consider how reductionist forms of agent-relativism have distorted much recent ethical thinking in the Kantian tradition. However, like others treated thus far, the topic can best be introduced by considering not a modern but an ancient example – extreme and therefore specially informative – provided not by Plato but by the Stoics: a group also claiming Socrates as a spiritual ancestor. If ontological or 'scientific' accounts of man threaten to leave out his personal responsibility and moral agency, extremist versions of agent-relativism will diminish the richness of his natural life, and therefore of the 'good life for man'.

Some philosophers maintain that an advantage of third-person (or impersonal) descriptions of man and his behaviour is that they allow us to concentrate on the results of human actions, emphasizing that what matters is less who does the good than that the good is done. A perceived objection to this is that in such depictions the individual seems dispensable; human beings are substitutable and their goods quantifiable, it making no difference whether this person or that is benefited: an impersonal fairness is all; no-one should be 'privileged'. Though this may depend on assertion of the equal value of all, it does little to obviate the possibility that no-one has any particular or intrinsic value. Humanity may matter, or be deemed to matter; individuals do not.

The Stoics go to the opposite extreme, looking at times like Socrates the agent-relativist gone mad, and thus tending to bring agent-relative morality itself into disrepute. For the Stoics, all that matters in and of itself is whether a man acts 'virtuously', acting 'virtuously' being construed as acting entirely in accordance with the obligations dictated by rationality (or attempting wholeheartedly to do so). The good life is reduced to the moral life and the moral life is reduced to rational (and therefore perfect) intentions and the scrupulous performance of obligations. A serious difficulty with this is that if nothing matters except virtue itself, then we can achieve virtue in promoting goals which have no value in themselves, and deploy the virtues to help people whose concerns (such as the saving of their lives) are in themselves of merely instrumental concern to the helping agent. The goods of ordinary life – such as the production of beautiful works of art or the search for knowledge – are 'indifferent' except that they may be 'preferred' insofar as they give opportunities for virtue.

The only answer the Stoic gives – or the only answer he has any right to give – is that rational behaviour is godlike behaviour and that, insofar as we act rationally, we act in the way God, of whom we are a part, acts by nature. We thus live up to or fulfil our potential *as god*, and it is clear that to be god by nature *is all that matters*. Admittedly by urging us to pursue (but not for its own sake) what is 'naturally good' (health, wealth, life, etc.), the Stoics try to modify this paradox, but the attempt is unconvincing since they recognize no 'real' goods but rationality, and identify rationality alone as the nature both proper to themselves and (insofar as it remains different) that of God.

The most obvious objection is that this is an absurdly restricted account of man's capabilities for excellence, which appear to call for recognition of a much wider range of intrinsic goods. Even if rationality is the greatest good, there may be lesser goods which are still 'really' good, albeit with an inferior perfection. What the Stoics need is a hierarchy of intrinsic goods, but what they offer is an arbitrary insistence that lesser goods are at best only good instrumentally. It is not accidental that, as 'academic' philosophers, the Stoics should come up with such an apotheosis of their own trade; therefore we should not mis-state (and improve) their position by saying that they were *merely* identifying 'moral virtue' as a good of a different order from other 'goods'. Certainly they were doing that, but it is not all that they were doing; their emphasis on rationality, narrowly conceived as tantamount to the only divine attribute, is merely arbitrary and, as is often the case, an impoverished account of man is defended by an impoverished account of God.

Nevertheless, one cause of so paradoxical a position in Stoicism is of great interest: namely that the Stoics were tempted, as is not uncommon inside as well as outside philosophy, to deny the reality of particular goods because they recognized that those goods are open to abuse. This temptation is the more attractive if one can argue that other supposed goods distract from the higher good, that a multiplicity of perfections impedes the greatest perfection. And the obvious corrective, that goods should be prioritized where possible, is neglected or dismissed, perhaps with a claim that no overriding measure of the different goods can be found. One can be perfect more easily, it would seem, if one's account of perfection is limited to 'all or nothing'.

Consider this in the context of more general ancient attitudes to 'commitment', in the sense of that concern for others which opens itself to the suffering which others experience. The extreme Epicurean solution (which, as we have seen, generates paradoxes over the role of friendship) is to deny commitment altogether, to regard human relationships as deals for the mutual use by individuals of one another so long as these are to the advantage of both. Ideally everyone goes into the deal with his or her eyes open as to its limitations, so no-one has grounds for complaint if the commitment is unilaterally terminated.

The Stoic view is less extreme; one stands by one's commitments, which are not emotional commitments. Hence the doctrine of 'reserved admiration', of preserving a safe distance between one's rational and benevolent act and any 'excess' emotional accompaniment: as Epictetus put it, when kissing your child goodnight, remember to say to yourself, 'You may die tomorrow' (*Discourses* 3.24.88).[30] The Stoics – in this respect at least like the modern therapist who tries to avoid becoming emotionally involved in the problems of his patient – were concerned not to be deflected from 'virtue' by the passions, since insofar as the passions can deflect a man from virtue, they are irrational.

The paradoxes which this outlook generates are particularly clear in the case of mercy. Mercy (and compassion) might be considered anti-rational insofar as they seem to involve treating similar cases dissimilarly. Mercy is shown when a man is given a less severe sentence than is normally awarded for the crime he has committed. That might seem to smack of unfairness – though such a description ignores the unique moral condition of each individual – and thus the Stoic would condemn the merciful as deflected by feeling from the rational and reasonable course. Is this defensible? What it neglects is that mercy indicates the limitations of laws and precepts by making room for 'equity', the specifics of which cannot be codified; it is not difficult to see the difference between a merciful judge (who perhaps takes repentance and remorse or provocation into account) and a judge who punctuates severity with arbitrary acts of 'kindness'. Although there is certainly a problem about how to reconcile the virtues of justice and mercy, the Stoic solution, which simply denies that mercy is a virtue, is procrustean, unless we allow for a godlike insight on the part of the ideal (Stoic) judge into the workings of the human heart – and of course in his moral character the Stoic sage is more (or less) than human.

In the extreme and psychologically impoverished version of agent-relative morality which the Stoics present, and in their concern for purity

---

[30] For more detailed treatment of the Epicurean and Stoic views respectively see (for example) K. Kleve, 'Lukrez und Venus', *Symbolae Osloenses* 41 (1966), 86–94 and 'Lucrèce, l'épicurisme et l'amour', *Actes du Colloque Guillaume Budé* (1969), 376–83; B. Inwood, *Ethics and Human Action in Early Stoicism* (Oxford University Press, 1985), 119, 205–15. And more generally Nussbaum, *The Therapy of Desire* (if used with care).

of motive, nothing else, even other people, seems to matter. (As I have already suggested, many neo-Kantians, some of them possessed of great benevolence and some of religious fervour, exhibit similar 'dark' sides to their morality and human concern.) The lesson to be drawn is that agent-relative morality will fail unless we can find a much richer and more responsible description of human goods than the Stoics were able to offer.[31] Indeed, one fundamental way of describing the weakness of such accounts is that they give too limited a description of what it is to be human, though it is of the essence of the views of Socrates and Plato, the pioneers of agent-relative morality, that the price of not living as one ought is to be less than human ('The unexamined life is not worth living for a human').

Even the Stoics showed themselves not entirely unaware of the difficulty when they accused their Cynic predecessors of a more extreme version of the philosophical offence of which they themselves were guilty, that of promoting a morality without adequate content, of being too narrowly obedient to the trivial command, 'Do the right thing', restrictedly conceived as 'that which will make your soul better'.

MORALITY, HUMANITY AND THE SOUL

Stoic extremism notwithstanding, agent-relative moralities do not have to be reductionist. Socrates' question, 'What is the right way to live?' finds a possible (if partial) answer in the advice to look after one's own soul, on pain of ceasing to be human. That is the sense in which morality 'pays' and therefore the foundational claim of Greek 'eudaimonism'. Its implications depend on the sense and the richness we give to the word 'human', and to the implications of the imperative that *I* become 'more human'.

The weaknesses of the Stoic morality of rational obligation, however, indicate a more basic problem in ethics. In a humanist or secularist world-view it is difficult to find room for a command like 'Love your neighbour' unless that command is purely prudential ('Take your neighbour into account') – and prudential 'love' is not love as most understand it.[32] Although commands may express prudential wisdom in other

---

[31] Plato is forced to exclude Homer from the city on moral grounds, but in the tenth book of the *Republic* he expresses a longing for someone to show him that such exclusion is unnecessary. That hesitation suggests that he is aware of the threat of being over-reductionist about human goods, but does not touch the problem of how, in our concern for our own 'salvation', we are (or must be) aware of a concern for other people.

[32] As we shall show in the next chapter, Platonic *eros* converts prudential desire into spiritual desire.

cases (like 'Do as you would be done by') – since a mutual contract and an encouragement to others to act according to such a contract may be recognized prudentially as in one's interest and perhaps within one's power – anything like 'Love your neighbour as yourself' is neither merely prudential nor necessarily within our own power, yet can be recognized as a peculiarly human ideal. Human ideals cannot be reduced to sets of performable duties and obligations, and 'being human', 'human excellence' and 'looking after one's soul' suggest more than recognizing the rational force only of those moral laws which it is apparently within our power to obey – let alone to obey without the emotional and other suffering that, *pace* the Stoics, attends genuine commitment. Broadly speaking, we seem to face the following difficulty: that within a humanist world-view certain sorts of apparently human (and therefore by definition moral) demands cannot be *grounded*, and thus that important entailments of the call to be human cannot be satisfied.

Be that as it may, this chapter has left us with openings on at least five major enquiries. In the first place, agent-relative accounts of morality are arguably misdescribed as concerned merely with one's personal well-being, as though their appeal lay in some egoism easily redescribed as selfishness. Their thrust is that we are willy-nilly potentially free human beings, yet if we do not value our own 'soul', we are in effect throwing away the humanity we have, and that not in favour of something higher, something more altruistic, even utopian, but of an impersonality, something which of itself has no evident worth, for it is senseless to claim to love the human race if, out of respect for 'fairness', we have no love for any of its members, or if we have no love for ourselves. Which raises the question, of what kind might be a genuine self-love?

Our second, related point is that Socrates and Plato challenge us to ask what we humans should do, not just as humans but as particular humans in particular circumstances – though to be particular is not to be concerned merely with one's own particularity. I shall argue that if it were, then such individualism would be not merely morally misguided but unintelligible.

The third point brings us back to moral obligations. We may notice their subordinate role in descriptions of the fully human life (under the aegis of Goodness) in the agent-relative accounts of Plato (and of Aristotle), and the excessive emphasis placed on them both among the Stoics and more recently among many who declare allegiance to Kant. According to these, all responsible moral relationships depend on (or can be reduced to) rational and universal obligations (and often their associated rights). I shall argue that such reductions must be resisted.[33]

Fourthly, while the agent-relativist must avoid giving too 'thin', too restricted, an account of human goods – and therefore of human behaviour and human nature – he must also avoid too cavalier an attitude to consequences under the pretext of seeking 'goodness of soul' and pure intentions. It is absurd to neglect the consequences (including the indirect ones) of actions when deciding about the rightness or wrongness of performing them; it is not only good intentions which matter, and it may often be better not to intend a good than to carry it through regardless of the undesirable side-effects it may produce. At its worst, such behaviour can be the moral equivalent of criminal negligence.

Fifth and most importantly: while Plato and Platonists (including Augustine) may underestimate the need to define man in terms of the ongoing metaphysical unity of his 'soul' and body, they must be right to insist that whatever account of such unity is given – Aristotelian or other – cannot displace but only complement their view of man as primarily a moral agent, responsible in some sense for his own acts. And if their emphasis on moral agency is only intelligible in terms of our constructing future souls from the collection of potential selves which at any given time are broadly oriented in one direction or another, that consequence has to be accepted.

---

[33] See the discussion of B. Williams, *Ethics and the Limits of Philosophy* (London: Fontana, 1985), 179–80.

CHAPTER 4

Division and its remedies

PSYCHOLOGICAL INCOMPLETENESS

If we are divided, less than complete wholes, it follows that we stand in need of completion, and it is further possible that we are incomplete 'externally' as well as 'internally'. By 'external incompleteness' I refer to a need for some external 'addition' or external 'factor' by which we may complete ourselves, with presumably an accompanying internal reintegration. By internal incompleteness I refer to my being a compound of less than integrated parts and therefore a less than functioning whole. The two forms of incompleteness are thus complementary, at least insofar as external completion promotes internal integration. That is what both philosophers and non-philosophers have often supposed, and many (at least since Empedocles) have thought that 'love' (in some acceptation of the word) could be the remedy by generating the desired unity.

At the end of the fifth century BC the poet Euripides indicates a typical concern of the 'Socratic' age with a striking representation of *acratic* division in the *Hippolytus* where his character Phaedra struggles with her passion for her step-son, and eventually yields to it. She is portrayed as, in the later classic phrase, knowing the better and doing the worse, and it is she, Phaedra, and no-one else, who knows the better and does the worse. But poets, we have noticed, have an advantage over philosophers for just so long as they do not succumb to the temptation to philosophize: they are able to present human experiences and dilemmas without having to subject them either to the test of experience or to explanation and so can show a divided self – as in our present instance – without having to ask how or why the self is divided, let alone whether such a division could occur in such a case or, if so, how it might have been overcome.

In Plato's *Symposium* the comic playwright Aristophanes is made to tell a tale of man's present miseries and their origin. Once upon a time we were 'rounded' doubles: some of us double men, some double women, the rest men–women. Because of our pride and Titanic desire to be gods, Zeus cut us in two, so that now we are in a state of seeking our proper and lost other half. Such seeking for completion and unification, says the poet, is called *eros* or the desire for what is beautifully fitting, or 'just right': in English, 'love' in one of its forms. Clearly in such a 'moral' tale there are two elements: a perception of our present incomplete and needy state – as well as its cause in our pride – and a mythological account of how we came to this pass. The comedy is in the story, of which the abiding appeal lies in the sense that Aristophanes has somehow hit the nail on the head as though his account were historical truth; we do feel our individual selves inadequate and long for completion.

'Quickie' explanations of this desire for completeness are readily available, some of them mentioned in the *Symposium* itself: nature has found a way to ensure that males and females come together so that the race may be preserved; homosexual couplings may or may not have 'higher' purposes. Doubtless there is something to be said for such explanations, but they do not account for significant features of human behaviour to which Aristophanes draws attention, and chiefly his claim that each of us is looking for *his own* other half. We should be satisfied (and incidentally satisfy the needs of nature for replenishment) if we found the *particular* other who would make us complete. Some kind of *identity* with another would unify us, or restore us to a lost unity. On the other hand, from Plato's point of view it is easy to see two reasons why Aristophanes' unmodified account is itself unsatisfactory and incomplete. First, Aristophanes – who persists in not seeing this point – is outside moral space, despite his account of our fall through pride, having nothing to say as to whether the 'other half' is morally good, bad or indifferent. Second, he assumes that the 'other half' is in this world, and has no appeal to transcendent being. From Plato's point of view, both omissions are of great importance: we should hardly be improved by linking our destiny to some other who might lull us into a false complacency while merely confirming our weaknesses and diminishing our moral (and hence productive) strengths. And despite the mythological framework, Aristophanes, like the sophist Protagoras, assumes that it is man who is the measure of all things, at least of all things that matter.

Moral and spiritual growth is unlike organic growth. If we are fed and cared for from the moment of conception, we shall normally grow to adulthood, but we shall not necessarily grow into fully moral beings. Otherwise put, without outside *moral* or *spiritual* influences we shall not develop well. Our needs in this sense are not material; we need not merely to be fed but taught and enriched. As we grow up, we shall learn to feed ourselves, but left to our own devices do not develop spiritually. We need to live in satisfactory moral space which allows us both to think and 'desire', and to be given examples and rules to help us so to grow. We need not merely nourishers of our bodies but especially spiritual nourishers who are adequately devoted to us: so the child-psychologist Winnacott postulates the 'good-enough mother'.

In many cultural traditions mystics use the language of sexual union to refer to union with God and sometimes assume (though rarely with argument) that the one is an alternative or a way to the other. Two explanations of this phenomenon are on offer: that sexual union is an image (or a shadow or a foreshadowing) of the union of God with the soul; or that an alleged or imagined 'union' with God is a projection, a transmutation into unreality, of the desire for a human sexual union. It is not our immediate concern to decide between these explanations, but two features which they have in common deserve attention. Both assume that our sexual nature – however explained – is fundamental not merely to our animality but to our humanity, and not merely to the survival of our species but to the maintenance of a *human* species; thus, in the language of the previous chapter, a 'moral' account of man, an account of man as primarily a moral agent, has to include an account of his sexual strivings. Both explanations also point to our need for 'external' fulfilment and strengthening and hence for internal integration through loving union with some 'other': that is, they both point – like the original story of Aristophanes – to our perceived external 'incompleteness'. If this incompleteness is radical, it makes nonsense of claims that we can be 'fulfilled' by pursuing a policy of extreme individualism, and suggests the futility of any hope that 'fulfilment' is possible in this present life or without reference to the transcendent.[1]

What are we supposed to want, or to need, when we sense ourselves to be externally incomplete? There are a number of possible answers in various mystical traditions. We may want to become *transparent* to the other. (That would seem to require a perfecting if we are not to be ashamed of what the other would 'see'.) Or we may feel we want to *disappear* into the beloved. Various forms of Indian and other 'non-dualist'

---

[1] A caveat is necessary, about 'fulfilment' and its associate 'self-realization'. Nothing we have argued so far entails that these should be *directly* pursued. Such language refers to recognition of something 'lost' or 'missing' and does not commit us to any account of how it may be recovered, let alone to the assumption that a direct pursuit of fulfilment could have any chance of success. Fulfilment or self-realization may be like pleasure (and knowledge of the self) in that they are received indirectly.

mysticism advocate this course, presenting our conscious self as little more than a harmful figment; really we are identical with the divine into which we wish to be merged so as to escape illusion. Or there is the 'contra-Indian' route – arguably the way the individualist *must* go – exemplified by Sartre in *Being and Nothingness*: the desire to *annihilate* the other, to reduce him or her to 'mere flesh', as being in fact no potential completion but a threat to our own freedom or autonomy.

For the 'pure' individualist, while agreeing with 'Aristophanes' that our well-being has to do with our present relations with others, and perhaps particularly with one other (or at least one other at a time), sees the 'solution' to such a problematic relationship quite differently: he must regard the other as a rival, since he can see no reason why the other should not wish to assert himself just as he himself does. For the Sartrian, any perceived incompleteness is an illusion which acts of 'annihilation' will, he hopes, dispel. Alternatively, the other might be 'deceived' into the false belief that he should not be an individualist, this deception being a more convenient and socially acceptable alternative to 'annihilation' – for individualists are still living in a world that hesitates to be thoroughly individualist. Perhaps deception would be a less successful means of dispelling the illusion of incompleteness; only experience could determine the outcome.

Such thoughts are not limited to existentialists. The contemporary libertarian Nozick seems (appropriately) to agree with Sartre in thinking that a proper self-esteem demands that one envy others.[2] Of course, if Sartre and Nozick are wrong and individualism is psychologically self-defeating, then the condition of the individualist is only made worse by his attempts to 'defuse' or destroy rather than to cherish that very person or persons who might enable him to flourish.

Sartre's notion of annihilation has a certain internal logic, for if it is true that the other is to be viewed primarily or even exclusively as a competitor (whether economically, in terms of prestige or in some other way), then even if he or she is *needed* to complete us, how can they be trusted not to take advantage of our need? At the very least we might suppose that to manipulate is the only way to avoid being manipulated. 'Romantics' may persuade themselves to the belief that 'love', at least, enables us to be wholly devoted to one another, but we need not go as far as Freud's characterization – not wholly new – that love is 'lust tormented into the mask of civility' to harbour doubts about the likelihood of a happy

---

[2] R. Nozick, *Anarchy, State and Utopia* (Oxford University Press, 1974), 245.

outcome of what is a necessarily ambiguous form of *égoisme à deux*. Even if the Romantics are sometimes right – human love is by no means merely a history of disappointment – nonetheless the incidence of disillusion and downright betrayal gives grounds for a fair degree of pessimism, and Sartre's brutal solution arises not least from the perceived failure of the Romantic ideal when confronted with the realities of our human condition. And his 'solution' is a (self-)justification of those realities.

God's love would not be thus unreliable – wherein is part of its attraction for the 'mystic' – but for most it is only an ideal, perhaps an object of wishing but no consciously experienced reality. Ordinary human love also appears to be 'dialectical', thriving on reciprocity and mutuality and seeming to demand that if we are to be whole internally, we must trust another externally. If, however, the Romantic ideal is something of a delusion, or at best an exaggeration, how can we inspire and require a trust without which we must logically become Sartrians or Nozickians? If trust and its effects are so necessary for contentment, shall we not despair of experiencing wholeness? And yet, if there is nothing at all in 'Romantic' ideas, why does it seem to make sense to say, for example, that we are *lonely* in a crowd? On the hypothesis that Plato's Aristophanes has proposed something important about external completion, one may try to develop his idea within a less mythological and more 'moral' framework. Thus: (1) Can we connect Plato's myth with our non-mythological account of the divided moral self, the would-be soul? (2) If we are divided wholes, as 'Aristophanes' says, why and how is this so, or what is the existential status of our incompleteness and our division? (3) Why are we not mutilated wholes, like an ox with three legs? The answer to this has to be because in the case of moral 'mutilation', that is, insofar as we are morally incomplete, we have lost sight of and indeed 'lost' (or never possessed) any stable internal principle of 'moral' unity. Though 'Aristophanes' in the *Symposium* does not explicitly place our search for the right 'other' in a moral context, he raises such moral questions.

Obliquely following both Plato and Hume, as I have already suggested, we seem to be – morally and intentionally – a bundle of selves, more or less loosely, at worst more or less casually tied together: yet not entirely casually, otherwise we would be incapable of any consistent pattern of action or of any regular tending in a certain direction. Nor could we be even dimly aware (as phenomenologically we appear to be) of what we might be and of what we might become (or, as in the myth of 'Aristophanes' and those of many other 'lost-paradise theorists', of what we once were). Thus we appear as merely 'morally' divided and disintegrated, but as each a morally divided *self*, which – according to the 'Platonic' thinkers we have been considering – can be united by love. What kind of love? Self-evidently – since we are divided – not love of oneself nor the disposition Augustine characterized as love-of-being-in-love.

TOWARDS INTEGRATION: LOVE AND REFLECTION

We have seen how we are not a 'fully unified' self now, nor, at least in the more obvious sense of the lost-paradise theorists, have we been in the past. Two options about 'full' selves remain: the 'Augustinian' hypothesis of the previous chapter, that we will be a 'full', completed self or soul – of whatever sort – some time in the future; or that the notion of a fully united self is a delusion, a mere projection, a utopian ideal or, as Sartre and others hold, an indication of our failure to assert our autonomy. If an integrated self does not exist and cannot exist in the future, our alternatives are self-deception or defiant acceptance of this tragic fact: a boast that the maximizing of apparently rational choices for our present unstable and multiple selves will get us by satisfactorily and that choice itself, serviced by instrumental rationality, can function as our 'good'. But how genuinely good will such a 'good' be? The quandaries which arise if we follow much contemporary philosophical advice and allow that human goods are indefinitely variegated and cannot therefore be usefully prioritized in our rational choices, have been highlighted by a much discussed example: was Gauguin right to abandon his family in order to exercise his talent as a painter in Tahiti?

Knowledge of human excellence – of the excellence of man *qua* man – cannot be immediately obtained by inspecting our own activities if we are morally divided. Yet, despite that division, our activities may perhaps be evaluated 'retrospectively', with reference to what we would be like if we could be complete. Even so, a divided self cannot supply from its own resources a reliable measure of the moral quality of its own behaviour. If we cannot discover what a 'full' self would be like because such a 'full' self is merely utopian, then we cannot determine, let alone explain, and only more or less coherently hypothesize – the degree of coherence depending on our present degree of integration – what human excellence might be or what we might intelligibly settle for as human excellence.

Insofar as we are a moral unity at all – and I will take it as agreed that we all experience some such unity – we function as individuals. The general planning his next campaign, the hit-man planning his next murder, is not a wholly different person from the father playing off-duty with his children. Yet since all of us will find tensions between the various 'roles' we play in the course of our lives and between the skills we deploy in these roles, it is impossible that our overall 'performance' be univocally the achievement (or failure) of a simple human excellence. For if it is excellence, why should it be in conflict with itself? Yet even Dr Jekyll and Mr Hyde have something in common; how otherwise would 'he' ('they'?) pose an enigma for us?

Plato, denouncing poets as inadequate educators, cannot afford to offer no explanation of the phenomena of moral division which he identified. Growing dissatisfied with the explanation of temptation as body pulling against soul, he came to realize that the problem (and any possible solution) lay in the latter. Thus to understand the continuing importance of what he tried to do, we must consider what he meant by 'soul': that *psyche* which is divided. Now for an ancient Greek to say that an object 'has' *psyche* was first of all to say that it is alive, that it is animate. Plants and animals, not just human beings, have *psyche*, and there are different kinds of *psyche*; in the *Republic* Plato claims that human beings possess three different kinds. A 'kind of *psyche*' is the way we live, and Plato wants to argue that each of us wants to live (with varying degrees of wanting) in three diverse, even potentially contradictory styles: we want a life in which our reasoned love of virtue governs our possessiveness, a life directed by a love of honour, status and self-respect, and a life of a Humean sort in which reason is (and *ought* only to be) the slave of the passions, for the satisfaction of which it plans and rationalizes.[3] By having Socrates argue thus, Plato both divides up our 'selves' and evaluates them, his valuation depending on the Forms as standards by which to measure human behaviour.

As an analysis of the different kinds of lives we simultaneously desire, at least until schooled and corrected, this is admirable, nor need Plato limit himself to three kinds of lives, though he may be right in supposing that other possibilities are subsumed under these; however, a huge question is left unsettled, indeed all but unbroached: namely, who or what is the 'we' which has the choice? – which surely must be the dominant (if 'narrative' and variable) 'we' which by second-order judgements morally evaluates our differing lifestyles and tends thus to identify us with one of them, but without succeeding in unifying them.

---

[3] For more detailed discussion see J. M. Rist, 'Plato says that we have tripartite souls. If he is right, what can we do about it?', in M. O. Goulet-Cazé, G. Madec and D. O'Brien (eds.), *Sophies Maieutores: chercheurs de sagesse: hommage à Jean Pépin* (Paris: Institut d'Etudes Augustiniennes, 1992), 103–24, reprinted in *Man, Soul and Body* (London: Variorum, 1996).

We saw Plato's suggestion that I have some kind of enduring inner core which really is 'I': the pearl-in-the-oyster. In opposition to that I have argued that something like a Platonic position can be salvaged only if we are progressing *towards* a 'soul', considered as our *eventual* moral and 'spiritual' self. But if such progression is to take place in a particular and positive direction, then over a period of time some of our subsidiary 'selves' will suffer defeat – not necessarily irrevocable defeat, for if we are only *more* likely to turn out to be one sort of person, we are only *less* likely to turn out to be another.

Each temporary self can be viewed as the composite or coagulate of certain deep-seated habits of mind – genetically allowed for, no doubt, but also dependent on experience: on our loves, hatreds, education, work, knowledge and ignorance in life, and above all, as it seems most probable, on our childhood experiences, including those which have been 'screened' from consciousness. Each individual 'self' may dominate our personality at times, yet its dominance cannot be absolute; if it were, we should not be a changing bundle but a self complete, even if impoverished and restricted, and in that case we could not substantially modify our lifestyles and dominant beliefs – which de facto is not our present condition. We know that people change their manner of living more or less radically and in circumstances where a merely behaviourist explanation seems wholly inadequate: examples range from religious or political conversion to the decision on medical grounds to give up smoking.

The phenomenon of such change requires that we explain how it comes about. If we cannot offer an explanation, the idea that we are a bundle but not a mere heap, and so that we are capable of movement in one or another more or less consistent direction – improving or deteriorating – looks implausible. I leave aside such radical possibilities as brainwashing, since they depend less on an overcoming or partial integration of one or more of our selves than a destruction or at least paralysing of them. More interesting is the phenomenon of the gradual shifting of beliefs remarked on by Newman when he observed of himself: 'Ten years later I find myself in another place.' The movement here considered is that of a man of imperceptibly changing habit which for the most part he can only recognize retrospectively – and who can know what the end will be, or could be? Arguably only one who knows what our moral identity – in Plato's language our soul – *will be* but *is* not yet, as also what we can make of the 'selves' we discard.

Consider what normally occurs when we engage in an argument about morality, and notice how different is what we assume from what Socrates and other Greek philosophers appear to have expected; then consider what misled them. If we get into an argument with a friend or acquaintance over some issue we both consider important – like pacifism or capital punishment or abortion – it is exceedingly rare that the discussion will end with one or the other agreeing that he or she was wrong and explicitly embracing the other's opinion, nor is it likely to be less rare even where the logic of our position has been shown up as deficient. We hold opinions not merely because they are logically well grounded, but as much because they are familiar to us and, like old friends, have been thus far part of 'us', and we are similarly loath to abandon them. We fear to feel part of ourselves torn away by giving a cherished opinion up, for who knows if we might not then become some caricature of the opposing position, and our tentative unity be further sundered? Besides, we have invested our self-respect in our stance; if we yield to the argument of another, we feel diminished, or, more crudely, that we have 'lost face'. In brief, to hold an opinion is not merely a matter of our rationality; it is also a matter of our emotions, our character, our loves. We do not usually want to change our moral opinions, and we cling the tighter to them if we sense ourselves becoming convinced on rational grounds that we should give them up. Hence we rationalize, procrastinate, change the subject. Davidson has classed such defeated beliefs as (now obviously) exhibiting 'weakness of the warrant',[4] a phenomenon somewhat analogous to weakness of will or *acrasia*, and perhaps equally difficult to resist. Just as we exhibit weakness of will when our willings are inconsistent, so our beliefs exhibit 'weakness of the warrant' when the original suasion in their favour is available but – unfortunately – so now is a stronger degree of argument to the contrary.

There are many Greek stories of quite other sorts of behaviour in philosophical defeat. Greek philosophical society was inspired by a strong – we might say overweening – sense of the need to live the rational life, and moreover that rational conclusions are transparent: hence the fairly frequent phenomenon of 'conversions' to philosophy. For us in contrast with at least some Greeks, it is not simply a matter of being more proud of our opinions – we may even be less proud – but of being more philosophically wary. Over two thousand years of philosophy have taught us that conclusions on substantive matters are almost always less obvious than they seem: there is so often some complication in the argument which we missed at first and even at tenth glance. Especially the last hundred years

---

4 Davidson, 'How is Weakness of the Will Possible?', 21–42.

of psychology have taught us to be more wary than were even the ancient Stoics of the likelihood of our own bad faith and associated inability to determine whether we are thinking about a problem honestly. In brief, we are more aware than the Greeks of something which they held Apollo had taught them: our need to know ourselves, and in particular to know how complicated (and hence potentially divisible) we are. Nor do we just recoil from wanting to know ourselves to a degree which the Greeks could not have suspected, but we have been taught that we are *incapable* of knowing ourselves – something which would have left the best Greek thinkers distressed – and so have despaired of finding firm ground for self-reflection.

Phenomena such as confirm these conclusions are those experiences of being 'swept away', or of coming to hesitate over what once seemed certain, or over a course of action once seeming obviously right. To be swept away is admittedly a metaphor, but an apt one, and being particularly though not exclusively associated with passion is our obvious, and Platonic, concern. It directs our attention to the now familiar problem of *who* is swept away, suggesting that 'we' lose our familiar bearings, not that it is someone else who is in love, or who now decides to embrace a new religious or political stance. Yet it appears some other and perhaps more 'basic' 'we' is also in question: we may claim that we do not recognize ourselves, or that having thrown off all illusions, we are now our true and proper selves –albeit in such self-discovery being perhaps the more deeply deluded.

Danger and fear provide us with similar 'empirical' data by introducing a kind of negative *acrasia*. All is plain sailing until a threat appears; then we find – perhaps to our shame – that we do not want to do what we intended to do, even if remaining in no doubt that we 'ought' to do it. We say that our sense of self-preservation or of prudence 'puts a different complexion on the matter'. In a sense we become *acratic*, though not now under the impulsion of pleasure but of pain, broadly understood. And this *acrasia*, like that of Euripides' Phaedra, is a state in which 'we' want contradictory things, and eventually 'we' decide for one of them which 'we' know, with 'our better selves', to be mistaken.

I have invoked Davidson's 'weakness of the warrant' to account for this persistence in hanging on to beliefs which we no longer have the right to hold. A similar notion may be invoked in that opposite case when we come to hesitate for no apparently good reason over what we previously held to be certain. It is not easy to know what happens in such cases, though extreme and persistent examples may be tagged as neuroses and a causal explanation offered by psychologists. What psychologists will not explain causally is our divided nature, but content themselves with the fact that in such and such circumstances we appear divided or 'schizoid'. It is thus by default the business of the philosopher to attempt an explanation of what it actually '*means*' to be thus divided.

If weakness of will, weakness of the warrant and our consequent proven unwillingness to give up our misguided 'selves', or to correct them, stand in the way of our unification, how is it possible for us to progress – as, it has always seemed, some of us do, though only exceptionally by the phenomenon of instant conversion? Since we have identified failure of 'desire' and failure of 'rationality' as the two sources of our weakness and consequent division, we can accept that only attention to both these 'sources' will bring moral unification. More specifically, since we both 'love' conflicting goods and 'hate' to correct our errors of understanding, through habit preferring to rationalize them away, we may enquire whether some unifying love, beyond fear of betrayal, is not prerequisite if we are to be 'simplified'.

Which brings us back to some 'Augustinian' attitudes already considered.[5] In praying for 'chastity but not yet', Augustine showed that he 'wanted to want' the good, though he did not yet want the good nor want to want the good strongly enough. If his prayer had been granted – as it eventually was – he would have wanted to want the good strongly enough to want the good, thus bringing his first-order wants into line with his second-order wants: that is, with what he by then unambiguously wanted to want! He would thus have become more unified – but, as he held and we must not omit to notice, only through an integration with an external force: the love and grace of God.

Not alone through 'love', however, for our failures in love are seen to be linked with our weaknesses of self-understanding. An essential condition for Augustine's increased moral unity could only be secured by a mental act – an act of intelligence –by which he reflected and accepted that his first-order wants were out of kilter with his second-order wants. Frankfurt (at least as revised by Stump) holds that the possession of second-order wants plus the capacity to form them by reflecting on first-order wants is a mark of a 'person':[6] that a person has free will if his first-order wants follow his second-order wants without tension.

---

[5] For recent developments of these ideas, see Frankfurt, 'Freedom of the Will' and Stump, 'Sanctification'.

[6] That would suggest that 'acratics' are 'persons' in some lesser sense. Frankfurt's account would identify (something of) the 'focal meaning' of 'person'.

Insofar as we are divided selves, our intellect may act, in differing circumstances, as the slave or as the master of our passions, but insofar as we are able to reflect on our life as a whole, albeit to a limited degree, we will recognize good reasons for wanting to want right things. Whatever the strength of the power to reflect – necessarily an indispensable function of that self (among our many) which exhibits the greatest harmony between its first- and second-order wants – it represents the best prospect we have 'thus far', as the most 'extreme' possible outcomes of our moral journeyings seem to confirm. For if our ability to reflect on our selves were lacking, we would resemble that mere 'heap', whereas insofar as we develop a capacity to correct by reflection the disharmony between the sum of our first-order and second-order desires, we are at least bundles and approaching that 'unity' which Plato would identify as a good soul. The good man (possessed of free and freed will) is thus transparent to himself, the bad man opaque to himself.

How then are we to increase this power of reflection, the power not only of practical but also of theoretical reasoning about who we are? Insofar as reflection is unitive, its motivating source must be love of perfection. Since this love, as distinct from the sense of need, cannot arise within ourselves as a whole, but only within any *one* of our incomplete 'selves' – otherwise we should be already advanced in unification – it must be aroused, or at least fanned, from outside ourselves, that is, from some object of our love. It follows that if some people seem to be growing more unified, they indicate a love *for* an 'external' source which is somehow caused by that external source, a source which thereby increases both their love itself and their power of reflection, so strengthening their awareness of the gap between their first- and second-order desires and diminishing their internal divisions.

In such a state of growth in unity, love will be the motor for a developing harmony of recognitions, desires and intentions. If the process were to reach completion, we would have a single 'will' or 'mindset' derived from the ongoing unconflicted interaction of reflection and love. It is easy to see why Augustine, whom I have taken to be the father-in-chief of the most cogently corrected form of the 'Platonic' tradition, identified the strongest form of 'will' (*voluntas*) with God's Holy Spirit (*On the Trinity* 15.17.31; 15.20.38; 15.21.41). For this Spirit, by definition, there is no 'external', as for human beings there is, and thus is met the requirement that our unitive love, to be fully effective, can only arise from outside itself. Such a love, driving and focusing our self-reflection, will in its double effects on our desires and on our thoughts tend to the overcoming of that otherwise ineradicable tendency to fragmentation which we have identified as the 'surd-factor' in our moral character as a whole: our erratic and rationalizing 'shadow self'.

What will be the attitude of our 'best soul thus far' to our other potential selves? As we have gradually shifted to our present (and *ex hypothesi* improved) condition, we shall have abandoned some previously possible selves which perhaps we shall have forgotten until reminded of them by others. If so, this is unimportant. What is important is that once reminded of them we shall not disown or deny them, nor merely take note while declining to accept responsibility for them.[7] To pretend that we are not 'responsible' for them is to pretend that what has been the case – that is, what *we* did or *we* thought or *we* intended (whether rightly or wrongly) – was *not* the case. Such pretence introduces 'the lie in the soul', so increasing the very division which our better self is aiming to eliminate. What further damages our single moral identity is not what we happen to remember or to *learn*,[8] but any unreadiness to *accept* our own personal or corporate history. Only when we take on responsibility for our past are we able to proceed without self-deception into our future. To proceed thus is to acknowledge that we are situated in an ongoing moral context.

In any case, however much we try to escape the responsibility for what we or our fathers and mothers have been, we cannot entirely succeed. Even should we commit suicide, the extent of our responsibility (in this life) would not change, while since we shall be responsible for what we know ourselves to have been just as long as we exist, if we continue to exist after death, we shall remain responsible. But if we do not so continue, there will even so be no time in our existence in which we have not been 'responsible'.

[7] If we accept responsibility for our past 'selves', we assume that some of our acts have objectively harmed others; thus that our moral division is no mere marker of harm done to ourselves (and for that reason alone to be avoided), but as a rule arises in the context of harm to other people. The importance of this will be considered in the next chapter.

I further note that, since we are 'social animals' developing within a particular and historical environment, responsibility for our past 'selves' needs also to be recognized at the institutional level. Thus though modern Englishmen are not guilty of past brutalities to the Irish, as continuators of an English 'tradition' and entity, they are especially responsible for ensuring that there be no repetition of these atrocities. Similarly Germans have a special responsibility not to repeat their past silences (during the Nazi period) over crimes committed in their name and midst, like Americans over black slavery. And so on.

[8] Thus the remark of R. Wollheim, *The Thread of Life* (Cambridge University Press, 1984), 163, that 'If we show ourselves unprepared to learn, or to try to learn, from the past in the way in which self-examination asks us to, we shall be forced to live in it' is incomplete. It is not only a matter of learning from and of our past but of accepting responsibility for it; that is, of treating our past as *our* past.

I have argued that if on reflection we harmonize our first- and second-order desires, we must recognize the activity of a unifying force, and so far we have recognized only love as a possible candidate: love, that is, for an 'external' transcendent worthy of total, undivided and unhesitant devotion, and which can only be for the Good as God (English is here the peculiarly apposite language): a God who by definition would subsume, not merely replace, all lesser 'goods'. If such an external transcendent does not exist, and if the 'Platonic' universe is merely a metaphysical fiction, then nor can 'souls' exist as unified realities – for no self-chosen life-plan, however inclusive, will be adequate for the unitive task required, and – though we might divide ourselves further by pretending otherwise – 'we' remain a set of irredeemably divided selves, as indeed much contemporary philosophy, by outlawing the 'theistic' alternative, is obliging itself to view us. Only love could induce us to take responsibility for our past; yet without taking that responsibility we cannot complete a *single* 'narrative' of our own life. Denied responsibility is history denied, and denied history is the condition of a divided self.

If only love can afford our moral selves, our 'souls', the possibility of completion – while by direct introspection we can identify such selves only in part – the question arises whether we can identify our selves at all while we are as yet too young to introspect or to recognize the need for unifying and completing love? Are we then to conclude that we only exist as persons when we are fully capable of active love and introspection? Not at all, for all we are at any point committed to is recognition of our capacity for progress *towards* being 'souls' and *towards* possession of the 'full' moral identity of loving and understanding which depends on our being capable of *receiving love*. For humane people – like almost all twentieth-century child-psychologists – have always understood that logically, biologically, and psychologically receiving love necessarily precedes giving love, and being the object of thoughtful concern precedes being able both physically and spiritually to give of such concern.[9]

TOWARDS INTEGRATION: LOVE AND FRIENDSHIP

I have argued that mystics in many traditions have endorsed something like Plato's view that erotic love finds its archetype in the love for God, and that a fully inspirational divine object can engender a unifying self-understanding able to overcome our defectiveness. Platonic *eros* is, of

---

9 For this now psychological commonplace see (e.g.) E. Fromm, *The Art of Loving* (New York: Holt, Rinehart and Winston, 1957).

course, not mere desire – a debased notion of it – but specifically desire for the good *as* beautiful. It cannot be overlooked, however, that within many religious traditions – not least the Christian – 'erotic' desire for the Good has seemed self-seeking, even selfish, and certainly devoid of altruism and loving kindness: concerned, that is, simply to grasp at something for oneself. Yet the charge has failed to dislodge *eros* from its role, not because irrelevant so much as because less damaging than at first appears.

Not to put too fine a point on it, *eros*, however well motivated, may present itself as grasping, or at the least in need of purification, and there seem to be two ways in which this purification may be obtained, one of which has already been considered. I have observed that to be able to show love one must first be able to receive it. While in the relation of a child to its mother such reception of love may be 'instinctive' or 'natural', in an adult something similar must be acquired (or expanded). For if love depends on being loved, the adult must be prepared to be loved; he or she must be prepared – something which natural pride may wish to forbid – to be the object not merely of desire but of affection, of the friendship of another.

In other words, as the pagan Platonic tradition was already well aware, and as the traditions of mediaeval Christendom made explicit, there is a sense in which *eros* must be moulded by friendship (*philia*), which – as Aristotle (in line with a natural interpretation of a key saying of Jesus) pointed out – must involve treating someone else as one's self, valuing another not, as undiluted *eros* might have it, because the other can minister to one's defectiveness or satisfy one's needs, or even inspire one to moral action, but because he or she is valuable *per se*.

We should not be surprised that human *eros* needs to be corrected; there is good reason why it too should be distorted by the wilfulness, backed up by manipulative rationalization, which seems to be 'natural' to the human psyche. Plato appears to have erred in thinking that *eros* is purified merely by being transferred to higher objects and ultimately to the Form of the Good. Although no doubt such transfer should be beneficial, there is no reason not to suppose the contrary is as likely, namely that love for a higher good can be transformed into, or rather remain as, something at least partly exploitative and lacking in affection.

That this would be obscure to Plato is likely for two reasons: because he considers the soul as, in its essence, already perfect, and because he views the object of *eros* impersonally, thus making the highest 'erotic' relationship lacking in reciprocity.[10] If these two conditions change, that is, if it makes no sense to suppose that the soul is already perfect and if the highest good cannot be impersonal, then we can return to *eros* with our eyes wider opened, recognizing both that it too can behave impersonally unless corrected, and that in any case, being the aspiration of an imperfect self, it cannot be of its nature pure. Thus, if our *eros* is to be perfected, we need not only to be filled and inspired by love of the transcendent God, but by a more kindly relationship with God. That it needs to be perfected we know, for if it had no such need – and given the existence of God – we would always and unfailingly be inspired, which manifestly we are not.

All of which would make considerable demands on God. Not only would we require him to promote love *in* us by *his* love *for* us, but to allow us to enjoy friendship with him. Clearly it would not be possible for any striving of ours to achieve such friendship; it would require not only God's turning to us, but his turning as a friend – which seems to be explicable only in terms of a Pauline theology of *kenosis*, of the condescension of God to our created level, enabling us to return, by a purified *eros*, to himself. And if God allows us to be his friends, we are enabled to be the friends of those others whom he wishes to be his friends. Thus it is less our desire for God, however real and inspiring, which enables us to value and respect – that is, to love – others, but our friendship with God, and hence our respect for what God himself is willing to respect. No true friend despises what his friend properly respects. As Plotinus put it, he who loves the father loves the children. Or as Jesus: who can love God whom he has not seen if he cannot love his brother whom he has seen?

AN ALTERNATIVE PROPOSAL: POLITICS AND VIRTUE
WITHOUT METAPHYSICS

Plato and many Platonists held that through some form of love we can overcome our internal divisions with the external incompleteness they produce. This love is directed to a 'Form' outside the self which, as Augustine held, is only reached by the help of external agency – though by seeking *within* the self. Plato had thought that *eros*, focused on the Good, would fulfil its unifying function through the experience of that Good, and indirectly through an important and necessary side-effect:

---

[10] Plato does allow for reciprocity between lovers at the human level, and even beyond this impersonality is interestingly diminished by the consideration noted above, namely that we are to try to attain 'likeness to God', not to the impersonal Form.

the perceived obligation of good men to political and social action. But what if there is no Good? Are psychological unity and human completeness then unattainable? I have suggested that this must be the case.

Nevertheless, in the remainder of this chapter I shall look at a popular contemporary route to integration which derives from that of those early modern philosophers who abandoned metaphysical supports for civic virtue but, unlike Hobbes, adopted something of the classical thesis that man's nature is essentially social; for convenience we may dub it the Way of Politics. Though rejecting a Platonic transcendent object of desire or any possible equivalent or improved version, its advocates hold the 'I' or 'self' to be constituted (rather than merely enabled to develop) as a properly enriched unity specifically by engagement in social and political life.[11] My present concern with this position will foreshadow the more wide-ranging consideration necessary for the philosophically more sophisticated 'naturalism' of Hume and his modern successors.

The Way of Politics may take on many forms – ranging from liberation theology through Marxism and Straussianism to Nazism, and though all these forms share a de facto rejection of anything like Platonic metaphysics, for present purposes it will be adequate to examine only the version currently most widely approved: that specifically concerned with the promotion of '*democratic*' societies.

Unsurprisingly, many ancient Greeks originated similar ideas, both as theoreticians and as citizens, Protagoras the Sophist being an early and distinguished example of the former group and his contemporary, the Athenian politician Pericles, of the latter. Though Aristotle did not himself subscribe to it, the theory can also be recognized in his drawing of a possible distinction between the good man and the good citizen, while some of the Greeks anticipated the more recent, and especially American, confidence in the humanizing effects of life in a 'democratic' state and of engagement in specifically 'democratic' politics. Realistically, such ideas are less applications of an unexamined Sartrianism than a trivialization of the genuinely Aristotelian axiom that we are social animals – which consideration may provide more hope to those who do not live in democratic societies, and help explain the ethically distinguished lives many manage to lead under anti-democratic régimes.

It is contemporarily easy to regard 'democracy' – however undefined – as end rather than means, yet even if we grant that some sort of democracy is the best available form of human government, it is far from

---

[11] See for example C. Farrar, *The Origins of Democratic Thinking* (Cambridge University Press, 1988).

obvious that being a democratic politician or activist is better *moral or spiritual* training than working in the context of a more autocratic, even a more unjust society. On the contrary it may just be much more cosy and hedonistic, and the more prone to corruption. The question thus raised needs further examination. We need to ask which sorts of delinquencies one is allowed and even encouraged to perform in which differing régimes, and then to consider how people are morally damaged (rather than, simplistically, which crimes are more serious) before pronouncing on the moral and psychological value of practising politics in a democracy or of promoting democracy itself.

Even those who profess belief in God often suggest that what is wrong with this Way of Politics is not its immediate exclusion of the transcendent – as neo-Hegelians they may wish to do without it in practice – but that the political and democratic ideals we normally espouse are too narrow and indeed out of date. In a fascinating account of our 'post-modern' predicament, in which he argues that the key to our present malaise is that we are still thinking in outworn terms of nation-states when the world of *homo economicus* is already operating in the global village with its global market, Nicholas Boyle concludes with the Kantian dream of perpetual peace expressed as follows:[12] 'We can and must learn to live (as Kant long ago saw), not as having an identity now, but as intending to have an identity in the future – specifically, the identity of world citizens.'

We can have some sympathy with this dream, for there is a sense in which our identity is in the future, and that it is indeed futile to deny obvious political and economic realities. What is left out of the equation, however, in Boyle's narrative, as in less universalist forms of democratic advocacy, is not just the role of the transcendent, but the surd-factor in man. There is little reason to suppose that political abuses, that is, the foreshadowings (or workings) of tyranny, will be diminished merely by political arrangements tending to a democratic world government, desirable though this development may be in important respects. For if the Platonists are right, our identity is not merely political, not merely realized in our role as citizens, but individual and moral, and if we wish to overcome our surd-factor we must look *outside* as well as inside any humanly constructed cosmos. As for tyranny, there is surely wisdom in Augustine's view that the multiplicity of languages 'after Babel' has at least diminished the would-be tyrant's opportunities for international *Gleichschaltung* – and this multiplicity is threatened by conditioned globalization.

---

[12] Boyle, *Who Are We Now?*, 320.

While there is no doubt that we are deeply affected by the society in which we develop, my present question is whether any society, even a democratic and fully international one, can of itself provide norms for our own *best* development, and how we can distinguish how the norms of any one society are better than those of any other. For immersion in strictly *political* life, even in the political life of an externally universal democracy,[13] insofar as it inhibits critical detachment from the principles of such a life and reflection on their internal consistency, let alone their foundations, is likely to induce an acceptance of the self-serving myths of that particular social structure – unless, that is, we have some external criteria for evaluating these myths. If we take them – as too many have done – as completed guides to a better self, only by luck shall we avoid disaster.

Directly to evaluate a society as a locus of nurture, we must already have a grasp of what we are trying to discover: the morally and spiritually good individual. Appeals to praxis as in itself the way to 'human development' or 'fulfilment' can be seen to collapse into a less blatant, and therefore more insidious, variant on the thesis that morality, and indeed the good life, is to be based on what we (or someone) – whether critically or not – want now: a variant, moreover, with peculiar risks, since history surely manifests how it leaves us open to a radical scepticism about moral values. Anything 'higher' than society itself being ruled out, there is the temptation – as also the licence – for a cynical or ruthless or alienated pursuit of immediate aggrandisement, whether for oneself, one's faction, or the promotion of one's personal ideology. It can be presumed to have been awareness of such risks that convinced Aristotle to distinguish between the good man and the good citizen: though the good citizen may be identified in terms of the good man, the good man cannot be identified in terms of the good citizen (*Politics* 1276B30–35, etc.)[14] – which is not to claim that it is not the nature of a good man to be a good citizen.

Nevertheless, even if we discard the proposal that man is 'made' merely by action in his political and social environment and that therefore the best man is made in what is to be the 'best' political and social

---

[13] I prescind from the further difficult question of the degree in which any individual could be an effectively *functioning* member of such a body – and of who would in effect replace him or her, whatever the constitutional facade.

[14] It is not enough to conclude, with Boyle (*Who Are We Now?*, 102), that the mistake is to say, with the French Revolutionaries, that the members of the *nation-state* are citizens, over against their world membership. The problem is with the inadequacy of the notion of man simply *as* citizen (of whatever earthly city), precisely as it is with describing him solely in the economic language of 'producer–consumer'.

environment, the problem of the divided self and – if this is to be harmoniously united – of how that unity has to be *achieved*, is no solely metaphysical question, but has necessary social and political ramifications.
And unless we are to conclude that the best life is made up solely of considerations which vary from moment to moment, we have to recognize
that there is no hope of identifying it without reference to some ongoing
individual life-plan within a social framework. This is not to say that
such a plan (even if constructed on 'transcendental' foundations) should
be regarded as fixed *a priori* rather than subject to constant corrections
demanded by individual circumstances; however, since these corrections
will be in comparative details, we are still ideally required to be aware of
the broad object of our quest, of what sort of being we are 'destined' to
become and what sort of unity we are able and should desire to form.

It is plain that in their several corrections people choose and often
follow over large parts of their lives more or less consistent 'plans' which,
as they proceed, will indicate the day-by-day condition of a 'soul' thus
far. That remains true even if we also recognize that in many cases these
plans arise at least in part from an initial set of decisions followed by a
drift along what appears to be the course of least resistance. We can see
the point negatively in that we cannot use all our talents, while we see
it in positive form insofar as we get immersed in what we do. Thus if a
man decides to become a surgeon and embarks on a course of medical
training, and if he is reasonably good at what he is doing, he will invest
more and more emotional and other capital in his project with every
day that he spends in it, so that, even if he has a talent also to play the
violin, it becomes correspondingly difficult for him to change his mind
and make the effort to become a violinist.

We have the advantage of trial and error in formulating our plans, and
perhaps the advice of more experienced acquaintance; hence what we
do – at best and if we have the opportunity – is constantly to *re*-formulate,
trying to fit our plans into a more and more suitable context and to
avoid the pitfalls revealed by our mistakes and the perceived mistakes of
others. Yet how much better off we should be if we could know what in
the long run could make us most happy and satisfied with our lives and
achievements: that is, if we could know what 'we' could best become!
That would require considerable knowledge of human nature in general,
and of ourselves 'as a whole' – however best arranged – in particular. And
that knowledge, in its turn, would be best achieved if we could recognize
our place in the largest possible helpful community of human beings
'Platonically' fitted out with a more-than-human dimension – I would

propose as paradigm case the Christian 'communion' of the living and the dead – but to fit into such a 'communion' we should have to recognize its communal values and build them into our life-plans: not of course what each fallible member may take from time to time to be his or her values, but what really *are* the common values, that is, the common loves and hates which if shared best promote the well-being of each and every one.

The posited advantages for 'soul-making' of membership in some such universal 'political' community (not merely of a world state) point us beyond the claims of those who say that our dividedness and incompleteness can be at best *improved* – quite apart from what I have shown to be the weakness of claims as to the necessary benefit of political activity as such, including 'democratic' political activity. They also indicate the weaknesses in many versions of individualism, taking for granted that no-one can profit even in the short run (let alone in terms of his best growth and development over time) *unless* he belongs to some kind of community, beginning with family and friends and expanding into wider groupings. Yet even that is insufficient: to speak of membership of a community is to say nothing about the attitude best adopted towards one's own membership – except insofar as members of a community recognize that their fellows require participation in common projects and acceptance of common conventions as well as a sharing in 'common loves and hates'.

Nevertheless, the attitude of the individual to himself and hence, at the level below surface conventions, to the other members of his group will be fundamental. Contemporary descriptions of a potential community of rational calculators are to be construed as envisaging that each member need *merely take account* of the existence of his fellows: a very diminished version of what Plato had in mind when he thought of his guardians as a community of friends, or Aristotle when he described man as a social animal. Both were expecting their (admittedly small) group of citizens not merely to take account of, but to have *respect* for one another; that is, in effect, to consider one another not merely as inconvenient necessities or unavoidable competitors but as valued contributors.[15] The problem

---

[15] J. Raz, *The Morality of Freedom* (Oxford University Press, 1986), 246, claims that the ultimate 'liberal' values are either individualism (free rein for all with basic liberties) or personal autonomy (involving respect for all persons with the necessity of collective goods). He hopes (as do others) to be able to separate liberalism from individualism. His distinction is interesting, and it is true that the two are conceptually distinct. But still at issue are foundations: is there any *reason* why liberalism should not collapse into individualism? Offering no groundwork for his liberalism, and personal autonomy being little more than a 'pious' hope, Raz can provide no protection – apart from a possible pragmatism – against the threat of moral solipsism. He admits that there is no basic right to autonomy (however understood): that it is an 'ideal'. The matter will be further discussed in chapter 7.

arising is how far our capacity to respect other people can be stretched, and what justification – surely it must be realist? – we could propose for such stretching. Can it be extended, for example, from the family to the city as a whole? For even if some people need only be considered under the 'rational' rubric of 'fellow calculators' – perhaps demanding only to be treated impartially – others, if their selves are to develop, will demand to be afforded respect, loyalty, love.

If some ever-modifying life-plan is going to demand our respect for a wider and wider group, it is also going to demand common values: what I have designated, in Augustine's phrase, 'common loves and hates'. How are these values to be arrived at? Each of the members of the community will try to reason to what is best for himself and to what he judges best in general (insofar as he is willing to distinguish the two). That again raises the question of the future of the 'self', for membership in any community requires each member to be *accountable* in the future for something he or she is in the present and has been in the past; that is, it involves him in duties and responsibilities as well as with claims, 'rights' and liberties. If, of course, he or she repudiates the notion of accountability (as part of an individualist repudiation of obligations or even of community at all), the outcome will be further fragmentation.

Membership in a group compels towards some form of *more* unified (though not necessarily unified or even unifiable) self; rejection of such membership under the plea of individual liberty pushes in the other direction, that is, towards maximum fragmentation. No-one in his right mind is going to pursue *in practice* an extreme individualism in a community – or at the least he will need to present a show of cooperation to cover his individualist purposes. That, however, would lead to another form of fragmentation, substituting a new kind of lie in the soul for an avowed disregard for others. Either way lies likely derangement.

But if the self or future 'soul' is supposed (but why?) to be uniquely valuable and yet to depend for its growth on merely human communities, paradoxes are to be expected. For if a recognition of group values promotes growth in the unity of the person, an insistence on the ultimately superior claims of the future soul (as an agent-relativist appears to demand) over against *every* group will generate further fragmentation – unless there is a wider and transcendent source of group unity available, and this the 'Platonic' thesis holds to be the case. Were the individual merely his conscious self, rather than his 'objective' (and growing) soul, there could be no other such source. But such an 'objective' soul lives in an objective – preferably a realist – moral world, that is a moral world recognizable as *given*, outside the boundaries of our minds and independent of them. Without that objective world the soul would become (or remain) a self (or rather a set of selves), making its own reality and able (if need be) to deny the moral reality of others. In such perspective, the power to criticize one's own wishes and preferences – traditionally associated with 'philosophy' and arguably with personal autonomy itself – must collapse into the power to deconstruct, in the first instance, the social institutions within which one lives. Of course, if successful, this would demonstrate the meaninglessness which deconstructionists proclaim – albeit commonly failing to allow that that meaninglessness must in logic embrace the deconstructionist's self and project.

In such a post-modern scenario not only does it make no sense to say that anyone can be made better (or worse), but the 'end' of the agent is his or her dissolution into potentially (and often into actually) conflicting selves, the desire for power remaining the only unifying factor. But, predicts the realist, the further the disintegration goes, the more the agent will be liable to actions which weaken his ability even to wield power: his intelligence yielding regularly to his passions so that he becomes dangerous to his associates who trust him less and less. Left uncertain as to which preference should be pursued, he can only swing from paralysis to random and arbitrary actions.

This portrait of the dictator is familiar, being summarized in Plato's vision of the violent, unpredictable, friendless and fearful 'tyrannical man' of the *Republic*: the man who abuses the public and social domain. Plato shows how such a man wants to maximize the satisfaction of his desires but that difficulties increase for him as, these desires being both multiple and contradictory, a successful accommodation of satisfactions becomes impracticable. In my preferred terminology, he becomes too many different selves, with only the still remaining desire for power and the maximization of pleasure binding the 'bundle' until the proper advancement of the 'person' is made unattainable, and with it even the hope of maximizing satisfactions.

It is apparent that we need some principle of unity, however precarious, if we are to function at all, and that there are three possible 'sources' of such unity: one, the most precarious, is the deconstructionist unity of power: at least the craving to dominate will give some sort of polarity in the form of what I have called our shadow self. The second is the shifting and ultimately directionless unity which comes with a total accommodation to societal and political correctitude, democratic or otherwise, or to what Plato called 'opinion' (true or otherwise); the third is only possible if one can relate oneself to objective norms and goals beyond the constructions either of oneself or of the group, which is to say of any human society. It is clear that the third option is out of the question if, transcendental metaphysics and religion being regarded as 'pie in the sky', we have to content ourselves with inventing a morality, either on our own or in company with comparatively like-minded others. Of course, if that is the road we take, we shall probably rely in the short term on the inherited capital of an earlier 'realism', but in the longer run it will seem vain to make claims for virtue, civic or otherwise (as do the Straussians and 'republicans'); such talk will become high-sounding, pious but unjustifiable prating. Vain too will be any hope of an end (or even a diminution) of the divisions in the self, whether more strictly 'internal' or generated by external needs and demands. The 'Way of Politics' is an alluring dead end: a deceptive short-term remedy for the human malady.

CHAPTER 5

Rules and applications

SOME USES OF RULES

As we have seen, there are two sides to the problematic of morality: moral agent and moral object or aim. In this chapter I shall consider a link between them, namely the moral principle or rule. From the role of rules and principles in possible accounts of moral behaviour we can shed light on both the nature of moral facts, if any, and on significant features of the genuinely moral agent.

I will begin by observing that unless rules perform as 'primitives' in a metaphysical universe – which is obviously impossible for the non-realist about values and also wholly implausible for the moral realist – they are to be viewed as means to ends, so we have to identify the nature and function of such moral means and their role in the formation of the moral agent. We shall then be in a position to consider two notorious puzzles in normative ethics: the problem of 'dirty hands' – believing oneself obliged to do things which seem morally wrong – and the problem of the relation between fairness and justice (in what circumstances and by what criteria should people be treated equally?). One of the reasons for the popularity of rule-based ethics is that rules seem necessary if fairness and 'rights' are to be enforced.

Since the proper status of rules and principles is obscured by the abuses of legalism and hypocrisy, as well as by difficulties about their application, we may usefully begin by determining how those with a proper respect for rules can be distinguished from narrow legalists and bigots with whom they are often (if sometimes malevolently) confused. The enquiry will further identify the moral agent capable of understanding the kind of metaphysics of morals which Platonists uphold.

The very word 'morality' can suggest priggishness, as in the phrase 'the morality squad', so that a distinction is sometimes made between ethics and morality, 'ethics' referring to the good life for man as a whole, while 'morality' is limited to what we are told we *ought*, or more probably what we ought not to do. 'Do-gooders' too have, if often unwarrantably (why or in what manner can it be wrong to desire to do good?), a bad name, and are held to be egregiously self-righteous in flaunting their 'morality'. From Dickens' Gradgrind, the 'man of principle' is a regular butt of novelists who sense the negative appeal of a person whose theories override considerations of empathy and straightforward understanding, or who has a new principle or rule for every occasion. Such suspicions may be misplaced, but in trying to understand how they arise – being particularly conscious of the matter of sympathy, while deprecating any natural desire to denigrate the good out of envy or malice, or in the interest of black comedy – we may gain a greater understanding of the place of principles, rules and even theories, in an account of virtue.

Part of the perceived objection to the 'man of principle' or the 'do-gooder' takes the form of a belief that he lacks that underrated but necessary virtue, the sense of humour which both graces the simple and unitary mindset of an integrated and harmonious self and, more specifically, encourages a sense of proportion about ourselves as about others. Lacking a sense of proportion, the 'man of principle' tends to make every piece of behaviour a matter of that 'principle', and thus to the Stoic absurdity that all sins are equal. As Hegel objected to Kant, if all sins are equal, it is impossible to avoid major sin, and the psychological need for hypocrisy becomes overwhelming. And insofar as the hypocrite denies his moral condition, he is liable to that lack of a sense of humour which is a kind of blindness, an inability to see and dismantle certain salient facts of human nature: not least of one's own nature, a proper perception of the funny or grotesque features of which is humility.

Hegel's criticism goes deeper: any moral system based on reference to rules and principles alone (and which thus discounts the emotions and intuitions, including empathy, as well as the proper *satisfaction* in doing good both immediately and habitually) is *unliveable* and necessarily leads either to hypocrisy or to the abandonment of morality itself. Hence it is that in literature the 'man of principle' is regularly *identified* as a hypocrite, like Joseph Surface in Goldsmith's *School for Scandal*, old Joseph in *Wuthering Heights* and the stereotypical Church of England clergyman in a series of English novels from Fielding through Jane Austen to E. M. Forster. Such hypocrites, combining lack of self-knowledge and moral dishonesty with lack of humour, make themselves a target for the humour of others. If Joseph Surface were not comic, he would have to be tragic; he could be both, as is Uriah Heep.

But to think of the man of principle as a hypocrite is to attend to the abuse, not the upholding, of principles. Are there objections to the very appeal to principle which would give a rationale to our unease about them and about the 'principled man'? Some 'Wittgensteinians' seem to think that principles are unnecessary in ethics; what we require is detailed and sensitive attention to the uniqueness of cases. Indeed, why should the man of principle need to appeal to principles or rules, as though he were *reminding* himself of what he should do rather than acting 'spontaneously' out of virtuous nature? He might be seen to improve if he appealed to his principles or rules not on any and every occasion (thus looking oddly like a Sartrean without the agony), but only when challenged by some Thrasymachean or merely puzzled onlooker. Does his behaviour suggest that whatever virtuous habits he has, they are not yet his 'second nature'? Does it also more constructively suggest that, whether or not we should appeal to rules before engaging in actions, it is important to do so when we have to justify what we have already done?

We have thrown up a second, not unrelated, complaint against our man of principle: that he has lost touch with, or lost interest in, the specific features of the case, and acts less out of concern for individuals than with reference to impersonal guidelines, which he follows with little empathy for those whom these guidelines should protect: that his is an impersonal point of view, cold and dispassionate. In light of our conclusion that rules are means to ends, this second objection is like its predecessor in presenting the 'man of principle' as morally incomplete: he lacks spontaneity; he has lost sight of the person among the general rules; perhaps indeed he is insufficiently aware of what the rules are for. Most of us would prefer to be helped out of love or kindness rather than from a 'virtuous' officiousness which acts from a sense of duty or from just following the rules – and that even where the same material assistance is received. This seems so obvious that we may wonder whether the man of arid principle can be said to be a good person at all, and if such doubts are taken seriously, then moral goodness, at least in high degree, is seen to demand the personal touch; so we come to recognize the general truth that 'impersonal' justice, though necessary in socio-political contexts, is a limited good: that duty is, at best, an etiolated form of love. Certainly if Goodness can only be intelligible as the nature of something like the Augustinian God, then impersonal justice, in the vital respect of personhood, is not strictly just.

Suchlike considerations underlie Aristotle's conclusion that he who acts out of a sense of duty or obligation is defective compared with the truly 'virtuous' man, the man of excellence of character. We have looked at the affective impoverishment of the narrow legalist earnestly carrying out his duties, and his relative unattractiveness to those he helps, who find his ability merely to follow right rules – put otherwise, to conform the mind to a set of obligations – disappointingly desiccated. Light is shed on his incompleteness by other sorts of cases. If I explain that, though I believe I could do it with impunity, on principle I have decided not to assassinate my business rival, you may wonder why I need to refer to principles and proceed to *decide* something like that. If I happen to have a gun in my pocket (rightfully owned and licensed) when I enter a bank, you might ask me whether I *decided* not to threaten the teller. I shall not merely reply that I would probably have been caught and sent to prison if I had done so, nor these days – unless perhaps I take the query as a joke – shall I recite the commandment against murder. I shall probably say that I am not violent or dishonest, that I am not *that sort* of person.

Such examples, however, may mislead. The man of principle may not always *decide* what to do on the spot; he may simply act in a principled way, having learned to obey the rules. His reaction will be neither ago-nized nor calculated, but automatic. There is no need to expect of him any consciousness of a general rule. Nonetheless, his position becomes problematic if, on reflection, he can *only* come up with a rule and can offer no context for that rule. For his 'second nature' is thus seen to be formed merely by rule-obedience, uninformed by an understanding of the nature and purpose of rules.

Though at times it would seem bizarre to expect an *immediate* appeal to principles to explain why one has done something right or has not done something wrong, examples such as these at least enable us to confirm our identification of two significant functions of such principles, and are useful both in explaining to those for whom we are responsible what we believe they ought to do – useful, that is, though not in themselves fully effective, as a teaching tool – and in justifying our behaviour even if its rationale seems self-evident to ourselves. The latter purpose recalls some Socratic behaviour discussed earlier. The traditional gentleman was satisfied to say, 'You just *don't* cheat at cards, kill the innocent, beat your wife.' The 'sophist' asks 'Why not?', and will not be satisfied by appeals to the *mos maiorum*.

It will be of little effect to say that our ancestors always condemned killing one's children to someone who will reply that in at least some instances they were mistaken. Nor, of course, will it be any better to reply, 'It is simply wrong'; that, even if true, is unconvincing, especially if the challenger is not only prepared to argue that traditional views are wrong, but to give some sort of 'scientific' explanation (or error theory[1]) of how people came to hold them. It is with the role of principles as justificatory devices, and not as more widely educative, that I am presently concerned, the aim of such devices being to establish in the minds of those who challenge our behaviour some *understanding* of why what is wrong is 'really' wrong, invoking all the relevant facts of the case and of similar cases.

There is a conceptual link between the justificatory function of principles and the philosophical function of what is often called 'Greek eudaimonism', the view regularly defended by Socrates, Plato and Aristotle that it 'pays' to be moral, not in any crudely materialist sense but in that one will become a better, more complete, more unified person, that one will be in that manner advantaged, 'happier', by living a 'moral' life. Though Plato would see no reason *against* wanting to become better and indeed many reasons why one should so want, in taking that view he, in particular, as we have seen, is not urging us to be good *because* it pays to be good, whether in this world or in another – though as a matter of fact it does – but because we are made to conform ourselves to the goodness of the gods. His immediate point is that when arguing with those whose only interest in 'morality' (or anything else) is whether it will somehow be profitable, it is material to point out that it will be – if indeed that is an arguable or demonstrable position; nothing else should expect a hearing.

Similarly, though we do not immediately appeal to moral principles when performing a good act of a kind to which we have become habituated, if required to defend and justify the 'goodness' of that act, we have no alternative but to explain why what is good is good, including good for us, and an appeal to rules or principles provides the context for this explanation. Any unwillingness to make it will, according to the intellectual preferences of the age, label a person as dogmatist, fideist or slave of convention. Of course, by appealing to moral rules, or more broadly to principles, we may still be unpersuasive. The principles, let alone the rules, may be unacceptable; yet to present them is to invoke comprehension of the kind of ethical structure in which we are trying to live, inviting the challenger to direct his criticism not at a particular action or even rule, but at a supposedly interlocking set of concepts.

Thus though relentless parading of one's principles in season and out is liable to provoke justifiable accusations of priggishness or hypocrisy,

---

[1] See for example Mackie, *Morality*, 48–9.

principles introduced *as justification* against some 'Thrasymachean' or more broadly sceptical challenger do not merit these rebuffs, though they may elicit them, since those with a 'guilty conscience' are prone to mock those they fear are more effective morally. Such hostility has to be dismissed; the good man will not seem instantly attractive to the less ethical and rather will often be dismissed as offensive to wrongdoers or people who claim unreasonably to be the victims of injustice, though he will attract those of good will if they are informed about the relevant facts of any particular case. To these the mere possession of principles will not make the good man unattractive, but their invocation in inappropriate circumstances, and the accompanying air of hypocrisy in their presentation.

Identification of the man of principle as a hypocrite derives in part from his perceived attempt to present himself as a moral paragon, human beings having an innate feeling – which may be well grounded – that moral paragons are as rare as the Stoic and proverbial phoenix.[2] Certainly there is no reason why it should be part of the character of the good man consciously to present himself as such a paragon, since to do so would be to exceed the truth. Even Aristotle's much-discussed 'great-souled' man only claims for himself whatever respect is deserved. Nevertheless, there is no reason, such as fear of unpopularity, for the good man necessarily to refrain from appealing to principles.

In addition to the role of principles as justificatory, I have noted their use in instruction, whether of the young or of the not-so-young. In society at large, the very existence of laws has the same effect, as was apparent in the southern States when racial discrimination was struck down. Parents have the duty of instruction, a duty to some degree shared by everyone from time to time, and there are certain persons (like judges, clerics, lawmakers) for whom instruction about principles is of the essence of their profession. Such people are regularly (often no doubt falsely) assailed as hypocrites; not only is that irrelevant to their role in society, but the most that fear of such criticism should furnish them with is a warning as to their own moral standards, and by no means an excuse to avoid the responsibilities of their role. Seeing that actions are regularly led by theories and by principles, if we – let alone if those whose job it is – are always inhibited about uttering principles or referring to rules, society will clearly be the loser.

---

[2] Cf. L. A. Blum, 'Moral Exemplars', in P. A. French, T. E. Uehling Jr. and H. K. Wettstein (eds.), *Midwest Studies in Philosophy*, vol. xiii: *Ethical Theory: Character and Virtue* (Notre Dame University Press, 1988), 196–221.

What matters about principles, whether justificatory or educational,[3] is the kind of principles they are, and whether, in given circumstances, appeal to them makes sense. Here at least two difficulties arise. The first is that what may appear to be such principles may in fact not be principles at all: that is, they are neither themselves *first* principles nor directly dependent on first principles and hence cannot be claimed to ground whatever later subsidiary behaviour is supposed to follow from them. They are thus ultimately arbitrary. Or they may be only what we could call 'external motivators', easily disguised as 'principles'. An agent would be externally motivated if he is under pressure to behave in a certain way and in accordance with certain principles which, though accepted, have neither yet been understood nor integrated as part of his 'second nature'. So the views of a parent might be external motivators to a child, and rules learned, followed, but not understood, are what I term 'external motivators' for adults.

Consider the historic question, 'Who is my neighbour?' The proper response to that was not a *theory* about the universalizability of moral propositions, or even about how to live well, though in other circumstances – say, a lecture on moral philosophy – the answer might be *reduced* to such a theory. One anxiety about a man who sees moral excellence as the possession of a theory or set of rules, as knowing the right answer, is that he may believe and proclaim external motivation to be a short cut to (or substitute for) moral improvement and even moral virtue. This is why possession of a set of rules can become a short cut (which contact with 'reality' might prevent one from taking) to fanaticism or bigotry – though it is not the only road to these conditions.

What, though, is wrong with being 'a fanatic or a bigot'? Not simply being mistaken about the importance of the material about which I am fanatical or bigoted: I may be a fanatic over an irreproachable cause like the teaching of medicine, and so willing to blackmail people into putting more money into medical research or indifferent to animal or human suffering or indignity caused by such research. There are at least two distinguishing features of the fanatic: like the 'man of principle' in the inferior sense of that phrase, he lacks a sense of proportion – and of course its manifestation in a sense of humour – about the weight to be attached to his chosen 'good' in comparison with other goods, many of which he may in consequence refuse 'on principle' to recognize as goods at all; further – as in my example – he is prepared to use 'any' means

---

3 There may be further uses of principles; we shall consider their *protective* role later in the chapter.

to secure the chosen end. Aristotle locates moral behaviour primarily in the quality of deliberations about the means to secure wished-for ends.

Since actions derive from a choice of means and a recognition or assumption of ends, right action must involve weighing the moral worth of the means in relation to the particular good which is being sought. The man who is prepared to use 'any' means towards a moral end can be seen to lack not only a sense of proportion about the end, but that false understanding – based on inadequate or diminished principles – of the end itself in which fanaticism and bigotry consist. For it is not that bigots and fanatics may not see the truth in part; one can be bigoted about what is perceived as true as well as about what is perceived as false (thus a Catholic can recognize a Catholic bigot as well as a Muslim bigot, a Muslim a Muslim bigot as well as a Hindu bigot, and so on), for the bigot ignores the surrounding circumstances and the 'context' of the truth, while the fanatic may behave disproportionately, even violently, to promote what the bigot values exclusively. The fanatic shows his bigotry in his acts, the bigot's thoughts providing the diminished 'principles' for the fanatic's actions. Both bigots and fanatics, as well as 'men of principle' (and hypocrites), can be abusers of legitimate rules and sound principles.

I have called the mere acceptance of the correctness of rules and principles 'external motivation'. Acts can be said to be *directly motivated* if they derive from principles which can be justified and grounded by an appeal to reason rather than merely to authority. (It follows that there is nothing wrong with an appeal to authority accompanied by an appeal to reason or justified by a reasonable account of the authority itself.) This distinction, however, should not be misread as endorsement for reacting to the question 'Who is my neighbour?' not by invoking some theory or set of rules, but in terms of feelings. To respond to a person or a circumstance out of feelings alone may lead to recklessness – otherwise known as neglect of the virtue of prudence: thus not only acting on rote principle alone (or being 'externally motivated'), but equally reacting merely from 'feeling', is an incomplete version of acting virtuously.

Possession of appropriate feelings and emotions *plus* the ability to refer – but not as a final court of appeal – to some interiorized and justifying rule are essential features of a well-integrated character. We must be able to justify our behaviour, but neither feelings nor the mere ability to appeal to rules will alone supply such justification. Except in the hypothetical case of the moral paragon, to turn the following of one's feel-ings into a rule of conduct is to invite arbitrary, irrational, inconsistent, cruel or stupid behaviour, though the good man will develop feelings appropriate to the decisions which he makes from time to time.

We thus arrive at the conclusion that to follow principle alone will promote a devaluing of the attitude or 'spirit' in which to do what we ought to do, leading to callousness and hypocrisy; conversely the influence of the *appropriate* feelings in situations demanding moral decision-making will challenge the morally inadequate pursuit of merely 'impersonal justice'.

Aristotle thought that the good man will enjoy doing good deeds and be pained at doing evil deeds. To which he added a caveat: the good man should be pleased at doing good deeds in the sense at least of not being pained by them. That seems clearly right; if I help a blind man over a road while fuming at the moral principles which I feel hold me in their grip and impel me so to act, my action must appear morally unsatisfactory, even if my principle of action is sound.

Other objections arise. We can envisage a principled advocate of capital punishment executing a murderer and admitting, 'Yes, I enjoyed doing that'; we have to grant that he was following Aristotle's rule unamended – doing the right thing and being pleased at doing good. Aristotle might prefer it if the executioner were rather 'not pained', since not to be pained is not necessarily to feel pleasure.

Still, the limit of Aristotle's incompleteness has not been reached. 'Dirty hands' aside, he takes no cognizance of circumstances where one unambiguously does the right thing and (even bitterly) regrets having to do it. Such cases arouse further concerns about impersonal justice. A judge handing down a severe sentence – or under a 'three strikes and you're out' rule being 'compelled' to hand down such a sentence – might understand the point. So might a parent having to correct a loved child severely. It would be disconcerting (even if other ages have not thought it so) to find someone happy, or even dispassionate (that is, feeling neither pleasure nor pain), while imposing, say, life-imprisonment on a fellow man.[4] When the good man acts in circumstances where he wishes that the world were otherwise, he will feel pain (in the form of regret) at the necessity of his actions. He will precisely *not* feel remorse because that would mean that he thought that he should have acted otherwise – that he has 'dirty hands'.[5] He feels regret because the world is as it is and he

---

[4] See Charles Taylor's discussion of the desire to limit the hardships and pains *even of the guilty* as a feature of 'modernity' in *Sources of the Self: The Making of the Modern Identity* (Cambridge, Mass.: Harvard University Press, 1989), 12–14.

[5] Cf. M. Baron, 'Remorse and Moral Regret', in *Midwest Studies*, vol. xiii, 259–81.

is in a position where he concludes (rightly or wrongly) that he has no moral option but to do as he does.[6]

Perhaps he would have felt more 'pain' if he had acted otherwise, but the moral world is not such that if I would feel more pain at one course of action than at another, then by avoiding the greater pain (say the pain of conscience) I also rid myself of the possibility, or moral necessity, of suffering a lesser one. At any rate, what such examples again show is that following principles, even well-founded principles, is in itself not enough for moral excellence, since the attitudes with which we follow them and what these attitudes reveal cannot be ignored. Such attitudes are an outcome of proper habits and dispositions and cannot be considered only in terms of emotions.

The man who habitually and *conscientiously* follows his principles might seem to require of himself that he do so *consciously*, but my account of the need only for retrospective justification eliminates this requirement. Indeed, such concern can easily lead to moral paralysis or to an over-proprietary attitude, verging on selfishness, towards the good life as a whole. While it is true that self-respect is a value, and selfishness its antithesis, a continual self-conscious concern with self-respect is likely to damage that virtue as others: as Plotinus points out, self-consciousness about a performance blunts the performance itself. Paralysis more plausibly occurs when we are perplexed by our inability to measure differing good courses, or specifically when we find it impossible to fudge the *consequences* of our putatively good actions. This brings us back to the priority of good habits over principles, for while paralysis may set in if one is immediately reflective over one's possible behaviour, for the person of good habits that will only be necessary in rare cases. Even when he is challenged to *justify* an action performed, his habits (though certainly reflected on if complacency is to be avoided) will provide him with the reply. Thus the good man, whatever his moral principles, need not normally be consciously aware of them or of the theoretical ramifications of his actions. It is important to reflect morally on our actions, to engage, that is, in serious self-examination, but usually away from the relevant actions.

While philosophers classically wonder why precisely Buridan's ass, confronted with two exactly similar bales of hay, would not die of starvation, having insufficient grounds for deciding on one bale rather than the other, one reason the ass – not to speak of a human being in similar

---

[6] The theme is trivialized when macho politicians and movie stars repeat that 'A man's gotta do what he's gotta do'. In such cases the apparent regret is a 'fig-leaf' protection against charges of ruthlessness or callousness.

circumstances – in fact does not starve is that he does not think of using principles to make a judgement in the case. He can be said to 'plump', and there is here nothing 'wrong' with plumping precisely *because* there is no principled reason to choose one bale rather than the other. It is if he were persistently to look for a principle that he would indeed die of starvation. However, the ass, being unable to reason or have an awareness of principle, could not (strictly) need, or be said to need, to plump; he would just eat at random one or other – or both – of the bales of hay. The man in similar circumstances, though able to reason and hence to act on conscious principle, would be foolish, even irrational, if he debated the matter. His *rational* course not being to make the matter one of principle but to act on the justifiable *instinct* that eating takes precedence over deliberating as to which identical meal it would be better to eat first, he can rationally get on with eating one piece of food or the other. I have already hinted at more difficult cases – and apparently not merely for the man of principle – which involve 'dirty hands', but these I shall defer until my survey of the uses of rules is complete.

So far I have argued that although principles and rules have both educational and justificatory value, rule-following is incomplete as a guide to or account or justification of moral behaviour as a whole. That is part of my contention that rules are means to ends; hence we can now add to our account of the importance of rules that, despite the claims of the 'man of principle', a further major function of rules (including, perhaps even especially, negative rules or prohibitions) is not simply preventative but as means to the positive end of freeing the agent from intolerable and selfish hindrances in his path through life. Under this aspect, the function of many rules is that of a bulldozer on a construction site, clearing the way for work to proceed; insofar as they fail to achieve that and merely protect people against themselves and others, their utility is diminished.

I am not saying that the protective function of moral rules is of no importance. What I am rejecting is the tradition, deriving from Hobbes and Hume, that this is their only or at least primary function. The Humean assertion that we are people of limited sympathy possessed of restricted means for material contentment and that we need moral rules to protect ourselves against one another is acceptable so far as it goes, but it presents a misleadingly incomplete overall picture. As Hume himself saw, by obeying moral and legal rules we become dispositionally different as we live with different institutions, the rules thus functioning educationally in a positive as well as in a restrictive sense. Rules not only prevent us from injuring others; they essentially tend to make us the kind of people who are capable of living, and perhaps bound to live, in a way that would be harder of attainment if we did not live under their guidance.

Perhaps the enabling function of rules is a subset of their educational function – and the same can be applied to protection. As Hume also saw, when I am prevented from harming others, I may learn *not* to harm them, as happens with children and puppies. That is not merely learning moral truths, but primarily learning to enact them. In this light, as I hope to have shown, the claim that it is not possible to legislate morality is both false and absurd.[7]

The foregoing comments on impersonal justice leave us with a dilemma: if love can embrace justice but not vice versa, and if impersonal justice is inadequate as a moral ideal, in that there seems to be a defect in a justice which fails to rise above the impersonal,[8] such justice is nevertheless the best possible character of much law, and therefore desirable and to be promoted. It follows that we cannot hope to produce a state where the code of public morality comes up to the highest personal standards or where it does not remain irredeemably incomplete, with the result that we have to be both more tolerant and more pragmatic about the moral possibilities of public policy, yet without misdescribing as pragmatism a lack of concern about the nature of our institutions and the behaviour of our officials. This difficult balancing act, we shall see, is not limited to the administration of impersonal justice.

DIRTY HANDS

Moral paralysis will not afflict the agent-relativist if he believes that a course of action will bring about a better outcome *both* in terms of its consequences for other people *and* in terms of his own 'moral' well-being. But what if the consequences look much less bad if an act is performed, and very bad if it is not, while the act itself, being for good reasons against some moral rule, or not readily harmonized with such a rule, seems likely to increase division and multiplicity in the character of the agent?[9]

---

7 My distinction between protective and enabling rules is parallel to that between protective and enabling rights.

8 The thesis that 'impersonal justice' is not enough has a long history. Recently, E. Stump has argued for a much richer notion in Aquinas ('Aquinas on Justice', *American Catholic Philosophical Quarterly* 71 (1997), 61–78), in reply to A. Baier, 'The Need for More than Justice', in V. Held (ed.), *Essential Readings in Feminist Ethics* (Boulder: Westview Press, 1995), 41–58.

9 Cf. more generally H. Frankfurt, 'Three Concepts of Free Action', in *The Importance of What We Care About* (Cambridge University Press, 1988), 47, on having to make a choice in a situation in which one is discontented about having to make the particular choice one seems 'compelled' to make.

This dilemma introduces the problem of 'dirty hands', to which I have alluded several times, and which we saw earlier was raised in a particularly challenging form by Macchiavelli's call for effectiveness in politics. Are there actions which may seem to the agent to be wrong, even – perhaps especially – if he reflects on the 'rules', yet which he feels morally (or otherwise) obliged to perform because of some appalling situation in which he finds himself, whether as a private individual or – arguably a different case – as an office-holder?

Such questions being best approached indirectly, I will set out the agent's dilemma in more detail. He does not wish to act wrongfully in breaking a rule made for others' protection; nor does he wish to be himself further divided, since he knows that it is wrong either to divide oneself directly (say by deliberate self-deception) or indirectly by breaking a moral rule and wronging someone else. That entails not that we avoid wrongdoing simply through a 'selfish' concern to avoid self-division – a bogey raised in chapter 3 – but that wrongdoing divides us precisely because it is wrong. The injured party, that is, has not only been hurt or disadvantaged; he has been wronged. If it is morally wrong to injure (and hence divide) oneself, it is morally wrong to injure another person liable to division:[10] as when victims of injustice are so traumatized by their experiences that they are hardly able to live a moral life, being dominated by the desire for 'getting even'. Thus, through the 'injustice' of another, they too have become divided, and even if they have not in fact been so traumatized, they have been wrongfully exposed to the risk of it, while if they do not survive, their possibilities of future development have been undeservedly curtailed. Such are the facts which lead the agent-relativist to conclude that he should not normally break moral rules.

With these preliminary observations, we can turn to a specific set of cases of 'dirty hands'. Victims may be said to suffer an injustice on the part of an agent who refuses on moral grounds to do what would prevent

[10] Whether more or less so need not be pursued. Aquinas at least thought that – to be intelligible – love requires that we love ourselves more than our neighbours (*Summa Theologiae* II.II.26.4). It is certainly true that there is a *logical* and *psychological* priority of love of self over love of neighbour. As recorded in what seems to be a plausible sequence of Platonic dialogues, the history of the Platonic Socrates, the first well-documented agent-relativist, suggests that the man who takes agent-relativity as a primitive, the man whose first concern is that his soul shall be 'as good as possible' may have to *learn* the logical necessity of 'altruism' and concern to give others their due, and in general an explanation of the virtue of justice. Perhaps it is no mere chance that, though justice is the primary virtue among the ancient Greeks, the Platonic Socrates needs time before he tackles it. He seems to have discussed other virtues in detail at an earlier stage of his philosophical development.

crime by an action which would normally – and by rule – be regarded as wrong. (An example would be refusal to extract information by torture from a prisoner who has boasted that he knows where a bomb has been planted and that it is shortly due to go off.) Now normally, if an action is wrong, it can be shown to be wrong, even if it does not directly harm another person, by its harming (and dividing) the agent. Does it follow that *any* action which will (at least *prima facie*) seem thus to divide and harm the agent will be wrong? Or will there be some instances – hence cases of 'dirty hands' – where even though the agent will seem to be damaged, he should act contrary to the rule; either to do someone else a direct good (the 'Robin Hood syndrome'), or to prevent him suffering injustice at the hands of a third party, as in the above example?

It is often thought – especially in politics – that there will indeed be such acts, but that the integrity of the agent is preserved, and his behaviour legitimately excused, if he regrets what he does, perhaps expressing such regret by determining to resign from office after the dirty work has been done. But it is not immediately clear that such attitudes and actions, even if diminishing the moral damage done to the agent, will enable him to escape it altogether. And even those who accept such a resolution of the dilemma are prone to insist that there are certain sorts of behaviour – usually involving the direct injury of innocent people – which remain beyond the pale.[11]

Clearly there will be no possibility of acceptable 'Robin Hood' behaviour in cases, if there be any, where we know precisely what counts as an act *never* to be performed. Our next question then will be whether there are acts which normally would divisively harm the agent but in the exceptional case would not do so unacceptably, the agent either not

---

[11] So Buckler, *Dirty Hands*, 100, citing A. Gewirth, 'Are There any Absolute Rights?', in J. Waldron (ed.), *Theories of Rights* (Oxford University Press, 1984), 90–109. Gewirth notes that rights language seems inappropriate in extreme cases, but the problem of how the line is to be drawn so as to bar the 'monstrous' or 'unthinkable' act still remains. If there is to be a line, then there are somewhere types of acts which should never be performed whatever the consequences: a conclusion many find (morally) intolerable. A common reaction to the dilemma is to give up: so Nagel (*The View From Nowhere*, 183, after an interesting discussion).

Nagel also raises the question (p. 184) of whether, if I ought to dirty my hands by, say, harming an innocent to save a number of others, those others have any 'right' to claim that the innocent should be harmed. (For the consequentialist, he adds, the victim may have no 'right' to object.) On my showing, the claim of the 'others' is itself both 'divisive' (that is, unjust to themselves) and unjust to the victim, whatever I decide to do. This does away with the suggestion that anyone has the 'right' to demand seriously unjust behaviour of others, and points to a more limited account of the place of rights in general within a possible moral theory. This is not the place to argue the (correct and) more general thesis that in agent-relative morality obligations are always prior to rights and that there are many important cases where the existence of a moral obligation does not entail the existence of a corresponding right.

suffering by breaking the rule, or suffering more if he refrains from break-ing it. To begin with, we must be clear what sort of damage is involved. We are not concerned with mental or physical pain in following the rule, but with cases where such pain would also mark a breaking down of the personality. Note that anyone who claims that some rule should always be followed, at least as defined, must also imply that non-following would always be worse than following. Now there would seem to be many in-stances where an agent, by reasoning, would not be able to make such a determination unless, of course, he believed that he had access to 'priv-ileged' authority (as God directly or through Bible or Church) telling him never to break the rule; when he would accept that contravention is indeed always *more* damaging to his 'future soul' than its alternative.

Augustine seems to have thought that there are instances of moral rule-breaking which cannot be avoided in this 'darkness of social life': that it is part of the misery of our present condition that human beings, and especially people in public office, cannot avoid such difficulties. Such 'venial' sins, though still sins – and thus, in our terms, cases of 'dirty hands' – can be atoned for through prayer and penance. In effect, Augustine condones certain instances of what we considered earlier: do-ing wrong provided that we make later reparation (and not merely by resignation but by mortification). But the reparation is still important; we are responsible for our behaviour, and must 'make it good' 'externally'. This is compatible with a thesis I developed earlier: that we must accept responsibility for whatever we know or learn of our own past if we want to grow to moral unity, and of course it also accommodates the politi-cian who, after regretfully dirtying his hands, should rightly resign. An advantage of Augustine's approach is that it starts from the reasonable premiss that all rules and prohibitions are not of equal importance: some can be broken, if not with impunity, at least without irretrievable damage to the agent.[12]

That relieves the difficulties somewhat, but Augustine also holds that there are kinds of actions (which they are does not affect the principle) which should never be performed whatever the consequences. Since, as we have seen, it seems beyond human calculation to determine in every

---

[12] It is incumbent on anyone agreeing with Augustine to offer some kind of list of sins, graded in order of seriousness. Most people would probably suppose (contrary to Augustine) that politicians may, at least in some circumstances, lie directly. Thus a Minister of Finance, trying to avoid devaluation, could – does – tell journalists that devaluation is out of the question – and then perhaps devalue next day. For present purposes the graded list of sins is a subsidiary matter, though most people now would be inclined to say that deliberate and direct violence against innocent individuals would count among the most serious and least likely to be permissible under any circumstances.

case which such actions are, it is fair to conclude that knowledge of this strong form of agent-relative morality is only available to a realist or rather a realist who believes in a providential God. I shall therefore defer substantive treatment of this matter until my final chapter, noting, however, that a disturbing feature of the present climate of discussion is that whatever the objective facts about morality, and despite any discomfiture caused to the theist, a greater degree of agent-neutral morality would seem to be available to the non-theist – and that he or she will find the stronger versions of agent-relativism unintelligible, even offensive. I also leave to that final chapter the further effects of the breakdown in moral debate between the theist and the non-theist, and the futility of wishing such breakdown away.

For the moment we may more profitably return to the case of the founding father of agent-relative morality, Socrates, who famously in the *Gorgias* states that it is better to suffer wrong than to do it. We will notice that in the first instance this is not a claim that it is better to let someone else suffer wrong than to do wrong oneself; yet there are two senses in which Socrates does make this claim. Firstly, it can hardly be denied that when someone gives up his life rather than do wrong, he leaves suffering to his family and friends: a persecutor can attempt to sway his victim by playing on this fact. Socrates himself states in the *Gorgias* not only that he would rather suffer than do wrong, but that he would endure his family suffering likewise. Although in the Greek context the severity of this may seem diminished by the reflection that a man's family is in a sense an extension of himself, that still hardly softens the rigour of Socrates' position.

Is Socrates a counter-example to our claim that it is only within a theistic context, indeed a providential context, that such claims, in extreme cases, make any kind of sense? Or is his position unintelligible? There is little doubt that Socrates, as presented by Plato, did believe in the providential ordering of the universe, and that his *daimonion* (guardian spirit) confirmed his special role in that universe, and so he provides no counter-example to the thesis that a coherent version of our strong form of agent-relativity entails theistic belief, is indeed perhaps embarrassingly unintelligible without it. Yet in Augustine's view even theistic belief does not entail a claim that all moral rules are equally unbreakable, even if some are.

The theist is thus left with the problem of how to proceed in less desperate individual cases and in most circumstances will come up with the Aristotelian answer: if a man has lived aright he will know how to act when he is faced with an option of suspending a moral rule. Our theist will also at times come up with the Augustinian caution that since such decisions are often beyond fallen human capability, we must pray for guidance.

THE LIMITS OF FAIRNESS

Rule-following assumes the possibility of impartial or at the very least non-arbitrary treatment of others. But difficulties about 'dirty hands' lead to more delicate problems about unfair, indeed unjust treatment, entailing doing people an injustice with the intention of benefiting others (or more others) to a greater extent. And that *inter alia* raises questions about the nature of unfairness. Have people some sort of claim or 'right' to be treated fairly, and does fairly mean equally, and if not, why not?

Such questions must be seen against their background. I have supposed that lack of feeling in dealing with individuals is a mark of moral incompleteness and so that the properly moral individual cannot be 'impersonal' in the sense of unfeeling. We should now consider whether he or she should be 'impersonal' in a second sense: that is, whether in following moral rules, he should always treat people in the same way, and if not, whether such apparent unfairness can be shown to be well-grounded. I am thus asking first whether fair in the sense of impartial treatment always also entails equal treatment, and can then proceed to ask whether – *whatever* the relationship between fairness and equality – justice should be viewed simply *as* fairness, and if so whether – because impersonal – it should be demoted from the summit of the pyramid of virtues.

It is not always fair to treat everyone *equally*; it can even be mockingly unfair, for example if a deaf individual were subjected, against his will, to the same musical instruction as normally hearing pupils. In cases where equality is characterized as fairness, it may again be unjust. If a subsistence-level labourer and a millionaire each are awarded a tax cut of a few pence, or each a 1 per cent pay rise, such 'fairness' has to be deemed unjust.[13] There is no reason to think that the person who attempts to treat everyone without exception in the same way will necessarily benefit either himself or anyone else. In the extreme case, individuals may be considered as similar and equals only as one well-made soccer ball is considered as good as another – and kicked in the same way.

---

[13] The fallacy of identifying the part with the whole is seen in adjudications and other legal or quasi-legal enquiries when the adjudicator is primarily concerned to make sure that procedures are correctly followed. The pursuit of fairness then replaces that of justice.

Insofar as we simply follow principles, theories or rules, we are acting impersonally, at worst even bureaucratically. Even if our guidelines have been drawn up after proper consideration of individual cases, they cannot always fit other such cases and agents. Aristotle famously observed that *equity* is the rectification of a *just* law. Rule-following, in and of itself, must entail a 'third-person' account of morality, whereby it would be morally ideal for each human unit to grant every other human unit (or at least every other unit covered by the rules) some form of impartially similar treatment, unemotionally dispensed. Of course, the target of *moral* rules *seems* to be the whole human race if one is talking about equal and impartial treatment as such rather than, say, for whites or blacks.

Impartiality is only a part of the concept of justice and obligation to fairness is not to be identified as the sum of deontological constraints on behaviour. Fairness (especially when seen as the demand for equality) takes on the appearance of justice itself when it is invoked 'negatively' to rectify inequalities of opportunity or to secure impartial protection against abuse and manipulation, but not when we are trying to identify and secure the best life for each individual. In such cases fairness is not justice itself, but indicative of a formal aim to rectify injustice. Thus appeals to fairness point to the protective character of rules rather than to their enabling force. Insofar as justice is also concerned with promoting an overall human good in diversified human beings, it will demand that all be treated impartially and fairly, but not always equally.

In speaking of fairness as a formal and on the whole negative aspect of justice, we cannot usefully refer to similar treatment – and hence to rules for similar treatment – or specify what sort of similar treatment, without asking whether fairness in the sense of an impersonal and impartial treatment of human beings is always going to achieve what it purports or is assumed to achieve, namely some advantage for each of its recipients. Unless rule-following and hence an emphasis on fairness and impartiality are accompanied by an adequate account of the subjects of moral discourse – namely ourselves as human beings – as well as of the moral space within which we operate, it is hard to see how they can provide us with reasonably adequate guidelines for action.

Such difficulties were recognized by Kant; however, Kant's insistence that the claim that all moral rules are universalizable can be *logically* connected with the intrinsic worth of persons,[14] who must thus be

---

[14] For some recent discussion (and criticism) of Kant's insistence on universalizable rules see L. Blum, *Friendship, Altruism and Morality* (London: Routledge and Kegan Paul, 1980); M. Friedman, 'The Social Self and the Partiality of Debates', in Claudia Card (ed.), *Feminist Ethics* (Lawrence: University Press of Kansas, 1991), 161–79; J. E. Hare, *The Moral Gap*, 142–69.

treated always as ends and never as means to ends, is – as I shall show – inadequately defended. To sympathize with Kant's failed attempt to make the linkage seems to be to exhibit concern that, if we are not to conclude that morality is a Thrasymachean figment, we must explain how the 'responsibilities' of moral agents comprise much more than a willed obedience to impersonal laws about equal or impartial treatment: and that firstly because such agents are themselves not impersonal – though they can and sometimes should act impersonally – and secondly because neither are the targets of moral action impersonal.

Impersonal rules – necessary as far as they go – remain an attempt to treat personal agents in an impersonal way. On the other hand, fairness as the awarding of *appropriate* treatment in each individual case – rather than merely equal treatment – seems to demand an agent omniscient about persons; to claim otherwise would be to reintroduce hypocrisy. But even so omniscient an agent's fairness need not be the summation of his goodness, nor even of his justice. Fairness (even if more than equal and impartial treatment) is important in that it provides guidelines for legislating the advantage and (in particular) the protection of people *en masse*; it is probably to be subordinated to justice and certainly to love and respect in promoting the overall good of particular individuals. The notion that a family, for example, is best organized on the basis of impartiality alone (or even of strict equality) is absurd – though it is far from absurd that it be run justly and lovingly. When Augustine said 'Love and do what you will', he at least should have implied that justice and fairness – insofar as they are virtues of third-person impartiality – can and should be viewed as part and parcel of a personal love, but that the proposition is not reversible.

The conclusions to be drawn from my discussion of rules and principles are limited. One of the wider implications is that the man of principle, in and of himself, is far from the highest moral type. I have identified a number of facets of morality and virtue which mere attention to right rules and principles seems to deform if not to disallow. Rules do require willed obedience, but not a blind or impersonal obedience, because both those who are supposed to benefit by the rules and those who enforce them are inadequately described as human units. Just as such considerations seem to demand the right kind of obedience, so do they demand as far as possible the right kind of affective disposition in that obedience. And just as the right kind of obedience and the right kind of feelings are required, so we require not a blind pursuit of fairness seen as equal treatment – or even as impartiality – but an alertness as to what kind of fairness is appropriate in the moral agent towards the particular moral 'target'.

A better appreciation of the relationship between love, justice and fairness may improve our understanding of the morality of those examples of unfair treatment which involve us in 'dirty hands'. Perhaps to ask how dirty I may allow my hands to become is often (though not always) to ask a form of the question: how unequally can I at times treat other people?

These conclusions about the relationship between rules and moral behaviour depend on the single proposition that talk about moral rules and principles without reference to the nature of man and of each man risks being if not literal non-sense, at least abstract, useless, even dangerous fantasy – such as those of abstract liberalism ('He loves the human race but no particular member of it'). If separated from an account of the virtues and habits which it must be our goal to identify and promote through, and beyond, the rules,[15] discussion of rules and principles cannot but imply two things: not only an impersonal, dispassionate identification of man as an 'ideal' type, but – even if we avoid the cruder reductions, such as man as economic unit or deliberating brain – a mentality whereby we explain away, or disregard as irrelevant, concern for and about the unique quality of each of *our own* voluntary and deliberate actions. By such moves we threaten the very possibility of agent-relative moral behaviour and moral discourse – thus, curiously, giving Thrasymachus an entry through a back door.

Consideration of human nature both general and individual – together with a determination as to the validity of Platonic 'realism' – must precede consideration of moral rules and principles, if the right habits and virtues, and the rules which will promote them, are to be identified. The identification of rules and principles without a corresponding account of their 'grounds' is as inadequate as an attempted identification of rights without a prior account of the nature of obligations and of who (if anyone) is obligated. What, though, are the implications for rules and principles if Platonic realism is an illusion and the 'nature' of man – and hence his 'virtue' – is a largely human construct; or if it cannot be discovered by us? In search of further light on these questions I turn first to various influential and seemingly objectivist alternatives to Platonic transcendentalism, pausing only to recall that from the beginning of this study I proclaimed myself a follower of Zeno's approach to a defence of Parmenides: if Parmenides is right, the world is strange; if Parmenides

---

[15] Cf. MacIntyre, *Three Rival Versions*, 139.

is wrong, the world is even stranger. Thus far I have delineated the demands of a developed and Christianized system of Platonic realism, fully conscious that I am requiring acceptance of a strange (though not unintelligible) hypothesis. In the following two chapters I shall indicate that non-Platonic approaches to ethics, and in chapter 8 also to politics, will lead us, like the opponents of Parmenides, into a yet stranger, even chaotic and unintelligible, universe.

CHAPTER 6

The past, present and future of practical reasoning

POST-REALIST MORAL DEBATE

The quest might reasonably begin with an academic happening of 1992, when the *Philosophical Review* published a survey of what its authors[1] saw as the principal trends in moral philosophy in the twentieth century. Since the survey may be taken as fairly representing the interests and judgements of the majority of Anglo-American philosophy departments, its emphases and omissions cannot but shed light on the present state of the subject. The authors begin with reactions to the work of G. E. Moore, treated as the last (if long expiring) gasp of 'Platonic' intuitionism,[2] and proceed thenceforward in roughly historical sequence. Yet though they mention historicist critics, one of the effects of their presentation is to suggest that the contemporary problems they discuss represent the remaining range of worthwhile debate in moral philosophy. They offer little hint that moral ideas exist within traditions considerably affected by historical circumstances; instead they give the strong impression that philosophical problems arise in an insulated intellectual environment and derive from one another in more or less coherent logical sequence.

There is no reason to believe that this is correct. It is true, as Warnock once noted,[3] that in regard to basic themes, assumptions and approaches in philosophy, as distinct from technical problems in logic, 'the way an influential philosopher may undermine the empire of his predecessors

---

[1] S. Darwall, A. Gibbard and P. Railton, 'Towards Fin de Siècle Ethics', *Philosophical Review* 101 (1992), 115–89.

[2] Cf. *ibid.*, 187, 'Now that Platonic ethical intuitionism has lost its following, the distinctions among forms of "moral realism", "constructivism", "quasi-realism" and so on can no longer be understood as turning upon commitment to (or rejection of) a domain of moral facts "independent of human capacities and interests". Moral realists, constructivists and quasi-realists alike look to the responses and reasons of persons, rather than some self-subsistent realm, to ground moral practice.'

[3] G. J. Warnock, *English Philosophy since 1900* (Oxford University Press, 1966), 9.

consists, one may say, chiefly in his providing his contemporaries with other interests'; that is to say, the best way to discredit an opponent or an unwanted approach, solution or methodology, is to induce people to concentrate on something else – frequently what the 'spirit of the age' finds attractive for reasons largely unrelated to technical philosophy. Latter-day spectators of the philosophical past can misrepresent such shifts of attention, as when, neglecting non-philosophical influences on the concerns of philosophers, they introduce an inauthentic adversarial relationship into their accounts of earlier philosophical views, or of the history of ideas, reading successive theories in opposition to one another even if they are more properly complementary. I have noted a signal instance of this: the allegedly antagonistic but more properly complementary accounts of man and the soul given by Plato and Aristotle.

The authors of the article in the *Philosophical Review* show no acquaintance with anything contemporary not written in English, and of earlier non-English speakers, only a few even of those whose works have been translated (Plato, Aristotle, and especially Kant) gain their attention. This limitation helps reinforce the authors' particular (and ideological) assumption that all worthy moral debate is more or less abstracted from time and place, and philosophy is to be viewed as is science, as continual radical progress marred only by occasional backslidings. Yet in moral philosophy even the very *flavour* of language is important, since nuances of speech reflecting varying cultures, local contexts and subgroup behaviour patterns are often not only untranslatable but at times difficult even to describe precisely in other languages.[4]

There is another, perhaps more significant (and not unrelated) lack in the article in the *Philosophical Review*: not only is there no direct reference to any theistic moral theory, or other natural-law theories (though they still flourish, Thomism being the most conspicuous omission); there is little even to the continuing influence of an unbowdlerized Aristotle, whose moral objectivism, as we shall see, is transformed, assimilated, reduced, de-Platonized and debased into a theory of the objectivity of 'practical reasoning'.

[4] Pace Donald Davidson, 'On the Very Idea of a Conceptual Scheme', *Proceedings and Addresses of the American Philosophical Society* 67 (1973–4), 5–20; for criticism of Davidsonian ideas on untranslatability see MacIntyre, *Three Rival Versions*, 113–14, 171, and *Whose Justice?*, 370–88. For recent deepening of the original debate see D. Bar-On, 'Conceptual Relativism and Translation', in G. Preyer, F. Siebelt and A. Ulfig (eds.), *Language, Mind and Epistemology: On Donald Davidson's Philosophy* (Dordrecht: Reidel, 1994), 145–70. MacIntyre defends himself against 'Davidsonian' criticism in 'A Partial Response to My Critics', in *After MacIntyre*, 295–7. For more of my own position see J. M. Rist, 'On the Very Idea of Translating Sacred Scripture', in J. Krašovec (ed.), *Interpretation of the Bible* (Sheffield University Press, 1998), 1499–511.

This means that, apart from Moore's supposedly Platonist intuitionism, the version of realist objectivism with which we have been primarily concerned thus far is mentioned only in the way of an obituary notice. What most ordinary people still believe are the most important questions in ethics have been banished from the moral philosopher's table, or at best relegated to *explananda* by some sort of error theory. So, at least, readers of the *Philosophical Review* are told, and presumably largely believe. The 'moral philosopher' as such has thankfully shaken off the concerns of the general public – except when he may take advantage of their gullibility – together with those of a number of his more traditionalist colleagues.

Nor do Nietzsche and the post-Nietzscheans warrant explicit mention in the *Philosophical Review*'s presentation, though their influence on ethical discussion both inside and outside philosophy departments has been immense. Their absence, combined with the absence of the most powerful version of realism, helps thicken the air of unreality which the historical parochialism of the article insistently exhales. Of course, in thus recording the developing situation in ethics as a whole, the authors of the article in the *Philosophical Review* are doing more than misreporting the present; they are hoping to construct the future of the subject, and in an unsuspectedly Nietzschean way; for though Nietzsche would despise their conclusions, he could not but be impressed by their single-minded claim to be concerning themselves with the only areas of traditional ethics worthy of their readers' attention.

ARISTOTLE'S ETHICS: BETWEEN PLATONISM AND 'PRACTICAL REASONING'

As I have indicated, one of the ways in which readers of the *Philosophical Review* are invited to approach questions of moral objectivism is through adaptations of the thought of Aristotle, duly cleansed of its 'Platonic' elements. A second and more prominent way is through Kant. Sometimes Aristotle and Kant are blended to suggest a certain anti-metaphysical analogue between the supposed relation of Aristotle to Plato and that between Kant and Christian theology. Various derivatives of Aristotle or of Kant, usually called theories of practical reasoning, purport to show that there are reasons for actions which any rational agent would accept and thus aim to identify behaviour which is objectively prudent or sensible, while in identifying morality as rational decision-making (rather than characterizing the moral as rational) they offer us an objectivism desiccated of genuine obligation, inspiration, affection or an adequate theory of value – let alone of the good – by admonishing us that in moral circumstances 'We ought to do this' is identical (with or without an affective flavouring) to 'It is rational for us to do this'. Morality, in other words, is once again reduced to rational calculating.

Even as an account of obligation and principled rule-following (which I have argued is insufficient for morality, let alone for the good life), such 'normative' objectivism without realism will prove insufficient for the task it purports to undertake. Even following Kant (or Ross), we must import the notion that it is not merely prudent but our *duty* to do what is rational. Without such an independent notion of duty or its equivalent, accounts of rational decision-making suggest consistency of behaviour while failing to explain the moral calibre of that lifestyle, as well as falling well short of an explanation of the force of the moral 'ought', let alone of the 'good life' in any wider understanding. Even more fundamentally, since they concern our ends rather than simply means to those ends, theories of practical reasoning, insofar as they treat reason as more than merely instrumental, maintain that by deduction and inference we can find or construct a compelling range of ends without resorting individually to arbitrary preferences or collectively to an arbitrary suppression of options.

This view that the moral is a mere subset of the rational is more than an insistence that morality make sense; it is a claim that intelligibility plus (perhaps) conviction, determination and conscientiousness is all there is to morality. One objection is that not merely the means to our required ends, but the ends themselves need to be intelligible, since there is little to be said for planning wisely for futile or crazy objectives. But to make sense of our ends is *inter alia* to understand the nature of human beings as changing and responsible agents. If human nature should turn out to be inadequately rational, we shall inevitably be drawn back to choices and preferences about our possible goals: to critical preferences, perhaps, but negatively critical, limited to the attempt to exclude what may seem incompatible projects.

If rational planning is all that is required for morality, why is Hume's notorious comment that there is nothing irrational in preferring the destruction of the whole world to the mere scratching of one's finger to be rejected? It has been proposed that such claims are to be excluded as 'unthinkable' – lunatic and therefore non-rational.[5] These protests, even if apposite – and we see them produced not merely to rule out the monstrous but also to find quasi-moral limits within the normal 'amorality' of politics – give no indication of why Hume is wrong or 'irrational'. It is no more than question-begging for Frankfurt to say that 'the unthinkable <not merely the impossible> defines his (*scil.* man's) limits as a volitional creature'; Hume can be shown to be wrong *only if reason is teleologically oriented*, not if it is the mere capacity to analyse and describe neutrally. If we refuse to move to a more teleological account of reason, we are left in the hole where Hume has dumped us.

What kind of teleological account of man is acceptable, and whence are its credentials? As the *Philosophical Review* points out, contemporary exponents of 'practical reasoning' – 'Kantian' or other – often suggest that Aristotle's *Nicomachean Ethics* presents an early, albeit still metaphysically tainted, version of their own views. Since there is a certain plausibility to this claim, before turning to such theories of practical reasoning, we should examine Aristotle's stance, to identify both how frequently it is travestied and its own weaknesses.

Aristotle believes that, if systematized, the proper practices of a perfected Greek society would be coherent and intelligible. He also assumes that these practices are founded on (or at least justifiable by) a vision of the best end which the virtuous man can identify and the best judgements he can make about the means appropriate to secure that best end. He is far from supposing that morality is merely a matter of finding good 'reasons for action', though he is interested in identifying such reasons. Nor does he suppose that the good man judges the best way to live by combining instrumental rationality with a moral sense, let alone by combining it with mere conviction or determination. Nor does he conjure up any primitive notion, metaphysical or other, of self-evident duties or rights.[6]

5 The comment is Frankfurt's, in *The Importance of What We Care About*, 185–8, who is perhaps on the right lines – but does not go far enough – in saying that Hume's remark is non-rational in a way other than can be accounted for by the discernment of a factual error. Whatever corrective should be applied to Hume, the problem is widespread and increasingly observed. Apposite is the comment of Melanie Phillips in *The Observer Review* of Sunday 18 February 1996: 'The reason the BMA has given [for its support of surrogacy] illustrates with chilling clarity how far this society has travelled towards a universal suspension of repugnance and an apparently limitless capacity to tolerate the intolerable.'
6 Fred R. Miller Jr. has attempted to read a rights theory into Aristotle's *Politics* in *Nature, Justice and Rights in Aristotle's Politics* (Oxford University Press, 1995); for compelling rebuttals see R. Kraut, 'Are There Natural Rights in Aristotle?', *Review of Metaphysics* 49 (1996), 755–74 and (damning anachronistic readings of Greek culture and the Greek language) M. Schofield, 'Sharing in the Constitution', *ibid.*, 831–58.

Aristotle's account of the good life is undeniably developed from an understanding of how man 'functions'. Just as, in the matter of the purchase of a pair of shoes, both buyer and seller assume that the buyer is trying to obtain a *good* pair of shoes – ideally the best possible pair of shoes, for to know what a shoe is is to know what a *good* shoe is, what a shoe is for and what a shoe ought to do for you – so Aristotle holds that to know what a man is is to know what a good man is: what he or she can do and what he or she ought to be in character.

Inevitably the Aristotelian approach demands further clarification, since shoes, unlike men, cannot be thought of as shaping their own destiny or as autonomous, or possessing any ability to deliberate or to distinguish means and ends. It is not the 'virtue' of a shoe to choose the best course of action. Yet it is not difficult to identify the features of a shoe which mark off a superior from an inferior example: bad shoes create bunions or let the water in; they 'ought' not to do those things. One of the more obvious differences between a good shoe and a good man is the range of possibilities open to the latter – starting at the biological level with the possibility of nutrition to support life and reproduction. But as Aristotle himself noted, if there are many 'excellences' in a man – as there are – his flourishing must at the very least involve his living in accordance with the best and most perfect of them. How then are we to identify that best and most perfect excellence?

To that question Aristotle *himself* (and unlike the 'practical reasoners') has an immediate and clear answer, however unappetizing it may seem to us: there is something godlike about man, and his best and most perfect excellence will have to do with that characteristic capacity of God which man to some degree shares, that is, his power of contemplation. There are many moral implications of this, but what should immediately strike us is that the excellence of man is ultimately to be measured by reference to something assumed to be imperfect in man himself but perfectly existing outside of man and independent of man's control. Man is not for Aristotle 'the measure of all things', but a variable creature and, to understand what by nature he is like at his best, we have to compare him with a superior being.

According to Aristotle, to understand rationality at its best involves knowing something of its best possible content and its intentionality towards that content. That is, roughly, if man is at his best when he contemplates, what does he contemplate when he is at his best? Certainly not himself, for in Aristotle's view the best object of contemplation must be eternal and unchanging, while man is constantly at variance with himself and in passage between generation and destruction from birth to death.

The *Nicomachean Ethics* discusses the best life for man, that is the way in which we can best flourish. In addition to considering contemplation, it distinguishes within our mental faculties the special faculty of 'practical reasoning' as one of the highest, but not *the* highest capacity we possess. Practical reasoning is roughly the ability to deliberate how best to achieve the good ends which we recognize with the 'eye of the soul'; it does not itself determine those ends by deliberated 'choice'. Aristotle assumes that good people will agree about excellences and ends and that someone brought up reasonably well in a reasonable society (especially in a Greek society, since he thought of Greek societies as the best so far achieved) will not dispute the place of the virtues of courage, moderation, prudence and the rest, nor the generally recognized highest practical aim of doing things 'for the sake of the fine and inspiring' (*to kalon*). Unfortunately he largely assumes the nature of that *kalon* and offers little specificity.

Let us reconsider two substantial difficulties in Aristotle's approach. Firstly, he feels no need to attack people who deny morality as such, although Plato, as we have seen, had devoted much effort to rebutting them in the *Republic*. Secondly, he pays relatively little attention to developing the distinction he has introduced between means and ends. Yet it is precisely these implications which underlie much contemporary debate about the nature of moral action and the overriding claims of morality itself. It is true that Aristotle insists there are actions which the good man will never commit (he cites matricide), but although he thinks such acts objectively wrong, he spends no time identifying any range of acts which are always wrong, nor discussing the problem of exceptionless moral norms in any general way, nor the moral uncertainty which may arise if 'forbidden' acts are performed not just 'under some kind of compulsion' to avoid worse outcomes – in the case he considers, compulsion is viewed as crude threats by a stronger party – but as means towards apparently 'greater' positive goods. He wants to say that there are types of forbidden act, while seeming to limit their number drastically, and to imply that virtually every moral prohibition is a guideline which the good man will respect in his specific judgements without regarding it as absolute.

Aristotle has such faith in his system of moral education that he assumes that the good man will make the right decision in given circumstances; hence the theoretical question of *how* precisely he gets it right is left aside, either as unanswerable or of no intrinsic interest, since what matters is to produce the right moral result. Aristotle is writing no merely theoretical treatise whereby we may know what is good, but a practical manual on how to live the good life and it is easy to see why he would *assume* that the good man would readily grasp the proper relationship between means and ends.

Aristotle and Plato agree that understanding the best life for man presupposes knowing what man is like and by what he should be measured, agreeing that it is false to hold, with Protagoras, that man is the measure of all things. For them both, man is to obtain 'likeness to God' (or to God's thought) as far as possible. But what Aristotle identifies as 'God' and 'God's thought' – the measure for man – is hard to comprehend, not in terms of any problematic about God's existence but rather what Aristotle wants to say about him since he exists. The God of Aristotle – thought-object of the Aristotelian contemplator – contemplates himself, but there is no suggestion that he is anything like a perfect moral agent, or that he contemplates anything like the Platonic Good or other kind of 'moral' goodness. Moral acts 'for the sake of the noble' may help to divinize us, but God himself is no morally active substance.

Clearly this must be contrasted with the claims of Plato, for whom we are also to attain 'likeness to god', but to gods divine by contemplation of the eternal Forms, especially those of Goodness, Beauty, Justice and Truth. These Forms, objective existents beyond any mind, whether human or divine, are the unchanging standards by which our achievements and those of the gods themselves are measured. Plato believed that without such unchanging and perfect standards it is impossible to measure and compare human behaviour, and it would follow that those Humpty-Dumptys who insist that words can mean whatever they choose could not be effectively answered. Nor did he see any essential difference between those who hold that the private beliefs of individuals about the sense or reference of moral language are all we have to go on and those who argue that morals are by agreement or convention between larger groups; such standards are made by men and can therefore reasonably be discarded by men; they have no foundation beyond men's claims (realistically stated or not), their whims, preferences, hopes or needs. At best, when they are formed by our taking account of impersonal descriptions of events in the universe adequately considered, they may generate prudent policy and enlightened self-interest; at worst they are instruments of deception.

From Plato's point of view, if Aristotle were right that the arguments for Forms 'by knowledge of which the gods are divine' are inadequate or invalid, then one of the necessary foundations for morality would have been removed. Certainly Aristotle's account of *moral reasoning* in and of itself and (like contemporary 'practical reasoners') divorced from that teleological account of human nature which invites us to contemplate the divine and act 'for the sake of the noble and inspiring', provides no more than a set of techniques to promote any given goal not obviously in conflict with the means employed to promote it. But will even contemplation and action 'for the sake of the noble' together serve as a replacement for the Forms? It is certainly reasonable to see acting for the sake of the noble as part of Aristotle's project for the good life, and, when grounding our limited capacity to contemplate, that it directs us towards divinization. The difficulty with pressing this is that Aristotle's god, as we have seen, is not a moral or prudential agent; indeed he is not an agent at all, except in the sense of final cause. Aristotle thinks that the Prime Mover 'moves' the world as 'an object of desire' and presumably objects of desire are *kalon*. However, if we act 'for the sake of the *kalon*' in our good acts, we are not thereby making ourselves godly *moral agents*, since Aristotle's God is neither moral nor an agent. Thus while it is true that 'acting for the sake of the *kalon*' enables an apparently transcendent good to function as a standard of morality, and indirectly to point towards divinization, Aristotle's position is paradoxically incomplete and leaves its author between two stools. Only by translating his God into a good and providential *agent*, as Augustine, for example, will do, could Aristotle offer a transcendent principle capable of functioning as the divine moral prototype required. With his *kalon* Aristotle may have explained the possibility of morality, but he has left a gap (even an antithesis) between morality and divinization. As in the case of the Stoics, an inadequate account of God produces (or upholds) an inadequate account of man.

From Augustine's point of view, if Aristotle could have made the necessary changes, he would have retained the Platonic thesis that the Good as object of thought is immaterial, strengthening it by his argument that thought must be a living 'actuality', while at the same time both improving on Plato's separation of God from Forms and providing a reconstructed God with the necessary 'Platonic' moral 'content'. Removed from such a God, Aristotle's *kalon* remains a wandering ghost of the Platonic Good.

Is it possible that *kalon* in Aristotle refers not merely to the act itself or to the agent and his intentions, but to the quality of the *performance* as a whole: both to the character and intention of the agent and to the rightness of what is done? On this showing, the 'rightness' would depend on the 'divinizing' capabilities of the act, which act (whatever the ontological status of acts) is thus saturated and informed by a teleological view of the world.[7] Such a reading seems not entirely alien to Aristotle, but it is hard to formulate precisely, and it would be easier to see it in the hands of an efficient-cause theist like Aquinas than in the 'non-providential' world of Aristotle's 'non-moral' divinity. What *is* clear is that Aristotle could not have viewed the 'fineness' or 'beauty' of a right performance as comparable with the secondary quality of an object (such as its colour). The redness of a red object is the way in which its primary qualities strike upon the human eye; although we really see red, the redness that we see can be described in physical and chemical ways which do not introduce the notion of redness. Aristotle would have denied that the moral qualities of actions are so describable;[8] insofar as they are qualitative, they would have to be primary qualities.

Still less would Aristotle have approved a comparable contemporary strategy, that of those 'quasi-realists' who, concerned that in practical morality we need terms ('good', 'right' and so on) which appear genuinely objective – comparably to secondary qualities appearing genuine qualities – want us to hold such moral terms to be 'quasi-objective': that is, to pretend or assume that they are objective simply in virtue of the fact that we 'really do' project them onto agents and actions.[9] Apart from such moves being an example of the perceived necessity of deception which seems to run through much contemporary ethics (and to which I shall turn in a later chapter), note that if we neglect the distinction between 'assuming' and 'pretending' (thus leaving open a further question as to whether we should be self-deceivers as well as deceivers), we find that the quasi-realist holds that moral language cannot refer to objective values, but is merely a set of value-laden redescriptions of non-moral facts, or even of emotional states. Aristotle neither holds nor could hold such a position. In describing an action as 'fine', he would certainly prefer the language of 'saturation', but would deny both that we merely assume

---

7 Sokolowski (*Moral Action*) seems to offer a view of this kind, which he roots primarily in Aquinas' distinction (as explicated by Husserl's account of intentionality) between the form and the materiality of the moral act (as between murdering X and pulling the trigger of a gun pointed at X's head); see especially chapter 3 ('Moral Action') and appendix C ('Intentions and the Will: Aquinas and Abelard').

8 Views of this sort are currently popular and treated with respect by the survey-writers in the *Philosophical Review*; see, for example, the so-called sensibility theories of J. McDowell, 'Projection and Truth in Ethics' (Lindley Lecture, University of Kansas, 1987) and D. Wiggins, 'Truth, Invention and the Meaning of Life', *Proceedings of the British Academy* 62 (1976), 331–78. Their philosophical origin – as distinct from their current attractiveness – can be traced largely to Hume.

9 For such 'anti-realism' see Blackburn, *Spreading the Word*, 171, 195; partially Humean origins are again apparent. The influence of Feuerbach is also curiously apparent in versions of anti-realism now popular with various theologians (predominantly the followers of Cupitt).

such saturation and that saturation refers to the way an action *looks to us* insofar as we admire it or rationally describe it. But I shall return to the sensibility theorists and quasi-realists when considering their origins in Humean naturalism.

Like Kant, Aristotle had a project for separating ethics from metaphysics and, like Kant's, his project failed. Some of his reasons for attempting the separation, however half-heartedly, were admirable. He thought that the existence of Platonic Forms could not be established, and even if it could that they are of no help in ethics. But Aristotle's criticism of Platonic ethics is part of a more general objection to Plato's philosophical procedures, which at times he took to be characteristic of metaphysics in general. In his scientific investigations too, he thinks that Plato invokes metaphysical considerations over-readily, thus depriving the particular sciences of the advantages of their proper methodologies. The *Republic* is certainly in his sights: as we have seen, Plato moves to metaphysical claims about the reality of the Forms in order to justify the possibility of objective moral judgements, and in so doing leaves all sorts of non-foundational questions – which he considered less urgent – inadequately treated or altogether neglected. Yet Plato is right that in ethics at least foundational questions, however settled, cannot be avoided, and, as I have shown, Aristotle's divinizing of 'the fine' (*kalon*), viewed as final cause of moral actions, bypasses foundational questions in evoking Platonic ghosts.

Man, according to Aristotle, is an animal capable of specifically human virtues, including 'moral' virtues; he is also an animal capable of specifically human vices. A more robust account of the role and nature of 'the fine' would have enabled Aristotle to explain exactly why we ought *qua* human to excel in virtue rather than in vice. To say that man is specifically rational – which he may well be – will not bridge this gap; we need to know more about the proper use of reason. Without lip-service to the 'fine', practical reason might be merely instrumental, a means to an end beyond its sphere of operation.

If Aristotle has only limited right to Platonic 'goodness', and any more transcendent theology or metaphysic is to be ruled out, a pair of 'post-Kantian' questions confront us in our quest for 'objective' alternatives to Platonic realism: can reason itself provide an adequate basis for morality?; or is reason alone capable only of being the dependant and servant of choice, albeit helpful in producing apt choices? Beyond this latter uncertainty – to which we shall turn later in considering Hume – lie deeper and more dangerous possibilities: what if while reason alone is incapable of the moral role some would assign to it, the contemporary advocacy of choice as the primary good turns out to be unintelligible? Put more bluntly: does the survival in the twenty-first century of 'ethical' theory depend on a blend of the inadequate with the confused? If so, it is clear that the demand for deception and self-deception must become all but irresistible (even if not viewed as simply desirable) – and as more than a means of handling the special exigencies of a political life (as in a democracy) where politicians require different sets of principles for different audiences and occasions. In which case, understanding and approving post-moral reasoning comes to entail not merely the death of traditional ethics but that of philosophy itself as traditionally conceived. Put otherwise, the surcease of ethics can be seen to be parallel to and inextricable from the replacement of truth by assertion and of truth conditions by assertion conditions, as in much contemporary metaphysics.[10]

ARISTOTLE, AQUINAS AND THE GOALS OF LIFE

Attempts to represent Aristotle as a 'practical reasoner' necessarily involve downplaying or even ignoring the claim in book 10 of the *Nicomachean Ethics* that contemplation – which must involve contemplation of God and indeed the attempt to 'immortalize oneself (to become godlike) as much as possible' – is man's primary goal. We strive to be like God because at some level – for Aristotle primarily at that of our mind – we *are* like God. Hence the notorious problem, which this is not the place to tackle in detail, about Aristotle's two goals of human life: first, and as far as possible, the life of contemplation; second the life of action and practical reasoning. Clearly the problem only arises because there exists a semi-Platonic object of contemplation – though, as we have already seen, Aristotle's account of God is too etiolated to serve Plato's purpose.

If the problem of human goals is difficult in Aristotle – and if we must recognize as un-Aristotelian the attempt of practical-reason theorists to forget about the contemplative side of the human good – it becomes even more difficult and of crucial importance in accounts of traditional natural-law theory, above all in that of Thomas Aquinas. For there is no doubt that Aquinas is a Platonist in that he believes in an 'eternal law' which is roughly the Platonic Forms seen in an approximately Augustinian manner as God's thoughts. The first issue, then, is

---

[10] For an introduction to how assertability depends on truth see P. Geach, 'Assertion', *Philosophical Review* 74 (1965), 449–65.

the relationship between this eternal law and what Aquinas and others call natural law. In brief, does Aquinas' (or any other) account of natural law depend directly on the metaphysics of eternal law, or can we show, as most recently Lisska has argued, that Aquinas' theory of natural law can be defended – and was intended to be defended – without reference to the existence of God?[11]

The reason such a defence is thought necessary is to enable a natural-law theory to be presented to secularists on their own terms, and to show such secularists – most of whom believe that Aquinas' theory of natural law depends directly on Platonic realism – that natural-law theories, when stripped of their religious and realist associations, can still be taken seriously: an unexceptionable project if possible. For Aquinas himself, however, obvious difficulties present themselves, not least such passages as *Summa Theologiae* I–II, q. 91 where he maintains that natural law participates in eternal law – in other words that its existence depends on that eternal law.

The problem of whether there *could be* a secular as well as a theistic version of natural-law theory (with necessarily different goals) is resolved not by showing that Thomas's (and Aristotle's) notion of human nature is no static essence but a theory of the dispositional nature of natural kinds – though this is true enough – but by asking what difference it makes to human nature and the possible goals of human life if God exists. Aquinas himself recognizes the problem – partly as a result of reflecting on the Aristotelian goal of contemplation – in his distinction between what he calls man's natural happiness and his perfect happiness (*ST* I–II q. 62 a. 1; cf. I q. 62 a. 1; I–II q. 3 a. 8). Roughly speaking, according to Aquinas, natural happiness, that is, the perfection of man's powers (presumably as possible for Adam before the Fall but no longer even attainable in this life) is Aristotle's goal; while perfect happiness is that perfection of man's potentialities (not only of his original capabilities) which would raise him to the company of the blessed and is only available through the sacrifice of Christ and man's adoption by God.

---

[11] A. J. Lisska, *Aquinas' Theory of Natural Law* (Oxford University Press, 1996), especially 91–138. Lisska's book also provides a useful survey of the various 'theistic' and 'non-theistic' interpretations of Aquinas' metaphysics of morals. In general he follows H. B. Veatch, *For an Ontology of Morals* (Evanston, Ill.: Northwestern University Press, 1971), and *Swimming against the Current in Contemporary Philosophy* (Washington, D.C.: Catholic University of America Press, 1990), the 'current' being represented by A. P. d'Entrèves, *Natural Law* (second revised edition, London: Hutchinson, 1970), and D. J. O'Connor, *Aquinas and Natural Law* (London: Macmillan, 1967). Our present discussion is less concerned with the interpretation of Aquinas than with the philosophical truths at issue.

Of course, the secularist's reading of natural law – as *ipso facto* that of the theist who wishes to cater to the secularist – has to assume that natural happiness is an actual and present (rather than a theoretical) possibility for man, in other words that perfect happiness is added on to it rather than informing it. Lisska, however, holds that 'Were there no trans-terrestrial ultimate end for human beings, the Aristotelian account as modified through Aquinas' theory of natural law would be sufficient for an adequate moral theory.' But this is misleading – even were it the view of Aquinas[12] – not only because the absence of Aquinas' trans-terrestrial end would eviscerate the contemplation, but because just as either there is a God or there is not, so man is either formed by God with an overriding, perfect, 'supernatural' end or he is not. And if he does have such an overriding end, then the natural end will remain not only incomplete but unrealized and unrealizable, a creation of analysis, not a phenomenon of human life. Man can only have 'two ends' if one is ordered to the other, the natural to the 'supernatural'. For Aquinas all human acts are ordered to the contemplation of God as an ultimate end (*Summa Contra Gentiles* 3.37).

Consider certain features of the two possible versions of natural-law theory, secular and theistic. Both rely on right reason to produce a list of goods, but depending on whether God exists or not, right reason will come up with different lists. On the theistic view, not only will the worship and contemplation of God appear as goods necessary for human flourishing, but making room for knowledge of God will affect our understanding of the nature and ordering of other goods which right reason can discover, as of the nature of human virtue itself. If God is love, the virtues will be modes of love and the good life will be a form of loving. If there is no God (or if God is not loving), then they and it will not be, unless loving in and of itself is and can be shown to be the rational course to follow. Or again, if there is no God, it will be no mistake to pursue the natural good without reference to one; but if there is a God, it will be, even though not necessarily a deliberate mistake. The notion that God, if he exists, can be bracketed out of an account of the nature of moral virtue and of human flourishing assuredly makes no sense.

Then consider the adequacy of our powers of reason – which question relates to our moral status as reasoners. Theories of rationality (like that of Rawls), which determine that the most moral course is that prescribed

---

[12] But for the correct reading of Aquinas see B. Ashley, 'What is the End of the Human Person? The Vision of God and Integral Human Fulfilment', in L. Gormally (ed.), *Moral Truth and Moral Tradition: Essays in Honour of Peter Geach and Elizabeth Anscombe* (Dublin: Blackrock, 1994), 68–96.

by practical reason from behind a 'veil of ignorance' about the actual circumstances of our lives, depend – fatally – on our reason operating in a mode, or with knowledge of a mode, in which it does not in fact perform. A similar problem arises with non-realist versions of natural-law theory, both if God (and therefore a supernatural end) exists and if he does not. For we are supposed, despite our present divided and confused state, to be able to recognize our natural end and to put ourselves in a position in which we can work out the rational course by which we are able to flourish. That rational course 'just is' the moral course. But even if our assumed theory of dispositional essence points to a goal to which we naturally 'strive', we cannot assume that striving will enable us to identify any complete set of 'goods', for if it did, we would all be able to recognize all of them. Our behaviour when we do wrong might then be 'acratic' in that we would know the better while doing the worse, but it could not be morally ignorant if, at least, we thought about it. This scenario plainly is not our normal moral world. Of course, if God exists, in terms of a non-realist natural-law theory we remain unable to acknowledge by any striving for our merely natural end any supernatural goods he may have planned for us. At best we can recognize only their natural shadows.

If we were living in our rational paradise, we would at least know that such rational behaviour would undeniably be prudent if we wanted to flourish. We could then say not, 'I ought to do X because X is right', but at least 'I want to do X because I then will flourish and *therefore* I call it doing right.' In default of the rational paradise, we cannot go even that far. If we come up with a 'rationally' acquired list of goods, the list must be more or less the result of intuition. This is the view Finnis seems to attribute to Aquinas, but almost certainly wrongly.[13]

Even supposing that we could come up with our rationally derived list, we would have shown no more than that if we want to flourish, as we have defined flourishing, we would do well to live in a certain way. Some defenders of natural law say we have shown more, following a procedure parallel to that by which Kant generated his categorical imperative. Lisska says that a 'natural-law' argument could parallel Kantian moves, and (p. 205) that 'both philosophers' (that is, Aquinas and Kant) 'have put forth a strikingly similar central theme. Immorality consists in striking

---

[13] For further discussion see Lisska (*Aquinas' Theory*, 157–61), who compares Finnis' position to that of Ross and Moore. It avoids deducing an 'ought' from an 'is', but at too high a price. Lisska's discussion is immediately a rebuttal of the defence of Finnis offered by Robert P. George, 'Natural Law and Human Nature', in *Natural Law Theory: Contemporary Essays* (Oxford University Press, 1992), 31–41.

at the very roots of one's humanity.' How misleading comment at that level of generality can be can be appreciated when we consider that in morality Kant is not concerned with human flourishing but only with the performance of duties, not with our wider humanity but with our rational agency. As I shall show, Kant's categorical (and not merely hypothetical) imperative lacks an adequate accompanying account of the relation between our rationality and our full humanity, and consequently an explanation of who properly counts as a human being. True, he professes a concern for humanity, but we have to consider how far and in what way his theorizing permits him to do so.

If we are a substantial set of dispositional properties tending to a certain end or good, there seem in a non-theistic naturalism to be no more than prudential arguments as to why the human race should *accept* that good. We incidentally may not *want* to be 'human' or 'fully human' in the sense towards which we are pointed, whether by an evolutionary or some other mechanism; so why should we not decline any 'obligation' to be moral, that is choose to make ourselves something else, something 'non-human'? Of course, if we are *designed* by God to go in a certain direction as towards our ultimate and individual end, and if that directedness is the plan of an ultimate goodness, the situation is quite other. In that case, and in that case alone, a choice of immorality is precisely a stupid pride: as Augustine would put it, a mere shadow of virtue. In choosing non-humanity then, we are choosing not only what we wish to be but what we cannot be, while in choosing virtue we are not only choosing rationally but choosing against the negation or at least diminution of our individualized being. In a theistic universe we cannot choose not to be human, but only to be humanly evil: in Platonic terms, bad humans. Typically, the non-theistic naturalist must underplay the significance of evil as an individual phenomenon.

We shall return to non-theistic naturalism; for the present we hypothesize that it can give us no more than a prudential 'ought', and in our present rational inadequacy – as indicated by our divided selves – not even clear guidelines to that. This is true even if we are – as we are only in a restricted sense – essentially sets of dispositional properties. It looks as though the function of Platonic realism – in its integral theistic form – will therefore be twofold: enabling us to test and correct information about 'morality' derived from our perverse and divided inclinations and, as we have noted, from our natural capacity for what is, in the words of Browning, beyond our grasp; turning a possibly plausible and prudential 'morality' of human self-realization into a rule of life where 'ought' bears a sense both objective and genuinely prescriptive, because dependent on a world transcending what is proposed and preferred by an attempted calculation of our self-determined interests.

As for Aquinas' version of natural law, it will stand or fall with the Platonic realism with which it is linked (and with the related and improved 'Aristotelian' account of man as more than rational agent), and not with its occasional overlaps with those Kantian claims about rationality and humanity the inadequacy of which will be shortly examined. There is no possibility (except in analysis) of separating man's 'supernatural' end, if he has one, from his natural end, if he has one, and it seems that Aquinas was of that opinion. For if God exists, any claim that a 'supernatural' end can be simply imposed on a natural end, and therefore that a natural end is an existential possibility without it, must be rejected. I do not have to consider further whether, in introducing an ultimate 'supernatural' end to which human nature is ordained, Aquinas gives an adequate account of whether or how the concept of human nature must be more widely transformed by the additional truths proposed to us in specifically *Christian* theism.

OLD BATTLES TRANSFORMED: HUME AND NATURALISM

'All morality depends upon our sentiments and when any action, or quality of the mind, pleases us after a certain manner, we *say* it is virtuous, and when the neglect, or non-performance of it, displeases us after a like manner, we *say* that we lie under an obligation to perform it' (Hume).

Aquinas offers us a theory of nature, including human nature, as founded and ordered by God. The universe, including man, is purposive, and human reason (aided by revelation) can determine God's purposes for man in that providential universe, which can be rationally approached through (Aristotelian and Platonic) metaphysics. One of the effects of the Reformation was to dethrone metaphysics, in the hope of replacing it by Biblical exegesis, Jerome being scheduled to replace Augustine as patron-saint-in-chief. Hence especially in lands where the effects of Protestantism were strong, we shall not be surprised to find an attempt to restate human nature in non-metaphysical terms:[14] if God is to be

---

[14] T. Penelhum, 'Hume's Moral Psychology', in D. F. Norton (ed.), *The Cambridge Companion to Hume* (Cambridge University Press, 1993), 143, suggests that Hume is 'a neo-Hellenistic thinker', who 'follows the Stoics and Epicureans and Sceptics in maintaining that we should avoid anxiety by following nature'. It is true that the period from Descartes to Kant is in a way the Hellenistic age of modern philosophy. Certain features of Hume's thought (not least the concept of sympathy) recall the Stoics, but he differs from them in his largely godless view of human nature as a whole.

introduced, he is to be the God of the voluntarists and his nature beyond the reasoning of metaphysics. From an unknowable God we move fast to an irrelevant God, and eventually to his elimination as superfluous. Yet atheism and scepticism are not the only options, for we might revert to some re-Platonized or Neoplatonized form of Christianity.

I adverted in chapter 3 to the fact that the origins of recent claims that human completion can be achieved by the Way of Politics – that is, paradigmatically, by engagement in the promotion of democracy or in democratic activism – are to be found in the early modern period. In light of the anti-metaphysical trends dominant in the Protestantism that developed in the sixteenth, seventeenth and eighteenth centuries, we can expect it to be among the Protestant states of northern Europe that civic virtue without metaphysics will appear. I have already considered Hobbes' view of the brutish 'state of nature', and there is a sense in which Hobbes was among those who set the stage for an extraordinarily transformed version of an old confrontation: between Thrasymacheanism and the 'new' naturalism of eighteenth-century Britain.

Hobbes, though, was not the only precursor of the clash between that Thrasymachus *redivivus*, Bernard Mandeville, and the 'moral sense' of his opponents, Frances Hutcheson and, most importantly, David Hume. For present purposes we need not linger over Grotius, Pufendorf, Locke or the Cambridge Platonists, but they deserve passing comment if I am to show how the new Thrasymacheanism of Mandeville represented a serious challenge.

Grotius offers an account of nature whereby morality can be justified and those who reduce it to self-interest can be refuted 'even if (which cannot be granted without the greatest wickedness) there is no God', or at least no providence. Certainly for Grotius, while the existence of God and our obligation to obey him provide an additional reason to be moral, nature alone, as interpreted by man's natural reason and in light both of his desire for society and his ability to formulate and act upon general rules of conduct, is an adequate source of moral obligation, in that we recognize an obligation to do whatever will best provide us with a well-ordered society. The importance of Grotius is that he thus raises the question as to whether nature alone (without God or any other 'realist' possibility) supplies the basis for moral obligation.

Hobbes, Pufendorf and Locke took up the challenge, denying morality any basis in nature. In Hobbes, as we have seen, there is a revival of the thesis that we contract into 'morality' and 'rights', which are contrary to nature, to save our skins; for Pufendorf (and Locke) God has to be reintroduced: God by *fiat* created a set of moral obligations (as part of natural law) by his absolute will imposed on creation. In response to that (as well as to various more directly Calvinist provocations), there arise more 'realist' proposals from Cudworth and other 'Platonists': God commands what is just (in the spirit of Plato's *Euthyphro*), and thus it is not solely by virtue of his arbitrary command that what is just is just.

Cudworth's position is 'old rationalist' in claiming that Neoplatonic realities like Goodness (understood more in the spirit of Proclus than of Plato or Plotinus) are accessible to (aided) human reason, even though more or less contemporary natural moralists like Pufendorf and Locke (not to speak of Hobbes) consider that without metaphysics rational morality can only be saved by positing a voluntarist God. In other words, where Cudworth offers a metaphysic laced with rather attenuatedly Christian theism, Pufendorf and Locke promote a voluntarist God as metaphysics substitute. The more fundamental question broached by Grotius and set squarely on the table by Hobbes was: what if there is no voluntarist God, no metaphysical deity of a Platonist sort, no attainment of *morality* through reason? Is it inevitable that in the long run Hobbes will triumph?

A way out of the impasse was offered first by Shaftesbury, then by Hutcheson. Hobbes – as we noted – had proposed a highly implausible thesis, for even if most of us on most occasions behave as Hobbesians, we are not all Hobbesians all the time. Grant that reason cannot find a metaphysical space for God or morality, yet our sympathy for others, however limited, must be accounted for, and it will transpire that we have a moral *sense* by virtue of which we at times act benevolently and even altruistically.

Shaftesbury's moral sense theory is primarily offered as a critique of Hobbes, and he concedes most of Hobbes' claims as to the instrumentality of reason. In contrast with Cudworth and agreement with Hobbes, he denies all metaphysical foundation for morality and *a fortiori* the ability of reason to guide us to such a foundation. The dispute between Shaftesbury and Hobbes is over the nature of human nature: is it or is it not entirely selfish? It was against the background of this dispute that in 1723 Bernard Mandeville, 'Epicurean' and 'atheist', published a revised version of his *The Fable of the Bees*, part 1 of which is entitled *An Enquiry into the Origin of Moral Virtue*.[15] If we prescind from his ultimate

[15] The text was edited by F. B. Kaye (Oxford University Press, 1924). For an overview of Mandeville's position see E. G. Hundert, *The Enlightenment's Fable* (Cambridge University Press, 1994). For his Epicureanism (not least on questions of language) see esp. 93–6.

aim – apparently to show how private vices are the necessary condition of public virtue and of the continuation of civilized society – we can recognize that Mandeville ('Man-devil') offers a theory of morality remarkably like that of Thrasymachus: we all are motivated by self-interest, though only a few recognize this fact. These few, as Thrasymachus had claimed, can take advantage of the doltish majority's easy acceptance of unexamined moral notions to exercise control over their fellows, duping them into accepting an invented 'morality' specifically in tune with their own purposes for society. As Mandeville magniloquently concludes (1.51), 'Moral virtues are the Political Offspring which Flattery begot upon Pride.'

Hume (following the earlier assaults of Hutcheson, Butler and Berkeley) alludes to Mandeville at the beginning of the *Treatise* (Introduction, xvii) and sets out to refute him, as also Hobbes and an assortment of rationalists and voluntarists. Mandeville had repeated Thrasymachus' mistake of treating largely of public rather than private virtues, and Hume objects to this. However since, like Thrasymachus, Mandeville's views could easily be rewritten in a more modern and totalitarian manner to include the private within the public and political sphere, more serious is Hume's objection – the same as he makes to Hobbes – that we are not all naturally brutal all of the time: 'It is sufficient for our present purpose if it be allowed, what surely, without the greatest absurdity cannot be disputed, that there is some benevolence, however small, infused into our bosom, some spark of friendship for human kind; some particle of the dove kneaded into our frame, along with the elements of the wolf and the serpent' (*Enquiry concerning the Principles of Morals* 9.1, p. 225, Selby-Bigg/Nidditch).

Still, we cannot but wonder whether Hume does justice to Mandeville's position. Even feelings of pity, according to Mandeville, arise because – for example over seeing a baby about to fall into a fire – we save ourselves the pain of remorse if we do not try to help it (1.56). Admittedly this is far-fetched and question-begging, but since Hume believes it is in virtue of an assumed moral sense or instinct, and not of reason, that we act 'mercifully', and since, as we shall see, his own objectivism in morals is inadequate, it is not clear why he should convince his Thrasymachean opponent that he has made a serious mistake.

For Hume rejects outright, as well as the God of the voluntarists, any sort of Platonism. Any transcendental being is beyond the reach of our reason which, being merely instrumental and inert, cannot distinguish right from wrong, good from bad, by appeal to a higher realm. Morality for Hume is simply written into human nature and so can only be grasped with reference to that nature: to know morality's foundations we would need to understand human nature and so recognize within it that moral sense in virtue of which alone he thinks Hobbes and Mandeville can be controverted.

Any Platonist will agree with Hume that we are all aware of moral issues, that, as Charles Taylor puts it, we live in moral space. But to be aware of moral issues is not to have a sense of what precisely is right and wrong, or even that there is a defensible difference between right and wrong. Hume divides the virtues into two groups, natural and artificial. Natural virtues exist in man *qua* man; they include generosity and concern for one's children. Artificial virtues arise in the course of time as a result of man's 'sympathetic' interactions with his fellows in society. So far we see no sense of moral obligation. Hume has stated that, as matter of fact, we possess as individuals certain benevolent qualities – that just is how we are: no need to ask why – and others we develop over time. From a philosopher who famously observed the fallacy of deriving 'ought' from 'is' (*Treatise* 3.1.1), we surely have the right to expect some reason why what is normally the case (Most people are at times and some are frequently kindly) ought to be the case. If Hume cannot provide this, then Mandeville can reply that while he grants most of us are benevolent (or seem to be so), there is still no reason why those who 'know better' ought to be benevolent rather than be such as to take advantage of the common run of naive fools and suckers.

It is important to recognize just how serious this possible challenge is, for it presumably is because they judge that Hume has failed to meet it that our contemporary quasi-realists proclaim that we must act *as if* there are real moral values 'out there' even though there are not, while our sensibility theorists want to liken such values to Lockean secondary qualities which appear to emerge from the interactions of persons. I doubt though whether Hume himself, their supposed progenitor, would have accepted these solutions. His account of obligation is rather different, depending in the first instance on a claim (which perhaps his own theory of personal identity might block) that human nature is fixed. Perhaps that looks acceptable: I have myself argued and shall argue again that there are limits both physical and mental which ideological reformers cannot traverse in their attempts to construct New Man (or New Woman). But Hume's claim is much more specific, namely that humans usually behave in particular ways and if individuals behave otherwise, they are blamed. They are blamed because they have failed to act rightly, which is, they have failed to do their duty or what is expected of them.

Hume's position is that moral obligation is the required performance of those actions which ordinary decent people expect, supposing them to be 'natural'. When we are thus properly disappointed with someone's behaviour, we say that he or she ought to have acted otherwise. Prescinding from the question whether, for Hume, it is possible to act otherwise,[16] we can predict Mandeville's likely response: 'I agree that most people expect, say, a parent to look after his or her children, but where is the obligation if self-interest tells him to act otherwise?' And there is further difficulty: just as Hume seems to confuse the view that we live unavoidably in moral space with the more dubious claim that we are able to sense the rightness and wrongness of specific behaviours (but only, it seems, by noting the approbation or disapprobation of our fellows), so if we noted, for example, that we all (unalterably by nature) value what we call beauty, would we have to conclude that we are all able to recognize by way of similar approbation or disapprobation more or less the same things as beautiful?

In light of the above, it is not surprising that Hume's list of virtues is conventional, and more or less fitting the standards of the eighteenth-century English gentleman. Hume thus incidentally resembles Aristotle in his inclination to suppose that his own culture provides the best models for moral worth – and indeed what else can he do, since he relies not on any reason to work out possibilities, but on a moral sense which can only be formed by local (and contemporary) societal conditions (whether or not taken to be universal conditions)? Nor, as we have seen, will he allow himself to venture beyond human nature as presently 'apparent': 'It is needless to push our researches so far as to ask, why we have humanity or fellow feeling for others. It is sufficient, that this is experienced to be a principle in human nature.'

Thus Hume does not commit his self-condemned error of deriving obligations from facts; instead he derives them from conventional expectations: we rightfully regard what is generally expected in a 'decent' society as an obligation. But we shall be more or less consistent in doing so, and Hume again, probably against Mandeville and his like, claims that since these more or less consistent expectations can be enunciated in a more or less coherent moral language, that in itself is evidence that they reflect a given state of nature.

Mandeville's view that our expectations result from the 'artifice' of political manipulators is far-fetched; yet he need not be discomfited by

---

[16] See recently on Hume's 'liberty of indifference' Penelhum, 'Hume's Moral Psychology', 130–2.

this either: a more sophisticated version of his position would be not that specific political manipulators invented the language of morality but that they contrive to take advantage of the 'pre-philosophical' phenomenon that given societies employ (unthinkingly) sets of moral terms. The political manipulator thus profits from the implications of a supposed second fact – viz. that moral *truths* lie behind linguistic encodings – to organize society with an eye to his preferred interests. Hume claims that Mandeville's position is like that of an optician who could show people without sight how to use colour terms correctly (*Treatise* 3.2; 3.3.1; *Enquiry concerning the Principles of Morals* 5.1.2.4). Mandeville could retort that the gullible public, while able to use moral language consistently, is victim to the self-regarding delusion that morality 'exists'.

We are now in a position to recognize how contemporary 'quasi-realism' is a consequence of Hume's position. Societies expect to use moral vocabularies, and we can treat *that expectation* as the source of 'duty', without believing that the injunctions it provides 'really' have more moral force than the conventions which the various societies can impose. In the wake of Hume these 'quasi-realists' argue that to accept the expectations of a 'decent' society as duties is useful, indeed necessary, for the maintenance of that society. Pragmatically and statistically this may be true: societies might well collapse if the majority in them followed the precepts of Thrasymachus/Mandeville. Mandeville's point is precisely that there is no fear of that, since only the select few will accept and exploit the actual *lack* of obligation to follow the conventional paths which the Humean naturalist proposes. In a sense the quasi-realist 'improves' on Hume by following Mandeville, having learned that deception is requisite if conventional aspirations and ideals are to be achieved, whereas Hume seems to suppose that we will accept his contention that expectation equals obligation if and when it is thought proper by the generality within the society itself. Apart from the weakness of calling an expectation an obligation, Hume seems to think that the would-be Thrasymachus will in fact profit from accepting the conventions – precisely what Mandeville (and Thrasymachus) deny, nor is any reason offered by the naturalists as to why their opponents should change their minds.

In light of the above we can finally return to the moral sense. I have argued that Hume confuses a sense of living in a moral universe with a sense of what materially is right and wrong – and that his conventionalism can only confirm such an error, as is precisely what we should expect of a 'moral sense' theory, since the moral sense must be governed by the unexamined consensus of the society around it. For Hume, reason cannot help in this. Reason can show the moral sense whether its objectives are within the realm of possibility, but not whether they are 'right' or 'wrong'. Then would a non-instrumental rationality do any better? The answer must be No, unless it were teleologically 'constituted' to aim (at least when purged of non-rational accretions) at what really *is good* for man (and not merely seems useful). Unless so constituted it might indeed identify certain goods as well as the means to attain them, but without the ability to order and rank them. I conclude that with or without merely instrumental rationality Hume and his naturalist successors – despite their legitimate correction of Hobbesian pessimism about human nature – are as naive in their attempts to salvage universal moral obligations as Mandeville might surely consider them.

Moral sense theories are thus no substitute for Platonic realism; the very most they can offer, if purged of wishful thinking about expectations, is the claim that we have moral obligations though we cannot know what they are, leading in practice to the substitution of a Pyrrhonist relativism ('Follow the customs of the country!') for the supposed 'expectation theory'. It remains to consider whether a Kantian rather than a Humean account of rationality can save the non-realist promise of daylight.

KANT AND POST-KANTIAN PRACTICAL REASONING

Despite the revival of various forms of virtue-ethics, philosophers claiming allegiance to Kant, together with consequentialists (whose inadequate concern with means to ends – as witnessed by their treatment of 'dirty hands' – has largely left them outside this enquiry), still dominate the contemporary ethical scene. For Humean naturalists reason is essentially instrumental, but Kantians claim practical reason as much richer since it can identify a 'kingdom of ends'. If Aristotle has to rely on a residual Platonism for a similar purpose, are we to suppose that Kantian advocates of the objective morality of 'practical reason' are able to do without something similar or does Kant himself not have an analogous though different sort of back-up? Kantianisms certainly are moralities of duty, but does the Kantian account of reason justify the duties specified? Kant introduced the concept of autonomy into ethics, but understood autonomy not in terms of choosing or the ability to express preferences, but in the very different terms of our rational ability to formulate maxims which allow no special consideration to be given to ourselves. Such universalizable maxims, necessarily impersonal in that they must allow no exceptions to be made in the interest of our own happiness, are the constructs of the rational will; as Kant significantly calls it, the holy will.

Kant offers several versions of his Categorical Imperative, two of which are of particular interest. He holds that we should act 'only on that maxim through which you can at the same time will that it should become a universal law' (*Groundwork* IV, 421); alternatively that we should act 'in such a way that you always treat humanity whether in your own person or in the person of any other never simply as a means, but always at the same time as an end' (*Groundwork* IV, 429). The strength of Kant's position depends on the practical equivalence he claims for these two formulations. In considering this equivalence, we should bear in mind that the Categorical Imperative is not intended to generate a specific moral code but to test the worth of proposals for moral action. Proposals are only morally worthy if they meet its rigorous requirements, and the chief of these has to be that they must depend on maxims which are universalizable and therefore themselves morally worthy. I suggest that the relationship between the two formulations is such that those maxims which are thus revealed as morally worthy will turn out to be those which treat persons as ends and never simply as means, and that this is what Kant means when he says that the formula of universalizability is the form of morality while the formula of persons and ends is the matter (*Groundwork* IV, 436).

If we ask why the test of universalizability will eliminate proposals which treat people as means, the answer seems to be that no proposal which aims to injure can do other than damage the victim's ability to act autonomously. A maxim that we should always coerce would entail that at least some (probably many) individuals would themselves become unable to coerce. Hence in acting upon such a maxim a man would be inconsistent in both willing that a maxim become universal law and at the same time preventing others from adopting it. We should notice, however, that Kant's construction depends on four claims: (a) that we are all similar insofar as we are rational beings; (b) the impersonality thesis: that it is rational to treat such similar beings similarly; (c) that we know who are to be counted as rational beings, since we know who are rational agents; (d) that being a rational agent in the required sense constitutes being human. All these claims – not least the last, as we have already observed – are dubious, and Kant's attitude to benevolent behaviour over and above the call of universal duties also suggests that he has further hidden premisses. For benevolence seems to be a duty precisely because some or all human beings (especially children) are *inadequately effective* rational agents when left to themselves. Of course, there may be little confidence to be placed in Kant's hope that if assisted they will be adequately capable of rational agency.

Kant formulates his concept of morality for rational agents, of whom humans are a subclass. But who precisely are to be counted as members of the class, and on what criteria? If all are *strictly* rational agents, that would, at the least, exclude children born as unborn and the senile – indeed the exclusion list would be much wider if we are required to act *fully* in accordance with reason. Kantians offer no adequate guidelines as to who is a rational agent and who is therefore, at least in what potential sense, autonomous. Nor is scope the only problem: I have argued that 'metaphysical' ethicists are right in denying that humanity is limited to moral agency, since this may not even be our highest capacity. Kant himself, in wishing to treat all persons as ends – persons certainly not being here limited to those capable of active moral agency – seems to allow that though moral activity is essential for rational agents capable of it, it does *not* sum up their humanity.

A further set of related problems for Kant himself, though not usually for neo-Kantians and 'practical reasoners', arises from Kant's bifurcation of the human being into his rational and moral self (which is autonomous) and his passions, desires, affections, inclinations, etc., which if followed make him heteronomous. It is questionable that human nature and functions can be so neatly divided, and if they can, the first casualties would appear to be virtues such as friendship and love, despite Kant's insistence that treating others as ends entails according them both respect and (love or) active benevolence. He holds that we have a duty to seek the autonomous happiness of others; yet we may reasonably wonder about the nature of the happiness that Kant is able to vindicate, since he sees morality primarily as the promotion of a strict and impersonal justice as fairness. I have argued in the previous chapter that respect for human nature and human excellence is diminished if advocated primarily in these terms.

Kant's problems, however, run deeper. Morality is concerned with imposing maxims on ourselves, with telling ourselves, *qua* rational agents, to respect other rational agents. But first, we are not substitutable agents, even if our rationality, *qua* rationality, is 'substitutable'. At the very least, even if *qua* rational agent I am exactly similar to someone else, I am not identical with anyone else *qua* person. Why then, ignoring that difference, should I refuse to make an exception in my own interest? And why suppose that necessarily where I do not ignore it I act irrationally, *ergo* immorally? In brief, even if my rationality is of the same kind as that of the rationality of others, it will not be irrational to suppose that it is still unique to me *qua* unique person.

There is more. How can I do my duty if I obtain no personal satisfaction *at all* from doing my duty, being allowed no such satisfaction under pain of acting heteronomously? Having abandoned the Platonic notion of rationality where only a conceptual distinction can be made between knowing (or believing) a good and wanting that good, Kant, operating on a rationalist (or Cartesian) concept of pure practical reason, must fall victim to Hume: if the dutiful man obtains no personal satisfaction from being dutiful, acting solely because it is his duty, he lacks motivation and *cannot* act at all. Kant condemns him to giving commands to himself which he has no intelligible motive and therefore no ability to obey.

Kant's moral theory can be shown to rely *inter alia* on a set of motiveless, if rational commands, and the useful but ultimately fortuitous test of universalizability which leaves a set of maxims identifiable by the common feature of treating humans as ends and not merely as means. We have seen something of the internal difficulties of these claims. In philosophy, however, as we have observed, ideas are not attractive merely because they are intellectually compelling, but often because they combine hitherto underestimated features of past thinking with the importunities of a later age. Kant's was an age which valued rationality and certain forms of freedom, Kant himself being in this matter under the influence of Rousseau.

With his attempt to separate the pursuit of happiness from morality, and with his claim that persons are privileged as sources of a 'holy will' and should *therefore* be treated always as ends and never as mere means, Kant has highlighted a fundamental question of ethics more effectively than had been achieved hitherto. The question, broached but rarely faced in post-Platonic philosophy, concerns the *precise* relationship between the strictly 'moral' life – that is, the life of decision between right and wrong – and the good life as a whole. We have observed a certain awareness of this in the Stoics, as also the narrowness of the Stoic solution in that the latter can be collapsed into the former. We are now faced with what can reasonably be construed as Kant's revised version of Stoicism, as well as with some of its roots. We are also in a position to raise what will turn out to be the closely related question of whether a Kantian moral life will resolve or at least diminish the problematic of the divided self.

Among a variety of themes introduced into ethics by way of Christianity, several persist subterraneously in Kant. One is the view of morality as obedience to the commands of an omnipotent and omniscient God – whence come urgent problems about the nature of such commands and the relation of the command itself to the morality commanded.[17] With only a few exceptions, Christian accounts of divine command morality have emphasized (even when they have often failed to explain) not that God has commanded an arbitrary moral universe which he could change by another fiat of his omnipotent will, but that he 'commands' us to act in accordance with the goodness of his own nature as being *ipso facto* the goodness of ours. This goodness may not lack appeal for the non-theist; however, for the theist wrongdoing now becomes *also* a matter of obedience, since to do wrong is not only to act against the Good, but *also* to be disobedient to God. It is no longer merely a question of proposing or arguing that certain acts are objectively wrong: we are now told that this wrongness can also be accepted (even where unargued for) on the authority of God himself. An ethical system thus developed under the banner of obedience – and its counterpart, inerrancy – is going to be more exigent than any secular version. For example, the problem of exceptions to moral prohibitions cannot be so lightly passed by.

In effect, what Kant (and some of his successors) have done – and what his Stoic predecessors could never do – is to retain the overriding claims of 'strict morality' and obedience to duty, originally backed by what was taken for God's will, and over against other (say, more Aristotelian) aspects of the 'good life', within increasingly secularized moral systems. Despite his exigent morality, however, Kant manages to retain the Christian claim that the good man is capable of self-unification (of which God is still the ultimate guarantor), but only by the agency of the purified moral will. For to provide psychological backing for his split between morality and happiness, as we have seen, he makes an *ad hoc* distinction – entailing considerable difficulties in motivation of duties – between our noumenal (mental/spiritual) self and our empirical concerns with happiness and self-interest. This distinction, even if plausible, would only strengthen the apparent divisions of the self which we discussed earlier, and so it is the normal practice of post-Kantians to dump the apparently 'impossible psychology', leaving Kant a virtual Stoic in that his real self

---

[17] Plato had already raised difficulties about the relationship between the preferences of the gods and morality in the *Euthyphro*, which has accordingly been much discussed. See recently especially N. Kretzmann, 'Abraham, Isaac and Euthyphro: God and the Basis of Morality' in D. V. Stump, J. A. Arieti, L. P. Gerson and E. Stump (eds.), *Hamartia: The Concept of Error in the Western Tradition* (New York and Toronto: Mellen Press, 1983), 27–50. Important though Plato realized the question to be, its importance is much enhanced if the gods (or God) are seen as omnipotent, as in Judaism and Christianity.

is the potentially pure and rational will alone and themselves as at best bastard children whose parent would certainly not own them. It also leaves Kant's a deist world in which we must think of morality as a set of rules and prohibitions – 'divine' commands given by us to ourselves which we must obey simply because they embody what we ought to obey as rational beings, and least of all because it is *good for us* so to do.

We thus seem to retain the 'theistic' imperative, but in the form of a command without a morally omniscient commander, and a command which is good because universally and rationally commanded, not because of its content or because of what it secures for us. Of course, there is some sort of commander in each one of us, not because we are able to command what we want but insofar as we command what is rational. Yet if obedience must be given to our self-commands simply and solely because they are rational, it follows both that rationality is the source of duty – which seems to be no necessity but a mere possibility – and that rationality is the most valuable feature of the human universe: a claim which, whatever value rationality has, we have no good reason to accept as it stands. Indeed for Kant, rationality should not only be the only intrinsically valuable phenomenon in the universe; it should be the source of value for everything else. In contemporary 'constructivist' accounts of Kant, this feature of his thought is much emphasized, rational choice appearing as a value-*conferring* property – a view directly opposed to the 'practical reasoning' of Aristotle.[18]

Kant seems committed not simply to the claim that good acts are rational but that they are good simply and solely because they are rational. It is true that he also thought that the existence of God is a precondition for ethics – in that it underwrites the conviction that obedience to duty *will ultimately* be compatible with happiness – but his inability to show how the effects of God as that precondition can be seen in 'moral' expectations and his de facto relegation of them to the moral sidelines might seem to justify the attitudes of those more recent 'Kantian' prescriptivists and constructivists who allow God to disappear altogether. For Kant, though insisting on God's necessity – and despite his secularized divine command theory – actively subverts God's significance, making him, like a *deus ex machina*, look like a concession to a bearable ethic, which concession should rationally only be allowed if he is given a far greater and more responsible role.

---

[18] For this sort of interpretation of Kant see, for example, C. Korsgaard, 'Kant's Formula of Humanity', *Kant-Studien* 77 (1980), 181–202. For Aristotle's opposite view, *Metaphysics* 1072A28–29.

Kant's splitting of the moral subject between reason and the inclinations, and his consequent diminution of the self, leads him to problems about duties to oneself. If persons are to be respected as ends and our moral deliberations and reflections are to be more than simply prudential, taking account of others only where logic and common sense demand it, then we shall respect all others and consider their good, insofar as we can, in the same way as we respect our own. Kant, however, wants to emphasize that our duties to others differ strikingly from our duties to ourselves. In the latter case – but markedly less in the former – our duties may well coincide with our inclinations; thus we are inclined not to commit suicide, but we refuse suicide on properly moral grounds only if we (hypothetically) decline to take our own life when we have lost the inclination to live.[19] Kant does not deny that self-regarding inclinations are necessary and desirable, but he holds that they are not moral. Morality is concerned with treating and respecting others in the way in which one would treat and respect oneself as a rational subject. The distinction between self-regarding and other-regarding duties is the origin of a more radical, though currently popular distinction between altruism and egoism: a distinction which, in its common form in which altruism (concern for others) is the essence of morality, is not Kantian. Yet in proposing that where there is inclination there can be no morality as such, Kant laid the groundwork for it, for it is at least plain that we are much more inclined to look to our duties to ourselves precisely because they correspond to our inclinations, and from that it is a short but fatal step to say that where there is duty it is always to others and that it is distinct from any inclination – hence arises the contrast between altruism and egoism, and 'egoism' is made problematic. It is, of course, in a combination of morality as dutiful altruism with a Kantian account of dispassionate rationality – and not in Kant's wider picture of the moral agent as a whole – that many recent theories of practical reasoning situate themselves. Such un-Kantian developments have the advantage, however, of being the more combinable with the 'Humean' view that morality is merely a set of rational constraints designed or agreed upon by each of us as protection against common selfishness.

In moralities of altruism, especially where accompanied by the abandonment of any Platonic or Augustinian realism, we can recognize a

---

[19] On self-regarding duties in Kant see M. Paton, 'A Reconsideration of Kant's Treatment of Duties to Oneself', *Philosophical Quarterly* 40 (1990), 222–32. Those who downplay Kant's retention of duties to oneself seem to feel obliged to attribute to him an unfortunately legalistic model of duty as obligation, thus raising the pseudo-problem of who is obligated to whom.

threat to yet another principle of a genuine Aristotelian, Platonic or Augustinian ethic, namely the concern to maintain and assert one's own worth. A sharp antithesis between egoism and altruism undercuts the thesis that the inclination to be concerned about oneself – by all admitted to be open to dire abuse – is nonetheless a positive, even a positively moral feature of human nature. Of course, all Platonizing theories judge self-concerned behaviour as moral not in terms of what, as we have noticed, is sometimes ambiguously styled 'self-realization' or 'self-fulfilment',[20] but, at least in part, in terms of its promotion of personal spiritual growth, of an integral flourishing, of the ability to use one's various capacities for the best, and so on. Very specifically, they invite us to keep asking whether it is appropriate, self-improving, even 'soul-making', for *me* to act in such and such a fashion.

Even in Kantian terms such questioning should hardly be misguided, though insofar as there is an inclination to it, it may not be allowed to be 'moral'. If I may not by experience know what will make my soul better, how can I know in any *enabling* way – rather than merely by way of restraints on my inclinations – how to benefit anyone else, or rather what is the *content* of my 'duty' to anyone else? If such experience is stifled, morality itself, as originally viewed as a striving for constructive altruism, soon degenerates and may not undeservedly acquire a bad name, at worst standing condemned as a set of 'puritanical' restrictions perhaps defensible (though not by Kant) as enlightened self-interest, but, as we see, making for hypocrisy.

The undercover Christianity of Kant's ethics is not limited to his secularized version of divine-command theory with its set of rational duties. We should consider why his formulation of the principle that one should treat others as ends and never merely as means is supposed equivalent to, or derived from, his rule that one should act in such a way as to follow a self-proposed general law to which one's own adherence is *mandatory*: as that wrongdoers should be punished, and that the lawgiver is not exempt from the law. As we have seen, such formulations depend on the claim that not only is the purely rational agent a source of prudential judgements, but that he is to be valued and respected *qua* rational, indeed respected above all else as the creator of values. But from that it must follow that I should respect and want to respect *myself*, *qua* rational agent at least to the degree to which I respect anyone else, in which case and

---

[20] These essentially Romantic notions are often wrongly presented as Aristotelian. See the interesting comments of P. Pettit, 'Liberal/Communitarian', in *After MacIntyre*, 193.

pace Kant morality here *confirms* inclination. More seriously, as I have already observed, that '"X is rational" entails "X is to be respected above all else"' – assumed for different motives both by Kant himself and by many 'practical reasoners' – goes substantially undefended, even if it is defensible.

For firstly, it is not self-evident in what sense rationality as such is supremely valuable as end rather than merely as means: we have already asked who would want to be *just rational*, and how, in any case, one could be conferring value simply in making a definitively rational choice. Secondly, if rationality is thus valuable, we can conclude that *only* insofar as an agent is rational should he be judged valuable by others and *only* insofar as they are rational. Such a conclusion might be inaccurate, but if correct, and if Kant were thus committed to what at times seems the Aristotelian position that human beings differ in value (and therefore deserve different degrees of respect and honour) *in proportion to* their rationality,[21] that would be clearly contrary to his view whereby *all* persons should be treated as ends. In fact, Kant (and many of his descendants) can be seen to have accepted on inadequate warrant a thesis not merely about rationality and the worth of persons but more crucially about their equal and also substantial worth. We will examine more precisely how this has happened.

Kant's moral theory invokes several arresting claims about persons: first that they should all be treated equally and respectfully as ends. It is not difficult to see that this produces for him results analogous to those which the notion of an inspirational and transcendent *kalon* secures in the world of Aristotle, namely the conversion of an ethic of prudently rational activity into a personalized morality: in Kant's case one of equal respect for desiderately autonomous persons.

Rather as the Aristotelian *kalon* seems to be a hangover from a general Greek 'transcendental' folk wisdom of which Plato had provided a very sophisticated philosophical justification – entailing the projecting of esoteric metaphysical entities – so the Kantian view, it has often been recognized, is a further secularization of Protestant Christianity. Equal and substantial respect for persons as ends is no mere variant on, let alone derivative from, the precept that we should follow universalizable maxims: it is either a desirable supplement to it or an incidental insight about the nature of the moral universe with which such maxims leave us, but

---

[21] See J. M. Rist, 'Aristotle: The Value of Man and the Origin of Morality', *Canadian Journal of Philosophy* 4 (1974), 167–79.

which derives its origin elsewhere: presumably from a (Protestantizing) understanding of the thesis that man is created in God's image.

Following Kantian maxims may prevent us from mistreating persons, but envisaging only our universal obligations, it will not account for the sum total of our moral obligations to others, let alone more personal, friendly or loving relationships. As for the post-Kantian practical reasoners, most wish to justify respect for rights, duties and even Kantian forms of 'autonomy', while specifically disclaiming even those fragments of Christian theology – and *a fortiori* the notion of man as created in the image of God – which in effect underscore Kant's portrait of man. Some modern Kantianisms, however, are in part re-Christianized to be offered in defence of an approximation to Christian ethics, as in the differing proposals of Alan Donagan and Germain Grisez.[22]

Curiously enough, hidden versions of Christian themes peep out from among secular post-Kantians more times even than from Kant himself. For example, returning to the 'post-Kantian' problem of altruism, we note that a prominent feature of that pietist Lutheranism familiar to Kant has never been more explicitly emphasized than by the twentieth-century theologian Rudolf Bultmann: namely that the correct interpretation of the Biblical text 'Love your neighbour as yourself' is as 'Love your neighbour [and not yourself] in the future in the way in which you loved yourself in the past [that is, in your unredeemed days].' This approach to the interpretation of basic Christianity, whereby the present is viewed not as renewing the past but as replacing it, has obvious resemblance to secular derivatives of Kantian theory and to certain versions of the contemporary contrast between egoism and altruism. The theological claim that it is correct to value others without restriction in the way in which one *used* to value oneself is paralleled in the post-Kantian

---

[22] For discussion of the latter's view see especially Ashley, 'What is the End of the Human Person?' Ashley examines the proposals of Grisez (as of J. Finnis, J. Boyle and other proponents of what is sometimes called 'new natural-law theory') who attempts – upholding an ultimately Christian ethic but eager to debate with secular moralists – to defend the autonomy of ethics and its liberation from much traditional (Thomistic) 'anthropology'. He argues that this project would be repudiated by Aquinas while still lacking the resources to defend natural-law theory against its contemporary opponents. He might have compared the new 'natural lawyers' with the 'transcendental Thomists' of an earlier generation, for just as these thought that to debate with Kantians they must take on Kantian 'metaphysics' (thus turning Aquinas into a Kantian epistemologist), so the new natural lawyers try to replace genuine Thomistic ethics with a combination of Hume and Kant. This gets them hopelessly bogged down (as Aquinas is not) both in problems of commensurability, and in a Stoicizing quagmire of the good life as in effect the moral life, inadequate room being left for a serious account of human culture and achievement. For similar contemporary mistreatment of Socrates see T. Irwin, *Plato's Ethics* (Oxford University Press, 1977), 100–1, with the comments of E. de Strycker and S. R. Slings, *Plato's Apology of Socrates* (Leiden: Brill, 1994), 130, note 9.

moral universe by claims that it is morally correct to respect others with no corresponding obligation to self-respect – reduced to, perhaps even defended as, egoism.

Of course, between the theological and the secular versions of the 'Lutheran' theme there are differences, and these are damning to the secular version. In the theological version, other people are to be valued for two reasons which may be connected (though to work out such interconnections would take us well beyond the scope of the present enquiry). The first is that to act in the theologically correct fashion is to obey a divine command; the second is that Lutheran Christianity retained something of the older Judaeo-Christian teaching that human beings are valuable because they are made in the image of God, the source of all value – and that despite the Lutheran theory they lost that value in the Fall.

Clearly, within a broadly Lutheran context these reasons fall within the overriding parameters of a belief in God which has almost disappeared from clear view in the Kantian shadow version – not to speak of avowedly secular post-Kantianism. In Kant the value of persons as rational agents is supposed to be dependent on the judgement of those rational agents themselves *qua* rational agents and good wills. But, as I have shown, the value of persons becomes more intelligible if there is reason to think that Kant's convictions about their equal and substantive worth should be treated less as derivatives of philosophical argument about reason or freedom than as surviving assumptions for which theological defences have been bracketed out and which Kant has attempted to justify in other ways.

We might even speculate that Kant's unrecognized but significant difficulty, namely that to treat human beings as equals can in effect mean to treat them as of *no* value, is itself a secular derivative of a problem in the earlier *theological* version of the theory: namely that from God's point of view too all human beings may be equally worthless: they are dust – a favourite comparison in Islam – or at best clay, an image the Hebrews were fond of, repeatedly pointing out that the potter can do as he likes with his pot. It is a regular problem in theistic systems, whether Islamic, Jewish or Christian, that the love and mercy of God need to be reconciled with the 'worthlessness' of God's creatures.

Kant's view of morality as primarily other-regarding or other-protecting is ultimately to be seen as a deformation of what is an important building-block of moral theory, though not of moral theory identified solely as a set of restrictions to protect people against each other's encroachments. The deformed dictum of Bultmann to which I have alluded (that we should treat others as we used to wish to treat ourselves) neglects an important truth in traditional versions of Christ's saying, and which Plato had already recognized: the proper distinction (*Laws* 731D–732B) between self-respect and selfishness, which in their different ways both Kant and Bultmann pervert, and which is a distinction not merely about duties but between psychological states. For self-respect – though it needs purging of selfishness – is a precondition of morality, whereas selfishness is morality's enemy.[23] But if self-respect is a precondition of morality, it follows that it is moral to develop and maintain it, and if it is moral to develop and maintain one's own (purified) self-respect, then it is a moral 'duty' to follow one's inclination to do so. Thus all absolutist post-Kantian antitheses between altruism and that 'egoism' which is self-respect crucially rule themselves out.

Kant has tried to replace much of the Platonic realism which, as far as we can see, a coherent moral theory seems to demand with an account of persons which has deep historical roots but which he has left philosophically ungrounded. So too a formalized version of Kant's account of practical reasoning, extracted from its wider context and assimilated to an 'Aristotelianism' itself torn from its native philosophical soil, has formed the basis for many more modern developments. Here we can recognize an interesting parallel with contemporary 'utilitarianism': practical reasoners seem similarly barren in their portrayals of man; unable to account for the respect for persons, or even for the duties, which they propose. This inadequacy may at times be masked by a 'quasi-realism' about moral characteristics, but this will boil down to little more than wishful thinking – a process which will be considered later in light of an examination of the moral significance of choice. But if even a stricter Kantianism than the emaciated versions of the practical reasoners fails (albeit supplied with hidden props) to secure the survival of an intelligible ethics, then readers of the *Philosophical Review* may be compelled to conclude that unless a different road – distinct from the forbidden route of Platonic realism – can be found, the moral quest is up. Thrasymachus has won and all that can be salvaged are devices to protect ourselves against him, quasi-realism being one such.

There follows a corollary to that: if we now find a philosopher saying, for example, that we should search for 'emotional integrity',[24] we

---

[23] For psychoanalytic discussion (with comment on both Kant and Luther) see (e.g.) E. Fromm, *Man for Himself* (New York: Holt, Rinehart and Winston, 1947), 124–45.

[24] So R. B. De Sousa, *The Rationality of Emotion* (Cambridge, Mass.: MIT Press, 1987), 332.

must ask whether by using the word 'integrity' he is speaking merely descriptively or also morally: that is, with 'moral' condemnation of lack of integrity, or deceit. Oscar Wilde observed that 'a sentimentalist wants the luxury of emotions without paying for them'; what we must ask is whether Wilde has any right to a moral judgement of the 'sentimentalist', or only the ability to point him out. If the latter, then in discussing 'morality' we are going to have to revise our linguistic uses much more radically than most of us have suspected or feared.

But before resigning ourselves to so dismal an outcome, let us take a further side-turning, revisiting the possibility of self-unification within the Kantian moral framework. Love, we have supposed, is the obvious candidate for a unifier of our divided selves, but love – despite being the supreme Christian value – cannot play this role in Kant's world, where there can be no unification, but merely an eventual *compatibility*, between the noumenal self and the whole man. The self remains fundamentally divided, in a manner parallel to that famously identified by Sidgwick:[25] that is to say that we find ourselves divided not merely between reason and the passions, or between what we are and what we ought to be, as older theories roughly had it, but between a belief that it makes sense to plan our lives in what we call our own interests and a hope that this can be done while retaining the overriding claims of some sort of morality of unloved duties.

So we are at an impasse, and no advance is possible – unless what we call our 'self', with its apparently conflicting goods, is indeed the desiccated and loveless shadow of some anciently understood 'soul', which once was held to have a destiny beyond our consciousness, even beyond our knowledge, and which could provide us with both a beloved goal and a beloved standard to resolve our present conflicts.

Because of his wish – despite his ambiguous title *Groundwork of the Metaphysics of Morals* – to separate metaphysics from morality, it followed that, since morality is to be 'autonomous', Kant could do no more than present us with an incomplete version of objectivist ethics: incomplete because non-realist. We have seen how his emphasis on practical reasoning also points towards an incomplete and diminished account of human nature, and it is clear that human nature would be enriched if it looked to more than merely rational behaviour as defining the human. In their different ways both Kant and Aristotle tried to separate ethics from metaphysics, but since Aristotle's attempt, as we have seen, is the

[25] H. Sidgwick, in the closing section of *Methods of Ethics* (eighth edition, London 1907).

more half-hearted, his residual theism and anthropology enable him to
depict a richer ethical universe.[26] I have argued that just as Aristotle
would fail without the hidden Platonism, so Kantianism fails without
the hidden Christianity, and that these failures point to the impossibility
of an ethical theory which is both substantive and non-metaphysical.

There can be little doubt, as the *Philosophical Review* suggests, that a
Kantian ethics – in however debased a form – lies behind many modern, and more formalist, accounts of 'practical reasoning'.[27] As a final
comment on how this has occurred, it may be helpful to compare those
parallel developments to which I have alluded within Kantianism's utilitarian rival. In the simplest, crudest and perhaps most powerful version
of utilitarianism, that of Bentham, the best life for man is that in which
each seeks to maximize the greatest good of the greatest number, that
greatest good being pleasure and measurable in units. As the nineteenth
century progressed and moved into the twentieth, and as the difficulties with that apparently simple claim became ever more apparent, the
content of utilitarian claims diminished towards vanishing point, leaving
the formal structure. We are nowadays invited to maximize the good
(whatever that is taken to be) for persons (whoever they are, whatever are
their individual differences, and assuming that their equal value is more
than zero each), just as in the Kantian parallel account we are invited
to construct whatever good or goods happen to be deemed rational by
a being deemed rational.

Such utilitarian claims may be of interest to economists who will tell
us, for example, that the greatest good for a country lies in its identifiable
wealth; hence that it is of overriding importance to increase the Gross
National Product (at least at any cost which is not otherwise counter-
productive); they are already of only limited interest even to politicians
and of no interest at all to moral philosophers. And as philosophers
rightly demand of the utilitarian an account of the goods which must
be maximized (in whatever sense maximizing is understood), similarly

---

[26] Note the comment of Sokolowski, *Moral Action*, 217: 'Kant thus works within the moral types
that Aristotle calls the self-controlled man and the man weak in self-control, the *enkratês* and the
akratês... The Aristotelian *spoudaios* has no place in Kantian moral philosophy.'

[27] J. Rawls, *A Theory of Justice* (Cambridge, Mass.: Harvard University Press, 1971), and other
'constructivists' claim to be Kantian both in their respect for the person and in their emphasis
on the formal elements of Kantian rules. Nagel and many other proponents of 'impersonal'
morality (whatever weight they give to impersonality) do likewise. In *The View from Nowhere*
(especially 185–8), Nagel still wants to say that the more impersonal (and rule-governed) we
can become, the more we are governed by 'moral', as distinct from other, constraints. In his
view morality (as distinct perhaps from ethics) is specifically concerned with such deontological
constraints.

they must demand of the 'practical reasoners' an intelligible account of what goods practical reason will or can deliver. It is of scant use to be told either that X must be maximized or that practical reason will tell us how to construct, identify and secure respect for persons, if our ability to perceive what secures such respect is vitiated by an account of persons which is at worst massively incomplete, or at best fuzzy or sentimental. In other words, we shall be left asking what *are* real goods, or what is the real good – or both – and if there is a plurality of goods, which, if any, are the more important and why.

In the event, utilitarians are liable to resolve these and other difficulties by identifying the required goods as the critically examined preferences of various groups. That sort of preference theory, of course, is no part either of original Kantianism or of original utilitarianism, though it is to be connected both with many revised forms of Kant's own theory of autonomy and especially with the variation proposed by Mill: autonomy as the 'freedom' of the person or agent – a freedom envisaged largely as the power to choose for oneself.

CHAPTER 7

Autonomy and choice

RIGHTS, NEEDS AND WANTS

It was Kant who popularized autonomy and identified it with the power of practical reasoning, and in the last chapter I considered some of the weaknesses of Kantian schemes and treated briefly of post-Kantian developments. However, it is not primarily Kant's autonomy which can be discerned in contemporary debate – let alone in contemporary assumptions – but something more like the autonomy of Mill: that is, autonomy viewed as the ability, in the absence of an overriding account of the human good, to pursue one's preferences. That is commonly subject to two constraints, one of which is a remnant of Kantianism: that our preferences should be subject to criticism, that they should be rational preferences. The second has a longer history, going back at least as far as Locke: namely that we should work out our preferences subject to the allowance of a similar opportunity to others. The latter position is often phrased in the language of rights: the right, that is, to as much liberty, viewed as freedom from interference, as is compatible with a similar freedom for others. I shall consider both these constraints, and not least how far they are or could be effectively constraining.

If we leave aside the Kantian claim that autonomy is the functioning of the practical reason, we must understand it in terms of our wants or of our needs, and if the latter, then claims about autonomy are the more easily connected with rights both positive and negative. To survive we have genuine needs, and it seems possible that these at least can be viewed as the subject-matter of rights claims. However, at the outset the status of rights is controversial. They are nowadays often taken to be fundamental in ethics. While in the absence of any metaphysical theory that can hardly be claimed for a natural right, it may be true of legal rights. But bluntly, while there is no doubt about our need for food and shelter, and it is widely held that we have a right to these, that right only stands if it matters and should matter (to others as to ourselves) whether we perish: if, that is, we have value – and even then depending on what sense we attribute to that value.

Whether we make rights depend on obligations (which gives us a better opportunity to describe obligations which have no corresponding rights[1]) or whether we assume that obligations depend on rights, we cannot evade the possibility that, lacking a foundation for either rights or obligations outside of our needs – whether broadly or narrowly defined – we have no basis for natural rights at all. Theists can hang natural rights on God's decree or on man's valued status as created in the image of God. Kantians, as we have seen, would hang them on claims about rational agents. If both these approaches are rejected, rights are seen to be no more than deified needs, even deified preferences. Without an adequate account of human value there is no justification for the claim that even my basic needs should be met, unless because that is what I want, choose or prefer; in which case, the basis of ethics is autonomy: my individual preference. Those who settle for such a solution usually, as we have seen, hedge that these preferences should be tested for rationality, so that, for example, if it is deemed irrational for my preference to be pursued at the expense of someone else's, then my preference – as Locke held – should be constrained. But the only rational ground for my agreeing to constrain myself is to protect myself against the similarly threatening preferences of others and thus a theory of preference merges into a form of Hobbesian contract. The contract could be as follows: we all pragmatically concede 'value' to each other (or at least to all those able to assert it) and then expect each to assert claims they can show do not infringe on others'.

Rights theorists may claim to derive other rights from a basic right to liberty in all areas where the right of another is not infringed. If, however, rights are merely deified needs or deified choices, the right to liberty itself is one of them, and in political thought, in particular, it will be important to recognize that it is no less tenuously based than the rest, seeming also to require a metaphysical foundation which most of its advocates are unwilling or unable to provide. Without this it reduces, as do other rights, to a mere application of a *preference* for liberty asserted as a claim to be valued (accompanied by the 'contract' to uphold the

[1] See for example O. O'Neill, *Constructions of Reason* (Cambridge University Press, 1989), 189–93.

preferences – within strict limits – of others). I matter simply because I say I do or because I choose to matter.

Though 'choice' – whether subject to rational scrutiny or not – might be a good in itself, or even the only ultimate good, yet choices are taken to be of goods or supposed goods. If we could identify our basic needs, we should recognize our basic goods (and hence what further 'goods' we may want without strictly needing them); then if we know how to satisfy our basic needs we shall secure at least that degree of autonomy and self-respect which will enable us to perform our moral obligations and duties if any. And if autonomy is necessary for our own well-being, it must be necessary for the excellence of others; hence if we could deduce any *duty* to promote our own autonomy, we would have a *similar* duty to promote – so far as possible – the autonomy of others. The possibilities for such autonomy might seem limited in the case of others in quite different ways from those in which they would seem limited in our own case.

Hence we must consider three related questions. What do we *really* need? This can be reformulated as 'What are our basic goods?', and it leads to the further questions, Are these needs the same for all of us if we identify them with reference to that self-respect posited as an essential constituent of autonomy?, and how far does an understanding of these goods (and perhaps of their ordering) depend on the already controverted questions of 'who' we are, of what is our 'soul'? Then there is the corollary: if the structure of our basic goods depends on who we are, and if we cannot determine who we are, what room is there for ethics?

At the outset, we should dismiss a fall-back position which invites us to suppose that even if neither strict Kantianism nor its modern practical-reason derivatives, nor Aristotelianism (in its Platonizing original form) can provide an adequate substitute for the realism about goodness which effectively *moral* theories seem always to invoke (surreptitiously or otherwise), we still do not need a realist account of what is good for us since *beliefs* about what is good for us – individually or collectively – will suffice, provided they are grounded or warranted by reason.[2] Or perhaps not beliefs but moral sentiments,[3] if they could be reasonably well grounded, are adequate. The latter view has the advantage of recognizing the role

---

[2] Something of this sort is the position of A. Gibbard (one of the authors of the survey in the *Philosophical Review*); see *Wise Choices, Apt Feelings* (Cambridge, Mass.: Harvard University Press, 1990).

[3] See A. C. Ewing, *The Definition of Good* (New York: Macmillan, 1947).

of those moral emotions which traditional realism can always call upon. Without admitting to self-deception, we may allow beliefs about which we feel strongly to serve our 'moral' needs.

The same difficulties arise in such cases as with the other non-realist theses considered thus far. We may be able to show that, so far as we can see in a world of increasing complication and resulting confusion, our beliefs are warrantable, but such merely provisional warranty only assures us that if we are very largely 'right' about what is good for us and others to do and to be – and hence about what is rationally to be sought and perhaps morally to be sought – then we 'should' live accordingly. But since practical reasoning in and of itself can only tell us with more or less certainty either how we can secure the aims we seek or whether we are pursuing logically incompatible ends, it is of limited help – unless we know the targets at which we 'should' aim. More significantly, it will have nothing to say as to whether some transcendent reality either exists or affects our moral circumstances; hence reliance on practical reasoning may even weaken our ability to recognize our most basic needs. In such cases, our moral sentiments and beliefs will merely enable us to experience the satisfactions of moral emotion whether we are pursuing X which is just or Y which appears so, provided we have reasoned adequately to their attainment.

But strong moral feelings can be dangerous unless our beliefs about moral goals happen to be 'right'. That, of course, is a possibility, and it might be held to be the more warranted by their progressive coherence – though only with the greatest difficulty could this test be implemented in a pluralist society. Hence it seems that the only safe way of avoiding moral chaos – unless we 'democratically' *assume* that pragmatism will always give the 'best' result – is to have at least a very good idea about what *really* is good for us, which implies also about who we are, as well as about what we hope to be if things work out right and we become progressively less divided.

Leaving aside, for the time being, the supposition that our goods may be simply what we desire, let us concentrate on those more limited wants which we may attempt to justify as needs. We will certainly want all we need even if we do not need all we want, so how do we identify those goods which we really need, and when is a want a need? The determination of which wants correspond to basic needs will settle whether we offer a richer ('thicker') or a more impoverished ('thinner') theory of human goods. At the very least we shall have to decide which goods, and in what circumstances, we must add to the personal goods of subsistence, shelter, and possibly the good of reproduction – which seems to be a good for the race though not necessarily for its every member.[4]

Perhaps all basic goods can be summarized under the Hobbesian account of self-preservation, broadly understood. Perhaps they are those goods which, as Aristotle explained, are the prerequisites for simple survival, for life itself as distinct from the good life. Once we pass from the goods of the former to those of the latter, problems increase. We cannot ignore that mere survival will fail to provide most of us with that self-respect which is a necessary condition for autonomy. Further and less tangible goods are required, but what they will be depends either on what we *choose* to be (in which case they are hardly describable as 'needs'), or on what we ought to be if we have reason to become one sort of (unified) person rather than another.

Before tackling the problem of the less tangible needs, we must look more closely at the goods of mere survival. In some societies even these will be more minimal than in others, as can be seen from a comparative consideration of the self-respect of the poor: now people seem more degraded, possessed of less self-respect, if they live (as in many parts of Western and especially North American society) as beggars among the rich than if they live where the great majority are in the same leaky boat. Envy apart, those who remain in poverty while the rest become richer are the more aware of the gross economic inequality as their society's 'ideals' as to a minimally tolerable lifestyle are upgraded.

Already our distinction between the goods of survival and what is required for Aristotle's 'good' life is threatened. Some will have enough to survive and enough perhaps even to advance in the 'good' life and ensure their dependants can do so, while others, with similar purely material comforts, will have less chance, or at least normally less success, in living 'well'. And we need to put more flesh on this concept of living well, which means that we must be able to list more goods and to prioritize among the goods. Prioritizing will always be difficult, and even to begin we need a canon, a yardstick that will tell us what above all we should try to be and – reverting to my earlier accounts of the divided self – what will enable us to be unified. But where – Platonism of some kind apart – can

---

4 As noted by Ashley, 'What is the End of the Human Person?', 73, Aquinas identifies health, reproduction, society and truth as the four basic goods of human nature (cf. *Summa Theologiae* I–II q.1, a. 2 c). Health and reproduction are roughly our present concern; we shall discuss society in more detail in chapter 9. Truth is more problematic. If some form of Platonic moral realism is true we need truth; if Platonism is false, people may be better without it, at least for a time, as Sidgwick realized. See also the discussion of ideology in chapter 9.

such an authoritative yardstick be found? And with no such yardstick, how can we avoid, both in private and in public, the more or less random satisfaction of now one, now another need – like politicians trying to satisfy one interest-group after another?

As we have seen, the 'thinnest' of all theories of goods is the Hobbesian claim that every one of us, other things being equal, seeks at least the preservation of his own life; yet even that claim is open to challenge. Many people act on the belief that it is not always good to preserve their own lives. In some this attitude might lead to a heroic death; on a more general theory – deeply rooted, at least since the time of Locke, especially in the United States[5] – that we can do what we like with what is our own, it is argued that those have a right to suicide who judge the 'quality' of their lives unacceptable. If that is right, then even our most basic need becomes merely another *chosen* good, chosen more commonly and arguably for better but still for less than compelling reasons. Present trends illustrating how it is a small step from desiring suicide to desiring more general 'euthanasia', we begin to perceive a 'culture of death' arising.

The possibility that practical reasoning can find us a reliable list of intrinsic goods seems to be vanishing, though a famous thought-experiment is supposed to show that we have overlooked something important. If we consider a number of recent philosophical accounts – of Rawls, for example, or Gauthier[6] – of what we mean by planning rationally for the good life, we find ourselves in an unexpected universe. Such planners assume that the choices we would rationally make behind something like Rawls' 'veil of ignorance' would also be 'right' (because impartial) in the differing conditions of our individual lives. A major objection to this is that to reason in a veiled world is not to reason in the world, and even if I lived my life as though it were, others would certainly do no such thing, nor would it be *rational* for them so to do. Whatever is excogitated in an academic utopia 'exists' in no more than a possible world, and contracts projected under such circumstances are like economic models where no account is taken of national politics. To say that we ought to reason in the actual world as we would behind the veil is to say that in the actual world we (and others) *ought* to reason irrationally![7]

---

5 For Rousseau's contrasting opinion see the discussion in Glendon, *Rights Talk*, 32–3.

6 Rawls, *A Theory of Justice*; D. P. Gauthier, *Morals by Agreement* (Oxford University Press, 1986).

7 For elaborate objections to using other-world models as guides to behaviour (rather than as ways of identifying odd features of our 'natural' mentality) see K. V. Wilkes, *Real People* (Oxford University Press, 1988).

Operating in a no more than possible universe entails more than logical weakness in contractarian theory. Modern 'contractarians' usually assume that everyone in the contract, or in a position to plan the best for him or herself or for the human race, is an 'autonomous' adult,[8] and that all adults are (or can be counted as) equally capable of reasoning out, or of recognizing with their reason, at least what would be their best advantage in given circumstances – whether they are reasoning in some 'ideal' condition (such as that posited behind the 'veil of ignorance') or whether they are working out in real life the deals, compromises, etc., which will maximize whatever they judge best for themselves.

All of which adds to the plausibility of a 'thin' theory of goods like that of Hobbes, at least for calculators in the 'real' world. The most dim-witted individual (not to speak of the child) might recognize the advantages of his own survival and of its 'good', while he would have more difficulty with the 'good' of knowledge, of 'art', or even of 'liberty', if this last entails – as it frequently and vacuously does – that he does not get enough to eat. Again, some people (and not necessarily only the most stupid or most desperate) can come to hold that personal survival is *not* the be-all and end-all of life, however misguided their intellectual or less courageous 'betters' may suppose them to be in such a belief. To take account of that sort of 'paradoxical' or 'quixotic' mentality, it might (again) seem better to the rational planner to think of protecting not what one might rationally be able to calculate as in one's own best interest, but rather the opportunity for each individual to judge (or choose) what he or she, the calculator, *wants* to be his best interest – whether, rationally speaking, he may be misguided or not.

We need to attend more fully to difficulties raised by 'minors'. The problem of children disappearing from modern ethics even more

---

[8] Again much of the trouble goes back to Locke (cf. *Two Treatises*, 218, and the comments of Glendon, *Rights Talk*, 69–70). See more generally R. E. Goodin, *Protecting the Vulnerable* (University of Chicago Press, 1985). There have been protests about the missing child among academic philosophers: see O'Neill, *Constructions of Reason* (187–205) and O. O'Neill and W. Ruddick (eds.), *Having Children: Legal and Philosophical Reflections on Parenthood* (New York: Oxford University Press, 1979); J. Blustein, *Parents and Children: The Ethics of the Family* (New York: Oxford University Press, 1982). The topic is also well aired by S. M. Okin, *Justice, Gender and the Family* (New York: Basic Books, 1989), 56, 93ff., etc. For more popular comment about a world where children – if not forgotten – become pawns in the battles over rights claimed by their parents, notice Melanie Phillips in the London *Observer* of 18 February 1996: 'A progressive decoupling of sex, parenthood and family, a culture of autonomous individuals, adults and children, competing with each other in a market of rights in which children have become little more than objects whose purpose in life is defined pre-eminently as the fulfilment of adults'. The 'option' for a child is either to be treated – grotesquely – as 'already' autonomous, or if not, to be fit for exploitation by those who are.

completely than from the societies in which these ethics are mooted, is only a part – though a peculiarly informative part – of the wider problem of maturity. Clearly it is wishful thinking to assume that everyone (or anyone), intelligent or stupid, can adequately calculate his advantage. So perhaps the only way he or she could salvage some part of their goal is to concern themselves not with maximizing those goods to which we incline, and which with some reason we claim we need – however 'thinly' we view them, and however mistaken we may be about their importance – but with maximizing choice itself.

Thus can be solved the problem of the immature adult – and most of us would fail tests of rationality of a stringency such as the moral philosophers might seem to demand – as well as alleviating that of the minor. Some minors are certainly as capable of *choosing*, and even of rational choice, as are adults who have learned little from their experience. Yet claims about the superiority of age in this activity are based not only on experience but on a common decline in impetuosity – even if it can hardly be denied that irrational emotions and behaviour are easily promoted among the far-from-young insofar as they become a mob or herd, a fact particularly relevant in an age of mass-man and mass communications, and which makes for peculiar opportunities to avoid individual responsibility for actions, allowing irresponsibility to become ingrained.

This, though, is not to disallow the conclusion that older people, on average, are more likely to possess mature judgement than younger, though it suggests that the principal reasons for this are not on clear display. These reasons may be connected with a relationship between being able to identify oneself and being a responsible agent; they are, however, rarely noticed by contractarians and probably cannot be fitted into any ontology which these would wish to own.

In any case, if we limit ourselves to maximizing the opportunities for choice as such, then questions of experience are less important. Even if we accept that as a rule experience makes a difference to the rationality of our choices – despite the observable fact that it may only make us over-cautious – we still have to recognize that it is precisely this sort of experience of which we should be deprived if we were taking our decisions behind a veil of ignorance. More interestingly, if experience is a promoter of rationality, and therefore a good, then there must be a second good, not dependent on choice but seemingly as important, for with experience some choices will be *better* than others, at least insofar as they are liable to promote a better result. What we would be looking at here would be some sort of *informed* choice, but then we are back to the question of the *direction* in which experience is going to push our choices. Choices really would be better for us, *qua* experienced people, if we knew *simpliciter* what a better choice for us would be, which implies if we knew what our good or goods are. But that is to beg the question, since this is precisely what we do not know, or certainly not well enough for our purposes – at the very least when we get much beyond Hobbesian basics, and assuredly not in the abstract.

Nor does even *instrumental* rationality seem to be a help, for if we mistake our goods, then a more rational approach to achieving them will in effect be harmful. Rationality, as thus construed, is a tool and like all tools in itself neither good nor bad. Again it looks as though every alternative to a morality of realism must be a variant on the claim that autonomy itself, expressed in choice, is the supreme, indeed the only ultimate value, replacing the Good which Plato advocated in the *Republic* and which later realist philosophers and theologians developed. In such an alternative world-view, whatever is 'ours', in the sense that it is what we have chosen, is 'good', simply because we have chosen it. Even our 'fulfilments' are significant simply because they are ours, or because *we* have achieved them.[9] And if we cannot choose, for whatever reason, we are presumably not fit to exist, or at best exist on sufferance: hence imbeciles may be eliminated.

Yet how can 'significant' be understood without circularity? Are we to say not that it is good to achieve specific goals, as Aristotle insisted, but that any achievement is 'good' and the categories 'virtuous' and 'vicious' are irrelevant when applied to achievements? If so, then we should stop talking about improving ourselves or the world – except as propaganda or to make ourselves feel good – and restrict ourselves to talking of *changing* ourselves or *changing* the world. An 'advantage' of such a conclusion would be that we should no longer have to make distinction between desires and needs: if we want it, we need it and can claim some 'right' to it. A 'disadvantage' would be an inability to distinguish theoretically between the reformer and the nihilist revolutionary: both want change.

It begins to appear that, unless each of us can be held to know that he or she wants to pursue even the continuation of his own life *just because* life has some sort of value in and of itself (which points us back to 'Platonism' and moral realism), all talk of whatever goods we are inclined rationally to want (even in the simplest case) reduces to the basic question of the

---

9 So R. de Sousa (mocking some earlier comment by C. Taylor) in his review of Taylor's *Sources of the Self* in *Dialogue* 33 (1994), 122.

prime importance of our choice itself: put otherwise, that 'autonomy' just is the opportunity to choose and that choice itself – far from being merely a possible condition of virtue – alone confers value on subsidiary 'goods', including experience and instrumental rationality.

Even if life *is* intrinsically good, it does not seem as though that is something to be inferred by practical reasoning, so perhaps our inclinations, themselves directed by our needs, must help us out at least in this case. Or perhaps not, for which inclinations are in question? Do we refer to our inclinations when we are wise and rational or when we are foolish, when we are informed or when experienced or when children? When we are young, confident and healthy, we normally (though not always) want to live; we hold life to be a good and do not wish to consider suicide or to let ourselves be killed. But when we are old, ailing, disillusioned and terrorized by neighbourhood thugs, we may lose inclination to go on living and more of us may opt – it may be rationally – for death. Why should we then not commit suicide? Some might say because in conditions in which rational judgements are made we should not want to do that, or that choosing suicide already indicates 'clinical' depression, or that it is making a choice opposed to integral human fulfilment. But why should human fulfilment seem like a serious option for us in circumstances in which it appears beyond our capacity? Unless there is some *further* reason beyond (not our possible but) our actual inclinations (and beyond unjustifiable habit) to urge us still to go for fulfilment, what *reason* could there be for us to do so – unless we 'smuggle in' some further good by which we can measure our present situation in the light of our future, even other-worldly, prospects and thus 'respect' the basic good (i.e. of life) which we are proposing to abandon?

The only apparently coherent alternative to Platonic realism – perhaps indeed the alternative underlying all other possibilities (as was already mooted in chapter 2) – is first to identify a selection – however limited and impoverished – of basic needs and hence basic goods (which cannot, of course, in this scenario be intrinsically good but good by the very process of selection), and then to maximize the opportunity for each person to choose, critically where desirable, for him or herself, such choice being held up as the incarnation of autonomy and the root of that self-respect which human beings are agreed to need. Of course, even the desideratum that choices be made 'critically' will not of itself be a *moral* constraint. Choice will be finally in the hands of the agent, whose optional use of his critical faculties is to be viewed similarly to his use of better material means for securing the relevant ends: he might prefer a mechanical digger to a labour-intensive pickaxe. Reason (like better technology) avoids disappointment, but then it may negate the very joys of arbitrariness and inconsistency.

Thus in any seemingly attractive lifestyle and behind all apparent goods, whether of survival or of some notion of the 'good life', will lie Choice itself, held to be the identifying mark and essential functioning of autonomy. The political correlate of such an ethic will envisage the state as a device for maximizing choices and where necessary regulating them to offer equal Lockean opportunities: the 'level playing-field' concept of the state, for a level playing-field is all that the state – desiderately neutral about human wants and human ideals – is fitted to provide. Later we shall consider the raw intelligibility of this solution to the human dilemma, as well as its consequences, but already even apparently basic goods are less secure than they seemed once Choice itself is seen as the Supreme Good. At some stage we shall have to decide between a theory of basic goods and the Supreme Good of Choice as the essence of 'self-respect', autonomy and value. And since, interestingly, autonomy as the right and power to choose whatever one wishes – however restrained by practicability and the covenanted concession of similar autonomy to others – becomes, on the Augustinian conception of the good life, not the supreme good but the supreme mistake,[10] the polarity between a developed form of Platonic realism and the Supremacy of Choice could not be wider.

CHOICE: HISTORY AND PROSPECTS

What if maximizing choice is the only good (or at least the only ultimate good) which the moral philosopher can propose? How is such a question to be understood? Does it mean that since no *other* claimants for the role of primary good can be found, we have fallen back, by default, on choice? Or are there positive reasons in favour of it, at least as something which we can all agree on as important? But then what are we agreeing about? Is it clear that choice, viewed as both prior to the goods chosen and self-evidently desirable of itself, is an intelligible concept, regardless of how many people think that it is? The least we can say is that choice, while it may be a precondition for some forms of goodness, is not self-evidently good if we have no idea of what it entails in concrete terms – for only in the abstract is there choice which is not choice of something. Or is the claim

[10] This contrast seems to be what Iris Murdoch has in mind when she mistakenly (though not entirely unreasonably) attributes the worship of choice and independence to Kant in *The Sovereignty of Good over other Concepts* (Cambridge University Press, 1970), 80.

that the opportunity for *any* choice is *always* better than having less choice or no choice at all? That claim in turn only makes sense if it makes a difference what we choose (that is, if some choices are in fact 'better' than others), and if some circumstances (such as being possessed of choice) are better than others by reference to some standard other than choice itself.

If doubt is cast on the intelligibility of raw choice as the highest good and hence as the source of other 'values', its defenders must either support their position or assume without argument that they are right, thus putting themselves outside the philosophic pale. If they have no argument, while insisting on their rightness and trying to persuade us (even compel us) to accept it, they must resort to deception, intentional or unintentional: if not arrant deception, at least a willingness to deceive, since while denying objective moral values in general, they are asserting one particular moral value, the good of choice. They say that we should, if necessary, go to any lengths – though perhaps, for pragmatic reasons, compatible with providing similar licence for others – to expand our own choices, even if we do not know who we are as choosers, nor how uncertainty on that score may affect the nature and goal of our choices, nor how to understand choice without reference to what is chosen.

As with other proposed goods, it is worth indicating some of the historical roots of choice as an absolute value before considering whether its difficulties can be resolved. Having observed already how much contemporary moral philosophy is a secularized version of earlier theological debates, we should not be surprised to find that some of the conceptual roots of modern theories of choice lie in religious anti-rationalism; already in chapter 2 we took note of the radical views of Kierkegaard, or rather of a perversion of them.

Kierkegaard's ethical theory (like Kant's practical reasoning) sprang from the failure of the eighteenth-century ethic of benevolence and moral sense, and from an unwillingness to go back (even had it been possible, given the state of knowledge of the day) to one of the alternative ethical theories of Graeco-Roman antiquity, or (given anti-Catholicism and in some wilful ignorance) to Aquinas' combination of some of those theories in his Christian synthesis. This state of ignorance should not be underestimated: even if the philosophers of the late eighteenth century had wished to revert to ancient or mediaeval positions, their attempts would almost certainly have been misguided. The theories of antiquity had for too long been seen through latter-day spectacles and many of their more important ethical features – such as the theory of *eros* as Plato had originally proposed it – were buried under latter-day deformations.

Kant believed that the ability of reason to prescribe universal rules for itself is the key to the nature of morality, and held that the ability to universalize and to *will* obedience to such universal 'moral' rules, is self-evidently valuable, and indeed the essential mark of humanity, that is, of persons. Why he thought this – as we have seen – is philosophically rather puzzling but historically less so. Our immediate interest, however, is in his identification of the *freedom* of our holy will. Whereas practical reasoners may want to emphasize his account of its rational *dictates* – that is, of the supposed contents of morality which practical reasoning can identify and prescribe – the choice theorists, with perhaps greater acumen, can point to Kant's concern with the freedom of the will itself. It is this side of Kant which brings him nearer to Kierkegaard and to a much larger group of secular descendants.[11]

It is not surprising – with hindsight – that theories about the leap of faith which in Kierkegaard are a sophisticated defence of the superiority of Christianity to merely moral thinking, were changed in more recent and godless versions of existentialism into claims that goods themselves are created as such by individual choices and that choice itself, for which no reason can ultimately be given, is the expression par excellence of man's (Kantian or other) freedom.

Such ideas have often acquired persuasiveness – especially since the Romantic period – by way of comparison of the moral chooser to the creative artist. Human creators of art or literature (analogously to parents) have the ability to create (procreate) something radically new, something which, though similar to its authors, has never existed in its present distinction before. The comparison should not be stretched too far, for the writer, composer or artist is creating neither *himself*, nor, like a parent, another *person*; he is making an object which in some way projects himself into the external world. By contrast, the moral 'creator' is trying to make of *himself* something different, and this he can up to a point, on condition that he objectifies himself uncritically.[12] But his limitations are

---

[11] It may be objected that Kant's emphasis on the freedom of the autonomous will is not particularly modern; it can be traced back at least to Augustine. There is obvious truth in that, but the eighteenth-century context is different – though contemporary choice theorists, as we have seen, can have little truck with the purity and rationality of the Kantian will, only with its autonomy. Further investigation of the pre-Kantian 'will' is impossible here, but it should at least be observed that the history of 'will' (Latin: *voluntas*) from Augustine through the mediaeval period is complex, variegated and still inadequately understood.

[12] Part of this false objectification can be traced to the Lockean idea that our body is some kind of 'property' which we own: 'Every Man has a Property in his own Person', and 'The Labour of his Body and the Work of his Hands' (*Second Treatise of Government*, chapter 5). But if bodies are property and owned, it is a unique sort of property and ownership: I cannot destroy my *body* and survive; with my house it is different. The notion of self-ownership is enthusiastically taken up by Nozick, *Anarchy, State and Utopia*, 273.

more fundamental than those of the artist who will either be inspired by something outside himself – an echo of the Platonic view – or can create something within or about himself. This he can 'worship' through some sort of internal inspiration and projection, but it is still some feature of himself – not just himself – that he creates. He can *create* a work of art and, within limits, *change* himself; he cannot create his substance; he can only change his qualities and his character; beyond that, often even in that, his creation becomes destruction.

If an artist cannot work effectively in a particular medium, say oil-paint, he can shift to another or come up with a new medium, but the frustrated creator of his moral self is limited to what the human frame and the human psyche can bear. He may talk about creating himself, but beyond certain decided limits can only pretend to do so or delude himself that he is doing so; or the one can lead to the other. Hence philosophers who, like Sartre, want to insist that man has no essence but only a history, no ongoing nature but only a set of experiences, or who, more recently, talk about human life 'before the institution of sexuality', can only end by deifying lying and self-deception, and one notes the recurrence of deception as an outcome; we have already considered it in connection with the hypothesized need for social *belief* in objective values even if there are none. As we can pretend that objective values exist, so can we pretend to create ourselves while actually failing to do so. It is easy to see how someone who goes down the road of self-creation will come to entertain delusions of grandeur, if not of divinity: he would be so much better off, as he imagines, if he possessed greater or absolute power; he could make others (or 'the other') do his will; above all he could make him refuse to challenge the lying claim that we can create ourselves and achieve what are then styled 'free' choices and autonomous acts.

All theories of morality thus far considered – insofar as they deny the existence of 'Platonic' standards independent of human reason or our present inclinations – have either fallen into incoherence, or have assumed such standards,[13] or have tended to self-deception.[14] This may be less than immediately apparent, not least because we recognize that in practice we can behave morally or immorally without being able to give an account of the foundations of morality or even seeing the need

---

[13] We recall again that Kant claims that without God ethics loses its meaning.

[14] Another possibility is to trivialize moral differences: to suppose, for example, that within the framework of liberal politics, radical disagreements can be resolved by arbitration. Recent work by Rawls seems to offer this option, but I disregard trivialization. The view that we can arbitrate away behaviour which many people regard as grossly vicious and immoral, though certainly trivializing, is also a subset of deception and/or self-deception, and is not less so for being dubbed 'democratic'.

for such an account. Or we can make the more sophisticated but false claim that uncontroversial first principles can be readily assumed.

Again there is a religious analogue to all this, as we might expect. Christians (and other believers) have had to recognize that in their day-by-day lives non-Christians may act as well as, or better than, professed Christians.[15] However, in the event of Christianity (or any other religion) being true, problems for non-believers arise less with what they do – though they may arise there too eventually – but with what they say when challenged to *justify* their courses. If the defence of those courses necessarily depends either on metaphysical claims which cannot be demonstrated (though they can be shown to be very plausible) or on facts which can only be 'revealed', then the inability of the good pagan to defend his moral foundations is intelligible enough. His situation is that of the Platonic man of 'true opinion': he does right things but cannot begin to give an account of them to others. This inability may eventually detract from his ability to maintain and live by his own beliefs; Plato thought that in hard times the man of true belief will necessarily cave in to pressure.

Of course, no-one should demand that a man be able to give an account of his beliefs to those – wilfully or otherwise – metaphysically or religiously blind. As Plato was reported to have told Diogenes, when the latter said he could see a horse but that he could not see Horseness: 'That is because though you have eyes you haven't got a mind.' Our man of 'true opinion' would not fail to explain himself merely when talking to a Diogenes; he is possessed of insufficient understanding ever to be able to do so. If he pondered his dilemma, he would either have to deepen his position, or, if he deemed no such deepening to be intelligible, to abandon his true opinions for false ones – unless he resorted to an acceptance of foundations or quasi-foundations in bad faith.

The epistemological difficulties confronting the Platonic moral realist should not be underestimated. If there are metaphysical or religious truths which validate certain systems of morality and invalidate others (because they give the best answers to questions about what we are and therefore what we ought to be), these truths cannot be *demonstrated* by ordinary methods of philosophical enquiry. That may seem surprising,

---

[15] That is not to suggest that either the content or the impact of a theistic morality can be identical to its secular equivalent. Acknowledgement of the existence of God, and therefore of his calls on our attention, cannot but alter our attitudes both to the nature of our importance as moral agents and to the consequent moral demands made upon us. The Christian virtue of humility (dependent on a proper attitude to the Creator) is not a possibility for an atheist.

but it is not fatal: there is no reason why there should not be truths which we cannot even know or discover for ourselves, let alone *demonstrate* either to ourselves or to others. Our minds may be inadequate to them or the data necessary for understanding them may not be available to us. Thus the Church Father Origen claimed that the reason why philosophers had not understood and could not understand the problem of evil is that philosophy can tell us nothing about the fall of the angels, and that if we do not know about the fall of the angels we cannot understand human wrongdoing.

Of course, to recognize that a Platonic foundationalism cannot be demonstrated is not to allow that it is implausible, let alone necessarily to open the doors to crude irrationalism; it may still be the most plausible, even the only intelligible, explanation of what we are and of the nature of moral experience. Of course, if and for whatever good reasons our minds cannot come up with an even plausible and coherent account of those metaphysical truths which would illuminate and support the foundations of ethics, all we should do is, with proper philosophical honesty, admit our failure. (But then honesty – the honesty of Hobbes – will also have gone out of the window.) We should acknowledge how unpleasant the world turns out to be where the deification of choice is the summation of ethics and where deception and self-deception about what used to be called morality – plus discourse in which considerations of truth are irrelevant – is the essential core of public as well as private life.[16]

It certainly seems that most currently acceptable varieties of ethical belief – or all, in the eyes of those who composed the survey in the *Philosophical Review* – are anti-realist: that, as Mackie puts it, we have to 'invent' our own foundations. With Choice thus lying in wait as the foundation of such foundations, it is easy to see why modern ethics textbooks look remarkably like textbooks of law or economics. Just as it is possible to be a competent case-lawyer without having any theory – at least any clear theory – of jurisprudence or of the foundations of law, so in applied 'ethics', students are invited to choose from a menu of first principles (Kantian, utilitarian, contractarian, etc.; all are assumed

---

[16] Cf. H. Frankfurt, 'On Bullshit' in *The Importance of What We Care About*, 117–33, esp. 132, 'He [the bullshitter] does not reject the authority of the truth, as the liar does, and oppose himself to it. He pays no attention to it at all. By virtue of this, bullshit is a greater enemy of the truth than lies are.' Frankfurt also compares 'bullshitting' to bluffing: both require you to talk without knowing what you are talking about; it is common in public life, and especially in a democracy where citizens are supposed to have opinions about everything. Cf. M. Black, *The Prevalence of Humbug* (Ithaca: Cornell University Press, 1985), 143, 'HUMBUG: deceptive misrepresentation, short of lying, especially by pretentious word or deed, of somebody's own thoughts, feelings, or attitudes.'

to be grounded) and then to work out, within those parameters, the consequences and entailments of specified 'hard cases'. Moral debate reduces itself to the solving of problems, and apart from questions of casuistry, wider disagreements only become visible because followers of schools with differing first principles talk insistently past one another.[17]

In practice, something like a Sartrian 'decision' has been taken at the beginning of each chain of moral reasoning – a situation unnoticed by the writers in the *Philosophical Review*, but not unrelated to their otherwise inexplicable silence about Nietzsche; though, as Taylor has observed, the very existence of moral dilemmas is inconceivable on the theory of radical choice.[18] Our applied 'ethicists' select some basic set of preferred moral assumptions, and in so doing ratify a historical process brought to fruition, as I have sketched, over the last two hundred years whereby the Platonic Good (or its improved successors) is replaced by a now fully secular thesis about the supremacy of Choice.

CHOICE, CONTINUING MORAL IDENTITY AND RESPONSIBILITY

Since moral debate, as we have seen, must identify both the moral target and the moral agent, choice (as the new Good) is not the only necessary phenomenon of our contemporary moral 'replacement'; parallel must be a specific set of answers to the sort of problems about moral identity we have already considered. Ultimately these answers too will be arbitrary, and their arbitrariness compounded by that further arbitrariness we remarked in the adoption whether of Kantianism, of utilitarianism, or of some other dogma as the chosen starting-point for current casuistry: to be able to choose in the sense required of an autonomous agent is to be (or to present oneself as) a single choosing self and not a (Platonic) divided self. Yet without the lodestar of the Good or some equivalent to provide a fix on what we may become, our moral identity itself is only a legal fiction, itself a matter of arbitrary or conventional selection, or of a series of such selections, a choice this time not of constitutive goods but of possible selves.

The majority of choice-based ethical theorists assume a strong version of moral identity and integrity: hence a typical slogan (at least since Locke) is, '*I* need to give *my consent* if X is to be done.' Claims of this sort demand both a strong sense of freedom (I am able to make real choices)

---

[17] As already noted, the point is splendidly made by MacIntyre in the opening pages of *After Virtue*.
[18] C. Taylor, 'Responsibility for Self', in A. O. Rorty (ed.), *The Identities of Persons* (Berkeley: University of California Press, 1976), 291.

and a strong sense of personal responsibility (I take responsibility for my choices). And they almost necessarily reduce to the thesis that we are individuals in a very particular moral sense, that is, individual 'atoms'. Not surprisingly, this representation of human autonomy evokes echoes of Kant, as well as of Mill; for Kant, to be human is to be autonomous: that is to be rationally and hence morally competent and responsible. Yet one of the recurrent features of modern thought, whether influenced by Freud, Marx, Darwin or Weber, is that there are overwhelming constraints on our autonomy. Those who take the view that it is freedom – seen as autonomy and the power to choose – which makes us human, voice their demand for freedom in a world in which their psychological freedom is seriously threatened, and find, as did many existentialists, that their most urgent human pursuit is to achieve the genuinely free act. In this view, all are striving to be autonomous and we only become ourselves if we are autonomous. Yet our psychological givenness, social environment and fellow humans acting in their own name and for their own autonomy challenge and oppress our own. As Sartre famously put it, 'Hell is other people.'

Again we must distinguish between the philosopher *qua* philosopher and the philosopher *qua* man in the street. Typically, as man in the street, the philosopher assumes he possesses the requisite freedom and is able to make choices. Yet as philosopher not only the existentialist recognizes the challenge of 'Platonic' division. He may retort that though 'we' play roles most of the time, the real 'we ' is also able – though with great effort – to make genuinely free and autonomous choices; typically he fails to explain the nature and mechanics of such choices. That arbitrariness normally will distinguish them is occasionally allowed, but the implausibility of an arbitrary act being 'my' act, in the required sense of 'my', has tended to bring this view of autonomy into disrepute among professional philosophers while non-philosophers have never accepted it, tending *merely to assume* the likelihood of our choosing both freely and rationally, despite the strong – albeit mutually contradictory – objections by Platonists, existentialists and other groups that they have no right to this assumption.

Suppose the idea of radical choice by free agents viewed as moral atoms makes no sense, or, if understood as arbitrary, gives no grounds for self-respect or autonomy. Since we are able to feel emotion about what is ours, about our choices in general and whatever we choose for ourselves, simply in virtue of its being ours; since too we can appropriate to our choices at least some of the intensity of the 'traditional' emotions which attach to beliefs about what is right and wrong, then if we want any kind of 'moral' universe (if only for the sake of social cement) we have no alternative but to persuade ourselves and others that beliefs in the supremacy of choice and our own moral integrity as choosers can be intelligibly and honestly held, *even though they are not and could not be*. Again deception, at some stage and to some degree, seems to accompany any alternative to a realist morality: a perception itself inimical to self-respect.

Choice theorists, open or closet, recognize that they need a strong version of free action and are seriously challenged if a given version is open to powerful objections. They normally also assume a strong theory of continuing moral identity, of the continuing nature of the 'I', the moral atom which makes the choices. Parfit, of course, can make them an intriguing if unwelcome proposition that they would do better with a much weaker theory. Certainly the need for a strong account of *my* 'freedom' would be much diminished if we could accept something of Parfit's revisionism about personal identity. According to Parfit, we do not need to suppose the existence of a 'self' over and above our conflicting 'selves', roles, or experiences, for we are less divided selves than – as Hume also supposed – sequential selves. What 'fundamentally matters', says Parfit,[19] 'in our concern about our own future [and our own past], is the holding of Relation R, with any cause' (289), and by Relation R he means 'psychological connectedness and/or psychological continuity' (262). So, for example, in estimating our responsibility for our past and future acts, it is connectedness or continuity, not identity with our past or future selves which is determining.

Thus according to Parfit we resemble a club whose members are constantly changing while it continues to function as a corporate quasi-legal entity. But a quasi-legal entity is not a moral entity, and one effect of such an analogy is that traditional concerns about truth-telling, promising, etc., turn out to be less worrisome than we normally suppose. Certainly we should feel diminished scruples of conscience (as distinct from fear of the police) about being responsible for 'unjust' behaviour if – already divided as we are – we also successively disclaim moral responsibility for our past 'selves'. If I am no longer (or hardly) the person I was when I married, 'I' am not self-evidently bound by vows made when I was someone else – and to a party who is now also a different person.

Of course, whatever my own (true) beliefs about what I was and am, society may still try to justify punishing me for 'my' past behaviour, so

---

[19] Parfit, *Reasons and Persons*.

long as my 'club' remains in existence (that is, insofar as it concerns
me or so long as I remain alive), by claiming that punishments are not
only exemplary and thus socially necessary but also collective: like a
sanction on Jews simply because they are Jews and it is impossible for
them to 'resign' from membership of the Jewish 'club'. Perhaps we must
be content with that sort of account of 'justice'.

One attraction of Parfit's approach to our continuous moral identity
is that it seems to reflect certain recognizable features of ordinary experience. If we think of our past, we shall almost certainly be surprised to
remember beliefs which we once held, perhaps passionately, but which
we are now equally sure are false. What puzzles us, at first sight, is that
I know that 'I' held beliefs of a certain sort, but cannot understand how
I could have not realized their fallaciousness. Now suppose such past
beliefs to include a belief in the importance of promise-keeping. If I have
come to think that it does not matter whether I intend to keep my *present*
promises, I shall obviously feel no obligation to keep promises 'I' made
in the past; nor shall I be able to understand how I did not see through
'promise-keeping' in the first place.

Perhaps if we know that we once believed in the importance of
promise-keeping but now think such beliefs mistaken, we have merely
changed our minds; but if we cannot understand how we could ever have
believed in the binding nature of promises, we may come to think that
we are not the people who once held such beliefs. It seems to us that we
have not merely changed our mind. There are beliefs which it is now
inconceivable that 'I' could ever have considered well grounded, and
the only other explanation is that someone else held them. That other
person is *connected* with me psychologically, and certainly is so connected
in law, but merely as a matter of convenience to a society which cannot
function without attaching importance to such connections, while at the
moral level I can disown such legal and conventional assumptions.

To say that we are not the same persons as once we were is not the
most obvious explanation of such divergent views on promise-keeping.
A more normal account of the man who says that he cannot understand
how he could have believed in promise-keeping in the past is not that
he was then a different person, but that he was then a fool and is now
older and wiser. Such an explanation, however, depends on precisely the
account of human nature which Parfit has put in question. If, despite
being 'self-movers', we really are psychologically like Hobbes' ship of
Athens, which retains the same name and shape though all its timbers and
other components have over time been replaced, then the explanation

that we have changed our mind can yield to the alternative view that 'I' never made such a commitment in the past and cannot therefore be held responsible for it in the present.[20]

From the point of view of 'common morality' and justice and traditional accounts of autonomy, it is a major objection to Parfit's position that it greatly diminishes our perceived responsibility (often cited, as we have seen, as a *necessary* feature of such autonomy) for what we now say no longer exists, that is, our past selves. Obviously the problem becomes greater the more distant the past self, that is, the longer we live. Newman said that ten years later he found himself in another place, but according to Parfit it is that ten years later we are (more or less) another person.[21]

Parfit himself attempts to defend a degree of both freedom and responsibility, but in his treatment of psychological continuity ignores the kind of continuity necessary if we are to make any sense of being historically aware of ourselves over time. For a special part of such awareness, as we noticed earlier, is of ourselves as existing within some kind of 'moral space': of living in a world in which we cannot but be aware of moral problems and moral ideas. This awareness is with us – as an importantly formative part of us – whether we live in a world of moral realism or whether we have to invent or agree upon the contents of the moral universe. Nor, in fact, does it matter if we change our moral opinions or forget or fail to comprehend what once we were like; what is essential to personality is that we have moral opinions to change. So that even if Parfit (or Hume) is right that we are successive selves with diminishing comprehension of our past selves, we shall end up as crude reductionists about human nature if, while allowing that we have some kind of psychological connectedness (and/or continuity) with those past selves, we have an inadequate sense of its specifically moral character. For the connectedness by which we and all other humans are linked with our past – fingerprints genetic and other aside – includes the belief not only that we live in the same moral space as everyone else but that we share that moral space with the former evolutions of our 'selves' for whom we retain responsibility.

If the choice theorist is ready to follow Parfit in effectively diminishing our sense of ourselves as moral agents, he may diminish the problematic

[20] Note that Parfittian accounts of personal identity already existed in classical times; for discussion see D. Sedley, 'The Stoic Criterion of Identity', *Phronesis* 27 (1982), 255–75; also E. Lewis, 'The Stoics on Identity and Individuation', *Phronesis* 40 (1995), 89–108.

[21] Parfit's example of the *Nineteenth-Century Russian* is particularly helpful (*Reasons and Persons*, 327–9): note especially Parfit's remark (p. 329), 'the young man whom she loved and married has ceased to exist'.

question as to which of our selves makes the free and autonomous choices he requires, but at the cost of adding new implausibilities to his position and in particular of undercutting the strong sense of autonomy and personal responsibility he desires. He, at least, will probably prefer to decline Parfit's proffered assistance.

Parfit, of course, can demand whether, if the choice theorist rejects sequential selves, he wishes to say that in the name of autonomy one can at any time simply repudiate one's past. This is Parfit's fork: if the choice theorist says Yes, he will look wholly arbitrary and forfeit any claim to trust, thus subverting all social relations; if he says No, he compromises that very autonomy of choice and action which he has professed as a good.

FREEDOM, HABIT AND THE GOOD LIFE

Kantianism apart, non-realist claims in moral philosophy must – I have argued – reduce to the attribution of supreme importance to personal autonomy seen as the power to choose, on the grounds that it is only through choice that we can enjoy self-respect – seen as a necessary condition for 'moral', indeed for 'human', activity. But if this notion of autonomy turns out to be indefensible and incoherent, yet still an apparently necessary condition for human 'dignity' and post-morality, then we are reduced to *attributing* intelligibility to it (as the quasi-realists in parallel fashion attribute an 'as-if' reality to moral 'facts'). And some self-appointed or co-opted guardians would be needed to understand the reality behind the deception.

Strong claims about the importance of choice compel us to consider the role of psychological determinism, that is, how our behaviour may be internally controlled by our desires and dispositions, and what are the implications of such control. Determinism is not logically entailed by the having of reasons for our actions; it would only be demonstrated if, in all circumstances, we could not do other than we do, and if that were the case we should also have to ask whether there is room for morality at all, since moral philosophy – not to say most public policy – is driven by the assumption that, at least in normal circumstances, we can act otherwise. Certainly without this assumption criminals could not be deservedly punished, righteous indignation would be ruled out and people's characters could be altered but not morally improved. Of course, the impossibility of moral discourse continuing as now practised, or of present public policy being pursued in the future, in no way affects the theoretical issue of whether psychological states are determining: the case logically is precisely the reverse.

Setting out guidelines for his successors, whether themselves Kantians, Sartrians or contemporary choice theorists, Kant tried to meet the problems of determinism by positing a 'noumenal' self which is autonomous to the necessary degree. Such a quasi-separate self is a most implausible metaphysical postulate, and as for non-Kantian claims about autonomy seen as the power to choose, they must take one of two forms. The weaker form, that any choice is significant merely insofar as I make it, regardless of whether it is or is not determined, is of no interest, since it depends merely on the *assertion* that what I choose, whether freely or not, has value.

The second and stronger form is that I have at least some genuine moral choices between 'worse' and 'better' courses, but that the power of choice itself is of far greater importance than the status of the choices I happen to make. Thus it is always better that I can make a wrong choice than that I have no choice at all – or than that I can only make right choices. The latter claim reveals its own absurdity in that it implies that if there were a God it would be better if he could make wrong choices than that he always *necessarily* make right ones, and thus, in one (non-Augustinian) sense, not choose at all; that is, in traditional language, that it would be better if God were able to sin, and man likewise.

Objections to the supremacy of choice as thus understood are not restricted to theology. An analogous objection can be sustained if we consider the nature of human habits. Even if we are divided selves in the sense argued earlier, it will still be true that if we develop patterns of action by a series of choices, we shall increase the likelihood of such patterns being repeated in the future. If we several times choose to help strangers in trouble, we shall become more likely to help strangers in trouble: in other words we shall become less likely *not* to help strangers in trouble, and less likely not to *want* to help strangers in trouble. We can then envisage a situation in which we would want never to disregard such people – even though we recognize that such a developed habit substantially diminishes the 'freedom of choice' we once had.

If by an extending series of such choices we were to develop a set of habits covering the great majority of our moral life, we would find our original freedom of choice – namely that proclaimed by some the highest or only good – diminished almost to vanishing point, but that would not burden us. We would not object to seeing it go, nor would we suppose our dignity or self-respect in any way diminished by such alteration, realizing that it does not depend on this sort of freedom, indeed that freedom of choice understood as a genuine option between moral possibilities is at best a *means* (for those who need it, and to the degree that they need it) towards an end beyond itself which would dispense with such so-called freedom altogether: an unavoidable *condition* of a stage of moral life which we rationally prefer to transcend. A glance at the theological parallel will illuminate the argument further: lovers of choice as an end in itself would have to prefer not to be 'in heaven' (as indeed *per impossibile* would God) because they are so addicted to the opportunity of being somewhere else. (In the case of God, this would mean he would prefer to be other than he is.)

Thus the addict of absolute moral choice should logically be compelled to be on his guard that his preferred behaviour, indeed any behaviour, does not become habitual. To take my previous example, he must be quixotic in his response to the needs of strangers – and even to his own family and friends – for fear that his freedom be diminished. His aim, therefore, must be to make his behaviour as erratic as possible – unless perhaps he fears becoming habitually erratic – an inconsistent fear if his love of choice is sincere. Clearly on his own terms he cannot be convicted of wrongful behaviour; however, his increasingly erratic character can be signalled – as Plato signalled it in the latter books of the *Republic* – as likely to lose him friends and influence.

If such disjointedness, at least in the form of having no reason to choose one moral course rather than another,[22] is the logical outcome of choice thus construed, it is easy to see why such theories are diametrically opposed to 'Platonism', which seeks a future unity, and why it makes sense to argue that the logical last stage of counter-Platonic argument is choice theory. That is not to say that 'Platonism is true': rather to argue – again Zeno-style – for the radical incoherence of the moral universe if Platonism is false: or better, that if Platonism is false there is no moral universe, only successor schemes to satisfy various wishes, desires, hopes and fears of rootless and dissatisfied humans, individually or in groups, as the power of each waxes and wanes. We may observe that the serious choice theorist's need to avoid forming moral habits of any kind, for fear of finding choice itself reduced, finds something of a political analogue in the wish for 'perpetual revolution' which Mao Tse-tung and others

---

[22] Note the perceptive comment of A. MacIntyre on Heidegger's Nazism in 'Existentialism', in M. Warnock (ed.), *Sartre: A Collection of Critical Essays* (New York: Doubleday, 1971), 26: 'We should not be surprised that Heidegger was for a short [*sic*] period a Nazi, not because anything in *Sein und Zeit* entails National Socialism but because nothing in *Sein und Zeit* could give one a standpoint from which to criticize it or any other irrationalism.'

have seen as the only alternative to the otherwise unstoppable growth of inveterate non-revolutionary habit. Choice, like revolution, can become an end in itself; indeed if it does not, it becomes superannuated.

Thus respect for choice in and of itself as the supreme good leads to positions as unintelligible in themselves as appalling to those who envisage their implications. But if all non-realist positions tend to collapse into an unintelligible version of choice theory, the Platonist must (and always did) have a rival theory of choice, and so of autonomy, human freedom and dignity. That theory is that while we still have the possibility of moral improvement we *cannot avoid* being more or less 'free' to choose the worse, and that we can say of this our present sort of autonomy, insofar as we still have it, that we are fortunate not to be 'freer'. Freedom as we should wish it is not the option to use or abuse, to choose the better or the worse, but a state, towards which we can only aspire to grow, in which we will be able only to choose the good.

Thus too the 'determinism' which marks the actions of the good man is distinct from the determinism raised in connection with the 'free-will problem'. The latter is a hypothesized inability to do anything better or worse or other than what we actually do. Now it is certain that we are not presently 'determined' to do what is good; if we were, no-one would be discussing ethics. And the best reason for thinking that we are not yet fully determined in either or any direction will be found in the recognition that we are as yet a set of immature selves, not congealed into a single 'soul' of whatever fixed type, but liable, in virtue of our plurality, to react to those events which Williams and others refer to as 'moral luck', which Plato often despises as indicative of a 'bourgeois' imperfection and weakness before the shifting changes of fortune, and which Christians interpret in terms of a providence. Such providence or grace is itself only pertinent to those who are not settled for better or for worse, for insofar as we try to direct ourselves without reference to such outside help or pressure, we proceed along the deceptive path of the only necessary determinism, that of amorality.

If either the 'secular' or the 'theological' version of our proper fear of an absolute 'freedom of choice' is well founded, then any 'Stoicizing' success in making ourselves invulnerably secure against moral luck will quickly reveal a psychological and 'amoral' determinism. Stoic self-respect – like all theories of human worth built on claims about such self-respect – will prove illusory.

Having, as I hope, indicated some important ways in which the word 'free' is dangerously and misleadingly equivocal, I conclude with a further point about the so-called free-will problem. If 'free' is properly understood as 'able to pursue the good', perhaps as 'unshackled', even, as Plotinus would have it, 'undivided' (*Ennead* 6.8.5),[23] then there is a harmless sense in which the ideally good individual (and the same will apply to God) is *both* free and determined – where determined means 'so disposed as to be *in effect* unable to act otherwise'. But if freedom, as commonly if unthinkingly supposed, is the right to use and abuse, or if it includes a right or privilege or capacity to do wrong, then any moral compulsion, 'internal' or 'external', to do this rather than that, will constitute an infringement of freedom and open up the possibility of a damaging form of determinism, even of the 'hard' variety: damaging, however, only within that set of philosophical parameters which generate the traditional philosophical *problem* of free will, which is thus seen to be largely misconceived.

Choice and autonomy thus remain paradoxical. I have argued that non-realist systems of morality collapse into an unintelligible version of choice theory, but have no wish to deny that there is – as now explicated – something good about choice, and even about the possibility (never the actuality) of making wrong choices. Autonomous choice is thus *a* good and one which historically has often been overlooked, sometimes for good if ultimately inadequate reasons – but it is not *the* good. Choice *of goodness* can easily be fitted into a 'Platonic', as into a Christian ethics, but we are still uncertain as to the *comparative* weight to be allotted to choice itself in a hierarchy of goods. Where and to what degree shall we promote the opportunity to choose badly? Presumably only when such opportunity is inseparable from the possibility (for us) of choosing well and thus of moral improvement. This is a dilemma close to philosophy itself: there is no doubt that not only Socrates but also his successors may 'corrupt the youth'.

Post-Cartesian philosophy, with its concentration in psychology on consciousness and in ethics on human freedom, has emphasized important features of the life of a man – made, as some still hold, 'in the image and likeness of God' – which had in the past been regularly and substantially underplayed. That new concentration went hand in hand historically with the assertion of the importance of the individual and individual judgement against the possible or actual tyranny of state or church. But in its zeal to rectify error, it brought in turn a new exaggeration of a most

---

[23] There are other possible reconciliationist senses, such as 'determined by compelling reasons', but they all arise within the ordinary parameters of the free-will problem as identified below and are not our present concern.

serious sort, and, coupled with the post-Kantian decline of metaphysics, produced a mentality for which autonomy as choice, in and of itself, is no longer an important and necessary *condition* for moral improvement, in the direction of an end state in which we only choose the good, but becomes the sole remaining 'virtue' of a world from which the Good has vanished.

CHAPTER 8

Ethics and ideology

RESPONSIBILITY, CORRECTION AND COMMUNITY

At this point in our story we move from man as a moral (and spiritual) individual to man as member of a community. For in arguing that anti-realism finds its starkest expression in the all importance of individual autonomy and 'free' choice, we cannot treat the individual as isolated in his own world. We must consider realism and its converse not only in terms of their effects on individual lives but of how those effects work themselves out in society, transforming society in their own image.

What then will be the proper role of society and the state in a realist and non-realist world? In the first instance I shall focus on the inculcation of responsibility, since I have argued that taking or declining responsibility for one's actions both present and past is a key to reducing or increasing that splitting of the self which indicates, in realist terms, moral progress or regression. In treating of such responsibility I must consider responsibility both *for* oneself and *to* other members of one's community – thus beginning to identify the interface between 'private' ethics and social and political concerns. My method in this political section of the book will again be 'Zenonian': in this case I shall consider the horrors in which we must recognize ourselves entangled if it is false that, as Aristotle, Plato and their Christian successors have always insisted, we humans are social and political animals. And I shall look at the specific sense in which we ought to be political animals if realism is true.

According to a theological theory developed by Augustine from the prophetic utterances of Paul, our 'individual' nature can only be understood in light of an interwoven communal nature: naturally we are one in Adam. If this view were correct, it would imply a radical interpretation of Aristotle's claim that man is a 'social animal': radical in that not only are we formed and developed in a social context, but that such development depends on the prior fact that we are, as it were, genetically social, rather as, in more recent times, it has been proposed that each of us shares in and is moulded by the collective unconscious. In contrast to all such speculations, dominant contemporary belief, taking a variety of forms but in every case emphasizing the sovereignty of choice, views us as moral atoms, and connects a liberalism – even if it calls itself conservatism – dependent on 'autonomy' as the highest value, with a radical political individualism in many respects recalling that of Epicurus. We are at base – so runs the theory – isolated individuals, each in some way – whether in public or in private – seeking his or her own individual good. Margaret Thatcher notoriously if crudely summed it up: 'There is no such thing as society; there are only individuals and groups of individuals.' In accordance with this view we often find a right to 'privacy' elevated into a basic right *on which other rights are held to depend.*

Turning to consider both the facts and their implications for public life of such conflicting descriptions of human nature, I note first that not only the more extravagant metaphysical speculations, whether those of Augustine or of Jung, are condemned by radical individualism, nor only those who, as we saw in chapter 4, hold that our psychological unity is achieved without benefit of metaphysics by mere immersion in specifically *political* life, more especially in democratic life. Anyone is so condemned who subscribes to a broadly 'Aristotelian' belief that our proper personal development is inextricably dependent on some form of constructive participation in the society in which we live: in the special sense that we are to treat the goods of our fellows as in some sort our own, and that in appropriate respects we are responsible for the well-being of others as inextricably linked with our own and our responsibility for ourselves.

This 'communitarian' view conflicts with the claims of the choice theorists in asserting that our good as members of society depends precisely not on whether we *consent* to be those members but on whether we *are* (and *need to be*) them. Its corollary is that, if we choose not to make others' goods our own, we cannot effectively choose our own good, the integrity of our choices depending as much on a concordance with our general ontological and psychological structures as on the mere fact of choice itself. And its further corollary is that if choice theory is confused and indefensible, and if the belief that we are moral atoms is an inseparable aspect of choice theory, then any belief that we are moral atoms will entail confused behaviour and damage to the selves who hold it.

As already noted, for reasons historical and political as well as philosophical, rights, especially ever proliferating individual rights, have come to play a major, even a supreme, role in contemporary Western debate – dominantly, in the United States – about both public policy and more abstract moral issues themselves. Apart from special circumstances leading to the quasi-divine status accorded to the American Constitution, the Bill of Rights and subsequent amendments, more general historical reasons for the modern emphasis on rights have broadly to do with the often violent rejection, in Western societies since the Renaissance and the Reformation, of absolute governments whether political or ecclesiastical. Against such governments – and later against any authority whatsoever – rights have been seen as quasi-metaphysical 'possessions' of discrete individuals: not only as correlative to all acceptable duties, obligations and responsibilities, but as the 'owned' claims of potential victims against potential infringers, and even – increasingly – as 'prior' to the duties, obligations and responsibilities themselves. As so-called 'negative rights', they are mobilized both against government (seen as the 'state') and also against society itself.

It belongs to their intellectual history that rights can be deployed and held as a threat against those perceived as infringers. In many contemporary versions of rights theory, where rights are claimed not merely against individual others but against society itself, society is seen as the enemy not merely in respect of requisite checks on abuse of power or privilege, but precisely in that it requires respect for the 'common good'.[1] Modern societies are expected to face not merely claims for protective and enabling rights against oppression, not merely the problematic of *conflicting* rights claims, but an insistence that the 'common good' itself is a fiction (being at best no more than the sum of individual goods) which poses a threat to the rights of individuals to which it must always yield precedence.

The mushrooming of such ideas has been promoted both by the perception of injustices, sometimes on a massive scale, and by the new political development of a secularized version of the Christian belief – first exploited selectively within Protestantism[2] – that all men are made

---

[1] The specific concept of a 'common good' goes back to Aristotle, where it refers at least to the promotion of those background conditions of a society necessary if its members are to flourish (such as peace, adequate resources, etc.). It probably also denotes the activities of communities united by a common goal, who thus constitute themselves not as individuals but as members of a team. A society can only have a common good in this second sense if its common goals are widely (ideally universally) acceptable to its members. It is lack of this consensus which makes much talk of the common good – when it goes beyond the mere provision of security – seem unintelligible (even proto-fascist) to many contemporary Westerners. The plurality of senses of 'common good' needs much further investigation; realist accounts will necessarily look to a divine Common Good which is the good of all God's creatures.

[2] Recall that the *founding* fathers of the United States were all committed slave-owners.

equal in God's image;[3] hence that secular authority and responsibility must depend on the free and informed consent of the governed. Problems inevitably arose, both in theory and in practice, as to how that consent could be achieved and given institutional substance in social and political structures. In particular, longstanding concerns, such as how to reconcile freedom – now, at least in theory, for all – with order and security, took on new urgency.

As we have seen, underlying all such politico-religious developments – and ever seeming the more urgent in light of the increasingly dehumanizing effects of industrialization, technological advance, the 'homogenization' required for total war and more broadly for mass society and a global market – was the growing 'theoretical' importance accorded to the choices of individuals. At first the individual was viewed more and more as alone with his God, identifying his own spiritual future and accepting whatever authority he judged best on earth. This mentality might lead to a new defence of authoritarianism as in Hobbes, or to the possessive individualism of Locke; all emphasized that the individual had his own supreme rights, to be suspended only – and then not always – by his own 'free' choice. Whereas broadly speaking – and despite such obvious exceptions as Cynicism and Epicureanism – the majority of earlier conceptions of the relation of man and society emphasized the communal responsibilities of the individual to the group seen as the matrix of individual growth, now, in parallel to the increasing mushrooming and power of established institutions – not to speak of a fear of their ability to suppress individual well-being altogether – arises a desire to minimize their authority and a growing scepticism about their contribution to the 'good life'. With such ideas important steps have been taken towards the thesis that the principal function of the state is to protect its members against one another (and presumably also against itself) rather than enable them together to work for a richer whole for all of its members than anything they could achieve individually.

Whereas for the ancients and mediaevals society at large is the framework within which an individual works out his duties and responsibilities, being responsible for the welfare, including the moral and spiritual welfare, of each of its members (at least in that structures providing for this

---

3 This is not to suggest that the idea had no influence earlier, but that after the Renaissance and the Reformation it increasingly took centre-stage. Compare the success of the abolitionist crusade against slavery in the British Empire and the United States with the intellectually powerful but less socially successful pleas by Vitoria and Las Casas against similar evils – including contemporary versions of the theory of 'natural slaves' – in the dominions of sixteenth-century Spain.

were recognized as better forms of community), there now developed
the idea that minimal government allows maximal 'freedom' for the individual to choose his own path, with the corollary, derived in no small
part from weariness of religious violence and repression, that toleration
of an ever increasing number of lifestyles and human goals is a primary
good. The state is to be viewed more and more as neutral in its attitude
to the choices and even the ideals of individuals, its role being limited – as
some at least hoped – to that of preventing the choice of one becoming
the coercion and denial of choice to another. If it passed beyond such
limits, it might be accused of transgressing on the 'rights' (normally still
god-given, as in Locke) of the individual citizen.

In the sixteenth century the word 'state' itself came to indicate less the
community or society as a whole than its government, itself frequently
viewed as in at least potential opposition to the citizen. Thus any state,
and later even any 'community', might be perceived no longer as a
means to the individual's growth but as a threat to his autonomy. In
more recent time such threats were seen as the greater insofar as the state
came to require a more and more complex, impersonal and 'faceless'
bureaucracy, thus tending to take on a 'corporate' life of its own.

All such developments tended to promote a concept of the individual as less and less dependent on the society around him, hoping to
'fulfil' himself by his own choices without reference to his societal context except insofar as he needed it to provide minimal security. In the
extreme Hobbesian version, he calls upon it for the protection and upholding of his fundamental desire for self-preservation; Locke and others
added, for the preservation of his own property seen as an extension
of himself. From this prospect the individual self could be considered
to 'own' what an Aristotelian would consider inseparable features of
his psycho-physical unity, notably his body; and so in more contemporary philosophy we hear of owning our emotions and beliefs. I have
already observed how suspect is this 'ownership', if not unintelligible –
albeit informative about the self-centred assumption of the philosophical
debate.

Though the development of such political and social ideas was neither continuous nor uniform in Europe and North America, by the
late twentieth century a set of attitudes could be identified which are in
marked opposition to the dominant modes of earlier 'communalism'. As
we have noticed, there is an almost ubiquitous tendency to emphasize
choice, which takes the pivotal role once played by the Platonic Good
or its theological descendants; it is by now customary to refer to rights

in terms *either* of protected goods *or* of protected choices.[4] But choice is limited by physical capacity, and although we may fantasize (encouraged by the commercially minded) that we may live for ever, never become frail, old or ill, we know that these physical limitations are real. It is a mark of much post-Nietzschean thought to 'forget about' death, in an interminable series of heroically self-deceiving aphorisms.

The older, 'pre-modern' world in which 'rights' were largely seen as legal rights available to citizens, responsibilities tended to take precedence over rights, and 'goods' were generally identified as common, depended less on political arrangements and philosophical theories envisaging the state as active promoter of each citizen's pursuit of his individual well-being than on the axiom that the individual is dependent for his good and for his development not on his wants but on his needs, broadly conceived,[5] less on his choices than on the communal nature of his personality itself, viewed as desirably participating (rather than just living) in a vigorous and active community.

Hence we can approach the problem of the intelligibility of most modern forms of individualism by asking whether the older 'communitarians' faced the facts: how much, that is, did the ancients, and Aristotle in particular, get right about man as social animal? For if man is a social animal he will suffer by not being social, and extreme versions of individualism will fall into the category of fantasy or stupidly wishful thinking. In the *Politics* (1253A ff.) Aristotle remarks on the differences between men and other social creatures like bees, observing not that we have two legs and cannot fly but that we are like them in the important respect of being social, though unlike them in the way our sociability fits with the rest of our nature. In a notoriously difficult phrase, he observes that we are distinguished from other social animals by the possession of *logos*, which word seems to refer to our capacity both to organize our thoughts and to formulate them. For Aristotle, the sociability of bees expresses itself as a quasi-automatic response to their surroundings; for humans it stands or falls with the use of their rational capacity to function in organized communities.

Aristotle thinks that all living creatures are possessed of 'faculties', and that the possession of a 'higher' faculty presupposes the possession of lower ones. Thus human beings, the sole possessors of reason (if we leave the gods aside), are affected by that possession in the way they exercise

---

4 Cf. Sumner, *The Moral Foundation of Rights*, 45–6.
5 See D. Wiggins, 'Claims of Need', in T. Honderich (ed.), *Morality and Objectivity* (London: Routledge and Kegan Paul, 1985), 149–202. The matter was treated in chapter 7.

their lower capacities to feel, eat, reproduce. This is clearly correct insofar as we know that we can eat in a human way, socially and not 'like a pig', or that we understand and experience erotic and romantic love as well as versions of 'sex in the head'. But Aristotle's primary concern is that we can use reason to determine how to achieve the ends to which we are *naturally* oriented, organizing our defences, planning our families, regulating our diet – or to defeat them by deciding to starve ourselves to death. Reason gives a chance not merely to live a prearranged life – above all not merely to survive – but to lead 'the good (as well as the bad) life', and that good life, which we arrange for ourselves, must be arranged within human communities suited to it. Hence it becomes a theoretical problem (as well as an urgent practical one) to decide what sort of human community will best enable us to live the 'good life', as also what this life consists in, for we cannot live the good life as individuals seeking only our individual good. He who cannot live as a citizen in a community, says Aristotle, is either a beast (like the Cyclops) or a god!

Aristotle's claim – and in this Plato's is similar – is that we cannot grow up without human communities and that we shall prove better or worse individuals, in part at least – room is left for differences in our 'nature', though perhaps more radically by Plato than by Aristotle – in proportion to the excellence of the societies in which we develop and participate, for to grow up in a society is not to be merely a 'sleeping partner', but an active member, acknowledging our fellows and respecting them as friends both as individuals and for the fellow-citizenship which we share.

Observe, however, that neither Aristotle nor Plato claims that we shall be more 'fulfilled' by membership of a better society; they say something which may look like that but is importantly different: namely that we shall better exercise the capacities that we have; that we shall be more fully developed. They put it that way because they have no concept of self-fulfilment[6] – because they have no modern notion of a 'self' to fulfil. Plato is concerned with 'how the soul shall be in as good a condition as possible'; nor does he identify any present 'self' with the 'soul', rather with what the soul could be again and once was. To fulfil – construed as to satisfy – the soul as presently constituted, would be both to pander to its multiplicity, and as the *Gorgias* shows, impossible in practice. Aristotle for his part discusses the exercise of our capacities 'in accordance with virtue', presenting this as good not because it satisfies or fulfils us as individuals – though insofar as it is good it will do that, if anything will.

---

[6] The Romantic origins of 'fulfilment' were noted earlier.

This ideal (like that of Plato) differs from the ideal of self-fulfilment in its emphasis on the achievement of actions and states of affairs in the outside world. In the contemporary climate, therefore, where happiness is often construed as pleasure (or a balance of pleasure over pain), it is, at best, misleading to use the language of self-fulfilment or self-realization to describe the Aristotelian ideal, and it is even less appropriate if we are to consider the nurturing of our *future* soul.

Thus to present properly human performance in a Platonic or Aristotelian way not only sidesteps the problem of who 'I' am, but more immediately indicates that although Plato and Aristotle recognize that we have specific wants and desires and that we cannot but suppose that the satisfaction of at least our 'better' desires is good, they do not treat such achievement as a matter of self-fulfilment. Indeed they would argue that self-fulfilment could be a good only if we avoid its direct pursuit, for such pursuit, like the direct pursuit of pleasure, is self-defeating. Self-fulfilment is only to be experienced as a by-product of virtuous performance in the pursuit of other identifiable and honourable goals.

Although it is misleading to attribute to Plato and Aristotle any interest in or sympathy for 'self-fulfilment' or 'self-realization', it would be plausible to say that if they were confronted with these notions they would allow that *as a matter of fact* they could only be obtained within a communal or social environment in which the citizens are well disposed to one another, and that attempts to deny this are mischievous. Aristotle observes that it is not natural for man to be alone, and that the superior form of friendship arises not for the sake of 'utility' but for the sake of 'excellence', while Plato, in his portrait of the tyrant, shows the fate of the man whose desire for his advantage, pursued in contempt of others, leads to social isolation and accompanying degeneration, surrounded only by sycophants.

Nor would Plato be impressed (as is shown in *Republic* book 2) by the argument that the bad man does not have to be a fool, but can use his intelligence the more effectively to pursue evil ends. He would counter by claiming that the worse his ends, the more divided he will become, and thus the *less* disposed to use his intelligence even instrumentally. And he sees the same divided intelligence 'writ large' in the evil state; he could have been contemplating the latter days of the Nazi régime when a variety of conflicting intelligence services, as hostile to one another as to their common foe, continually rendered their rival workings ineffective.

Plato and Aristotle are unconcerned with self-fulfilment, at least directly. Their primary concern is pedagogic: with how the city can educate its members to belong to itself and to one another. And they will be members insofar as they identify their interests, some directly, others indirectly, with those of all the other citizens – directly, in being willing to fight for the city, for though the city's *raison d'être* is 'the good life', it arises for the sake of the survival and nurture of its members and in that respect is the analogue of the family: man and woman come together for primarily biological reasons, and marriage is in the 'interest' of the survival of the human race – though it will not follow that the generation of children and their nurture is the only reason for marriages to exist or to continue after these ends are concluded.

Obviously the good life which the city pursues depends on the physical survival of its citizens; yet they do not count themselves as citizens merely in order to survive but because the city affords them the opportunity to live and exercise their talents in ways otherwise impossible. A man with great musical talents may live in a small community but probably cannot obtain good teaching there; he certainly would not be able to play in a symphony orchestra. A community of desirable size is as much a necessity for certain attainments as for survival itself, and as is the family for the education as well as for the birth of children. Plato illustrates the point by the story (*Republic* 1.329E ff.) of the Athenian politician Themistocles' retort to an inhabitant of a remote island. Agreeing that had he been born on that island he would not have achieved political renown, he added that nor would this islander have gained renown even had he been born an Athenian! The combination of individual talents (nature) with opportunity provided by the city (nurture), is required for great achievement. We need the minimum protection of a society, such that if that society does not wish us to survive we probably shall not. But we also need that society for the exercise of talents such as musical ability, as for many 'parts' of virtue, such as courage and generosity. For a 'full' individual is required the opportunity, which only a community provides, to grow physically, morally and intellectually, and to exercise his talents when developed. Generosity and courage involve relationship with other human beings, and without a sense of community cannot be deployed, for my community, however defined, will be composed of people whose interests are considered comparable, at times even prior in importance to my own. Best citizens will be best friends.

The modern anti-Aristotelian individualist will deny much of this, allowing that at certain stages of development people need the society of their fellows, indeed their active benevolence, but insisting that such a 'natural' situation carries with it no later obligations of benevolence when their interests are threatened; indeed that it is often 'best' to be parasitic on the society, to use it and take advantage of its help when we need it, to exploit it and manipulate it to our own advantage when opportunity (or 'need') arises. Of course, the principal Platonic reply to this is that the person who so acts will not profit but rather become 'unhappy'. But this has to be a particular sense of 'unhappy', for it is hard to argue that the wicked do not prosper materially; they often do, and many instances when they do not are no rebuttal of the 'immoralist' position, since it can be claimed – Platonic objections to the extreme cases notwithstanding – that the material failures of criminals are often due less to their criminality (involving their diminished sensitivity) than to their stupidity, or to sheer bad luck. A different sense of 'unhappy' has to be deployed, as Plato knew, that different sense being imbedded in an argument that the good life is not merely the exercise of our talents, however 'godlike' (as the Greeks would put it), but rather their deployment in an active concern with what we 'ought' to do to make our souls better, in the specifically moral and spiritual sense.

Within a strictly *Aristotelian* framework, as I have observed, it is some-times hard to see where the sense of moral, as distinct from pruden-tial, obligation comes from, though it assuredly operates. This probably contributes to the belief of a number of modern writers influenced by Aristotle, such as Williams, that overriding moral obligation should be removed from ethics altogether, that we should talk simply about living the good life and exercising our talents in a productive way; nor should we assume that aesthetic considerations ought always to yield to moral ones: so Gauguin arguably was right to abandon his family in order to paint in the South Seas. In cases like this, however, it is not unreasonable to wonder whether Williams relies, contrary to his professed intentions, on consequentialist considerations: millions admire the pictures, while the family is remembered only by a few tiresome biographers. In any case, Aristotle, who in his own will neither mentions his library nor even refers to himself as a philosopher,[7] would hardly endorse such a reading of his ethical project.

What Aristotle fails to do, thus leaving himself open to Williams' alien interpretation, is to explain adequately how moral (and therefore social) obligations are related to the good life as a whole,[8] let alone consider whether, and if so in what sense, such obligations lie at the heart of the

---

[7] With Aristotle's attitude as typical of classical Greece, we can compare Aeschylus whose epitaph noted that he fought for Athens, not that he was a playwright.

[8] We noted in chapter 6 the importance of Kant's 'discovery' of this weakness.

good life, or whether without them life cannot be good. It is probably this neglect – due to his unspoken acceptance of Platonic premises – which also generates another notorious problem for readers of his ethics – at least in times when the social context of pre-modern ethical writing has largely disappeared from view; this is the problem of the relationship between the 'practical' life and the life of contemplation. Here what is often missed in modern debate – as we have noticed in the practical reasoners – is that Aristotle *assumes* that any 'contemplative' will recognize certain 'moral' obligations as overriding: that there are some things which he simply would not do, others which he would insist on doing. No Aristotelian contemplative would be able to desert his comrades on the battlefield for the sake of meditation on God.

Nevertheless, it would be easier for Plato than for Aristotle to defeat the notion that as individuals we are moral atoms, of which the essence is that we have no responsibilities for *others*, let alone for society as a whole, unless we choose to assume them, and that we risk no psychological incompleteness if we choose to neglect them. Plato and Aristotle are more or less in agreement that there are two sides to the good life: the exercise of our abilities and the acceptance of some sort of moral ought (giving duties to ourselves as well as to others); Plato, however, because of his emphasis on man as primarily a moral and 'spiritual' – if divided – agent, and because of his more direct emphasis on a strong form of moral realism, can insist more effectively on what Aristotle would not want to deny, namely that, if correctly derived, obligations to others, both public and private – at best seen as welcome responsibilities – are an essential constituent of the good life. (One difference between them is that Aristotle, whose account of happiness is characteristically more tied to this present life, is more preoccupied with the damaging effects – even on the happiness of the virtuous – of ill-luck and material deprivation.)

What both Plato and Aristotle (and their successors) would always maintain against the moral atomist is that a sense of public and private responsibility for others is an inherent part of human nature (and not merely of culture, let alone of choice), that this sense provides a basis for any account of obligation and a field in which social and personal inspiration may be sown, and that unless our capacity for responsibility is nurtured, we develop awry. To have a developed sense of responsibility is not a want, not something we can choose to have, but something we *need* in order to 'live well'. And, as we have argued earlier, our sense of responsibility is an essential link with our own past, and helps to enhance the growing unity of the self which will mark our success in moral living.

Responsibility can only develop in a social and political framework; hence membership in a community, and on no piecemeal basis (for the sense of responsibility would then be diminished) is a fundamental human need without which human beings are the worse off – indeed less than fully 'human'. In a community we both live out our responsibilities and are corrected if we fail to do so. The community develops the responsible and corrected individual member, thus eliminating the moral atom and emphasizing man's communal role. In accordance with such beliefs about the best life for man, both Plato and Aristotle view the basic distinction between good and bad constitutions (and *ceteris paribus* among human beings insofar as they are publicly effective) not in terms of the size of the governing group (for example, aristocracy or democracy), but of whether or not rulers take on responsibility and rule for the sake of others as well as (but not excluding) themselves.

In contrast to the ancient view, however, we have noticed that several more recent accounts of personal identity, of what it is to be the same human being over time – especially those of Locke, Hume, and more recently Parfit – suffer from lack of attention precisely to that particular activity in 'moral space' which is the development and exercise of our capacity for responsibility.

Since we possess a sense of responsibility and cannot describe ourselves without reference to it, and since that sense must be exercised within a community whose members accept and respect each other, not only is an *unconstrained* individualism in conflict with something ineradicable in human nature – the development of which has greatly contributed to whatever moral identity we have thus far attained – but almost equally unsatisfactory will be the *prudential* individualism which calculates how we can all agree to maximize our advantages by game-theoretic or other means. To concern oneself only with what is rationally in one's immediate interest is not to develop a sense of responsibility, but to plan to act *as though* we were responsible whenever it makes sense to do so.

The problems with prudential individualism are analogous to those previously considered in the case of Epicurus' attitude to friendship. Friendship purely for the sake of mutual profit will not sustain itself, and to adopt what merely *advertises* itself as a responsible attitude to others is no more to acquire a sense of responsibility than to enter a 'trial marriage' is to enter a marriage. Of course, it is possible to convert a trial marriage into a marriage, but then a new action is required by which we constitute ourselves married people by a commitment. Practising quasi-responsibility might teach us something about responsibility, even help us to become responsible, like holding 'mock' elections in schools; it is not itself the practice of responsibility, which, like marriage, is constituted by predictability.

Curiously, both the life of duty ('moral' life in the narrow and constraining sense) and the life of achieving what we are capable of insofar as we have the opportunity, can be diverted towards individualism and moral atomism: in the first case because our sole concern can be our own (negatively construed) moral performance, pursued 'whatever the consequences' in rule-driven courses of action regardless of social effects direct or indirect. To act without consideration of the direct effects of our behaviour is to be willing to use people as means to the end of our own 'perfection', while to act without concern for the indirect effects is to incur imprudence and culpable negligence.

Directly to actualize one's potential and use one's talents obviously also risks moral atomism and anti-social individualism, for side-constraints, such as the principle that no-one should be worse off as a result of one's behaviour, or that the weakest and most disadvantaged members of one's society should not be worse off, certainly cannot be squeezed out of the principle of developing one's talents and using one's skills without invoking further (probably arbitrary or fashionable) premises. In a libertarian world there need be no rational constraint on doing what one is able to find means of doing, in accordance with the skills which seem the most attractive and 'worthwhile' to deploy.

The basic theoretical problem in developing an account of the social and political ramifications of the best life is to identify obligations which enable us to develop in accordance with a disciplined and rational evaluation of our talents while simultaneously constraining skills and excellences when required by considerations of the 'common good': put alternatively, to identify how far it is the mark of any genuinely human skill that it be exercised only within the context of adequate moral restraint, sense of obligation or sense of responsibility, however that sense of responsibility or obligation be ultimately grounded.[9] As we have seen, a desirable proportion between these elements of the best life can only be rationally determined if we have some idea of what we are 'at our best' and without which we can only 'hope for the best', while often – especially under pressure, as the reading of history ought regularly to remind us – only securing what is far from the best.

---

[9] As noted, such grounding is lacking in much contemporary 'communitarian' thought: again a result of the quest for ethics (and politics) without the inescapable metaphysics.

Learning to be socially responsible is not just a question of acquiring well-adapted habits: of running to become a runner, as Aristotle at times suggests. Nor is it merely a matter of *enjoying* being responsible, though normally the responsible man will prefer to act responsibly, even when that entails doing things which are far from enjoyable or even highly unpleasing. It is also a matter of learning to respect the members of the community for which we wish and ought to feel responsible, and being mindful of the difference, so distinct from the mentality of the hired bureaucrat (who could be an out-and-out Thrasymachean), between respecting someone and taking account of him, as perhaps an inconvenient perplexity.

Consider attempts to eliminate hatred based on race or class. In order to achieve a society in which any possible citizen can flourish, his fellows must learn to respect those of other races and classes. If we are in some sense to feel responsible for the whole human race (including future generations) – the most urgent reason for being concerned, for example, with the ecological condition of the planet – we must feel respect, and understand why we feel respect, for the entire human race. To underpin this, we need a theory as to why all or any human beings should be 'respected', in the same way as we need a better rationale for why all or any should be accorded rights than that they are powerful enough to choose, assert or grab them in virtue of their being active 'moral' agents.

If our problem may be seen as whether or not we should *respect* our fellows, it still cannot be dissociated from whether we need them and the kind of need in question. I have pointed to certain essential needs if we are to develop to something generally labelled 'maturity', but have asked whether our concern for those we need (and who otherwise may not be fit for our use) will not be limited when, after using them, we find that it no longer 'pays', at least in the short term, to treat them with the respect we previously evinced. That in turn relates to the *kind* of needs we hope to have satisfied by the other members of our community. Might it be the case, for example, that the older and wiser we get the less we (normally) need the help of others and the less we need to 'respect' them?

Leave aside the consideration that if we antagonize our immediate fellows we risk losing their support even in emergency, and so may fail to satisfy even our basic need for self-preservation. Notice again, however, that those who would rationally plan the best life for themselves habitually think of the participants to the contract (or whatever other rationale they come up with to underpin their prudential policies) uniformly as adults. In explaining this, leave aside more sociological questions about why we have developed a society which disregards the young, particularly the very young. (We no longer say, as was and is often said in more traditional societies, since our society has repudiated patriarchalism and, significantly, so far failed to substitute matriarchy, that offspring are included with the head of a family.) We must recognize that the omission of children – or their self-serving misdescription as adults – highlights a wider lack of concern to exercise *responsibility* for others, that is, *inter alia*, for their physical and moral education, which when necessary will include correction.

Why then do we appear to fail so signally in this particular? Because in seeking, as rational adults, to improve our own lot, usually in material terms or in terms of increasing our 'freedom', we rarely see the necessity – if my account of our self-division is roughly adequate – to *correct* our own behaviour and outlook, let alone *extend* our area of responsibility – which would itself be a major correction. As rational agents we adults do not need correction; we may correct ourselves, but if we choose to, not because we ought to. Even if we admit good reason to change, we do not accept to be *corrected* by our society. We are not children!

Rational planners will be concerned with satisfying their wants, as far as is convenient without harming others rationally wishing to do the same thing. But for most people, and certainly for self-seeking rational agents, correction is merely an unpleasant experience, unwanted, and, we hope, hardly needed. If we are only to be concerned with our choices and wants, our community will by default be viewed solely as the means of enabling us to secure them. Yet whether we *need* to be corrected is not a matter of choice; it depends on what sort of people we are, on our character. That 'surd-factor' of our nature which we considered earlier precisely calls for correction, and not least when we do not choose or like to be corrected. And moral correction means correction of our sense of responsibility towards others, but also, *ex hypothesi*, towards ourselves: not least, that is, in relation to holding ourselves responsible for our own past.

If the community – and perhaps immediately *only* some form of community – can fulfil an inevitable *need* for personal correction, then we need such a community to play such a part in our lives that extreme theoretical positions like moral atomism and radical individualism are seen to make no sense. Our wants may be the grounds, when negotiated, for *civil* obligations, where the society is viewed as 'external' to its 'members',[10] but the need to correct ourselves demands a more 'Aristotelian'

---

[10] H. L. A. Hart, *The Concept of Law* (Oxford University Press, 1961), 88.

community not merely as supplier of goods and services and as enabler of functions, but as the 'organism' to which, if we are to make *moral* progress, we have *no choice* but to adhere wholeheartedly.

We are thus brought back to a now tedious question: are we now or could we now be in an optimal condition, and on what does the possibility of such an optimal condition depend? Few people believe themselves to be in optimal condition, whatever their material or professional satisfactions. That being so, have we to accept that we cannot even approach an optimal condition, or are we to say that to do so we require an ongoing correction of our natures – and above all of our sense of responsibility – and thus the abandonment, as a delusion, of the assumption that we can 'go it alone' as properly human beings? If this conclusion, namely that we stand in need of correction, entails the rejection of individualism and the return to a wider and Aristotelian sense of needing to belong to a community not merely of unavoidables but of friends, then so does the pursuit of individualism entail either an acceptance of whatever we can make of ourselves, however horrific it may be – which is roughly the Sartrian option of salvation in and through chosen praxis without regard to what kind of praxis – or the acceptance that we are already the best we could be, which latter option Nietzsche expresses in the subtitle to *Ecce Homo*: we must become what we are.

Notice how different is this Nietzschean aspiration from a traditional claim which superficially resembles it. Older dualistic (and Platonizing) models of man suggest that we can recover a hidden self, the pearl-in-the-oyster, if the excrescences which have accumulated around it (perhaps seen simplistically as bodily) are stripped away. The Nietzschean view is quite different; it entails accepting ourselves as we are *now*, not in any responsibility for our actions, but simply in the being what we are. Clearly such a view, unlike the pearl-in-the-oyster theory, wholly contradicts any realist morality. Foucault (rightly from the Nietzschean standpoint) rejects even Sartrian praxis as a kind of terrorism – and in this akin to traditional morality – in favour of an all-accepting way of living in which the traditionally 'darker' and 'lighter' sides of human nature receive equal weight. Such a twentieth-century proposal corresponds descriptively with the dark pictures of original sin given by the sternest Christian moralists. But while 'Pelagian' utopians deny original sin and Augustinians maintain it, claiming that only God can free us from it, Nietzscheans, at least according to Foucault, hold that the moral quagmire condemned by the Augustinians is simply our existential condition, and thus that not only is there nothing sinful about it but that we have no option but to try and live it, and indeed 'should' live it – though it is hard to see where the 'should' comes from, unless (after all) it is a ghostly image of Sartrian authenticity.

None of us, of course, should have any illusions that, if this is ultimate individualism, it is also the way to madness, suicide and even murder: whether or not stories circulated about Foucault are fair to him, it is at least likely that just as he wagered his own life, suicidally, in the bathhouses of San Francisco, so he could have wagered the lives of others. One of his disciples has objected ('rightly', from the individualist's point of view) to any such hypothesis about his behaviour being considered under the 'moralizing' canon of 'truth' or 'falsehood'.[11]

At least we can see that this version of self-realization has little to do with the traditional Platonic or dualizing sort, the primary difference lying in the earlier assumption that the present 'empirical' self needs *correcting*, and that whether or not it once existed in a perfect form, as Plato seems to have supposed and as some Christian accounts of Adam also suggest, or whether that perfect form is something towards which our various roles, some dominant, some weaker, are – given 'moral luck' or whatever it takes – all tending. But if our 'self' needs correcting, there is an unassailable case to be made that the correction must come largely from a community where the traditional virtues have been exercised. If we could correct ourselves we should not stand in need of correction.

The traditional moral virtues, saturated with respect and hence a sense of responsibility for others developed within the social setting, diminish the empirical self. They certainly point us beyond becoming *what we are now*. Yet to the individualist, strictly speaking, 'what we are now' *is* all that we are or could be or 'should' be, and we had better face the amorality of that fact, if fact it is and if we want truth – even 'truth' in scare-quotes – rather than social control. That much Nietzsche certainly got right. If, on the other hand, there is an objective morality, effectively grounded in some theistic version of Platonic realism, we must maintain a distinction between a present empirical (and divided) self and a 'real'

---

[11] D. M. Halperin, in 'Bringing Out Michel Foucault', in a series of papers on James Miller's *The Passion of Michel Foucault* (New York: HarperCollins, 1993) in *Salmagundi* 97 (1993), 69–89. Note especially the ambiguous reaction to the suggestion that Foucault may have intended murder (p. 84) and the (deliberate) echo of Goering's reaction to 'Geist' (p. 89): 'The example of Miller's book demonstrates with particular vividness, then, why it is that whenever those of us who felt themselves to be in Foucault's embattled position, or who share his political vision, hear those who don't do either invoke the notion of "truth", we reach for our revolvers.' For Goering's attitude to truth (and to recognize its similarity to Halperin's) see J. C. Fest, *The Face of the Third Reich* (Harmondsworth: Penguin, 1983), 121: 'I thank my Maker that I do not know what objective is. I am subjective.'

self and insist that my real self is at least in part communal, that is, living and emerging (and, we hope, improving) over time in a respected community – and willy-nilly. We become what we will to be, and not on our own but in some sort of respectfully – better lovingly – corrected and correcting solidarity with others. We grow in community, and the better the community – 'better' meaning more saturated with accurate moral theory – the more likely we are to grow well.

REALISM OR IDEOLOGICAL DECEPTION?

Thomas Aquinas – confident about the transcendental foundations of ethics – argued for the importance of four basic and 'Aristotelian' human inclinations. In earlier chapters we have met two of these: the desire for life (self-preservation) and the desire for reproduction; to these Aquinas added a third, which we have just introduced: the inclination (and the need) to live in society. If, however, choice is to regulate all these goods as their ultimate arbiter, and if, as has been argued, the notion of choice, thus understood, is incoherent, then a choice-based morality has to reject Aquinas' fourth and final inclination – that already identified in the opening lines of Aristotle's *Metaphysics*: the inclination to truth itself. We have seen how the collision of choice with inescapable fact points in an anti-Thomist direction, sacrificing truth in the interest of choice, and how in this respect Nietzsche and Foucault are the New Prophets.[12]

Conceivably we must accept that first principles cannot be established for ethics, that to seek a secure and non-arbitrary basis on which to construct a set of ethical propositions is quixotic, that 'foundationalism' is an outdated aspiration. Conceivably neither reason nor realism are necessary or even plausible foundations, or perhaps they can be introduced, if deemed necessary or useful, at some later stage of the process of moralizing by those whose first principles (even in contrast to their actual practice) are ultimately defensible only in terms of the most brutal self-assertion, such self-assertion being a variety of the deification of unexamined 'choice', carried to its 'absurd' extreme: we opt for 'choice'. In any case, there would seem to be ground for concern – if not for despair – if our historically most valued beliefs and ideals turn out to be either ultimately arbitrary or merely a consistent set of self-supporting and supposedly prudential theses dependent on circular reasoning and established by human agents whose nature and goods are substantially uncertain.

---

[12] For Aquinas' view see *Summa Theologiae* I–II q. 94, a. 2 c.

Of three ways in which ethics could be devoid of necessary foundations, only one is our present concern. Ethics would lack foundation if it flouted basic principles of reasoning such as the law of contradiction, and it would be irrelevant to human action if it flouted the first principle of practical reasoning (without which all 'moral' statements make no sense), namely that the good (whatever it is) should be done and the bad avoided. Nonsensical utterances are beside the point. What must concern us – and in the most practical sense – is the third possibility: the situation in which we would find ourselves if there were no *non-stipulative* way of *evaluating* the behaviour of particular agents. Thus we could describe the six-inch blade penetrating the throat of the unwanted and friendless Brazilian 'street kid' clinically enough, but we could say nothing authoritative about whether it is good that he should be stabbed for the amusement of those who have thrown him into a police cell or about whether we should regard his captors and killers as noble or ignoble.

The most basic *stipulative* suggestion for handling such problems has already been canvassed, namely to propose a certain determination by ourselves, individually or in groups, that certain kinds of inconsistent, irrational, frightening or otherwise 'shocking' behaviour should be stigmatized not merely as inconsistent, irrational, frightening, or shocking, but also as '*wrong*'. The suggestion, however, is not that wrongness is something additional to the other characteristics or a way to refer to them as a sum greater than its parts, but only that it is a term to be attached to one or more of those characteristics when they appear in specified circumstances. I thus avoid banishing 'wrong' altogether, for, as noted, the paradox still appears shocking if a moral philosopher replying to the question 'Did Hitler ever do anything wrong?' states baldly 'He certainly did many things which I detested and which destroyed the lives of many millions of people, but strictly speaking I could not say that he did anything "wrong".' That might be the strictly truthful answer; however, to avoid shocking, I might prefer to use 'wrong' to refer to the characteristics which my own society, or the 'enlightened' segments of it – often designated 'we' – have come to label morally and socially 'inappropriate'.

But, as I have also noticed, a major difficulty in the way of this 'stipulative' solution is that – as Socrates showed Callicles – we find it hard to be consistent in our usage. Our belief in an objective standard is deep-seated, error theories notwithstanding; hence instead of consistently rejecting the realist sense of 'wrong', we may apply it to different kinds of actions. We laugh at 'Victorians' for saying that fornication or serial partnerships are wrong (our laughter depending on a widely varied set of assumptions, not all of which may involve relativism or perspectivism), but normally say, or at least feel obliged to say, that discriminating against blacks or Jews is just wrong; alternatively, if we are adherents of the National Front *et al.*, that allowing racial intermarriage is. Etc.

What are we doing in such cases? Leave aside the possibility that there are objective and prescriptive truths in morality after all, and that, being realist, they are not dependent on what we, or the Victorians, or the National Front, find reason to think from time to time. Rather, in default of these truths, we must either *pretend* that they exist and have practical entailments or we invent a practically effective substitute for such now discredited moral thinking. In either case we need to be clear that not only are we to fashion our morality; we (most of us) are also to believe in it,[13] and for it to be effective, we have to accept its prescriptive force with the same devotion as we did in the bad old 'Platonizing' days. Of course, the non-prescriptive aspect even of invented or postulated 'truths' may be 'objective' (though not realist): it can be allowed as a fact that certain behaviour really does damage the agent or the victim, or both – in which case we can *decide* that it is wrong, or conversely that it is not. Reflection on the social role of moral beliefs shows why we need to feel strongly about them, whether such feeling is 'realistically' warranted or no. Unless appropriate people are prepared to *feel revulsion* at the arrest and random killing of 'street kids' as well as recognizing propositionally that it is bad luck for someone else, namely the 'street kids' in question (I will assume they are not merely worried that a murder committed in the next district will affect their own), and unless that revulsion arises from a belief that killing 'street kids' is 'wrong', they will be insufficiently concerned about killing 'street kids' to provide us with much hope that the practice will be stamped out. The social machine not merely runs on the nuts and bolts of the propositional recognition that some sorts of private actions and some types of public policy and public behaviour are irrational or hurtful, but is fuelled by the emotive insistence on justice which only a belief (whether justified or not) that morality is something different from a prudential self-interest will provide: a sense of personal outrage which springs from a belief that what has been done damages a world for which

[13] Notice again an analogous situation in theological writing: followers of Don Cupitt, such as David A. Hart, *Faith in Doubt: Non-Realism and Christian Belief* (London: Mowbray, 1993), would have us accept that it is the part of the mature Christian (indeed of the mature theist) first to invent his own God – the projection of his highest ideals – and then to worship him. The form of argument goes back at least to Feuerbach.

one recognizes oneself as irreducibly responsible insofar as one has means to exercise that responsibility – perhaps even beyond normal means.

In the last days of the old régime an anti-apartheid campaign might have been attractive to some inside South Africa on merely prudential grounds. ('If we oppress the kaffirs further it could be the worse for us in the future.') But such prudential considerations would have had little appeal in, say, the United Kingdom of the 1950s, where 'It couldn't happen here'. Virtually all international campaigns for civil rights depend not on their supporters' prudential beliefs, but on the belief that something is more seriously and primarily wrong than merely judicious suasions suggest. Fortunately appeals to relativism (It's all right in South Africa or Tibet, but not here) or to various forms of perspectivism seldom succeed in dissuading the supporters of such causes; however, if non-realists, we might wonder whether, despite its being to our advantage that supporters of good causes should believe that female circumcision (for example) is 'just wrong', they are not ultimately 'useful idiots'. But from whose standpoint is such a judgement to be made? Are we to assume a group with *no* delusions, and able to manipulate the delusions of others? If so, for whose advantage?, and if not for mine, why should I encourage them? In any case, I should be unwise to do so, for even if their original intentions are 'honourable', it is likely that those who regularly mislead others will develop a contempt for the misled. Moreover, the propagandist, if he is to be successful, cannot readily keep himself from believing the beliefs by which he manipulates others.[14]

Philosophers have often expressed unease about the behaviour of any thinker, propagandist or not, who claims to know the truth himself but to keep it from others for their good, and this unease is not merely on account of moral corruption overtaking those who so behave but over the moral dubiety of the behaviour itself. Williams has dubbed such an attitude as found in the utilitarian tradition 'Government House Consequentialism', and Sidgwick's clear concern about it may show that he was more moral than his theory; he had less opportunity for supposing such behaviour immoral than has a twenty-first-century thinker who

---

[14] Plato had already made the point, 'correcting' Thucydides, and deception by the élite about the fundamentals of ethics may be attractive even granted a 'realist', but widely unrecognized, moral world. In such a world strict justification for condemning, for example, ecological vandalism could only be achieved by arguments which at some point will suggest premises about the existence and nature of God. Such premises will make no impact on atheists, who can only be convinced (irrationally) of the 'truth' about the environment by arguments – or in some cases mere appeal to self-interest – formally inadequate when purged of theistic features. Publicists (and self-appointed philosophers) often, wittingly or unwittingly, resort to such arguments.

should have relearned from intervening history the corruption endemic in self-appointed political and moral élites. Thus much at least in mitigation of what Sidgwick committed himself to in writing, namely that, 'It *seems* [my italics] expedient that the doctrine that esoteric morality is expedient should itself be kept esoteric. Or, if this concealment be difficult to maintain, it *may be* desirable that Common Sense should repudiate the doctrines which it is expedient to confine to an enlightened few.'[15]

Sidgwick thus betrays a measure of unease about concealment. Rawls and Williams too find it objectionable. Yet in the confusion in which, given the death of realism, we find moral philosophy presently mired, effective alternatives seem almost to necessitate self-deception and deception of others: as the dilemma imposes itself, either we ignore the fact that we operate in an apparent world of objective and realist values which, were we to examine it, we could not sustain, or we deliberately foster, or allow others to foster, the emotional accompaniments of the old morality within our own wholly different post-moral context. Perhaps this second alternative appears to involve less deception, or perhaps with it deception is no longer a problem, the emotional accompaniments of the old morality being there to be attached to any set of beliefs about human action. Such questions are part of the wider problem of the nature and status of ideologies.

This is not the place for a detailed comparison of ideologist and moral philosopher, though – *pace* contemporary Nietzscheans – there are great differences, as there are also important common features. Both are convinced of the rightness of their ways of understanding the 'moral' world of human action and behaviour, and though one wants his hearers to be ideologically, the other morally, driven – and my account heretofore should suffice to indicate how this distinction is not merely question-begging – both expect not merely an intellectual commitment to 'truth' as they see it, but an emotional commitment, with its concomitant loves, hates, preferences and aversions, and the consequent choices and refusals. Normally, they both will expect their adherents to accept their beliefs as 'true' and not be wittingly deceived, though some ideologists may think it necessary to go through a stage of deliberate self-indoctrination – not to say deception – in order to arrive at 'the truth', while others will follow the more stipulative route whereby what is true is *defined* as what we declare to be true.

[15] H. Sidgwick, *The Methods of Ethics* (eighth edition, London, 1907), 490; regretted but still maintained, 395–6. For Williams see 'Utilitarianism and Beyond', in Smart and Williams, *Utilitarianism: For and Against*, 16. Rawls also thinks that moral beliefs should be public, and attributes such views to Kant (*A Theory of Justice*, 133, 338, note 4; cf. 182, note 31).

Observation of the workings of the appeal to ideology shows that the enthusiasms, loves and hatreds of believers mimic the emotions that arise from 'untaught' moral beliefs, that is, the moral responses which grow up 'naturally' in pre-philosophical societies, as also that such emotional responses – and their related stirrings of 'conscience' – can attach to lies put about by ideological puppet-masters. Nazi propagandists were successful in inducing in their populations a revulsion and fear towards Jews such as many 'naturally' feel for rats or other rodents, thus facilitating a popular acceptance that Jews should be treated as such, even to extermination. Emotional responses are the necessary triggers for action, whether for crudely ideological ends or for more authentically 'moral' ones, and if 'objective' moral judgements of the traditional sort are held to be based on bogus metaphysics, that in no way inhibits attaching 'moral emotions' to some other and more acceptable social 'glue'. It merely requires something more 'acceptable' to be available: most of us – arguably on 'intuitive' rather than fully reasoned grounds – do not find Nazi-type ideologies the acceptable 'glue' to which to attach our sense of righteousness and accompanying emotions.

Those philosophers who would find it disconcerting if any or every harnessing of our emotions were to involve deception by an ideological controller or some other 'rational' social planner or institution, might be brought to accept such deception if they believed that the self-evidently useful emotional commitment to justice could *only* be promoted if the wider public still assumed (falsely) that moral judgements are objectively true or false and that they ultimately depend on the existence of such real 'items' as God or Goodness: hence the encouragement of such false beliefs might seem necessary for the organization of the best possible society.

But 'best' in whose judgement? It is obvious that the ordinary citizen wants the best possible society, but less obvious that he would approve of a society the essential precondition of which is that some or even most of its members will be deliberately or effectively deceived: at best the society of the Platonic 'noble lie' – so excoriated following Popper – in which the omniscient philosopher thinks it best for most, if not all, of his fellows to remain in ignorance.[16] Plato aside, however, in a non-realist world the vanguard consequentialist will not only argue with his peers that it is *rational* to deceive most people (the view, I have maintained, at which most people will balk), and try to persuade the public to accept what he himself 'knows' to be false; he will ignore or underplay the significant risk

---

[16] Plato's defence, of course, would be that all deceptions are not equal, that he would have men deceived only in the interest of what *really* is the best city – itself only to be constructed in a 'realist' universe.

of the deceiver succumbing to his own deception, of losing the ability to recognize that he has opted to deceive other people. And if he finds that his sophistries alone will fail to secure this deception, he must resort to forms of public fraud such as large-scale media manipulation. Nor will he necessarily exclude various forms of coercion – such as we already find employed, in decreasingly hidden ways in, for example, appointments influential on medical ethics.[17]

Of course, since his credit is damaged or destroyed if his deception is discovered, our non-realist guide must be not only a liar but an effective liar – with 'psychological' – i.e. soul – effects I have no need to repeat if my account of our present divided self is authenticated. Lying will be personally divisive even if there exists no Platonic realism to under-write more constructive behaviour. Even if inventing 'Platonism' may (at least in the short run) help the social fabric, it is liable to be at the cost of 'happiness' and peace to those who invent it, and devastatingly so if they are led into the paradoxical situation of believers in their own deception.

FROM ETHICS TO POLITICS

Plato it was who first pointed out that any theory of man, implicit or explicit, will be reflected in a theory of the state. In his analysis of our three competing loves and lifestyles in the *Republic*, the organiza-tion of the 'tripartite soul' is paralleled by constitutions indicating the potential arrangements of the 'parts' of its citizen-body. In a modern context there will be no perfect examples of textbook constitutions; so-called democratic societies will have non-democratic elements built in, while dictatorships may exhibit democratic or aristocratic features. That is unimportant theoretically; all we need recognize is that insofar as, for example, a society is 'multicultural' (which is to exclude those where the cultures are sealed off, as largely happened in 'apartheid' South Africa), the self also will be to some degree multicultural. As I have shown, we can-not avoid being affected by our surroundings, sometimes 'pluralizing' our selves to the point of living not merely different but contradictory 'lives', without realizing we are doing so – unless we put ourselves through the intellectual processes needful to reconcile our 'lives' in a more coherent synthesis.

---

[17] We should recognize that a call for force may lurk behind any adoption of choice theory, in that there will often be no logically or emotionally compelling reason why anyone else should willingly accept my choices.

Such diversity, in the individual as well as in the society, community or state, poses problems for public policy as well as for the individual members who will need to reconcile their lifestyles as best they can. Two extreme possibilities will emerge, neither of which will be adopted in its pure form, though each forms the pole towards which 'impure' mixes will tend; these I will dub Tolerant Diversity and Corporate Unity. The former signals acceptance by the society of any and all the goods proposed by its members; in practical terms its obvious weakness is that individual goals will be destructive of the goals of others, so that they cannot exist side by side without regulation whereby the state curbs some to allow opportunity for others. But at the theoretical level that means that the principle of toleration is breached, and debate, issuing in perhaps arbitrary decisions, will ensue as to its limits, and as to a further principle to determine those limits, which will be viewed as existing to maximize toleration in accordance with guidelines themselves dependent on some principle of 'fairness'. Thus it will be argued that it is *unfair* to some to tolerate the 'excesses' of others, or that there is no *reason* to tolerate the claim of one at the expense of another, such arguments assuming the role of the state to be that of providing a 'level playing-field'. The 'playing-field' metaphor, however, is ambiguous: either the state offers 'equal opportunity' to all *or* it adjusts opportunities in the interests of certain concerns deemed 'fair' (or even actually so).

Here we can isolate an instructive dilemma of 'post-modern' Western democracy evinced strikingly in debates about public policy on issues such as violence and 'hard' pornography. It used to be said that pornographic material will become merely boring; there is no need for censorship – stigmatized as a cardinal intolerance – since it will disappear on its own, or at least people will become unaffected, if it is freely available. The predictable objection has been that *even* if it be found that most of us are not attracted by 'hard' pornography – finding it merely 'inappropriate' or distasteful – catastrophic results can ensue if it impresses only a small minority of individuals, when tolerance as mere theory is then liable to give way before the rampages of two or three serial killers or child-molesters; then something of a lynch-mob mentality develops, with far from tolerant pressures on both suspects and the police. Individualism too is discounted, though in fudged rather than principled fashion, so that the honest thinker will question whether a degree or two more censorship is not by far the lesser of evils.

A popular variation on individualism, offering each individual a 'fair' chance to satisfy his wishes or choices, is what might be called group individualism, whereby the roles of individuals are played by pressure-groups whose leaders view their organizations as extensions and organs of themselves. Much North American politics is now to be viewed as clashes between the claims of individuals and those of larger or smaller groups, self-identified as women, gays, native peoples, Hispanics, the 'moral majority', etc. Formally left-of-centre organizations which may have verged towards mild forms of socialism, as even the Democratic Party itself, can view themselves as umbrella-holders for such pressure-groups, while in opposition the Republicans stand up for good old individual individualism. Typically, group-rights people describe themselves in neo-Marxist terms or terms derived from the Frankfurt School, the traditionally Marxist proletariat being replaced by the favoured group of the moment. It should be needless to say that Marx himself would not have touched such groups with the proverbial bargepole, and nor, not long since, would they have touched Marx!

Toleration, the 'letting of a thousand flowers grow', stands as the principle by which the state, as Rawls has put it, exists to arbitrate – on whatever basis – between competing freedoms. The opposite extreme is some form of corporatism, often dubbed 'fascism', though by no means exclusively the province of the political right. Its roots are in a longing for community, for a sense of solidarity with our fellow humans – at least for those of them deemed worthy to inhabit the Promised Land, for in extreme cases the unworthy are killed, expelled, locked up in mental hospitals – or merely kept out of influential positions. Its appeal is to a fragmented sense of unity in which all work together for a common good; in Western practice it usually takes the form of an ideological movement operating quasi-messianically and as a religion-surrogate, replacing the community of heaven, the unity of the faithful in God, with a man-made dream of perfect satisfaction for me and mine.

A theoretical reason why such schemes end up in brutality and oppression is indeed that they surround the utopian state, and that vanguard who know how to manipulate and run it, with a divine aura.[18] For in the theological original – one notes how yet another standard concept

---

[18] An intriguing example of the substitution of the state for God appears in a number of secular Zionists' outlooks, for example in formerly American Israeli Prime Minister Golda Meir, for revealing comment on whom see A. Orr, *The unJewish State: The Politics of Jewish Identity in Israel* (London: Ithaca Press, 1983), 172–84. The case of Israel is unique in that secular Zionists ground the secular state on a religious tradition which they reject. If Zionism were so simply secular, it would have no other than a pragmatic or sentimental case for the establishment of a Jewish state *in Israel*. Yet if it is religious and its ideals founded on Biblical and traditional faith, it is hard to see why it should issue in a secular state at all: hence the attempt of 'ultra-Orthodox' groups to produce an anti-modern theocracy, comparable here to parallel attempts in Muslim states.

seems easier to defend in a theological context – an infinite God can be supposed to understand the single good that is his nature in the manifold forms in which each of us strives for it or fails to lay hold on it. In its secular guise, corporate utopianism deifies finite goods in the restricted aims of an individual or group and suppresses all other goods and aims, thereby diminishing the individuality of those who legitimately seek them.[19] Thus whereas the tolerant state overemphasizes the individualizing features of the human psyche, the 'fascists' overemphasize, and through restriction necessarily abuse, the psyche's need for unity and homogeneity of goods.

The specious unity appealed to in 'fascism' is reduction to a lowest common denominator, and there is an important sense in which some more apparently democratic forms of egalitarianism are similarly impugnable and can thus be seen as 'fascist'. The basic economic problem of political life is that for whatever reason, whether it be poor agriculture, incompetent management, corrupt government, excessive demand or losses arising from war, there is never enough to go round of necessary material goods, let alone of luxuries or less tangible cultural, artistic, even spiritual assets. Idealists often proclaim that this would not be the case if man behaved more rationally or less sinfully; by itself this is not intelligent *political* comment, since there is no reason to suppose that human behaviour will greatly improve in these respects – though the establishment of 'fail-safe' institutions may do something to counteract its worst effects.

If there is in effect insufficient for all, how should public policy be formulated to deal with that reality? The lowest common denominator answer is an egalitarianism easily fuelled by envy. But it is apparent that to take away from those who have is often easier than to give to those who have not, and hardest is to raise the cultural opportunities of those who have not to the level achievable by those who have. This is not intended as a lazy answer to the problem of distributional injustice, but to point out a rule of the world of supply and demand, namely that if there is insufficient available, we make political problems – not to speak of human opportunities – worse by radical redistribution of goods if such redistribution means taking away from some without giving enough to others.

Take Britain as an example, where the problem cries out in the field of education. Prescinding from educational effects deriving from differences

---

[19] For the 'classic' liberal introduction to the problems of single-minded utopianism see I. Berlin, *The Hedgehog and the Fox* (London; Weidenfeld and Nicolson, 1953).

in children's home backgrounds and from the disadvantages which would accrue if an invariable form of state education were imposed on all, those who attend private schools are more often than not given a more thorough-going education than those in the state system. In the most obvious sense this is unfair and requires a remedy. But abolition of private schools – as was shown by abolition of those 'grant-aided' by Labour ideologue Shirley Williams – would in itself do nothing to improve general standards of education but – to put the matter in simplified terms – only mean that under the reformed system even fewer have a good education and therefore the possibility of passing this on. It is hard to see how egalitarianism of that sort caters to anything but envy, that is, the desire to take away from someone else merely because that someone else has more. Economic expediency – the inability or unwillingness to fund an overall improvement in education – thus finds a licence for political destructiveness with benefit to no-one and the result of cultural impoverishment of the whole.

If excess of tolerance produces an egalitarianism which, unless tempered, promotes envy because supplies of all kinds fall short of demand and expectation, it appears that what the state can do best for its citizens is to encourage them to accept inequalities of wealth on the understanding that promoting the advantages of all is its highest priority. Clearly a society will become more unified if, with basic requirements of justice fulfilled, there is a restraint on the claim of further rights, whether those rights be claimed as human and inalienable or merely as contractual and civil. If anything is to be done to promote the sense of community which Plato and Aristotle assume and for whose desirability I have argued, then this kind of restraint is essential, and it will have to be recognized by the individual that his or her own 'rights' may have to be limited or declined in the interest of the common good, as regularly happens in wartime even in the best ordered societies. It may also require that we tolerate in actual states of society what in some theoretically better society might be intolerable.

Contemporary Western society appears to be largely developing in the opposite direction, not least because in attempting to sort out public policy on the basis of the rights claims of groups or individuals, it has no yardstick by which it can arrange such claims into a plausible list of priorities, for that would offend against the equal toleration of goods or perceived goods. The result is necessarily either no planning, or the constant neglect of long-term goals in favour of more immediately obtainable short-term ones, or alternatively the specious deferral of short-term goods in favour of the (alleged though not planned) claims of goods further 'down the road'. Of course the whole political landscape is simultaneously disfigured both by the short-term imperative of winning elections through satisfying conflicting interest-groups simultaneously and by the immensely complicated social equations which demand solution when politics and economics are played out on a global scale.

Furthermore, although we may like to suppose we belong to a 'global village', we seem to assume that our village has to be full of feuding families or groups. Indeed with all local traditions in the melting pot to which I alluded in reflecting on the diverse origins of our various cherished moral beliefs, it is likely that factionalism only increases as we maintain the special goals of Western individualism. Already the way to power and influence in a typical Western democracy is being seen less as to push one's claims – which as Hobbes observed will soon fall victim to the 'warfare' of ideological and political anarchy – than to identify oneself with a lobby group whose well-being can be assimilated to one's own. As I have remarked, the development of lobby-group politicking in the United States – the most 'advanced' Western democracy in the sense that 'rights' depend on legal interpretations of a document, the Constitution, man-made and therefore flawed, but treated as a holy writ – is an indication of how to expect things to go in the global village. On Hobbes' war of all against all – supposing that to occur within a single national political unit – is superimposed the war of group against group, reflected in institutions as diverse as multinational corporations, gun lobbies or environmental protection agencies and operating not only within but well beyond the boundaries of often arbitrarily constructed nation-states.

At this point the 'fascist' appeal to order and overall unity, preferably in the form of a world-state, can seem attractive, but the danger of 'fascism', constructed globally, is transparently the danger it historically has introduced at a local level writ hundreds of times larger. Appeals to comradeliness, fraternity or 'community' are the more sinister the more they are issued in the name of a single, unchallengeable authority, and if absolute power corrupts absolutely, 'fascists' are the more dangerous the bigger their power blocs. Confronted with the gradual materialization of the global village, its ever expanding demands fuelled by advertising and consumerism at the economic level, and potentially even more destructive at the political level: threatened, that is, by an exteriorized unity of mankind without community, what sort of public policy should we advocate?

Desirable would seem to be a policy which, while retaining a sense of community and avoiding envy-based and destructive egalitarianism, would at the same time inhibit the Hobbesian clash of interest-groups, seen, and indeed functioning, as individuals writ large. Unless that is achieved, the prospects for the individual 'soul' become year on year more daunting, as he or she becomes ever more multiform in his principles, as by tolerating all ideas he soon comes to value none of them – unless the arbitrary choices of fascist fanaticisms – while at the same time he grows ever more homogenized in the preferences and prejudices affecting his material living. Looming over us is loss of all sense of 'native' traditions, combining with an externally fed, unending series of material desires and a constant clamour for rights for those groups with which each individual, in lieu of a genuine sense of community, opts to identify. Such a state of affairs cannot but promote the increasing instrumentalizing of the intellect, indeed to renewed claims that the intellect is nothing but instrumental, for the loss of native traditions leads to a parallel 'democratic' tendency – as noted already in contemporary moral philosophy – to fudge differences about fundamental beliefs.

At the political level we can expect the problem to have reached the same proportions as it has at the psychological. At the worst, we have to fear that though the trappings of democratic societies remain in place, their citizen members become so rootless – no-one has a vocation, only a three-year contract – and so homogenized in their banal desires and aspirations that they can be manipulated with ever greater success by political operators supported by articulate 'opinion-formers' who provide a rationale for the developing 'unity', at the same time retaining an intellectual élite's contempt both for the public and for their political executive. One need only remember that in the 1960s distinguished professors of logic would urge riot- and mayhem-disposed 'radicals' to 'think with their gut'. As in the Weimar Republic, such will readily imagine that the politicians are ultimately their creatures, nor do we need an Orwell to tell us how seriously they could be mistaken.

Perhaps more expectable is the American-style scenario by which 30 per cent of the population, supposing themselves to be free citizens of a democracy, vote in an assortment of millionaires whose liberal individualism is skilfully packaged to suggest that real choice is available to their backers – though the options of these will lie between a group of competitive individuals who hope to secure their personal successes through 'big government' and another group advocating the devolution of power and reward to more locally based winners at the expense of more broadly or nationally based losers. At this political level the supremacy of 'choice' which we met in moral theory is metamorphosed into the status accorded aggressive success. Sir Ronald Syme remarked that 'Nobody ever sought power for himself and the enslavement of others without invoking *libertas* and such fair names.'[20] Admittedly he spoke in the context of ancient Rome, but expand 'himself' to include 'his faction or interest-group' (seen as an extension of himself) and the scene is widely recognizable.

Already we can see how difficult it is for even the best informed to distinguish truth from falsehood in the public domain.[21] 'How can you tell whether a politician is lying? See if he moves his lips.' The popularity of such jokes shows that many realize this, but still we are willing to suspend judgement in just those 'few' cases where the politician is able to appeal to our immediate and individualized interests. So, by use of public money and the control of information, politicians continue to be able to induce the voters – who in any case may know that the 'other crowd' are equally bad – to give them this last chance.

Nor is the problem reducible to wilful deception by *politicians*; indeed politicians can be victims (willing or otherwise) of deception by those on whom they rely for 'facts', needing to make rapid decisions on a formidable array of topics. Journalists and others stand ready to supply that information, whether or not they have had time to acquire it, digest it, or even understand the languages of their sources. Some, of course, in print or on television, succeed in supplying accurate or not inaccurate information, but there is a sense in which this can even make the problem worse, if, knowing that much 'information' can be reliable, we find it the harder to detect where it is misleading.

The reliance of reporters on 'sources' who speak the language and can read the papers not infrequently leads to the blind being led not merely by the blind but by the corrupt. One effect of such misinformation can be seen in our time in the surprise of almost all Western 'experts' at the collapse of Communism in the Soviet Union, or – to go back many years to a less earth-shaking change – at the attainment by Khrushchev of the position of First Secretary of the Soviet Communist Party. If you do not know the explanation of an item which must be reported tomorrow, hazard a guess. You might get it right, and the chances of being caught

---

[20] R. Syme, *The Roman Revolution* (Oxford University Press, 1939), 155.

[21] Note the comment of a former civil servant, Adrian Ellis, in 'Neutrality and the Civil Service' in R. E. Goodin and A. Reeve (eds.), *Liberal Neutrality* (London: Routledge and Kegan Paul, 1989), 101, who refers to 'the information officer . . . quoted as calling at his union's annual conference for "a code of ethics . . . to protect those members who are expected to expound untruths on behalf of government, produce dodgy material or leak documents in the government's interest"'.

out – let alone of being remembered – as wrong are small. It may be that politicians will be even more grateful for your errors than for the truth, if they can put them to more immediate use.

Alasdair MacIntyre, attempting to answer the view that independent moral and cultural traditions are of equal moral standing and that it is impossible to regard any as superior, has argued that when traditions meet, the one which is still alive will be able to assimilate, on terms set by its rival, the best in the alternative tradition. His principal example is of how mediaeval Christianity managed to embrace within itself the best of the Aristotelian tradition from classical antiquity without losing itself (and specifically its Augustinian self) in the process. But the Western tradition since the Renaissance and Reformation, let alone during the twentieth century, has found itself confronted by so many different traditions – quite apart from itself generating a series of alternatives to that broad tradition which survived from the Middle Ages – that it has had no time to assimilate or reject them. The result is an uncritically respected cultural pluralism, needing justification by *ad hoc* theories of toleration.

All that leaves the contemporary politician – and the new professional opinion-former – in an unprecedented situation. His or her general aim, acceptably enough, might be to promote harmony within the national and the international community. Yet even within his own society, he is confronted with radical disagreement – compounded by massive half-ignorance about complex facts – among the intellectuals and political élites about any kind of common good, while among the populace at large there *is* a general sense that there is a common good (seen as 'What any decent person knows . . . '), but no clear notion of how it could be worked towards or whether its justification must ultimately introduce realism. In such a situation conflicts seem unavoidable and civil unrest lurks, making civil strife an ever present possibility, and giving the more reason to fear the ability of demagogues and populists to stir up either class or xenophobic hostilities.

Similarly at the international level, where a Hobbesian war of all against all has always seemed a more present threat in the absence of an effective international police force or its equivalent – and leaving aside the times when 'gun-boat diplomacy' by one or more of the greater powers may impose a semblance of order and even of justice – we can observe the possessive individualism of factions struggle in a more or less unconstrained way until fear of unsuccessful war or economic ruin may drive them to parley and even to prate of human rights, the rule of law, or the common good: this in practice to be understood as what will maximize benefit to the parties preferably short of so damaging others as to lead to further acts of desperation. This at least is the best outcome one can normally envisage.

The impossibly complicated nature of modern politics, the fear of losing popular support, even such outbursts of idealism as occur, all seem to impel the modern politician in the same direction: the public must be soothed into believing that harmony can be achieved by some kind of non-divisive politics of healing or at least of caring. When the leaders do not agree on their ends any more than the general public, when even if they agree on their ends, electoral advantage and the complication of modern economics, with its massive array of factors to be considered, will combine to confuse them, virtually all Western democratic leaders – if not by deliberate choice, at least by the logic of pragmatism – will fall into pursuing a programme of deception. Indeed with deception and self-deception a necessity of moral theory, it is hard to see what principled resistance there could be to its extended deployment in the public domain, or how contemporary democratic politicians, themselves 'formed' in the prevailing chaos of moral theory, could flourish without both massive deception and also the opportune exposure of deception.

The leaders will deceive either because they do not agree on the end, or because they cannot identify the effective, let alone the moral, means to that end, or because they are indisposed to evaluate short-term against long-term political goods: even because they will not understand that the pursuit of short-term idealism may only be maintained at the price of long-term confusion. Like their constituents, they may sigh for a community with common goods and common goals, and at least a measure of agreement as to the appropriate means to attain them. In the absence of any clear sense of common good or community, they resort to litanies of soothing platitudes.

Basic security aside, in the absence of a widely accepted 'common good' there can be no properly common standard by which even intermediate success may be measured; therefore how can the modern politician know whether he has been successful (apart from the accolade of re-election)? Certainly he can know whether a specific economic policy has produced a specific, even if temporary, effect: for example, whether inflation has been reduced or unemployment increased. What he (and the rest of us) cannot know is the degree to which this enables individuals within the community to assess whether their own multifarious 'goods' have been promoted, for with no final objective in the series of goods to be pursued, there seems no reason why even for each individual the

achievement of an intermediate good will not lead to an equivalent dissatisfaction over the non-achievement of the next one; indeed the advocacy
of 'consumerism' is designed to promote such permanent dissatisfaction.

It may be said that there is no alternative: politicians have to deceive
because the concept of a common good, though psychologically appealing, is both impractical and theoretically indefensible, since it supposes
and tries to impose an unrealistic restriction on the diversity of human
wishes and possibilities, and at worst promotes the vicious homogeneity of 'fascist' or otherwise totalitarian societies. That, of course, would
be true if the common good were a choice or preference rather than
a need: some national, racial, or class-driven ideal reified into an un-
alterable goal. Those who uphold a realist ethics have not proposed,
and cannot logically propose, so restricted a substitute for the common
good. For us the common good can only be identified by reference to
the overall nature and purpose of man.

A measure of the confusion now apparent even in 'traditionalist' circles
can be seen in attempts to argue that a theory of politics consonant
with moral realism can be constructed without appeal to a transcendent
Common Good in light of which the more restricted common goods of
particular historical societies – whether these be the conditions apt for
human flourishing or the joint activities which themselves constitute that
flourishing – can alone be understood. To be unable to invoke such a
Good is as destructive to a coherent theory of political goals as is the view
that the Common Good is no more than the sum of individual goods
(such as might be proposed by utilitarians).[22]

For realists there is no alternative to whole-hogging in political theory
as in ethics, for a defensible common good, as a defensible moral rather
than prudential *ought*, requires a transcendent and overriding Common
Good. Without it the politician, whether he appeals to positive law, traditional ideals, cynicism or enlightened self-interest – like also the moral
philosopher when speaking in the public domain rather than among
'friends' or in a closeted academic milieu – will either have to assume
such an overriding good in some emaciated and disingenuous form or,

---

[22] The confusion appears from time to time in attempts to determine the nature of Aquinas' theory
of the common good, and connoisseurs of polemic will enjoy the contribution of C. De Koninck,
'In Defence of St. Thomas: A Reply to Father Eschmann's Attack on the Primacy of the Common
Good', *Laval Théologique et Philosophique* 1.2 (1945), 9–109. This earlier instance of debate about
the common good centres on whether, for advocates of the common good, the individual is to
be sacrificed to society, thus paralleling the motivations (and the weaknesses) of Karl Popper's
roughly contemporary attack on Plato. For more recent disputes note the arguments of Ashley
('What is the End?') against Grisez, Finnis and others.

if he goes through the motions of ignoring or denying it (say on grounds of cultural pluralism), to continue to imply it when convenient, on pain of forfeiting public confidence.[23] In the United States his talk will take the form of discourse assuming 'civic religion'.

Thus for the politician in public, as for the philosopher in his study, the alternatives to realism and to the political 'applications' of realism are deception (whether or not accompanied by confusion) or the forfeiture of credibility. Large sections of a half-educated public, flattered as 'sophisticated', may be ready for the death of God; they are not (yet) ready for the death of public (or of private) morality. Yet they will be cheerfully deceived where the alternatives are too unpleasant to contemplate, and the politicians and opinion-formers are willing to oblige them.

As in private life, so in public, we find deception a plausible, even a necessary alternative to realism and to the political applications of realism, but before further analysing the particularly informative example which we introduced earlier, namely the deceptive aspect of egalitarianism, we may recognize a selection of topics about which there is good reason to think Western democracies already addicted to regular (even systemic) misrepresentation. The list would include claims about the possibility of full and continuing employment within an advanced capitalist society; or that the United Nations (or anyone else) can maintain peace without substantial (and costly) military deployments, and that loss of life of UN or other troops can be avoided if peace-making is embarked on; or that a Western state can reduce its spending on defence in favour of social services while remaining able to protect its legitimate interests and nationals abroad and maintain a serious commitment to peace-making, let alone to protecting human rights; or that a 60–80 hour working week among young professional women can be combined with the successful rearing of small children; or that 'free' trade can be expanded without multinationals shifting factories to sites where desperation will induce workers to accept intolerable conditions and slave wages – and deprive their better paid colleagues of jobs in countries offering a human degree of social welfare; or that violence against women and young children can be stopped while little challenge is mounted to freebooting sexual lifestyles pumped up by pornography, easy divorce and readily available abortion. The list could be prolonged.

Egalitarianism, however – the attempt to construct a morality out of the view that human beings can all be treated without 'favouritism' – is

---

[23] Thus he may, in practice, rely on some political analogue to Blackburn's 'quasi-realism'.

an especially informative example of how, in the absence of a common standard for value judgements and with the help of a formal principle of fairness, the most absurd consequences have to be accepted, with or without the aid of deliberate deception. I allow that, at least potentially, any society, insofar as it is impelled towards justice, will generate a certain egalitarianism. The original impulse to egalitarianism, as to theories of rights and emancipations of all kinds, in the West finds its origin in the Judaeo-Christian principle of the equality of all men and women before God, which principle in no way involves that God endows all equally in respect of talents and needs. It does not follow that if all have the god-given right to a fair trial, all are to be held equally proficient at mathematics, at playing the violin, or at cheating at cards or – an example favoured by Macchiavelli – at planning political assassinations – or to have a 'right' to any of these attainments.

Insofar as any egalitarian politics suggests that human beings are *substitutable for* one another because they are all 'equal', it can and does only thrive on some version of the scientistic claim that we would indeed all be equally able if we had equality of social and political opportunity, and that if we are *genetically* endowed in an unfair way, that should be levelled up by appropriate engineering.[24] What moral objection could there be to our providing such equality if someone is unable to enjoy the opportunity he deserves, for example to play the violin, because of a merely genetic 'injustice'? To raise such a question is not to offer a plea against helping the defective, but to consider the limits of the description 'defective', and ask what it could conceivably mean to claim that we have the right to be equal in every respect. Have I more *right* than the now proverbial chimpanzee to write the plays of Shakespeare?

Orwellian fantasies aside, such egalitarianism has to depend either on an arbitrarily determined 'thin' theory of goods – only 'basic' goods (survival, shelter, etc.) matter – or resort to the fiction that people are not or should not be regarded as significantly different. In the clearest example, it may be – is – claimed that there is (or should be) no significant difference between men and women, the reproductive roles of each being fenced off as unconnected to the core 'personality'. In all such unreality, one can discern the politics of deception or self-deception – if indeed it is possible, as we have denied, to separate the two.

---

[24] One of the advantages of Parfit's book is the attempt at an *argument* that we are more substitutable than we had supposed. Contemporary scientific research on cloning provides additional reason for taking seriously the moral implications of some of Parfit's examples about Replicating.

The political analogue to a world where 'choice' is the highest value is a world without any sense of the common good. But if realism is true, there will be a common good which will provide a focus for the varying individual goods of individual members of society. But, if defensible, that common good will itself depend on the fact of God as a transcendent Common Good, who has made man with his specific needs and limitations and thus gives intelligibility to a common good which is (or should be) the object of human striving in social and political life.

If, however, such transcendent Goodness exists among and 'above' men, its effects in our human environment will be mediated by fallible human beings and its name can be hijacked in the interests of merely sectarian or factional projects. Hence its political and economic manifestations must be scrutinized as rigorously as those of any other political programme. Neither the existence of a final Common Good nor the search for the common good in society can justify any unscrutinizable 'theocracy'; such a 'theocracy' would imply the impossible this-worldly perfection of some or all of the human race. We have no cause to be complacent about the threat of corruption among those believing they are in search of the common good. As the old Platonic adage had it: *Corruptio optimi pessima.*

THE END OF HISTORY AND THE AHISTORICAL INDIVIDUAL

The negative aspect of my argument thus far has been that Nietzsche was right to think that in the modern world the death of God would be followed by the death of morality as traditionally understood, and by implication that something else, whether or not called 'morality', would succeed it. This new thing could have emerged before Nietzsche, and at times tended to do so, but it had never been an 'establishment' ideology in Western society, which may thus be said now to have openly split in two. Increasingly dominant since Nietzsche's time is a choice-based, rights-claiming, largely consequentialist individualism, usually dressed up in democratic clothes; the alternative, a continuing and struggling successor of traditional Christianity, comes in weaker or stronger forms, some of which are still nominally Christian. (In view of the success of Christianity in the pre-modern Western world, it would seem impossible to go back to the polytheistic conditions which formed the backdrop for the writings of the classical philosophers.) There might appear, however, to be a second alternative, namely a post-Christian 'morality' without the theology, but this seems intellectually unsustainable (i.e. reducible either to

'Thrasymacheanism' or to incoherence) and to survive merely by force of institutionalized habit.

Moralities of the past developed in specific historical circumstances, and in the case of the realist tradition, whether in its religious or its more purely Platonic forms, the immediate contexts in which key texts such as Plato's *Republic* or the New Testament have appeared have been critical moments in the social, political and communal history of their times. Such texts have thus both contributed to urgent contemporary debate and challenged wider audiences in time and space. It is not difficult to see how different and more ephemeral would have been their effects had they appeared in an age like our own when all sense of the past is being lost and when it is widely believed that history has little or nothing to teach us. For we must recognize in the 'ahistoricity' of contemporary man a phenomenon which can only further promote both his materialist homogenization and his necessary dependence on that very deception – both public and private – which will simultaneously divide his 'soul' and expand his moral anarchy.

It is dangerous to generalize about the spirit of an age, but it is easy to recognize one feature of that 'modern' world which began with the Renaissance and the Reformation, and continued through the early developments of modern science and the agricultural and industrial revolutions into a twentieth century of ever-accelerating technological change: namely this increasing sense of the irrelevance of the past. Even scientific theories become outdated, of interest for the most part to the historian of ideas rather than to the active scientist – let alone the general public, avid though that public is for the very latest opinions of science and medicine. Indeed, once discovered, scientific laws become public property. Thus Newton's laws of thermodynamics are impersonal 'facts' which happen to have been formulated by Newton, in that respect quite different from the plays of Sophocles or Shakespeare, which though the products of particular historical eras, are at the same time saturated in the personal life and character of the author.

In the case of the scientific discoverer, while the *process* of discovery is to an extent a personal affair, nothing new is 'created', and one effect of the impersonality of scientific truths in a world overawed by science is a growing sense that what matters is only what is timeless and ahistorical: therefore that history itself is little more than antiquarian pottering. This mentality is forwarded by those historians who teach social history with a minimum backing of political history to students who – it may be unlike their teachers – can have no sense of what it does to wrench beliefs and practices out of their context. (Comparable are the procedures of teachers of literature who suggest that context and authorship are 'unreachable', and the text is all one has to consider.)

Nor is it only among the educated classes that such anti-historical views flourish. It seems likely – as one might expect – that by now they have penetrated among the relatively ignorant, who are victims of authoritarian 'enlightenment'. Among the educated are those whose professional work or amateur interest lies in the past, and other intelligent people may for various reasons become conscious of the degree to which we are prisoners of our local cultural assumptions. The many who travel enhance their awareness of continuing cultural diversity and indirectly – as by visiting museums or archaeological sites – become aware of cultures of the past. The educated may even combine philosophical individualism with an ongoing, if incidental, interest in history.

Yet such a one is necessarily a member of an élite. The uneducated, unless they happen to be in an army or to have some other occasion, such as business, to move outside their normal habitat, have less chance thus to understand their cultural and historical situation. Not unlike many of the more educated, they may also attempt to shield themselves from the disturbing effects – and not necessarily just the poverty and squalor – of 'foreign parts': a travel agency in Toronto advertised holidays in Mexico during which, they guaranteed, one would not need to meet an actual Mexican.

For despite 'historical' programmes on television (with their huge variations in accuracy of fact and sensitivity to cultural implications) and despite the proliferation of books, it has never been easier than it now is for Westerners to forget, deny or ignore the past, thought of as 'replaced' by the present or reinterpreted in terms of the present, as happens haply under the timeless auspices of a 'Great Books' programme in many universities. Our forebears were most often told that they were inferior to their ancestors, pygmies on the shoulders of giants; now we are told – and most of us have little way of checking the assertion – that if not better than our fathers, we are at least quite different. But if we do not know our fathers, or if we despise them, we cannot know ourselves or how we differ from them, but have become displaced like perpetual immigrants, thrown back on our solipsistic resources, encouraged yet further to believe that we must 'choose what we shall be'.

Up to a point we have indeed no option and are prisoners of our time. Each of us must make a life for himself; we cannot ultimately rely on parents, friends or the state to do it for us. At the end we die alone, in the sense that no-one can die in our stead, and though we try to deflect it, this realization is as old as humanity;[25] in the past, particularly during periods of social upheaval coupled with great migrations of peoples, it has led to the adulation of the heroic individual warrior; thus Homeric man lived with and by his tales and legends, his historic past only descried in a mythological haze.

We too have all been variously nourished – for worse or for better – on national and cultural myths which are part history, part nostalgia, part patriotism, part religion, but which always linked us with a valued tradition. On parallel traditions were nourished not only the great empires of Rome and ancient Egypt, but also the nation-states and empires of more modern times. While these traditions, as blends of myth and history, might have much in common, they always also served to identify peoples as distinctive: not *necessarily* as better than others, or not better in all respects, but as unique, an unrepeatable combination of past and present.

The modern West sees the fading of such traditions in the light less of necessary ignorance than of an ignorant contempt for the past, a feeling that it is at best irrelevant, and at worst inimical to our present desires and aspirations, to our current obsession with production and with what advertisers and politicians wish us to see as progress into the twenty-first century. Ignoring such posturings, we note the end of a tradition in the rootless individual who frequents (or haunts) our city streets, or in his often suicidal and frenetic avatars in contemporary literature and popular culture seeking to hide their isolation in mindless sex, drugs and whimpers about their alienation and how 'screwed' they have been by their parents or society. As they have in that, lacking any inherited sense of the past, they can only lament the meaninglessness of their lives, while their literary inventors find it lucrative to 'expose' the meaninglessness of life itself, thus contributing to that sense of meaninglessness. These would have life understood solely in terms of timelessly monotonous power relationships.

The quest for rootlessness is usually not carried to logical completion, and politicians and opinion-formers still find it convenient to appeal selectively to history, real, mythological or instant – like the radical appropriation of 'acceptable' (or for 'revisionists' unacceptable) icons from a valued past seen as significant for future glory. Figures such as Lincoln in the United States, in England Elizabeth I, and many others have

---

[25] Heidegger served us well at least in insisting that our ability to comprehend our situation is subverted if we try to ignore the fact that we are 'framed' by physical death.

always been grist for propagandists, until in our age their re-written image can be served up with unprecedented rapidity, the name surviving merely as a counter to be deployed by spin-doctors equipped as never before to 'target' selected publics. Diminished respect for the past allows whatever information is in circulation to be the more readily turned to ahistorical purposes; thus have the legend-makers of many stripes of John F. Kennedy been effective in print, on stage, and on all broadcast media. Such currency, unlike older, more slowly developed myths, is usually ephemeral: easy to come by, easily gone.

Before looking in more detail at examples of the fading of historical or imaginary traditions, I here enter the obvious caveat that what is to be sought in place of the lost sense of the past is not merely a new selection of myths but the more sedulous pursuit of history, that is, of historical truth. Those who point to abuses of national, racial and religious myths, whether long-standing (as in Serbia or Ulster), or more recently generated (as those of the Aryan race or the Stakhanovite hero), have concerns too genuine to be overlooked. That is why we need the replacement of myth not by ignorance but by history, of self-serving and self-indulgent appeals to a selected folk memory by the recovery of the intricacies of past events and of the divided though genuine motives of past heroes as of ourselves.

Rootlessness cannot remain myth-free, as Goebbels should have taught us; where truth should claim its place, the interests of politicians, bigots or commerce will always push to fill the vacuum. The only lasting protection against rootlessness is that proper sense of the past for which national, religious and racial myths are but bastard substitutes. The United States, now dominant in the Western world, and with its founding ideology of a break with the tyrannies of Europe, is peculiarly susceptible to suffer from a general contempt for the past and to export that contempt elsewhere. And being thus insulated against awareness of history, Americans can also be peculiarly blind to the antics of self-serving mythographers within their borders.

Now consider two specific but *prima facie* very different examples of the fate of national traditions when confronted with timeless 'reality': the decline of Canadian identity and the loss of religion among the British (especially English) working classes. Both examples show that a growing lack of awareness of the past promotes (and in turn is further promoted by) social rootlessness and devotion to material 'well-being', themselves to be viewed against a background emphasis on the immediate rights of each individual or of each group with which that individual can identify.

The national myth on which Canada developed, by which it was nur-tured since Confederation in 1867, was of two founding nations: the English (by which more accurately was meant the Scots and Irish) and the French. Whatever the historical basis of the 'contract' between these two founding peoples – and tendentious versions were widely if diversely circulated in the two communities themselves – the myth was broadly founded in historical fact, and survived for many decades. Even after many of the 'English' were in origin Ukrainians, Germans, Italians or Portuguese, in the North American setting they were 'culturally' English in that the language of their political and ultimately social success was English, the history they learned in school was English, and so on; they were English in the sense in which in the empire of Alexander the Great, Egyptians and Syrians, if politically and culturally adjusted, were 'Greeks'.

Two historical realities changed that situation: firstly the numbers of immigrants grew so large that many of them tended to feel more soli-darity among themselves than among the 'founding' peoples with whom they now shared their destiny. That alone would not have damaged the pre-existing Canadian national myth to the extent that actually oc-curred; to understand what happened next we have to look, as ever in recent Canadian history, south of the border. The United States had faced a similar problem: how to identify its huge waves of immigrants as Americans, to induce them to abandon – or so it was hoped – the feuds, loves and fears of the Old World in the brave new country across the Atlantic.

The preferred solution was the 'melting pot'; all were to be drilled in school, in homestead and in every area of social life – not least in the military – to become new Americans, equal in rank before God and the law and equal in the legitimacy of their aspirations in and for their new motherland. To a considerable degree it worked, but there was a darker side. For various reasons which need not be considered here, but not least because of the special difficulties of assimilating a depressed class of black former slaves, one of the effects of this process of homogenization was to deprive many among the second and third generations of immigrants of knowledge of their past without giving them an adequate 'new past' with which to replace it. That, coupled with the intense competitiveness of a 'new-frontier' American society, led to a combination of theory-based possessive and aggressive individualism with an immense susceptibility among the dehistoricized masses to sloganeering and advertising: a com-bination which, as has been widely recognized, helped to generate the rootless and violent society of many American cities of the late twentieth century.

Seeing the risk of such criminal wildernesses developing in their own hitherto comparatively peaceful domain, and under the same pressures from immigration, Canadians attempted a different solution: not the melting pot but the mosaic. All sorts of hyphenated Canadians (Italian-, Ukrainian-, Japanese- or Chinese-) were to co-exist, each going very substantially their own way. Thus was virtually blotted out the national myth of the founding peoples on which the country had thus far developed, replacing it (at worst) with national or regional interest-groups whose primary goal was to promote their own identity in terms of economic and social advantage. With little awareness of their own history beyond tendentious memories of ancient feuds (as between Poles and Ukrainians, Greeks and 'Macedonians', Serbs and Croats), these local groups either had to find new national myths (or even truths) in a hurry (and in a transplanted state) or merely symbolize the loss of whatever inadequate awareness of the past the old myth of the founding peoples for a time preserved.

Thus Canada ran the risk of a cultural debasement in which individual groups of immigrants – increasingly merged in culture with the *déraciné* descendants of the 'English' founders – mistook the survival of their tribal identities for genuine history – as happened with the Protestants and Catholics of Northern Ireland. At the same time they could not but 'massage' the more negative responses of the original French-speaking minority who thus tended to reduce themselves to yet another set of embittered seekers after their own 'rights': in a post-referendum speech in 1995 the then Premier of Quebec complained he had been defeated by 'money and the ethnics'. An outcome to be feared is that under similar economic and commercial pressures to those in the United States, Canada will experience similar massive alienation from society and its political processes, as from its earlier national traditions, society being viewed solely as a vehicle for a possessive and self-dividing individualism.

In this regard, it is significant that the number of non-voters (by choice or apathy) in American presidential elections – generally higher than in corresponding elections in Europe – shows little sign of decreasing, for the homogenization and depersonalization which goes with loss of any sense of the importance of the past and of the need to extend and improve inherited and intelligible traditions shows itself in a moribund democratic process in which the consumerist, politically apathetic, often violent masses – convinced that voting will hardly affect their lives – abandon their governance to a diminishing élite. And I leave aside for the present how, even within those who vote, the option of making choices based on sound information about the alternatives available can – as already noted – be distorted to a disconcerting degree: in the first Clinton election a majority of the voters did not know which party controlled the Congress.

The *word* 'democracy' remains untouchable for the foreseeable future. But in the absence of a clear idea of what a good democracy would be like, or of its historical context, reference to 'democracy', like other ordinary terms of moral language, remains ambiguous. Those who utter the term are often like a man who enters a jeweller's shop to ask for a watch without any clear notion of what a good watch would be like because he does not know what watches are *for*. In the absence of a clear idea as to what democracy is *for*, we treat it as an end in itself, or perhaps as a political analogue to 'Choice'. So long as we have 'free choice', we believe we can achieve our status as human beings; so long as we live in a 'democratic' society, we believe we have the structure within which we can be 'free'. If choice is the idolatry of private life, democracy has become the idolatry of public life.

And if the United States is the trail-blazer for the West, we can predict a nominal democracy, with all the institutions of democracy intact but which has ceased to be democratic at all, where the competent few can manipulate, with a view to securing their own political power, the consumer-driven individualism of a population which, deprived of its historical roots as well as of its sense of the common good, will work as long hours as possible as variously paid productive cogs in a vast, impersonal and increasingly multinational economic machine. For to those manipulating the historically lost, not the least significant tool will be the provocation of 'patriotic' outbursts, while the only check on governmental misdemeanours (real or imaginary) will be a constant self-seeking litigation dignified as the appropriation of human rights. On this scenario the loss of a proper sense of the historical past also aids and abets that very proletarianization of the citizen-body which, seasoned by the names of equality and opportunity, invites and needs the politics of deception from its élites. For if, as individuals or nations, we throw away any concern for our past, there is less to prevent the manipulation of our future and the further loss (or at least gross deformation) of that very sense of personal and national identity which our flattering politicians successfully pretend to enhance.

For it is to be noted that some of the goals of Hitler, Stalin and other promoters of man remade can be achieved in a more anodyne but equally mindless society, the more comfortable totalitarianism of egalitarian because rootless and envious individualism. It is no accident that such individualism, coupled with ignorance and contempt for the past, can flourish under some versions of the 'democratic' umbrella; indeed such characteristics may become the illusory Three Pillars of any future 'democracy' itself: riven by class divisions, devastated by crime, corrupt in its political dealings and judicial processes, massively philistine and illiterate (though led by a highly articulate, educated and sophisticated élite), tasteless and brutal in its entertainment – and self-devoted to 'freedom' viewed as choice. The United States has moved far in this direction and Canadians, being next in line and now comparatively unprotected, have much to fear beyond their present anxieties about separatism.

Our second example of the effects of the decline of a sense of history is *prima facie* very different. In the latter part of the eighteenth century the Church of England began to lose touch with the poor of the new industrial cities so that the proletarianized masses, as Wesley and Whitfield realized, needed a new evangelization, if they were not to all intents to be lost to religion and eventually to moral tradition as well. The reasons for this Methodist anxiety are easy to understand, for as the poor, driven by fear, starvation or greed, flocked to the towns, they left behind a more stable social world over which the Church of England had for two hundred years presided, linking them, in imagination if not altogether in historical fact, with further centuries of Christian tradition. Anglican Christianity was not the only source of the set of fixed habits they inherited, of respect for one's 'betters' and understanding of one's place in the scheme of things, but it underpinned or coexisted with the rest. Mass emigration to industrial life threatened not only revolutionary violence on the political stage, but loss of the traditions of Christianity itself which, however inadequately preached, were grounded in land and village and the local churchyard where one's ancestors had lain for generations.

The Church of England failed to recover the masses, and though the chapels picked up some of the slack, the rapid dechristianization of England – at work below the surface conventions of the Victorian age – left such high-falutin' movements as Tractarianism to the circles of those few, normally university men and their womenfolk, who could still reach behind the new urban culture to a more stable and historically stabilized past.[26] Hence the phenomenon of earnest religious and moral revival among those retaining a sense of the past, and a simultaneously increasing amoral homogenization of the urban poor, become targets for mass ideologies or what Talmon has called 'totalitarian democracy',[27] that is, identification of the masses as the raw material of the General Will by those few whose self-appointed role is to 'discover' that Will among the many. Had the people of Britain not been promised outlets in Empire, such ideological pressures might have made as devastating an impact among them as were – *mutatis mutandis* – made among some peoples of continental Europe. As religion followed the flag, so the national myth took the Church of England in tow, to take on a new if temporary lease of life.

This curiosity of nineteenth-century English history has to an extent repeated itself in the twentieth-century, with effects less dramatic if similarly revealing. Newman's abandonment of the Church of England for the Church of Rome was effect as it was cause of intellectual movements within nineteenth-century Christianity. Since then the Roman Church in England has been nourished by waves of largely intellectual converts, as by internal intellectual growth, notwithstanding a decline in recent years in its regular churchgoers.

Like the nineteenth-century Church of England, we find a persistence in religion of part – a surprisingly high part if we consider the social disadvantages of professed Catholicism – of the educated élite of the country. Again those who broadly speaking possess their own roots, their own past and traditions, have persisted in their beliefs against the push of consumerism and the cult of instant gratification by media, spin-doctors and PR people. Again we note the survival, at least to a degree, among the historically conscious of what cannot survive among those not so conscious. We might conclude that such persistence of religious belief among the educated is particularly striking in an age of unprecedented scientific and technological change.

But the contemporary situation differs significantly from its nineteenth-century forerunner in that the homogenization which in the nineteenth century affected the poor and depressed urban masses now embraces a superficially informed and comfortable middle class, which

---

[26] On the locally *theological* rather than broader ethical motivations of Tractarianism, and the consequent 'datedness' of the movement, see now D. Callam, 'Christopher Dawson on the Oxford Movement and the Relationship of Development to Authority', *Communio* 22 (1995), 488–501, especially 500–1 with the letter there quoted of Sheridan Gilley.

[27] Talmon, *The Origins of Totalitarian Democracy*.

having come into being through increased wealth, remains proletarianized and in a sense classless. Elites aside, Britain (like the United States) is moving towards something like a classless society of the lowest common denominator, in which the TV and tabloids (or their 'broadsheet' emulators) exacerbate the hopes and fears of the half-educated middle classes as much as of the new, largely immigrant, urban poor. A classless society is not necessarily an improved society; it may be merely a discontented and aimless mass.

Religious survival in contemporary Britain can only be explained in terms of a personal self-awareness incorporated into an Ecclesia freed from the pliability and polymorphousness to which it would succumb without its traditional resonances. The phenomenon is not limited to Catholic intellectuals but exists to a degree among those who derive their ethics from the evangelical tradition (now largely secularized and thus deprived of its theoretical roots) of nineteenth-century philanthropy and idealism. But it is particularly striking among the Catholic educated classes for reasons which cannot but be connected with their maintenance – even if often in an attenuated form[28] – of traditions in which individual self-awareness, together with the possibility of minimizing psychological pluralism, was and can still be developed. Beyond this more historically aware section of the community, there is evidence that erosion similar to that which affected Anglicanism two hundred years ago has affected the Catholic working classes in the mid-to-late twentieth century, and there is every reason why this should be expected, for if the individual is deprived of his past, he can be expected to assume the persona put upon him by current fashions and pressures, which in the present age will most often mean reduction to economic man.

There are other ways of neutralizing the unwelcome liberating effects of history, thus tightening the stifling embrace of present concerns, than merely ignoring them. As Orwell, observing the practice of contemporary (and earlier) dictatorships, knew, the past can also be rewritten or invented. And – especially in the early twenty-first century – we do not need a dictatorship to do this; we can rely not only on self-interested politicians and publicists, but also on the authoritarian mentality of more or less ideological academics and humanists,[29] not least of historians of

---

[28] For an informed treatment of one of the more important features of this debasement see E. Duffy, 'Rewriting the Liturgy: The Theological Implications of Translation', *New Blackfriars* 78 (1997), 4–27.

[29] We can even afford to overlook as untypical such blatant cases as denial of the Holocaust.

philosophy, or, on the contemporary ecclesiastical scene, of theological partisans. *Quis custodiet ipsos custodes?*

The technique is roughly as follows: I first argue that my predecessors were great but somewhat naive philosophers (a sop is often thrown to Plato and Aristotle); then I set about rewriting their logically 'unsophisticated' efforts into a more contemporary mode, in so doing changing the tone and temper of their work. The advantage of such a proceeding is that if past thinkers say something which is out of kilter with contemporary philosophical fashion, one no longer has to face the dilemma of whether X (Plato or whoever) is mistaken or whether it is I, with my contemporary approach to the problem, who am the misguided one. Past philosophers can thus be simultaneously venerated and neglected, since the opportunity to *learn* something striking from them has been neutralized. By this move Plato (or anyone else) can be either patronized as primitive or turned into something reassuringly contemporary. If past philosophers have anything radical to offer, the contemporary professor can prevent this from reaching the contemporary student by explaining away their most interesting claims or by setting these in a systemically confusing context: the 'poisoning of the wells' approach to the history of philosophy.

There is an interesting parallel between those who wish to deny our differences with the past, that is, with the views of those who differ from us in time, and the attitude we often wish to adopt to societies which differ from our own not in time but in space: that is, to contemporary non-Western traditions. That may seem surprising in view of the common concern of intellectuals to rid themselves of Eurocentrism, and to do justice to what are assumed to be very different but equally valuable modes of thought from other sources. There is no present need to linger over which if any such cultures offer much help to us, or even to themselves. An *a priori* reason for studying them is often suggested by an unexamined inference: since all at least non-threatening cultures should be equally tolerated, they *must* all have something of value to teach us, and probably are of 'equal' value – however that is supposed to be assessed.

For the sake of argument let us grant these dubious premises. More immediately relevant is the way we go about appropriating non-Western cultures, frequently taught as they are *by* the ideologically motivated – the ideology taking the form of uncritical hostility to 'Western' traditions – *to* the conspicuously and dangerously ignorant, that is, to those ignorant not only of the alien culture but of sufficient of their own to be able to make just comparisons. The phenomenon of the blind leading the blind becomes the more striking when one considers the further fact that the great majority of those engaged in formulating such material not only are ideologically driven, but have no significant knowledge of the languages and cultural traditions in which the outlooks they profess to teach are expressed, sometimes even denying the benefit of such knowledge. The result is that such cultures are read simplistically through Western, and at that mainly ignorant Western eyes. The net effect of such 'instruction', in Indian, Chinese or 'Amerindian' ideas, may be compared with that of instruction in classical Greek philosophy – as sometimes occurs – by those with no notion of the cultural setting of the concepts they handle, or rather mishandle, presenting ancient societies naively as versions of our own.

Thus the death of history may be said to have spatial as well as temporal aspects; we become the more ahistorical the more we pride ourselves on freeing ourselves from the limitations of Eurocentrism. I note also a perhaps slightly preferable alternative to the Westerner teaching about ancient China or India; that is the deracinated 'native' who aspires to rewrite his own tradition in a contemporary Western mode.

Our current ability to destroy the past by rewriting it in the idiom of the present is peculiarly startling in that it comes at the end of two centuries of scientific historiography; that is, at the end of a period when historians have learned better than ever before how to study events in their context and to understand the behaviour of historical individuals in terms of the norms of the societies in which they lived.[30] Thinking people will not pass blanket condemnations on ancient slave-owners, who, like their slaves, could hardly imagine the possibility of a world functioning without slavery. And together with recognition of the indispensability of historical contexts has arrived recognition of the importance of cultural traditions. Yet that we are, though for different reasons, as willing as were the ancients to assimilate all philosophical questions to immediately contemporary ones and to deny in ethics the truths about society which we don as spectacles through which to inspect history, is because we allow ourselves to be deluded into denying our history, and because we have come to suppose that such a state of ahistorical existence is normal and normative. Our ancestors may have known far less detail of history than we do, but normally better understood the importance of history itself.

---

[30] The limitations we continue to recognize as due to our own historical standpoint and to our own questions to the past have to be unambiguously admitted and constantly taken into account; they in no way weaken our claim to enhanced historical understanding.

I began this section of the present chapter by noting that the thesis that traditional morality (in whatever version) is to be replaced by acclimatization to a world of competing individuals has developed at a time when for reasons connected with the advance of science and technology, and especially of our powers of mass communication, the past widely appears irrelevant and to have virtually disappeared; and that it has not always disappeared unwittingly but has been displaced by a willed ignorance. If such loss of our history, and the attendant further loss of knowledge of ourselves as anything more than ephemeral numbers in the market, combine with democratic egalitarianism, the latter's worst features can only be exacerbated. The results will vary, but psychological divisiveness will be a constant: predictable are cynicism and deceitfulness among the rulers, envy and pliability among the 'consuming' ruled. In a mass society such attitudes, if blended with an increasing powerlessness (or at least an increasing sense of oneself as disenfranchised), will push us towards the alternatives to which I have alluded: pseudo-democracy or more blatant forms of totalitarianism; and I suggested that despite the nightmares of an Orwell, the former may in the long run be the more insidious, not least since it has turned out more difficult than was expected to induce a populace to love Big Brother rather than cower before him in impotent apathy. Mass populations seem to be brutalized by their masters rather than to love them, as will appear when, in a palace revolution (as with Ceausescu), a mob has opportunity to wreak its will on the thug on whom formerly it fawned.

In raising within our present ahistorical society the possibility of pseudo-democracy and its more obviously totalitarian alternatives, I must finally revert to an institution which contributes in a distinctively contemporary manner to the further development of proletarianization and rootlessness: the institution, that is, known as bureaucracy. Bureaucracy is unavoidable in an elaborated society, but while it 'oils the wheels' of such a society, it plays into its impersonal and ahistorical features. And insofar as bureaucracy is necessarily impersonal (and hence disliked and resented even when efficient), it can function under both pseudo-democratic and totalitarian régimes. For the bureaucrat, the client has no past but only a file, no personality but only a number or a place in a queue. Of its nature bureaucracy discourages institutional responsibility, which is another reason why its officials can so easily move from one political master to another.

Yet as a necessary instrument it cannot be abolished, only subjected to surveillance. Within any comparatively healthy bureaucracy, 'whistle-blowing' will be encouraged, and the cult – to which such organizations have been prone since Byzantine times – of the organization as outside the law actively discouraged: especially at its upper levels a sense of history should be expected as a necessary qualification, under pain of removal. Bureaucracy, of course, does not in itself promote Thrasymachean individualism; rather is it one of the instruments of which the rampant individual (be he dictator or corporate mogul) can make fearsome use.

I have offered only an introduction to the ramifications in political and social life of combining choice theory and atomic individualism in ethics with the necessity of deception and/or a widespread sense of the irrelevance of the past among both political élites and the ordinary members of a 'democratic' state. It remains to draw preliminary conclusions about some of the dangerous phenomena which such combinations seem to evoke. The first is that an over-heated demand for individual or group rights – apart from developing litigiousness at the cost of a diminishing respect for the common good – is a call for what cannot be achieved, since infinitely expandable resources are required if these rights are to be carried into law. In practice there may in consequence be a tendency for the latest and faddiest rights to triumph in the cut-throat competition for funds; in any case the satisfaction of endless rights without duties can only lead to an increase in the arbitrariness of resource distribution. Thus the search for unlimited rights – in this like the search for unlimited choice – will result in the pursuit of a power necessarily to be used against others, with socially dangerous consequences at both the personal and the economic level. Even demands for more and more jobs may generate a situation where a new job for me leads to job losses for others.

Secondly, just as there are insufficient resources to satisfy the endless demand for rights – not least for the right to possess – so this insufficiency (when combined with a failure in moral theory to identify and justify claims about public and private goodness) must provoke deception not only about human nature but about economic and social realities, especially the possibilities of endless economic growth – thus calling for a vast array of opinion-formers to perpetuate (and cover up) such deception.

The third danger is a corollary to its predecessors. Despite the near certainty of an eventual decline in economic expansion (and more immediate problems about the just distribution of rewards), the incessant demand both for material goods and for unjustified 'inalienable' rights will not correspondingly decline, or not enough, so that life, as we have seen, will seem more and more a 'zero-sum' game. An obvious effect of this will be that few will 'afford' to have children further to 'consume' their time and resources: this indeed is already a European phenomenon. In moral theory, particularly in accounts of the formation of rational contracts, we have noticed the phenomenon of the disappearing child. In a social and political world where zero-sum competition has replaced classical 'community' and the common good, such 'theoretical' disappearances will find their analogue in an ever more aged citizen-body. Of course, migrants may be invited to fill out the workforce (and keep the pension funds in the black), but they are to be not responsible citizens but exploitees – until the time comes for them to settle their cultural accounts. It remains only to observe that the prospect I have sketched is the terminal condition of a social and political world in which substitutes for Platonic realism and its political applications have been finally put in place. Advance towards this world is rarely in a straight line and is therefore the more easily overlooked.

CHAPTER 9

God and ethics

REALIST ETHICS AND DIVINE COMMANDS

Finally let us return from the macrocosm to the microcosm, from society to the individual. I have argued that our self and our coming soul are such that we shall be unable to fulfil our moral obligations and live well – assuming such obligations and standards are real – until we are adequately unified and our plural selves harmonized as a single self. That in turn means that the possibility of living good lives will depend both on the reality of moral standards and on help from an external source necessarily 'more than human' in view of the effectiveness required. Or to put it bluntly in traditional Christian terms: if we are to be supported by God's grace, we can be so empowered, at least progressively, while without such empowerment, 'ought' (if there is an ought), so far from implying 'can', would rather imply 'cannot'. Insofar as morality would then make any sense, it would function similarly to Paul's reading of the Jewish Law: to make us aware of how we cannot fulfil our moral aspirations. Thus, and in traditional terms, for morality to function God must function both as final and (at least in great part) as efficient cause of our moral life.

A number of contemporary theists and moral objectivists think they see a way round a contemporary shyness of introducing God into an account of first principles of morality, both as object of moral action and ultimately as the necessary support for its performance. Debate about fundamentals of morality can, they suppose, be effectively carried on with agnostics and atheists on the basis of data supplied by our inclinations to our human reason as it is. The philosophical attempt is – one acknowledges – worth undertaking, and if successful would leave the theistic moral philosopher less intellectually isolated and more secure – presumably in some adaptation of Kantianism. In such a spirit Germain Grisez, John Finnis and many others – proponents of what has been called the New Natural-Law Theory – have offered a defence of exceptionless moral rules which they hold achievable without recourse to metaphysics, let alone to theology or revelation.[1] They argue that we can identify certain 'pre-moral goods' (life, friendship, knowledge, etc.) and that since there is no general reason – the goods being incommensurable, like apples and oranges – to prefer any one such good at the expense of any other, we have never to act intentionally and directly against any one of these nor directly and deliberately sacrifice one good for a greater good, or as means to a greater good: as they would put it, we must always refuse directly to do evil in order that good may come, that being precisely – by the same principle of incommensurability – the rational thing to do.

It is unfortunately not as easy as that – though I have intimated that the appearance of incommensurability between alternative goods may be less threatening if we think not of choosing in some posited atom of time between goods in the abstract, but recognize that choice will normally flow easily and imperceptibly from the style of life we are living up to this point.[2]

Yet the problem cannot be entirely exorcized in this way: there seems a desperate need to sacrifice one good for another in those hard cases consigned to 'dirty hands' where a normally 'evil' deed must still apparently be envisaged to avoid what may seem a worse outcome. In confronting this, first observe that if we grant that it makes no sense to sacrifice any of the pre-moral goods to secure another – that is as a means to what may appear a greater good – and that *simply* because such goods are incommensurable, then we are doing no more by refraining than following what seems a *rational* course; we are saying not that this act *ought not* to be done, but that we have no sufficient reason to say that it *ought* to be done. By assuming both that obligation is the inseparable partner of presumed rationality and that lack of guidance must always be taken as

---

[1] Perhaps the most accessible and tightest exposition of their views is 'Practical Principles, Moral Truth, and Ultimate Ends', *American Journal of Jurisprudence* 32 (1987), 99–151. A more casual account of the self-evidence of moral first principles (in themselves and to us whatever our tradition) is offered (and attributed to Aquinas) by J. M. Boyle (commenting on MacIntyre) in 'Natural Law and the Ethics of Traditions', in R. P. George (ed.), *Natural Law Theory: Contemporary Essays* (Oxford University Press, 1992), 3–30.

[2] Note that Aristotle says that flourishing can only be properly recognized in a 'complete life'. To make abstract choices between incommensurable goods involves stopping the clock of one's life. There is an analogy between claiming that in a temporal continuum we cannot make such choices and Zeno's paradoxical claim that Achilles will never catch up with the tortoise in a race if the tortoise starts in front: for by the time Achilles reaches the tortoise's starting-point the tortoise will have advanced, and by the time Achilles reaches that point of advance the tortoise will have further advanced, etc.

a moral inhibition on exceptional action ('I cannot show the rationale for doing this exceptionally; therefore I should not do it'), we get the required result.

Let us consider positive courses before moving to the more difficult matter of prohibitions. In the world of realist morality, the 'determination' that this *ought* to be done is not something secured by a human will reacting to human inclinations, but something to be first recognized by the human mind de facto, simply because the world is as it is. Though human reason may give the command that X should be done (in the belief that X 'morally' ought to be done), that 'ought to be done' – rather than the mere 'would be rationally done' – implies further authorization – and that not merely because of the inability of the human reason to determine correctly even when it determines sincerely. In justifying itself as moral rather than prudential or at best constructively rational in the Kantian sense, fallible human reason requires – as Suarez may at least have glimpsed[3] – some sort of external warranting. In default of the Platonic Form (which does not give commands) that external can only be God, whose 'nature' – and therefore *ex hypothesi* our 'original' nature – is communicated by way of non-arbitrary commands. Insofar as practical morality provides us with *obligations* rather than simple appeals to our (limited) reason, it requires the justification not of an impersonal and inactive Form but of an omniscient, providential and preceptive deity. It would make no sense to say that God is good but does not want to show his goodness, or that he knows what we ought to do without telling us (by intelligible command if necessary) what we ought to do. And if unaided practical reason cannot explain why one good may or may not be 'sacrificed' to another, our aided reason may be able so to do – but *ex hypothesi* only on the terms of the God it thus implies.

We are forced to concede that moral obligation – the only obligation clearly separable from prudence or enlightened self-interest – remains a utopian dream in a non-theistic (and therefore, if our earlier arguments are correct, non-realist) universe, and vain are the attempts of theists to deny this in the hope of persuading secular moralists that the debate between them can be resolved in purely this-worldly terms. As they should have foreseen, philosophers who, like Grisez and Finnis, attempt to argue that God need not be invoked in such debates are no more able to avoid him than was Kant, who, attempting to show that morality needs no metaphysical foundations (in his understanding of metaphysical), had

---

3 See J. Finnis, *Natural Law and Natural Rights* (Oxford University Press, 1980), 338–9.

to allow that without the ultimate sanction of God, his moral universe would collapse: a side of Kant, as we have seen, well appreciated by Nietzsche, who held that after the 'death' of God there could be no foundation for morality. The notion that Kant enables religion (viewed as faith) to survive without metaphysics is but a current version of the old fideist claim that religion, though true, is indefensible, while the related claim that Kant pointed to morality surviving in the absence of God is itself un-Kantian.[4]

If God cannot be excluded from contemporary debate about traditional ethics, we can the more readily understand why, when reading Finnis, and more especially Grisez, we find it hard to know whether, though they try to distinguish philosophy from theology, they are clear in which of the two they are engaged. Lurking unacknowledged behind many of their incommensurable goods – which include, absurdly if proposed to atheists, religion – are views about kinds of behaviour which they hold that God, through Scripture and magisterium, has proclaimed as forbidden, albeit intelligibly so. It would be preferable if such claims about the origins of desirable behaviour were straightforwardly admitted at the start (as they were by Maritain[5]), even if the result were that debate between theists and non-theists on strictly moral questions (or at least on the *foundations* and the *justification* of morality) has to come to an abrupt halt before what is the effect of the theistic brick wall. God, we see, is not only necessary for the performance of morality, but cannot be excluded from discussions about its foundations and imperativity. We shall soon also see, what Augustine and Aquinas implied, how God can enable us to free ourselves from that paralysis in decision-making to which squeamishness about dirty hands will otherwise condemn us.[6]

To say that the foundations of realist morality must include the existence of a God who is also the source of commands is not – be it repeated *ad nauseam* – to be committed to the view that the good is simply what God commands or that all there is to morality is obedience to god-given obligations. Rather it is to say that an explanation of the nature of moral action – as distinct from mere true belief about 'moral' facts – must include an account of divine commands. Of course, that further fact has

---

4 But for Kant's failure to explain dogmatic Christianity in terms of 'religion within the limits of Reason alone', see most recently John E. Hare, 'Augustine, Kant and the Moral Gap', in G. B. Matthews (ed.), *The Augustinian Tradition* (Berkeley and London: University of California Press, 1999), 251–62.

5 See R. McInerny, *The Question of Christian Ethics* (Washington, D.C.: Catholic University of America Press, 1993), especially chapter 1.

6 See Ashley, 'What is the End of the Human Person?'

over the centuries and in some religious traditions led to a deformation of moral awareness in itself, for although, as the Psalmist put it, fear is the *beginning* of wisdom, it is not wisdom's equivalent or fullness. To see why this is relevant we must consider the nature of a moral command, and in particular the nature of the commander insofar as he commands morally. In so doing we must look back to my earlier distinction (especially in chapter 5) between acting from a sense of principle and acting because one loves the right and the good. If we recognize that while the first is right, the second is superior, to claim that morality is mere obedience to divine power and divine fiat is to assume a wholly inadequate account of God.[7] And inadequate accounts of God, as I have also observed, supply or support correspondingly inadequate accounts of man.

It has often been argued that if to do good is to do what God wants merely because he wants it, then morality has been left out altogether. It may be good sense so to do good – one might be a literally damned fool not to – but it remains mere calculation, and leaves us still lacking a fully 'realist' explanation of *morality*. To suggest that it is specifically moral to obey God because he is 'stronger' is a mistake tantamount to that which reduces moral behaviour to the performance of obligations *qua* obligations. As has been observed, we prefer to benefit from a helpful or merciful act done out of love than one done simply from obligation or fear of punishment.

The core of the difficulty about 'raw' divine command theories thus lies in the presumed account of God's nature. Since God is normally viewed by theists as creator, power will be prominent among the divine attributes: God is omnipotent and, as psychologists early made us aware, omnipotence is a salient feature of a parent as perceived – and as resented – by a child. But if God's other attributes are swallowed up by the emphasis on his power (as in the common religious image that views us as dust in his hands or clay in the hands of the potter), then to say that what we are commanded is right is no more than to say that the power disposed by God is right. That, as I have allowed, seems to point towards a 'morality' of obedience hard to justify as morality at all. If, however, God's love is an attribute inseparable from his power, we can be certain that what he commands will not be right *merely* because he commands it

---

[7] P. Geach (despite his own caveat) seems to come near to this mistaken account in 'The Moral Law and the Law of God', reprinted from *God and the Soul* in P. Helm (ed.), *Divine Commands and Morality* (Oxford University Press, 1981), esp. 172–4. (Note p. 173: 'We shall have such fear of God as destroys all earthly fear'.)

(even though he will and 'must' command it if it is right), but right because it is good as God is good. There are two possible forms of 'divine command morality', only one of which – that which assumes the loving goodness of God – is compatible with our sense that if something is to be right it is not right merely because it is the will of a superior.[8]

Granted the truly divine commands of a God whose nature is love, we can assume that actions are wrong because alien and hostile to that divine nature, and against his will because God does not command what is contrary to his excellence. Thus a viable 'realist' morality – the alternative to the ethics, or better 'moralities', of choice, rational calculation or obligation for obligation's sake – involves obedience to divine commands not merely because they are commands, but, as the Platonists always put it, because what is good is in itself inspiring to us, just as, analogously, it is to God. A loving being will not use power unjustly, even though he or she may have the physical capability of doing so; I have already observed that to say that I could not shoot a man in cold blood means not that I have insufficient strength to pull the trigger, but that I could not 'bring myself' to do so.

I conclude that within a realist morality the element of inspiration to do right comes from whatever capacity we have to be motivated by the good, but that since we are insufficiently empowered to follow up these inspirations – we grow tired, cynical, hedonistic or self-interested (even irrationally so) – we cannot ground the perduring obligation – derived from and informing our inspirations but outlasting their weaknesses – without reference to a divine command, itself revelatory of the unchanging divine nature.

In considering inspiration, 'pure' Platonists would appear to have underestimated our inability to do as we want, and even to do what we are more weakly inspired to do. They thus fail to provide an answer to the sceptic who (quite properly) never gives up his challenge: 'What do you mean by "ought"?' On the other hand, as we have seen, the theist – not to speak of the secular post-theist – inclines to neglect what the original Platonists identified as necessary features of a morality transcending mere obligation, namely love and inspiration which – as Plato knew when he told the *Republic's* Guardians to return to the Cave – reveal obligations and promote just actions, and – I extend Plato – are capable (given an appropriate object of desire) of stimulating compassion. It is precisely

---

[8] Virtue, said Augustine, is 'nothing other' than the supreme love of God (*On The Life-Style of the Catholic Church* 1.15.25). Contrast this with the possibly Socratic and certainly Stoic view that it is a mode of knowledge. Augustine goes on to identify the cardinal virtues as modes of love.

this neglect which entails in some religious traditions what becomes little more than a worship of power from which 'morality' has in effect been excluded.

I have tried to show how an adequate analysis of morality demands the existence of a God whose attributes cannot be subsumed under power. It is, of course, our human need for morality (even our need in a godless universe) which drives one to attempt such an analysis. I cannot therefore reasonably conclude this discussion without sketching a reconciliation between certain features of our perceived moral awareness and the analysis of ourselves as divided selves: above all our experience of moral weakness, of an inability to follow the goodness which we recognize, by which we are inspired and to which we feel obligated.

What we need is to recognize those features within ourselves which indicate we are such that God alone can give us cause for rational hope or even intelligibility. I have already considered our 'surd'-factor, our self-expanding capacity to lose sight of our 'desired' moral unity, the nature of which Augustine subsumed under two interlocking categories, *ignorantia* and *concupiscentia*, which he claimed to be results of the Fall. I am not here concerned with his theological explanation, only with his organization of the data and his suggestions – which may be little more – of its relation to a divided present 'self'.

First, we do not always recognize the good for what it is: we are perplexed and do not know how to apply our principles to actual situations. Such *ignorantia* is not always simple ignorance. Because 'we' are divided, we may be inclined 'not to know' or 'not to want to know' what we should do. That brings our 'ignorance' (insofar as it begins by a perverse act of willing) closer to our *concupiscentia*, our lack of will to *do* what we know to be right, our weakness for various forms of attractive malice: our ability, as the poet Ovid put it, to 'know the better and follow the worse'.

In the absence of a unified self, since we are divided as to the nature of the 'we' which is knower and agent, it would seem impossible always to know what we should do. Furthermore, if and when we have knowledge of what is right, we are unable to act on it because 'we' are unable consistently to carry through the implications of our moral beliefs. To act consistently requires the activity of a single individual or self (or of a set of totally harmonized and mutually organized selves) – which is what we are not and cannot be, except in hope. Thus, as I have argued, in a non-theistic universe not only is there no place for the foundations of morality, but even if we could establish such foundations – and so come to know (*per impossibile*) that morality is a reasonable demand on us – we should still be unable to live morally because of the divided condition in which we find ourselves and our consequent need (in a non-theistic world beyond all possibility of satisfaction) for the assistance of God, God's commands and the grace enabling us to become single in the recognition of real Goodness.

GOD, 'DIRTY HANDS' AND THE POSSIBILITY OF POLITICS

If goods are incommensurable, it is hard to conceive of a rationale for acting directly *against* any one of them. If a good can only be obtained by doing something which would normally be directly wrong, and the loss of that good is always incommensurable with the further good sought, it is not easy to see how the apparently 'greater' good can be rationally chosen. In some cases such would-be rational failure to act has resembled paralysis, and has appeared peculiarly dreadful in politics, the rational agent sitting by while horrible things are done around him.[9]

These difficulties are diminished by taking a less abstract view, when some forms of the problem of incommensurability become less threatening than they appeared. Abstractly considered, the claims of piety may seem incommensurable with those of justice, but will not necessarily appear so in the individual case. The choice between different kinds of virtuous action will be determined not by an abstract and perhaps rationally impossible choice, but in accordance with the moral status of the agent at the time the action is to be performed. Although he or she may not be able to know in advance which course of action to pursue, and thus may be unable to formulate a rule of priorities for those in similar situations, he yet may be in no doubt at the time, nor have any regrets afterwards. But though this, as I have noticed, diminishes difficulties of incommensurability, it does not resolve the question of prohibitions – not least because prohibitions may themselves be incarnated in the mindset of the moral agent at the time when he is required to decide and act.

I first considered 'dirty hands' in connection with Macchiavelli,[10] who, as we saw in chapter 2, seems to offer a choice: either we can live a Christian life, based largely on the mediaeval version of moral realism; or we can enter politics, attempt to become a 'prince' and learn, where

---

9 See the arguments of J. Porter, *The Recovery of Virtue* (Louisville: Westminster, 1990), 21, against G. Grisez, *The Way of the Lord Jesus: Christian Moral Principles* (Chicago: Franciscan Herald Press, 1983), 184.
10 The key role of Macchiavelli is recognized in a modern treatment (Buckler, *Dirty Hands*) which sets the problem out well, though offering little solution.

appropriate, the arts of cruelty and lying, and in general when *not* to be 'good'. Macchiavelli's claim, echoed frequently since and still influential, is that ordinary morality is unsuited to politics, indeed that it will cause the failure of those politicians who are constrained by it, since, as it has recently been expressed,[11] consequentialism, the judgement of actions by their results, is the only morality – one might almost say 'the only language' – of politics.

These Macchiavellian attitudes and claims find curious confirmation in the relative withdrawal from public life effectively implied by the 'New Natural Lawyers'. If politics demands 'immoral' behaviours which are strictly forbidden (such as deceit or, more generally, the purveying of misinformation, let alone cruelty or callousness), then the good man cannot, it is said, rationally be a politician, and if he attempts to become one he will soon either have to resign over some invitation to dirty his hands, or fail dismally in his chosen task. To take immediate examples, it would seem that no position in the armed forces of a modern Western state will be open to the good man, nor any position of political control over such armed forces.

The caveats soon multiply. No Minister of Finance can avoid intervening to promote an assurance which he believes untenable when the currency he has to protect is under threat, but must assert, when he fears he may be forced to devalue, that he has no intention of doing so. To do otherwise – even to refuse to answer a question posed by a reporter and irrespective of whether the reporter has a right to know or not – can only damage the currency it is the Minister's responsibility to protect. In brief, it looks as though, given contemporary or foreseeable political conditions, no follower of a strict anti-consequentialism can enter public life: he can only sit by and protest the iniquitous behaviour of politicians. He can criticize from a standpoint which amounts to paralysis and proffer no viable alternative.

Consider problems of warfare. Strict observance of the spirit of a rule that the innocent should not be targeted would make life impossible for the modern general or Minister of 'Defence'. In the event of war these may try, by policy decisions and the use of sophisticated technology, to minimize '*collateral*' deaths, but they know they cannot avoid them altogether. In a major conflict, even with conventional weapons, collateral deaths will be numerous, though this will commonly be denied by a spokesperson who will be known to be lying. A commander may even

---

[11] Cf. R. Holland, *Against Empiricism* (Oxford University Press, 1980), 126–42.

avoid a direct intention of threatening the innocent, but he knows he profits from the fact that he is perceived to be threatening them in numbers. In confrontation with a ruthless and cynical enemy he will also know that strict adherence to a policy of refusing *knowingly* to kill the innocent will leave him and his political masters helpless in the face of a curiously obnoxious form of blackmail. Thus to keep his palaces the more secure, Saddam Hussein filled them with 'human shields', and in Kosovo Milosevic is believed to have copied him, 'escorting' Albanian refugees with Serbian convoys to decoy NATO planes into bombing them. Such actions, which have their analogues in private life, can be seen at their most dramatic in the public domain; the Macchiavellian rationalizes them by taking consequentialism as the 'morality of politics'.

A few years ago Williams introduced a famous example into the debate about consequentialism.[12] The setting is a village in a South American dictatorship. A visitor comes upon a scene where a captain in the militia has rounded up a group of Indians whom he is about to execute. He tells the visitor that he can have the guest's privilege of shooting the first Indian, and that if he does so the remaining thirty will be spared. If he refuses, they will be shot. On consequentialist grounds the position of the visitor may seem clear. If he fails to persuade (or threaten) the captain into sparing his prisoners, he should execute the one to save the many. Yet the objection to this is obvious: that I should not murder someone in order to prevent someone else from murdering someone else: in other words that I should not give way to moral blackmail.

Why exactly should I not give way? There are at least three possible answers, two of which I have already considered. I should not give way because I am imperilling my soul in doing so – in secular language because I do not want to compromise my moral integrity, and thus – in the language of this essay – increase my 'multiplicity'. Secondly, I should be unwilling to allow blackmailing to gain ground as a weapon in political and social life; on consequentialist grounds too this is a powerful argument. Finally and most simply, it is unjust for me to kill the Indian. The latter argument, which should be powerful with a Kantian, cuts little ice with a consequentialist.

Jonathan Glover dismisses the 'secular' notion that I should avoid dirty hands in such a business as a rather squeamish and excessive concern with my own integrity.[13] In secular terms he might be hard to

[12] B. A. O. Williams, 'A Critique of Utilitarianism', in *Utilitarianism: For and Against*, 77–150.
[13] J. Glover, 'It makes no difference whether or not I do it', *Proceedings of the Aristotelian Society: Supplement* 49 (1975), 171–90, especially 187–8.

answer – though his essay is in fact aimed at the non-secularist stance of Solzhenitsyn, whose attitude, according to Glover, we should admire despite its philosophical inadequacy. Even if Glover were to accept my analysis of loss of integrity, he could argue in utilitarian terms that I should sacrifice my self-regard in such a case: a greater good would more than counterbalance the loss. However, this answer would be less compelling if given to a believer to whom death is less important in light of eternity – and Nagel may rightly suspect that believers in an afterlife are less likely to be hard-line opponents of capital punishment.[14] Against which might be set the fact that one of the best-known believers, Pope John Paul II, *is* against it, and that believers perhaps ought to make much of the argument of the harm done to the executioners and those who endorse them.

Holland's discussion of Williams' Indians is broadly helpful, and particularly revealing when, falling immediately into non-secular language, he wonders what a 'saint' would do in the circumstances. One thing, he thinks, is clear; the saint would not shoot the Indian.[15] Holland may be thinking primarily of what has been called the 'moral saint'; but if so is misled and misleading; 'saint' is a term of religion, and to use it outside a religious context is either to lapse into inexact and populist phraseology, or – wittingly or unwittingly – to appropriate the emotional force of religious terminology in a context where it is strictly inapplicable and indefensible.

Although a 'moral saint' may exist without realist (and therefore religious) beliefs, yet his stance as moral saint cannot be *justified* without recourse to realism. Holland opines that such a person would probably have no *moral theory* at all, but would simply know how to act. A better explanation is that he would not need to *work out* his position – in the present case his refusal to shoot the Indian, with perhaps his willingness to lose his own life in the Indian's place – but that if one has to *justify* such acts, it can only be done in terms of moral realism.

How does any of this help us with dirty hands? Holland, while denying the possibility of moral politics, seems to think that what he sees as impossible in politics can be achieved in private dealings: there will be a few moral saints who will somehow intuit the right answer to their

---

[14] Nagel, *The View from Nowhere*, 230, note 4.
[15] Holland, *Against Empiricism*, 141–2. Behind Holland's remarks seems to lie the empirically plausible claim that everyone would have *some* 'stopping-point' or limit on the amount of dirt he would tolerate on his hands. It is a serious objection to any strong form of consequentialism that this seems undeniable.

personal dilemmas. But if in private actions, why not in politics? Holland is clearly right that avoiding dirty hands may in some circumstances – which could be in public as in private life – entail giving up one's own life; the famous English case is Sir Thomas More, who tried and eventually failed to find devices whereby he could both avoid compromising his integrity and keep his head on his shoulders. The more pressing question arises when it is a matter not of saving one's life but of preserving a political position in which one may expect to be effective in doing more good than any replacement. More had been forced to resign his position of power, and so his immediate effectiveness, long before he lost his life.

However, Holland's 'intuitionism' about the moral saint may still be illuminating. Perhaps it is the case not, as Macchiavelli supposed (and as Holland agrees), that politics is out of range of the good man, but that the good man must be willing, when called on, to enter politics (though never forgetting that at some time he may be forced out of it), because he cannot be sure in advance if he will be unable to avoid dirty hands, nor where his personal 'stopping-point' will turn out to be. In that public morality would resemble private life (from which we cannot 'resign'); in neither do we know when we shall have to refuse to act. The demand for dirty hands, though always a fearful possibility, may not materialize, or not immediately, and for the time being there will be much good to be done.

The paradigm case of dirty hands arises when one is called on to make decisions any one of which one would prefer not to make, and so is tempted to remove much of the difficulty by keeping out of situations in which such decisions are liable to be needed.[16] Under this aspect, the claim that politics is morally impossible shows itself to be an attempt to escape such decisions by calculated withdrawal or by avoidance of certain types of life, many of which might otherwise seem to require the good man's participation. That claims about the impossibility of politics turn out to be evasions of responsibility and not just the avoidance of temptation can be seen since, although hard cases can arise more dramatically in the public domain, they arise also in private life. How then is one to avoid them? Here advice regularly proffered by Augustine may be helpful. Repeatedly asked by politicians and generals confronted with dirty-hands dilemmas whether they should withdraw not merely into private life but into monastic, Augustine – who at times seems to have an over-optimistic view that monastic seclusion could free men from

---

[16] There is a curious similarity between this attitude and that of the Stoics (and Epicureans) who advocated a play-safe attitude to desires and emotional commitments.

such dilemmas – usually responded to enquiries about withdrawal from 'this darkness of social life' with an unequivocal No!

Augustine seems to have thought of two ways to diminish the problem of dirty hands, one 'religious' and the other pragmatic (though he would be the last to admit the ultimacy of this distinction). He urges trust that in difficult circumstances we will be shown what to do by God: whether to act or to refuse to act. He is also willing to admit a degree of consequentialism into the public behaviour of officials and more generally people operating in the public domain which he would not allow in their private lives and in those of ordinary citizens. To take an extreme (and to us intolerable) case, while forbidding killing in self-defence to a private citizen even if his life is threatened, he has no hesitation in countenancing service in the imperial army, which among its regular duties included the ordering and carrying out of executions as well as torture. Why would he make such a distinction? Certainly because he held that it is one of the fearsome responsibilities of public life that one must find – or rather be shown – a way to secure certain desirable results, and prevent intolerable evils, without serious sin.

This is not merely to assert that, for example, allowing thousands to die by refusing to act would be a demonstration of trust in God's ultimate providence; rather it is to urge recourse to God in prayer and to trust that we shall be shown how to secure the best result even in 'this-worldly' terms, and so shall not dirty our hands. Far from refusing to take part in a politics where consequentialism is the current language, we are to play our part, and play morally – recognizing the extreme seriousness of the consequences of failure[17] – until our part is ended and in all probability we are forced out by someone else. Such advice will cut no ice with an atheist or agnostic, nor should these be despised for not following it; on the other hand they should acknowledge that, from the 'realist's' point of view, the advice is good. Moreover, my whole argument implies that if the atheist or agnostic is brought to accept that he has a dilemma (here lurks an ambivalence), he should by this recognition be brought to reconsider his position. For such trust in divine guidance is no mere intuitionism, and only a realist metaphysics of morals can justify it – which is not to say non-realist 'moral saints' may not act on it. Despite Glover's dismissive implication that such *justification* shows an obsessive concern with one's own integrity, in a theistic world it appears as nothing more than an

---

[17] It may have been some kind of recognition of this that kept John Paul II from an outright condemnation of the Western nuclear deterrent many demanded of him, a demand with which he was by temperament likely to sympathize.

acceptance that the most important facts about the universe and its maker are 'moral'.

The rational theist thus will refuse both horns of Macchiavelli's original dilemma, neither declining political obligations where appropriate, nor engaging in politics for the sake of glory, honour or even a ('republican') sense of *noblesse oblige*. For though he is a 'social animal', his social loyalty, dependent on his theistic realism, is not limited by any one political community. Immediately, he shares in the society of which he finds himself a part, but his fundamental loyalty is transcendent and to that wider community – certainly no mere nation-state posing as the proper home for the 'virtues'[18] – which Augustine identified as the City of God, and in terms of which his more local loyalties are to be determined and ultimately judged.

Seeing that I have argued that moral perfection is impossible in this life and we are all morally incomplete, what is the position of the ordinary saint, let alone the 'moral' one? Saints sometimes seem puzzling in that they exhibit obvious, even flagrant, moral failings: Jerome is one notorious example, but so, even, is Francis. Their sanctity certainly does not consist in living a perfect or necessarily a conspicuously saintly life, but rather in performing an act or set of acts which surpass 'ordinary' capacities and testify to an extra-ordinary life, however hidden. Constrained by the 'level of sanctity' achieved thus far, they yet display behaviour not only extraordinarily, even astonishingly, adapted to *enhance* their integrity but which bears witness to the 'realist' nature of goodness itself (Socrates), that is to God (Francis). But even saintly behaviour will not be comprehensively 'right', in that it will still reflect the imperfect and divided human condition. In light of this, the 'moral' saint would appear as one who behaves similarly, though lacking the explicit conviction as to his or her reasons for so doing. In Augustine's terms he is a denizen

18 We noticed in chapter 1 how republicanism is in many respects parallel to Straussianism, though lacking the bizarre theories of exegesis which usually accompany that curious American movement. Republican and Straussian virtues are similar not only in asserting, against individualisms of various sorts, that man has virtuous obligations specifically as a citizen (in the modern world as the citizen of a nation-state), but in their claim, as against realism, that such virtues can be grounded without appeal to metaphysics and theology. Much Straussian exegesis is devoted to the impossible project of showing that even Plato was 'really' committed to a non-metaphysical programme. For modern republicanism and its roots see J. G. A. Pocock, *The Machiavellian Moment: Florentine Political Theory and the Atlantic Republican Tradition* (Princeton University Press, 1975); Q. Skinner, 'Machiavelli on the Maintenance of Liberty', *Politics* 18 (1983), 3–15; and for the suggestion that republicanism is a *via media* between individualism and communitarianism – that is, a variety of social or civic individualism governed in its social activities by a blend of obligation and self-respect, as in Macchiavelli himself – see P. Pettit, 'Liberal/Communitarian: MacIntyre's Mesmeric Dichotomy', in *After MacIntyre*, 176–204.

of the invisible 'City of God'; in those of Jesus he is of 'the other sheep I have not of this pasture'.

PHILOSOPHY AND THEOLOGY: TACTICS
AND HONEST TRADITIONS

As philosophy in general raises questions about all aspects of the world that confronts us through our minds and senses, so philosophical ethics in particular is concerned with making sense of what seem to be our goods as presented by our wishes, hopes and desires, and accordingly with what look, on reflection, to be 'right and wrong' ways to behave – which may be cashed out as more or less effective routes to our good. Throughout this essay I have argued that the only genuine alternatives for the ethical theorist are on the one hand a realist theory of moral foundations, of a Platonic sort or (better) overtly theistic, on the other an ultimately unintelligible view that acceptable or less acceptable behaviour depends on what we determine or choose, rationally or otherwise, as our goods, needs, rights. The realist position thus is unashamedly theological or at least metaphysical, being the more or less expanded metaphysical claim of Plato that there exists some eternal principle of goodness and intelligibility independent of the human mind.

An embarrassment with which this leaves us is that, apart from offering to explain the uneliminable diversity of secular theories, a realist or theological moralist is granted little room for debate about basic principles with secular counterparts – even though at the level of the application of ethical theories to practical moral problems and dilemmas, he or she may come up with similar recommendations for (particular) behaviour or for public policy. I have noticed how this apparently unfortunate situation can induce realists to subvert their position by committing themselves too deeply to terms of debate set by their opponents, accepting to argue 'philosophically' only in the restricted sense of that term as defined in contemporary ethics.[19]

---

[19] Like many features of the current chaos in ethics, the split between the supposedly different subject-matters of 'philosophy' and 'theology' has important historical roots. It was unknown to Augustine and is rooted in the attempt in the twelfth century to identify theology as an 'Aristotelian' science. In the end this mischievous project helped to generate a desperate search for *any kind* of subject-matter for theology. By Protestants that subject-matter was assumed to be the Bible alone, but in light of the historical criticism of recent centuries the possibilities for such restricted 'theology' have been much diminished. For the beginnings of the confusion see especially M.-D. Chenu, *La théologie comme science au xiiie siècle* (Paris: Bibliothèque Thomiste, 1969); for further comment on the contemporary scene see J. M. Rist, *On Inoculating Moral Philosophy Against God* (Milwaukee: Marquette University Press, 2000).

The apparent advantage of behaving 'philosophically' (I use quotation marks for the term as tacitly defined by the secularist) is that by ignoring their own foundations and starting anew with the tools and problems of secular philosophy, realists can both hone their analytic skills and secure the illusion of being accepted by the contemporary intellectual world, diminishing the risk of being instantly dismissed as dependent on 'religious' but non-existent entities or indemonstrable premisses. The disadvantage is that they may come to suppose that substantial agreement and common ground can be obtained despite unresolvable disagreements over foundations – a supposition exploited by secularists such as Rawls who like to claim that at least their political proposals are based on non-controversial foundations. But it must be recognized that this supposition is a delusion, since the realist, on pain of ceasing to be a realist, has to admit that by the methods of secular philosophical enquiry he or she can come up with only hypothetical structures of ethical obligation and inspiration, and the best he can hope to work out with secular counterparts is a set of moral positions which might, given good enough logic, form a consistent and coherent basis for practice. It would still require something analogous to an 'act of faith' to accept that this basis of belief is more than at best the most rational, most prudential ethical construction achievable – without realism – by consensus. In fact, experience shows that in practice one does not get anywhere near even that measure of agreement.[20]

The realist must insist that his opponent can no more assume an inalienable value for the human being than the existence of a God or of a Platonic Form. He should add (in our Zenonian style) that secular schemes which claim or assume such value are even less plausible than theological structures, insofar as they make a series of (normally) unadmitted metaphysical claims *ex hypothesi* at least as indefensible as his own. By the same token Kantianism is ruled out – or should be – but he could allow the possibility of a scheme such as utilitarianism which accepts the significance (though not value) of rational calculation merely. He could then engage in evaluations of sets of behaviours in terms of a calculation of what kind of actions would probably lead to what kind of results, so that scenarios could be laid out for human beings – or some at least – to be in a position to select.

But he should recognize that in pursuing such evaluations he will find it as hard as his rival to ward off claims of, say, the 'animal liberationist'

---

[20] For the role of the will in belief see J. Ross, 'Cognitive Reality', in L. Zagzebski (ed.), *Rational Faith* (Notre Dame University Press, 1993), 226–55, esp. 237–46.

who wants the good of every animal put on a level with that of every human, against whom he would have no justification beyond the claim that *I prefer* that my kind survives rather than that an animal survives. Logically, that is, only some variety of Hobbesianism remains for him, which realization should reduce him, as it did Hobbes, to espousing some sort of contract – in which animals can be deemed not to participate – to secure his own advantage and that of his own group (hypothetically, it may be, but not necessarily identified with mankind) and (in the first instance) its preservation.

In any case it will remain true that if the moral realist wants to talk to those who deny the possibility of realism, he has no option but to talk to them on their terms, since they have ruled out being in a position to talk to him on his. Yet for the realist to attempt to proceed without sacrificing his principles is to load the scales against him, the best way to make a deal – as any labour mediator knows – being to have the parties talk on the assumption that a deal is possible, at least if they can develop a friendly or 'collegial' relationship. The analogue illustrates the snare for the realist, for much apparent agreement can be secured by such means, and there is much he might seem to gain, provided he does not allow himself to slide into a tacit or confused acceptance of premises, however wrapped up, implying that realism is de facto ruled out.

And what more, from the point of view of the moral realist, stands to be gained from such an exercise? The greatest challenge will be to demonstrate three theses: firstly the by now familiar one that we cannot operate within a virtual morality, an *as-if-realist* ethic, without deception – either of ourselves or of others or of both; secondly, that if realism is possible, a consistent morality can be constructed – even though, in view of the lack of personal unity under which we now labour, it will be imperfectly achievable in our present life; thirdly, that to demonstrate the consistency and harmony of a conceptual system is not to demonstrate that such a system exists outside our own minds, this precisely being the boundary between realists and non-realists in ethical debate.

For if – a big but not unthinkable if, as we have seen – we were to reach the situation where the realist and the secularist moral philosopher agreed that, given a theological framework to the universe, we could ground our ethical claims on something which both enriches them and gives them more than provisional sense, the secularist would have to opt either for his own 'act of faith' (or of defiant irrationality) – as that beliefs about the value of the human person just are true – or for commitment to a realist metaphysic as a solid grounding for such beliefs.

Such an interesting dilemma might be supposed rarer than the phoenix, since, as we have seen, a theory about the human being who is the subject of ethics, formed outside a theological or metaphysical universe, would seem hardly to satisfy the conditions the theist seems to require for an understanding of human nature, while without the common but improper assumption of secret theological or metaphysical notions, the most the secularist can find in common with his theological counterpart is a set of empirical, physical and psychological facts about human beings. Arguably the psychological facts are the most promising, but their extent cannot be determined in advance.

There will come a point, therefore, where the secular and the theological philosopher of morals will have to part company, as often in North America and continental Europe is represented by the divisions between (or within) philosophy departments themselves, theological and secularist moralists being separated geographically and institutionally as well as philosophically – even if the separation is to an extent obscured by members of one group keeping a 'low profile' in disputed areas if they wish to receive an academic appointment in an institution of the other persuasion, or alternatively choosing to attend to less controversial topics such as logic and the philosophy of science.

Let us leave the determined secularist to his choice between open or clandestine importation of moral foundations and the more honest but anarchic claim that such are not needed anyway, and rather consider the situation for the realist who reaches the stage of claiming, in virtue of a metaphysical or theological belief, that his moral theories with their attached lifestyles, their sets of virtues and vices, their collections of exhortations and prohibitions, not merely are rationally defensible as logical possibilities but can be intelligibly grounded. *Ipso facto* what he will be averring is that problems about how to live and how not to live cannot be viewed merely in the domain of 'morality', or as problems in philosophical psychology about the recovery or discovery of a hypothesized wholeness or integrity. He will recognize that to describe such questions *solely* as moral questions – at least in the normal acceptation of those words – is reductionist, and the fact that 'I ought to obey God' and 'I ought to do my duty or carry out my obligations' are of quite different logical order is sufficient to show this capitulation.

Although Plato has a reply for the critic who accepts the existence of the Good but is unwilling to order his life accordingly, there has often seemed to philosophers of the Christian era to be an important distinction between knowing the Good and doing it. We recall Plato's normal view that if we do not aspire to do good we cannot have known the Good, or its impact would overwhelm our resistance. Plato may eventually have realized that he had to allow for the fading of inspiration and that realism must fully acknowledge the soul's weakened and divided state: that it *is* possible and even likely that people hear and at least partly understand the calls of goodness and still fail to carry them out or choose to ignore them.

This is where divine command moralities have their appeal, since fear may offer support where love and inspiration cannot, or cannot yet. To the objection that mere *obedience* to moral command is not *moral* obedience at all, the obvious reply – as we have seen – is that the divine command does not add or subtract to or from the goodness of what is commanded. It does, however, draw attention to the 'personal' nature of the Good as well as aid the human being to habituate himself to doing the right thing – and Plato would agree that if we become sufficiently so habituated we shall at least have the opportunity to learn to understand that it is right.

Thus the realist and theist I have begun to portray follows what is good because he sees it as appropriate to do so, and that because the only account of God worth considering supposes him to require what is good not primarily because he has the power to do so, but because to do so is in accordance with the goodness that is his nature and being. And if it is also in accordance with the goodness of his nature to do so because he has already created mankind to be like himself, what better could he have done?

The theist can claim (against his secular counterpart) to be significantly Aristotelian, and so be rescued from morality in the narrow sense, that is from an ethics of mere prohibitions. He is conscious of needing to act well because to act wrongly is like trying to walk without using his legs, or better, while pretending that he does not have legs. For the Aristotelian to act immorally is to try to act as though he or she were a different creature from the creature he is and was designed to be. It is in this sense that immorality is irrational – and only the theistic believer can see just how irrational.

Accordingly the theist who tries to argue that we can identify moral behaviour without reference to the divine purpose in creating human beings puts himself, willy nilly, in the same shackles as the secularist: little wonder if he falls back on Kantian assertions about the dignity of man, or human rights, or treating human beings as ends and not means – correct sentiments but – as I have already argued – unsupported. The advantage of the theist is to be able to treat such claims as mere, or brute, facts, the moral 'ought' being for him an offer by God to rescue us from multiplicity to a state of psychological uniformity which is far from the narrowness of the mere 'repression' it has been in fashion to decry it as. Thus too divine commands cannot be arbitrary; indeed in any adequately conceptualized theistic universe whatever is arbitrary will be seen to point away from this best possible end. We reach the position, therefore, that to be moral is not only to be rational, but also, far more importantly, to be godlike insofar as we are able – as Plato also said, agreeing with the Old Testament's 'You shall be as gods.' Conversely, we have only one alternative and one we cannot choose rationally, since this non-moral 'alternative' is to become irrational because more pluriform and to disintegrate further while at best staving off the disintegration of ourselves and our society by pretending that the world is other than it is.

We have thus identified the position of the theist. The corresponding position of the secularist, if he is honest, is to accept the inevitability of disintegration and to go down heroically inventing or paying lip-service to a morality whether in favour of the goods which the theist asserts are real or of those which the secularist chooses; otherwise to resign from the unequal contest and watch the ship sink. Nietzsche offered a third alternative: to decline to lie and to will the creative power of man to pull himself out of the abyss. This the theist can only dismiss as the heroics of futility, buttressed by the denial of death.

In default of such a naked choice, there are of course many pathways to multiplicity. If theism is no wishful thinking, it follows that an element of human freedom remains. Yet the drift into multiplicity cannot be avoided merely by making choices, but only by making choices directed implicitly or explicitly by the theistic turn, whereby the theist dismisses misguided anxieties about 'freedom' and becoming godlike gains a freedom analogous to that of God: in a sense, no more and no less. Though not free to use and abuse, he is free to act well and in 'godly' fashion. And should someone wish to deny that this is 'freedom', it will matter to him who experiences true freedom only as a tragic mistake and limitation of the objector. For it is of the essence of a theistic claim that we are not simply free to determine what is the good life. If the good life is the life of God, our choice cannot make it otherwise, and nor is it available without God's bestowal.

Where does this leave us in the debate between the theist and the secularist about 'morality'? Certainly in a rather embarrassing position. At a theoretical level agreements may be reached; at the level of public policy common ground may be found at least temporarily, especially, as we have seen, if the secularist continues to operate within a theistic framework while maintaining that he is no theist. We should normally expect his non-theism to harden and the gap between the two parties – representing what Augustine called the Two Cities – to widen. Yet there is a ray of hope that this will not always be the case. If the theist is right that secularist policies, consistently pursued in what Augustine would again refer to as a 'shadow unity over against our Unity', will necessarily point the human race towards disaster both psychological and political, since they point man towards a nature specifically contrary to that which God's goodness provides for, the wise and Hobbesian fear of self-destruction will reassert itself at least in the direction of further pretence, and perhaps in that of dawning suspicion that the theist was right all along. But it is no part of the business of a philosopher to be a prophet, and it is a lesson of the Nazis' planned extermination of the Jews and others that even fear of self-destruction can yield to man's futile rage to destroy his chosen enemy in a suicidal campaign waged in the last analysis against God himself.

And though philosophy is not the same activity as prophecy, it may be able to offer some reasonable predictions. If the only coherent position in moral philosophy is realist and theistic – our individual philosophical selves being bearers not only of incomplete souls but of limited insights into moral thinking and its effects through time – it behooves us to consider not only how we can observe our limitations but how, by taking account of the realism which is the necessary groundwork of our belief, we can preserve the conclusions we and others before us have uncovered. In other words it behooves philosophers to bethink them of the maintenance of philosophical traditions and therefore of the institutional rock on which such traditions can be maintained.

If there is no hope for a viable or even intelligible moral (as distinct from prudential) theory on a basis of individualism, moral philosophy cannot avoid talking about communities, for if there is again no point in talking about our individual moral identity except insofar as we belong to one another in some sense, then we have to assume community not merely in name but in fact. The character of a particular community is evinced by its various institutions, and by institutions are to be understood not merely families, law-courts, parliaments, schools, hospitals and barracks, but the social, educational and cultural practices of the society for which these are erected and maintained.

Such institutions and practices are undergirt by public rules, above all by the traditions of the society which both embraces those rules and transcends them in the consciences of its members. And if it is hard to replace visible institutions like schools or monasteries if they are dismantled or destroyed, how much harder to repair the traditions they maintain if these are attacked or otherwise brought into disrepute or just allowed to lapse with the passage of generations. Whether for good or ill, if traditional institutions fall into desuetude, then the traditional virtues, practices and goals of the society will sooner or later be forgotten, misunderstood, misrepresented. Whatever wisdom a society has acquired can only be passed on if it is institutionalized in structures designed to maintain the memory of the inherited practices, beliefs and mentality. Traditions are threatened if their external structures lose touch with the ideals and practices they were designed to promote: that is, if they lapse, as they are always liable to do, into a merely historical connection with their own past and *raison d'être*. The existence of such lapsed institutions, or rather the fact that all institutions may display debased characteristics, may encourage the belief – currently widespread – that 'spiritual goods cannot be institutionalized'. That belief, in turn, leads to the disappearance in ensuing generations less of the external institutions than of the very goods which, in however relatively unsatisfactory fashion, these institutions alone are fitted to hand on from one generation to the next.

The role of tradition in an ideal society (and *ceteris paribus* in any society) is above all to provide a context and an opportunity for the growing young of that society to interiorize rules, goals and values, while at the same time shaming its adult members and guardians from giving in to weariness and discouragement. Yet a tradition, being defended by its own antiquity, is liable to be untouchable by criticism, while as it ages in the changing circumstances of the world, its upholders are increasingly liable to confuse the letter of tradition with its spirit. Thus a tradition needs not only to be a repository of the past wisdom of its society, but to be for ever able to update the expression of that wisdom in different historical contexts, enriching our understanding of it in face of continually new and unexpected challenges. If it fails in this challenging role – which is to say if men fail it – it begins to die. Its death may be protracted or occur quite unexpectedly – like political empires and dynasties which (like Soviet Communism's glorifying of the bodily shells of Lenin and Stalin) project a corpse-like persistence before suddenly disintegrating.

Traditionalists are liable to be represented, and often misrepresented, as merely reactionary. That cannot be avoided, but the force of the charge can be minimized by emphasizing – as I frequently have – that the only sort of tradition with which we are to concern ourselves is no fossil but contributes to a growing and developing spiritual universe: a

tradition, indeed, which without abandoning or deforming its enunciated principles and foundations is able to learn both from reflection on
itself and from the criticism of its opponents. Thus the Catholic Church,
having learned much from reformers both within and without, in our
own times has (for example) to assimilate the better account – freed as
far as possible from the impediments of outworn or false scientific (or
scientistic) theory – now available of the nature of women not only into
its theoretical depiction of the common good but into its corresponding
social and ecclesiastical structures, including those regarding the family and religious life. In pursuing this aim it is challenged not only to
retain the essence of its own tradition but simultaneously in the 'solving' of new challenges such as, frequently, those of ethical theorizing, to
avoid conceding too much to its opponents or to those of its members
overwhelmed by fear of ephemeral unpopularity.[21]

The task – banal but immensely difficult – confronting those who wish
to maintain the sort of living tradition in which a moral system can be
perpetuated, is to combine knowledge and respect for the past with the
spirit of serious self-criticism – by which alone the perpetuation of evils
accruing to the tradition itself can be prevented – and of openness to
whatever is new, whether this is to be taken on board, rejected wholly
or sifted for the gold in the dross. It is, as I have insisted, the role of the
realist moral philosopher who wishes to practise what he or she preaches,
to point this task out, and, insofar as he is able, provide suggestions and
advice as to how it is to be accomplished. Nor ought he, as he often does,
to reduce the good life for man to sets of moral rules or to any 'morality'
narrowly understood; human perfection is culturally, but critically, all-
embracing or it is mere perfectionism.

Clearly traditions play an ambiguous role in human societies: on the
one hand vehicles of the civilization into which new members of the
society are to be initiated and repositories of whatever is ennobling in
the society's past, on the other transmitters and preservers of what is
misleading or corrupting – which negative aspect may be more readily
obscured if the society is more or less homogeneous, as was mediaeval
Christendom, at least for some periods, and as are some 'modern' Islamic
states. If the society is so homogenized as to have little place for internal
criticism, it may fall asleep to awaken when disaster threatens, as the

---

[21] Those who debate as to the possibility of women priests often fall into errors of this sort, particularly in arguing that women have a 'democratic' *right* to be ordained – a 'right', incidentally, that
men do not have – where the proper context for the debate can only be the question of whether
the Church has the authority to ordain women.

Catholic Church awoke – often in an abrupt reaction ruled by fear of the enemy – at the Reformation.

If, on the other hand, a society is constantly struggling – as is Western liberal democracy – to retain some received principles when confronted with an unlimited array of alternative claims, it may so lose sight of its past as to rely on one principle alone, and one I have argued is ultimately self-destructive – that of nigh unlimited toleration of the gamut of possible human wishes. Acting thus, it will come to tolerate demands which must subvert the principle of toleration itself.

To retain a critical attitude to one's past is difficult even within a genuinely moral tradition, since to criticize institutions is necessarily to criticize the people who control them. In brute terms the situation then is of a 'traditional' body of corruptible individuals in power opposing and being opposed by a corruptible band of critics who wish to replace them. Even were the critic (*per impossibile*) not corruptible, his activities cannot but undermine the authorities he challenges in the minds of his more self-conscious fellows. We might concede that a tradition is the more effective, at least in the short and medium term, if it is unselfconscious. Some would argue that an over-self-conscious moral tradition risks becoming its own subverter.

In the contemporary world, short of assorted fundamentalist groups securing government, we can assume that an unselfcritical tradition cannot survive. We are like the classical Greeks after the Sophists, for whom, as Plato saw, there was no going back. The intellectual future of our traditions, as of his, cannot be identical with their past, and therefore, for those who espouse a realist (and theist) morality, that future can appear daunting. We need to be aware of the past and of what traditions have been generated, while at the same time allowing a critical spirit to flourish, yet if our criticism forgets its roots, its success will kill the tradition itself. Conversely, if tradition tries to suppress or ignore not only those critics who wish to destroy it – but who can also serve as its teachers – but also those who speak as informed friends from within, it is doomed to stagnation.

The realist tradition in moral philosophy is under threat in the West, where the majority of its remaining adherents – though not necessarily always the most effective of them – are my fellow Roman Catholics. There is no point in our going on the defensive, becoming merely nostalgic or trying to impose continuity merely by impressing rules on our surviving supporters. In a liberalizing world oppression incites to further reckless scrapping of the achievements of the past, and – as one often sees with former Christians – reaction to an authoritarian implementing of rules normally takes the form neither of critical belief nor of critical unbelief, but of authoritarian secularism: the ex-nun animating the pro-abortion campaign.

Mood swings are inevitable in a tradition critical of itself, as Hegel realized. It is easier to criticize than to reconstruct, and – as revolutionaries from Robespierre to Lenin and many more contemporary dictators demonstrate – it is easy in preaching of injustice to delude people into thinking that such preaching will necessarily indicate the path to justice. Constant mood swings may lead to the death of the tradition itself, for in the continuous change what once appeared permanent easily disappears from sight. Authentic revolutionaries such as Mao Tse-tung suppose rightly that in the maelstrom of conflicting moral and political proposals the nomenklatura charged with the maintaining of traditions (here Marxist traditions) cannot but lose sight of their original ideals and objectives under the impulsion of power and the allure of compromise with alternative lifestyles. The revolutionary's only hope of combating his or her weaknesses lies in constant recourse to revolutionary first principles. Nor can more 'respectable' traditions afford to ignore this warning.

In very recent times a number of advocates of Thomism – that tradition in Western moral philosophy which presents the most detailed version of the realist theory of moral and spiritual life – seem perplexed as to why, despite their own devotion to their tradition, they have largely failed to pass it on to the next generation.[22] Some of them, rightly impressed by the importance of institutions, have gone the nostalgic route of promoting small foundations where Thomism will be taught, sometimes largely by rote as in the 'good old days', normally in a philosophically more purified form.[23] Perhaps they hope that the West will fall to a

---

[22] Cf. R. McInerny, 'Reflections on Christian Philosophy', in V. B. Brezik (ed.), *One Hundred Years of Thomism* (Houston: University of St Thomas Press, 1981), 63–73; again in *New Blackfriars* 80 (1999), 195: 'For the foreseeable future, students of Thomism will be largely autodidacts.'

[23] J. Haldane has argued on several recent occasions that Thomism must be revitalized by analytic philosophy – and it is certainly true that an increasing number of younger Thomists are analytic (see, for example, 'Thomism and the Future of Catholic Philosophy', *New Blackfriars* 80 (1999), 158–71). Insofar as 'analytic philosophy' is a neutral set of techniques, the suggestion is an admirable call for better thinking. But Haldane ignores the 'mentality' of much analytic philosophy. The problem is not that analytic philosophy is to be read crudely as logical positivism, but the fact that most of its practitioners operate with a set of philosophical problems from which realism (and religious claims in general) are excluded. Several commentators on Haldane made this point: 'This does not sit well with the anti-religious bias of analytic philosophy … religious thought is unwelcome in many academies' (Haydon Ramsay, in *ibid.*, 198); 'analytic philosophy … is a mixture of a style of philosophizing on one hand, that stresses rigour and clarity, and a tendency towards a narrowing of the philosophical imagination, on the other' (Charles Taylor, in *ibid.*, 206). In other words there is much to learn from analytic philosophy, but if one sups at that table, it is important to remember who is supplying the available nutrition.

massive revival of Catholic Christianity or on its knees to a return to the spirit of mediaeval Europe. Short of these unlikely scenarios, however, Thomism so revived is doomed to comparative failure – unless, indeed, by a narrow interpretation of Christian teaching, such failure is to be deemed success! Such institutions are wanting as intellectual upholders of their tradition and continue to fail to impress non-realists, let alone non-Christians, not least because their students, unlike earlier Thomists, are so largely ignorant of relevant parts of their own past and present, both Christian and non-Christian – whereas Aquinas would have assumed familiarity with both historic realism and Christian (and some other) theology in detail.[24]

The realist tradition in Western ethics begins with Plato, and if it is to be pondered in the first instance in non-theistic versions – which is how it can first attract – to the literary and philosophical genius of Plato it must return: not only for the historical reason that – as I have contended – Aristotle assumed, and thereby diminished, the 'realist' elements in his master's ethical thought, leaving to Aquinas via Augustine, Ps-Dionysius and others, the 'replatonizing' of the Aristotelian tradition, but also because immersion in Plato's writings promotes a clearer understanding that philosophical error is identified and undercut by self-referential arguments that expose the false assumptions in opposing positions rather than by fundamentalist assertion. This procedure, indeed, is what will distinguish a genuinely Platonic (Socratic) inculcating of philosophy – as of other humane subjects not excluding even 'virtue' – from indoctrination.

Following Plato, upholders of the realist tradition must work through its history – which includes the history of those who have misrepresented it – down to the present day and continue its development into the future, learning from the skills and insights (though not the ideologies) of their secular contemporaries, and so develop a theme to which this book is offered as contribution: namely that those who cannot face up to the realist position in ethics must ever be challenged to own to the Nietzschean alternative route with all its licence to *force majeure*, lies, hypocrisy and the intellectual dishonesty or triviality which make it palatable to a credulous

---

[24] My criticism of such 'Thomistic' moves should, however, be sharply distinguished from the apparent defeatism of Haldane who elsewhere ('MacIntyre's Thomist Revival: What Next?', in *After MacIntyre*, 101) criticizes contemporary historians of Thomism (such as those who inspired McInerny's contemporaries) with failing to generate 'a living philosophy generally acknowledged to be able to engage with and be proven superior to Davidsonian philosophy, Nagelian moral psychology or Parfitian moral theory'. In reply to that, one can only ask who does the acknowledging. Like many others (but not MacIntyre) Haldane seems to assume that the Davidsonians, Nagelians and Parfitians are able to debate with Thomists from a common (and neutral) standpoint, which patently they are not!

and largely pre-philosophical public. The task is long, indeed unending, and there is no reason to suppose it will be successful, at least in human terms. I – along with Augustine and his line – have argued that we are not human beings enough to know who we are who make the attempt. Augustine was right in concluding that to *want to want* the right thing is the only sign of progress.

Broadly understood, then, the present book has argued that Platonism or deception are the only moral and political alternatives available to us; that the West's deception about choices – other false promises are available elsewhere – is shown to be incoherent; that Platonism is intelligible – as it was in simplified version in Plato himself – against any other available account of human nature, indeed that it contributes to the intelligibility of other accounts: in other words that Platonism (broadly understood) is shown to be the only viable theory available to philosophical psychology, as to moral and political philosophy. None of that makes Platonism 'true', though I have advanced various reasons why it is not only consistent, but also capable of offering, for all its difficulties, a more rationally convincing account of human life, human reasoning, human desire and in general human experience than any alternative: in short that it is the only *coherent* account of ethics.

Nevertheless, were Platonism to be false, that reality would need to be faced, by truth lovers at least, if not by the ordinary man or woman. It may be more consoling to induce ourselves to believe that the results of Platonism can be secured without benefit of Platonism itself, yet that seems a mistake. In any case, it is no self-evident function of a philosopher to induce people, for whatever gratifying reason, to believe what is demonstrably, or even probably, false.[25]

If truth is to be preferred 'especially by a philosopher', there is no reason for me to attempt to obscure the prospect that, if Platonism is false (as possibly even if it is true), it will increasingly come to be thought to be false, and the more widely it is believed to be false, the darker the future will be for the human race. Such darkness is not to be understood rhetorically but in concrete terms of vanishing respect for human life: daily more 'unjust'[26] killings, torture, and every form of 'callousness' and neglect both in public and in private. With morality, aesthetics will also

---

[25] In the absence of realism there is no possible 'moral' objection to deception by the well-meaning, as by the 'evil'.

[26] The quotation marks are inserted to indicate that all such 'value terms' have become transvalued in a non-realist universe. It is this very perception which makes way for 'diabolical' transvaluations such as the Nazi; Heidegger is the ghastly warning figure.

disintegrate, as it did under the rule of the Nazi 'artist' Hitler, for where there is no God, 'beauty' is a matter of choice and merely (ultimately official) taste.[27] Moreover, in the event of the disappearance of the human race, nothing beautiful would *matter* nor indeed *be*, because it would not matter or be *to anyone*. There is irony but little relish in the prospect of those who have long argued against realism finishing up among the abused and eliminated by those whom they have persuaded that the worse argument is the better.

---

[27] For the success of British democratic officials (both Labour and Conservative) in such matters see G. Walden, 'Contemporary Art, Democracy and the State', in J. Haldane (ed.), *Philosophy and Public Affairs* (Cambridge University Press, 2000), 85–95.

Bibliography

Annas, J., *The Morality of Happiness* (Oxford University Press, 1993).

    Platonic Ethics, Old and New (Ithaca: Cornell University Press, 2000).

Anscombe, G. E. M., 'Modern Moral Philosophy', *Philosophy* 33 (1958), 1–19.

Ashley, B., 'What is the End of the Human Person? The Vision of God and Integral Human Fulfilment', in L. Gormally (ed.), *Moral Truth and Moral Tradition: Essays in Honour of Peter Geach and Elizabeth Anscombe* (Dublin: Blackrock, 1994), 68–96.

Aubenque, P., *La prudence chez Aristote* (Paris: Presses Universitaires de France, 1963).

    'La prudence aristotélicienne porte-elle sur la fin ou sur les moyens?', *Revue des Etudes Grecques* 78 (1965), 40–51.

Badhwar, N. K., 'Social Agency, Community and Impartiality', *Social Philosophy and Policy* 13 (1996), 1–26.

Baier, A., 'The Need for More than Justice', in V. Held (ed.), *Essential Readings in Feminist Ethics* (Boulder: Westview Press, 1995), 41–58.

Bar-On, D., 'Conceptual Relativism and Translation', in G. Preyer, F. Siebelt and A. Ulfig (eds.), *Language, Mind and Epistemology: On Donald Davidson's Philosophy* (Dordrecht: Reidel, 1994), 145–70.

Barney, R., 'Is Plato Interested in Meta-Ethics? Commentary on Rist', in J. Cleary and G. Gurtler (eds.), *Boston Area Colloquium in Ancient Philosophy* 14 (1999), 73–81.

Baron, M., 'Remorse and Moral Regret', in P. A. French, T. E. Uehling Jr. and H. K. Wettstein (eds.), *Midwest Studies in Philosophy*, vol. XII: *Ethical Theory: Character and Virtue* (Notre Dame University Press, 1988), 259–81.

Bellinger, C. K., 'Kierkegaard's Either/Or, and the Parable of the Prodigal Son: Or, Three Rival Versions of Three Rival Versions', in R. C. Perkins (ed.), *International Kierkegaard Commentary, Either/Or, part II* (Macon, Ga.: Mercer University Press, 1995), 59–82.

Berlin, I., *The Hedgehog and the Fox* (London: Weidenfeld and Nicolson, 1953).

Black, M., *The Prevalence of Humbug* (Ithaca: Cornell University Press, 1985).

Blackburn, S., *Spreading the Word* (Oxford University Press, 1984).

Blum, L. A., *Friendship, Altruism and Morality* (London: Routledge and Kegan Paul, 1980).

'Moral Exemplars', in P. A. French, T. E. Uehling, Jr. and H. K. Wettstein (eds.), *Midwest Studies in Philosophy*, vol. XIII: *Ethical Theory: Character and Virtue* (Notre Dame University Press, 1988), 196–221.

Blustein, J., *Parents and Children: The Ethics of the Family* (New York: Oxford University Press, 1982).

Boyle, J. M., 'Natural Law and the Ethics of Traditions', in R. P. George (ed.), *Natural Law Theory: Contemporary Essays* (Oxford University Press, 1992), 3–30.

Boyle, J. M., J. M. Finnis and G. Grisez, 'Practical Principles, Moral Truth, and Ultimate Ends', *American Journal of Jurisprudence* 32 (1987), 99–151.

Boyle, N., *Who Are We Now?: Christian Humanism and the Global Market from Hegel to Heaney* (Notre Dame University Press, 1998).

Braine, D., *The Human Person: Animal and Spirit* (Notre Dame University Press, 1992).

Brunschwig, J., 'The Cradle Argument in Epicureanism and Stoicism', in M. Schofield and G. Striker (eds.), *The Norms of Nature* (Cambridge and Paris: Cambridge University Press, 1986).

Buckler, S., *Dirty Hands: The Problem of Political Morality* (Aldershot: Avebury Press, 1993).

Callam, D., 'Christopher Dawson on the Oxford Movement and the Relationship of Development to Authority', *Communio* 22 (1995), 488–501.

Chappell, T. J. D., 'The Virtues of Thrasymachus', *Phronesis* 38 (1993), 1–17.

Chenu, M.-D., *La théologie comme science au xiiie siècle* (Paris: Bibliothèque Thomiste, 1969).

Crawford, D. D., 'Intellect and Will in Augustine's *Confessions*', *Religious Studies* 24 (1988), 291–302.

Darwall, S., A. Gibbard and P. Railton, 'Towards Fin de Siècle Ethics', *Philosophical Review* 101 (1992), 115–89.

Davidson, D., 'On the Very Idea of a Conceptual Scheme', *Proceedings and Addresses of the American Philosophical Society* 67 (1973–4), 5–20.

'How is Weakness of the Will Possible?', in *Essays on Action and Events* (Oxford University Press, 1980).

D'Entrèves, A. P., *Natural Law* (second revised edition, London: Hutchinson, 1970).

De Koninck, C., 'In Defence of St Thomas: A Reply to Father Eschmann's Attack on the Primacy of the Common Good', *Laval Théologique et Philosophique* 1.2 (1945), 9–109.

De Sousa, R. B., *The Rationality of Emotion* (Cambridge, Mass.: MIT Press, 1987).

Review of Taylor, *Sources of the Self*, *Dialogue* 33 (1994), 109–23.

Dodds, E. R., *Plato's Gorgias* (Oxford University Press, 1959).

Donagan, A., *The Theory of Morality* (University of Chicago Press, 1977).

Duffy, E., 'Rewriting the Liturgy: The Theological Implications of Translation', *New Blackfriars* 78 (1997), 4–27.

Ellis, A., 'Neutrality and the Civil Service', in R. E. Goodin and A. Reeve (eds.), *Liberal Neutrality* (London: Routledge, 1989), 84–105.

Emilssen, E. K., *Plotinus on Sense Perception* (Cambridge University Press, 1988).

Ewing, A. C., *The Definition of Good* (New York: Macmillan, 1947).

Farrar, C., *The Origins of Democratic Thinking* (Cambridge University Press, 1988).

Ferreira, M. J., 'Faith and the Kierkegaardian Leap', in A. Hannay and G. D. Marino (eds.), *The Cambridge Companion to Kierkegaard* (Cambridge University Press, 1998), 207–34.

Fest, J. C., *The Face of the Third Reich* (Harmondsworth: Penguin, 1983).

Finnis, J. M., *Natural Law and Natural Rights* (Oxford University Press, 1980).
Fundamentals of Ethics (Washington, D.C.: Georgetown University Press, 1983).

Firestone, S., *The Dialectic of Sex: The Case for Feminist Revolution* (London: Jonathan Cape, 1970).

Flanagan, O. and A. O. Rorty (eds.), *Identity, Character and Morality* (Cambridge, Mass.: Harvard University Press, 1990).

Flew, A., 'Responding to Plato's Thrasymachus', *Philosophy* 70 (1995), 436–47.

Fortenbaugh, W. W., 'Aristotle's Conception of Moral Virtue and its Perceptive Role', *Transactions and Proceedings of the American Philological Association* 95 (1964), 77–87.

Foucault, M., 'Qu'est-ce un auteur?', *Bulletin de la Société Française de Philosophie* 63 (1969).

Frankfurt, H., 'Freedom of the Will and the Concept of a Person', *Journal of Philosophy* 68 (1971), 5–20.
The Importance of What We Care About (Cambridge University Press, 1988).
'On Bullshit', in *The Importance of What We Care About* (Cambridge University Press, 1988).

Friedman, M., 'The Social Self and the Partiality of Debates', in C. Card (ed.), *Feminist Ethics* (Lawrence: University Press of Kansas, 1991), 161–79.

Fromm, E., *Man for Himself* (New York: Holt, Rinehart and Winston, 1947).
The Art of Loving (New York: Holt, Rinehart and Winston, 1957).

Furley, D., 'Antiphon's Case against Justice', in *Cosmic Problems* (Cambridge University Press, 1989), 66–76.

Fussell, P., *Wartime: Understanding and Behavior in the Second World War* (Oxford University Press, 1989).

Gauthier, D. P., 'Why Contractarianism?' (unpublished lecture).
Morals by Agreement (Oxford University Press, 1986).

Geach, P., 'Assertion', *Philosophical Review* 74 (1965), 449–65.
'The Moral Law and the Law of God', in P. Helm (ed.), *Divine Commands and Morality* (Oxford University Press, 1981), 165–74.

George, R. P., 'Natural Law and Human Nature', in R. P. George (ed.), *Natural Law Theory: Contemporary Essays* (Oxford University Press, 1992).

Gewirth, A., 'Are There any Absolute Rights?', in J. Waldron (ed.), *Theories of Rights* (Oxford University Press, 1984).

Gibbard, A., *Wise Choices, Apt Feelings* (Cambridge, Mass.: Harvard University Press, 1990).

Gill, C., 'Is there a Concept of Person in Greek Philosophy?', in S. Everson (ed.), *Psychology: Companions to Ancient Thought*, vol. II (Cambridge University Press, 1991).

Glendon, M. A., *Rights Talk: The Impoverishment of Political Discourse* (New York: Free Press, 1991).

Glover, J., 'It Makes no Difference Whether or Not I Do It', *Proceedings of the Aristotelian Society: Supplement* 49 (1979), 171–90.

Goodin, R. E., *Protecting the Vulnerable* (University of Chicago Press, 1985).

Green, R. M., *Kierkegaard and Kant: The Hidden Debt* (Albany: State University of New York Press, 1992).

Grisez, G., *The Way of the Lord Jesus: Christian Moral Principles* (Chicago: Franciscan Herald Press, 1983).

Haldane, J., 'MacIntyre's Thomist Revival: What Next?', in J. Horton and S. Mendus (eds.), *After MacIntyre* (Cambridge: Polity Press, 1994), 91–107.

'The Individual, the State and the Common Good', *Social Philosophy and Policy* 13 (1996), 59–79.

'Thomism and the Future of Catholic Philosophy', *New Blackfriars* 80 (1999), 158–71.

Halperin, D. M., 'Bringing Out Michel Foucault', *Salmagundi* 97 (1993), 69–89.

Hare, J. E., *The Moral Gap: Kantian Ethics, Human Limits and God's Assistance* (Oxford University Press, 1996).

'Augustine, Kant and the Moral Gap', in G. B. Matthews (ed.), *The Augustinian Tradition* (Berkeley and London: University of California Press, 1999), 251–62.

Hart, D. A., *Faith in Doubt: Non-Realism and Christian Belief* (London: Mowbray, 1993).

Hart, H. L. A., *The Concept of Law* (Oxford University Press, 1961).

Holland, R., *Against Empiricism* (Oxford University Press, 1980).

Hundert, E. G., *The Enlightenment's Fable: Bernard Mandeville and the Discovery of Society* (Cambridge University Press, 1994).

Inwood, B., *Ethics and Human Action in Early Stoicism* (Oxford University Press, 1985).

Irwin, T., *Plato's Ethics* (Oxford University Press, 1977).

Kahn, C. H., *Plato and the Socratic Dialogue* (Cambridge University Press, 1996).

Kleve, K., 'Lukrez und Venus', *Symbolae Osloenses* 41 (1966), 86–94.

'Lucrèce, l'épicurisme et l'amour', *Actes du Colloque Guillaume Budé* (1969), 376–83.

Korsgaard, C., 'Kant's Formula of Humanity', *Kant-Studien* 77 (1980), 181–202.

Kraut, R., 'Are there Natural Rights in Aristotle?', *Review of Metaphysics* 49 (1996), 755–74.

Kretzmann, N., 'Abraham, Isaac and Euthyphro: God and the Basis of Morality', in D. V. Stump, J. A. Arieti, L. P. Gerson and E. Stump (eds.), *Hamartia: The Concept of Error in the Western Tradition* (New York and Toronto: Edwin Mellen Press, 1983), 27–50.

Lewis, E., 'The Stoics on Identity and Individuation', *Phronesis* 40 (1995), 89–108.

Lillegard, N., 'Judge William in the Dock: MacIntyre on Kierkegaard's Ethics', in R. L. Perkins (ed.), *International Kierkegaard Commentary, Either/Or, part II* (Macon, Ga.: Mercer University Press, 1995).

Lisska, A. J., *Aquinas' Theory of Natural Law* (Oxford University Press, 1996).

MacIntyre, A., 'Existentialism', in M. Warnock (ed.), *Sartre: A Collection of Critical Essays* (New York: Doubleday, 1971), 1–58.

After Virtue (London: Duckworth, 1981).

Whose Justice? Which Rationality? (London: Duckworth, 1988).

Three Rival Versions of Moral Enquiry (London: Duckworth, 1990).

'A Partial Response to My Critics', in *After MacIntyre* (Cambridge: Polity Press, 1994), 295–7.

Mackie, J. L., *Morality: Inventing Right and Wrong* (Harmondsworth: Penguin, 1977).

Matthews, G. B., *Thought's Ego in Augustine and Descartes* (Ithaca: Cornell University Press, 1992).

McDowell, J., 'Projection and Truth in Ethics' (Lindley Lecture, University of Kansas 1987).

McInerny, R., 'Reflections on Christian Philosophy', in V. B. Brezik (ed.), *One Hundred Years of Thomism* (Houston: University of St Thomas Press, 1981), 63–73.

The Question of Christian Ethics (Washington, D.C.: Catholic University of America Press, 1993).

'Reply to Haldane', *New Blackfriars* 80 (1999), 192–5.

Miller, Fred R. Jr., *Nature, Justice and Rights in Aristotle's Politics* (Oxford University Press, 1995).

Mitsis, P., *Epicurus' Ethical Theory* (Ithaca and London: Cornell University Press, 1988).

Murdoch, I., *The Sovereignty of Good over Other Concepts* (Cambridge University Press, 1970).

Nagel, T., *The View from Nowhere* (Oxford University Press, 1986).

Nozick, R., *Anarchy, State and Utopia* (Oxford University Press, 1974).

Nussbaum, M., *The Therapy of Desire* (Princeton University Press, 1994).

O'Connor, D. J., *Aquinas and Natural Law* (London: Macmillan, 1967).

O'Neill, O., *Constructions of Reason* (Cambridge University Press, 1989).

Towards Justice and Virtue (Cambridge University Press, 1996).

O'Neill, O. and W. Ruddick (eds.), *Having Children: Legal and Philosophical Reflections on Parenthood* (New York: Oxford University Press, 1979).

Okin, S. M., *Justice, Gender and the Family* (New York: Basic Books, 1989).

Orr, A., *The unJewish State: The Politics of Jewish Identity in Israel* (London: Ithaca Press, 1983).

Osborn, E., *Tertullian: First Theologian of the West* (Cambridge University Press, 1997).

Owens, J., 'The *kalon* in the Aristotelian Ethics', in D. O'Meara (ed.), *Studies in Philosophy and the History of Philosophy* (Washington, D.C.: Catholic University of America Press, 1981), 261–77.

Parfit, D., *Reasons and Persons* (Oxford University Press, 1986).

Paton, M., 'A Reconsideration of Kant's Treatment of Duties to Oneself', *Philosophical Quarterly* 40 (1990), 222–32.

Pears, D. F., *Motivated Irrationality* (Oxford University Press, 1984).

Penelhum, T., 'Hume's Moral Psychology', in D. F. Norton (ed.), *The Cambridge Companion to Hume* (Cambridge University Press, 1993), 117–47.

Pettit, P., 'Liberal/Communitarian: MacIntyre's Mesmeric Dichotomy', in J. Horton and S. Mendus (eds.), *After MacIntyre* (Cambridge: Polity Press, 1994), 176–204.

Piety, M., 'Kierkegaard on Rationality', *Faith and Philosophy* 10 (1993), 365–79.

Pincoffs, E. L., *Quandaries and Virtues* (Lawrence: University Press of Kansas, 1986).

Pocock, J. G. A., *The Machiavellian Moment: Florentine Political Theory and the Atlantic Republican Tradition* (Princeton University Press, 1975).

Poole, R., 'The Unknown Kierkegaard: Twentieth-Century Receptions', in A. Hannay and G. D. Marino (eds.), *The Cambridge Companion to Kierkegaard* (Cambridge University Press, 1998), 48–75.

Popper, K., *The Open Society and its Enemies* (second edition, London: Routledge and Kegan Paul, 1952).

Porter, J., *The Recovery of Virtue* (Louisville: Westminster, 1990).

Rawls, J., *A Theory of Justice* (Cambridge, Mass.: Harvard University Press, 1971). *Political Liberalism* (New York: Columbia University Press, 1993).

Raz, J., *The Morality of Freedom* (Oxford University Press, 1986).

Rich, A. N. M., 'Reincarnation in Plotinus', *Mnemosyne* 7 (1954), 232–8.

Rist, J. M., 'Aristotle: The Value of Man and the Origin of Morality', *Canadian Journal of Philosophy* 4 (1974), 167–79. *Human Value* (Leiden: Brill, 1982). *The Mind of Aristotle* (Toronto University Press, 1989). 'Plato says we have tripartite souls. If he is right, what can we do about it?', in M. O. Goulet-Cazé, G. Madec and D. O'Brien (eds.), *Sophies Maieutores: chercheurs de sagesse: hommage à Jean Pépin* (Paris: Institut d'Etudes Augustiniennes, 1992), 103–24. *Augustine: Ancient Thought Baptized* (Cambridge University Press, 1994). 'On the Aims and Effects of Platonic Dialogues', *Iyyun* 46 (1997), 29–46. 'On the Very Idea of Translating Sacred Scripture', in J. Krašovec (ed.), *Interpretation of the Bible* (Sheffield University Press, 1998), 1499–511. 'The Possibility of Morality in Plato's *Republic*', in J. Cleary and G. Gurtler (eds.), *Boston Area Colloquium in Ancient Philosophy* 14 (1999), 53–72. *On Inoculating Moral Philosophy Against God* (Milwaukee: Marquette University Press, 2000).

Robinson, H., 'Aristotelian Dualism', *Oxford Studies in Ancient Philosophy* 1 (1983), 123–44.

Ross, J., 'Cognitive Reality', in L. Zagzebski (ed.), *Rational Faith* (Notre Dame University Press, 1993), 226–55.

Rossi, J. and M. Wreen (eds.), *Kant's Philosophy of Religion Reconsidered* (Bloomington: Indiana University Press, 1991).

Rudd, A., *Kierkegaard and the Limits of the Ethical* (Oxford University Press, 1993).

Savage, D., 'Kant's Rejection of Divine Revelation and his Theory of Radical Evil', in J. Rossi and M. Wreen (eds.), *Kant's Philosophy of Religion Reconsidered* (Bloomington: Indiana University Press, 1991), 54–76.

Schama, S., *Citizens* (Toronto: Random House, 1989).

Schofield, M., 'Sharing in the Constitution', *Review of Metaphysics* 49 (1996), 831–58.

Sedley, D., 'The Stoic Criterion of Identity', *Phronesis* 27 (1982), 255–75.

Skinner, Q., 'Machiavelli on the Maintenance of Liberty', *Politics* 18 (1983), 3–15.

Skorupski, J., 'Liberty's Hollow Triumph', in J. Haldane (ed.), *Philosophy and Public Affairs* (Cambridge University Press, 2000), 51–74.

Smart, J. J. C. and B. A. O. Williams, *Utilitarianism: For and Against* (Cambridge University Press, 1973).

Sokolowski, R., *Moral Action* (Bloomington: Indiana University Press, 1985).

Sorabji, R., *Animal Minds and Human Morals* (London: Duckworth, 1994).

Steiner, G., *Real Presences* (London: Faber, 1990).

Strycker, E. de and S. R. Slings, *Plato's Apology of Socrates* (Leiden: Brill, 1994).

Stump, E., 'Sanctification, Hardening of the Heart and Frankfurt's Concept of Free Will', *Journal of Philosophy* 85 (1988), 395–420.

'Aquinas on Justice', *American Catholic Philosophical Quarterly* 71 (1997), 61–78.

Sumner, L. W., *The Moral Foundation of Rights* (Oxford University Press, 1987).

Syme, R., *The Roman Revolution* (Oxford University Press, 1939).

Talmon, S., *The Origins of Totalitarian Democracy* (Harmondsworth: Penguin, 1986).

Taylor, C., 'Responsibility for Self', in A. O. Rorty (ed.), *The Identities of Persons* (Berkeley: University of California Press, 1976), 281–98.

Sources of the Self: The Making of the Modern Identity (Cambridge, Mass.: Harvard University Press, 1989).

Veatch, H. B., *For an Ontology of Morals* (Evanston, Ill.: Northwestern University Press, 1971).

Swimming against the Current in Contemporary Philosophy (Washington, D.C.: Catholic University of America Press, 1990).

Walden, G., 'Contemporary Art, Democracy and the State', in J. Haldane (ed.), *Philosophy and Public Affairs* (Cambridge University Press, 2000), 85–95.

Walzer, M., *Spheres of Justice: A Defence of Pluralism and Equality* (New York: Basic Books, 1983).

Warnock, G., *English Philosophy since 1900* (Oxford University Press, 1966).

Wiggins, D., 'Truth, Invention and the Meaning of Life', *Proceedings of the British Academy* 62 (1976), 331–78.

'Claims of Need', in T. Honderich (ed.), *Morality and Objectivity* (London: Routledge and Kegan Paul, 1985), 149–202.

Wilkes, K.V., *Real People* (Oxford University Press, 1988).

Williams, B., *Ethics and the Limits of Philosophy* (London: Fontana, 1985).

Wollheim, R., *The Thread of Life* (Cambridge University Press, 1984).

Index